The Economics of Regulation:
Principles and Institutions

The Economics of Regulation:
Principles and Institutions

VOLUME 1   **Economic Principles**

VOLUME 2   **Institutional Issues**

The Economics of Regulation:

Principles and Institutions

VOLUME 1
Economic Principles

ALFRED E. KAHN

Cornell University

JOHN WILEY & SONS, INC.

New York · London · Sydney · Toronto

Library of Congress Catalogue Card Number: 74–116769

ISBN 0–471–45430–3

Printed in the United States of America

10 9 8 7 6 5 4 3 2 1

To Mary

Preface

The purpose of these volumes is to explore the contribution that economics can make to government regulation of business.

When governments try to influence the performance of particular industries, they must first define the purposes of that regulation. Second, they must devise the social arrangements best suited to those purposes.

The economics of regulation has two corresponding aspects. First, traditional theory provides guiding *principles*: these define the goal of economic efficiency and provide rules for achieving it. The development and the application of these principles are the subject of Volume I. Second, there exists a branch of economics dealing with the relations between various *institutional* arrangements—market structures, systems of incentives, laws and administrative procedures—and economic performance. Volume II examines the major institutional issues in the field of regulation, in relation to the goal of economic efficiency. Together, the two volumes are an attempt to join neoclassical theory with "institutional economics." The latter is aimless if it is not informed by theory. And a normative theory of public policy is not of much use if it cannot be related to the selection of the best set of social arrangements for achieving those norms. Therefore, each volume is written with continuous reference to the other.

As this dichotomy suggests, I see validity in both the quest for generalizations about the economic process *and* the view that every actual market or industry is unique—in its technology, in the nature of the service involved, and in the package of social and political goals that the institutions of economic control are supposed to promote. In order to make the informed judgments necessary for understanding and for prescribing public policies, we must bring to each problem a knowledge and understanding of the relevant general principles, and we must assess and apply them in terms of the particular circumstances of each case.

This study attempts to develop the tools and the general guidelines, and to analyze the common institutional considerations and tendencies. The numerous references to specific regulatory problems and particular regulated industries are intended only as illustrations of generalizations, not as solutions of the policy issues raised. I regard with equanimity the probability that the specific policy judgments I offer may be good or bad; the generalizations, I trust, are always relevant, valid, and useful.

Since understanding requires not only a grasp of the common principles but also the experience of trying to apply them to particular cases, I suggest, if these volumes are to be used successfully in teaching, that each student be required to do the second kind of exercise on his own: to dig deeply into the facts and issues relating to a specific case or policy problem and to try to apply to it the principles developed here. The numerous footnotes and illustrations provide suggested topics for this type of individual study. But an hour's perusal of several *Wall Street Journals* would serve the same purpose.

Over the years I have incurred so many debts in connection with the preparation of this book it is difficult to know where to begin or end my acknowledgments. First, let me express thanks for the many profitable discussions of these problems that I have had with Herman Roseman, Peter Boone, Rachel Simmons, David Kadane, Anna Holmberg, Lynn Silverman, Jules Joskow, and Caleb Rossiter. Then there are people who have supplied very useful criticisms of particular portions of the manuscript: among them it is a pleasure to acknowledge Daniel Gray, George Cook, Thomas Simmons, Joel Dirlam, J. David Mann, Lisa Pollack, William Freund, Jane Bryant, and Lippman Vodoff. Just as I did her namesake twenty-five years ago, so now I gratefully acknowledge the editorial help of Hannah Kahn, who taught me among many other things never to say "literally" unless I meant it, literally.

My special thanks to Agnes Sasaki Stelzer, who took a thousand IBM belts and with care, patience, and unbelievable efficiency converted them into drafts whose only fault was that they were physically so beautiful it was painful to lay pencil to them, and to Mertie Decker, who has somehow kept me from flying off in a hundred directions during the first year of a new and demanding job and in so doing made it possible for me to finish the book.

Throughout the volumes are reflections of the help and suggestions of my present and former graduate students, notably Irwin Stelzer, Douglas Greer, John Landon, Kenneth Fraundorf, and Keith Anderson—and of my research assistants, Rachel Kahn and Sharon Morris.

It would take another entire preface to acknowledge adequately my debt to Irwin Stelzer. The imprint of our discussions of these subjects appears throughout the two volumes. And it is the simple truth—literally—that I could not possibly have written them without his continuous advice, encouragement, assistance, stimulus, and support.

Ithaca, New York   Alfred E. Kahn
January 1970

Contents

VOLUME 2

Introduction

CHAPTER 1

Introduction: The Rationale of Regulation and the Proper Role of Economics

Economics emerged in the eighteenth and nineteenth centuries as an attempt to *explain* and to *justify* a market system. This is an oversimplification, but it is a broadly accurate characterization of the mainstream of Western economic thought. The purpose has been to describe how an essentially uncontrolled economy, in which the critical economic decisions are made by individuals, each separately pursuing his own interest, can nonetheless orderly and efficiently do society's work. The coordinating and controlling mechanism is the competitive market and the system of prices that emerges out of the bargains between freely contracting buyers and sellers. The competitive market guides and controls the self-seeking activities of each individual, so that, as Adam Smith stated in 1776, while "he intends only his own gain . . . he is . . . led by an invisible hand to promote an end which was no part of his intention"[1]—that is, to maximize the wealth of the nation.

This rationalization and description of the competitive market is still in large measure relevant to Western economies today. The economic reforms initiated in the 1960s by many Communist countries were short steps in the same direction. For all the great modifications to which market economies have been subjected in practice during the last century, and for all the qualifications that must be attached to the case for such an economy, the competitive market model is still in important measure (some economists would even say essentially) descriptive both of reality and of the community's conception of what an ideal economic system would look like.[2]

---

[1] *An Inquiry into the Nature and Causes of The Wealth of Nations*, Edwin Cannan, ed., 4th ed. (London: Methuen & Co. Ltd., 1925), I: 421.

[2] Apart from the fact that no two economists could agree on its precise formulation, it is impossible for even a single, nonschizophrenic, informed observer to make any brief statement that would adequately characterize the extent to which the model remains descriptively or analytically valid. There are large segments of the economy to which the model applies only peripherally—the governmental, public utility, and nonprofit sectors, including in the latter the entire household economy. See, for example, Eli Ginzberg, Dale L. Hiestand, and Beatrice G. Reubens, *The Pluralistic Economy* (New York: McGraw-Hill Book Co., 1965). Even where it does apply, the competition that actually prevails is highly imperfect at best. It may be agreed that even when the model does roughly characterize the functioning of the economy from some perspectives—for example, explaining how resources are allocated—it is almost entirely silent about other essential aspects—for example,

THE REGULATED SECTOR

There are at least two large chunks of the economy that the competitive market model obviously does not describe or even purport to describe. These are the huge and growing public sector, the allocation of resources to which is determined not by the autonomous market but by political decisions, and the public utilities, in which the organization and management is for the most part (in the United States—not in most other countries) private but the central economic decisions are subject to direct governmental regulation.[3]

To be sure, the government influences the functioning of the private, competitive sectors of the economy as well in many ways—for example, by regulating the supply and availability of money, enforcing contracts, protecting property, providing subsidies or tariff protection, prohibiting unfair competition, providing market information, imposing standards for packaging and product content, and insisting on the right of employees to join unions and bargain collectively. In principle, these influences, however pervasive, are intended to operate essentially at the periphery of the markets affected. Their role is generally conceived as one of maintaining the institutions *within* whose framework the free market can continue to function, of enforcing, supplementing, and removing the imperfections of competition—not supplanting it.[4] In these sectors the government does not, or is not supposed to, decide what should be produced and how or by whom; it does not fix prices itself, nor does it control investment or entry on the basis of its own calculations of how much is economically desirable; the government does not specifically control who should be permitted to do what jobs, nor does it specify the permissible dimensions and characteristics of the product.[5]

---

how the decisions of the assumedly "sovereign consumer" are really made. See Thorstein Veblen, *The Theory of the Leisure Class; an Economic Study of Institutions* (New York: The Macmillan Company, 1912) and John Kenneth Galbraith, *The New Industrial State* (Boston: Houghton Mifflin, 1967), Chapter 19 and *passim.*

[3] See the reference in note 2 to the large private nonprofit sector, also.

[4] Professor Hayek greatly stresses the distinction between governmental interventions consistent and inconsistent with the preservation of competition as the central economic regulator. It is the latter, not the former, he argues, that pose a threat to political and social freedom. Friedrich A. Hayek, *The Road to Serfdom* (Chicago: University of Chicago Press, 1944), 88–100.

Professor Clair Wilcox organizes his excellent text, *Public Policies Toward Business,* 3rd ed. (Homewood: Richard D. Irwin, 1966), under a similar set of headings. See also Lee Loevinger, "Regulation and Competition as Alternatives," *The Antitrust Bulletin* (January–April 1966), XI: 104–108.

[5] It is important even in a general introduction not to leave the reader with the misleading impression that government policy is more

logical, consistent, or clear-cut than it really is. We shall point out the fuzzy and frequently inconsistent shifting line that various governments have drawn between the essentially competitive and the regulated sectors of the economy. The Food and Drug Administration has determined that bread baked according to a formula developed by Cornell University may not be sold as white bread because it contains 6% soya flour. And that a perfectly healthful confection cannot be labeled as "jam" or even, clearly, as "imitation jam" unless it has at least 45% by weight of the purported fruit ingredient. See *62 Cases, More or Less, Each Containing Six Jars of Jam et al. v. U.S.,* 340 U.S. 593 (1951). In this instance the Supreme Court overturned the FDA. Heavyweight champions may be denied the right to defend their titles if they have had the temerity to make unpopular statements to the press. In many states professional wrestlers, veterinarians, and undertakers may not practice their trade without taking loyalty oaths. And we shall have occasion to note the many ways in which government restrictions on entry into supposedly competitive trades do in fact have major economic consequences, consequences often intended by those who administer them. On the other hand, the rationale or justification of such interventions, of which the foregoing

In contrast, the government does do all these things with the public utilities. Here the primary guarantor of acceptable performance is conceived to be (whatever it is in truth) not competition or self-restraint but direct governmental prescription of major aspects of their structure and economic performance. There are four principal components of this regulation that in combination distinguish the public utility from other sectors of the economy: control of entry, price fixing, prescription of quality and conditions of service, and the imposition of an obligation to serve all applicants under reasonable conditions. This book is an analysis of the economics of that regulation—its characteristics and consequences, the principles that govern it, and the principles that ought to govern it.

THE LEGAL RATIONALE

For some 67 years, roughly in the period 1877–1934, the United States Supreme Court took the position that there were certain more or less readily identifiable industries, peculiarly and sufficiently "clothed" or "affected with a public interest" to justify legislatures subjecting them to regulation despite the Fourteenth Amendment's injunction that "No State shall . . . deprive any person of life, liberty, or property, without due process of law." In a series of landmark decisions in the field of constitutional law, it drew tight boundaries around that group of industries, holding that outside those boundaries the Fourteenth Amendment prohibited any such drastic interferences with the freedom of contract. It admitted into the select circle grain elevators,[6] banks,[7] fire insurance companies,[8] and insurance agents.[9] In so doing it recognized also the long-accepted right of legislatures similarly to regulate the suppliers of gas, electricity, water, and transport services on the ground that these companies operated under governmental franchises giving them the right to make use of public streets or to condemn private property; these, being contracts freely entered into, could legitimately impose various regulatory conditions on the franchisee. And, typically over the vigorous dissents of such justices as Oliver Wendell Holmes, Louis D. Brandeis, and Harlan Fiske Stone, the Supreme Court declared "essentially private in nature"[10] and therefore beyond the reach of state regulation the manufacture of food, clothing, and fuels,[11] and the operations of theater ticket brokers,[12] employment agencies,[13] gasoline service stations,[14] and ice plants.[15]

---

represent an almost infinitesimally small sample, is not the direct control over economic performance. The purported and often real purpose is either a political one—harassment of the "disloyal"—or to see to it that consumers are not misled in making their free choices, that is, to assure that competition itself functions more effectively.

[6] *Munn v. Illinois*, 94 U.S. 113 (1877).

[7] *Noble State Bank v. Haskell*, 219 U.S. 104 (1911).

[8] *German Alliance Insurance Company v. Lewis, Superintendent of Insurance of the State of Kansas*, 233 U.S. 389 (1913).

[9] *O'Gorman & Young, Inc., v. Hartford Fire Insurance Co.*, 282 U.S. 251 (1931).

[10] *New State Ice Co. v. Liebmann*, 285 U.S. 262, 277 (1932).

[11] *Chas. Wolff Packing Co. v. Court of Industrial Relations of The State of Kansas*, 262 U.S. 522 (1923).

[12] *Tyson & Brother—United Theatre Ticket Officers v. Banton, District Attorney*, 273 U.S. 418 (1927).

[13] *Ribnik v. McBride, Commissioner of Labor of the State of New Jersey*, 277 U.S. 350 (1928).

[14] *Williams, Commissioner of Finance, et al. v. Standard Oil Co. of Louisiana*, 278 U.S. 235 (1929).

[15] See note 10. In a way it is ironic and somewhat misleading to trace the restrictiveness of this doctrine back to *Munn v. Illinois*, since in that decision the Supreme Court deferred to the judgment of the legislature in finding in the strategic position of the grain elevators (their importance to the public and purported power) a sufficient justification for regulation. It

Since that fascinating chapter in constitutional history was completed in 1934 and since the story has in any event been well told in other places, there is no need to reproduce it here.[16] Suffice it to point out that the varying views of the court and its members seem to have hinged on the following closely interrelated factors:

1. The extent to which they adhered to the precepts of judicial restraint, of which Holmes was the principal proponent—restraint in substituting their judgments for those of the legislature about what might be construed by some as essentially legislative, by others as essentially constitutional issues.[17]

2. The extent to which they interpreted the "due process" requirement of the Fourteenth Amendment as subjecting legislation only to a procedural test as against calling for a determination of its substantive merits or imposing a substantive commitment to a policy of *laissez faire*.[18]

3. The degree to which they identified freedom from government regulation of *economic* activities as inseparable from or essential to the preservation of the basic human freedoms protected by the Bill of Rights.[19]

---

adopted from the common law the notion that "property does become clothed with a public interest when used in a manner to make it of public consequence, and affect the community at large" (94 U.S. 113, 126, 1877) in order to support this extension of regulation to companies that were not franchised or given monopolistic privileges by the state. It was only later Courts, notably in the 1920s, that converted the doctrine into a straightjacket.

[16] See, for example, Dexter Merriam Keezer and Stacy May, *The Public Control of Business* (New York: Harper & Brothers, 1930), Chapter 5; Emery Troxel, *Economics of Public Utilities* (New York: Rinehart & Company, 1947), Chapter 1; Charles F. Phillips, Jr., *The Economics of Regulation*, rev. ed. (Homewood: Richard D. Irwin, 1969), Chapter 3. See also the useful compendium by Irston R. Barnes, *Cases on Public Utility Regulation* (New York: F. S. Crofts & Co., 1938), Chapter 1.

[17] "For protection against abuses by legislatures the people must resort to the polls, not to the courts." Chief Justice Waite, speaking for the majority in *Munn v. Illinois*, 94 U.S. 113, 134 (1877).

"We have no right to revise the wisdom or the expediency of the law . . . we would not be justified in imputing an improper exercise of discretion to the legislature of North Dakota." Shiras, for the majority, in *Brass v. North Dakota*, 153 U.S. 391, 403 (1894).

"I think the proper course is to recognize that a state legislature can do whatever it sees fit to do unless it is restrained by some express prohibition in the Constitution . . . and that the Courts should be careful not to extend such prohibitions beyond their obvious meaning by reading into them conceptions of public policy that the parti-

cular Court may happen to entertain. . . .

"I am far from saying that I think this particular law a wise and rational provision. That is not my affair. But if the people of the State of New York speaking by their authorized voice say that they want it, I see nothing in the Constitution of the United States to prevent their having their will." Holmes, dissenting in *Tyson v. Banton*, 273 U.S. 418, 446–447 (1927).

[18] "The Fifth Amendment, in the field of Federal activity, and the Fourteenth, as respects state action, do not prohibit governmental regulation for the public welfare. They merely condition the exertion of the admitted power, by securing that the end shall be accomplished by methods consistent with due process. And the guaranty of due process . . . demands only that the law shall not be unreasonable, arbitrary, or capricious, and that the means selected shall have a real and substantial relation to the object sought to be attained." Roberts, for the majority, in *Nebbia v. New York*, 291 U.S. 502, 525 (1934).

"The Fourteenth Amendment does not enact Mr. Herbert Spencer's Social Statics. . . . a constitution is not intended to embody a particular economic theory, whether of paternalism and the organic relation of the citizen to the state or of laissez faire." Holmes, dissenting in *Lochner v. New York*, 198 U.S. 45, 75 (1905), involving a law fixing the maximum permissible workweek for bakers at 60 hours.

[19] "If this be sound law, if there be no protection, either in the principles upon which our republican government is founded, or in the prohibitions of the Constitution against such invasion of private rights, all property and all business in the State are held at the mercy of a majority of its legislature." Field, dissenting in *Munn v. Illinois*, 94 U.S. 113, 140 (1877).

4. The extent to which they were prepared (a) to confine the powers of the state to regulate price—"the heart of the contract"[20]—or entry, or to impose an obligation to serve, to situations in which the very ability of the firm to do business required that it obtain a franchise from the state, which admittedly gave the latter the contractual right to insist on such regulatory provisions as it saw fit;[21] or (b) to extend it to specific businesses that had been recognized as "public" in character under the common law because, similar to inns, ferries, hackmen, grist mills, and other "common callings," they "held themselves out to serve the public" anyhow or for some other reason had been held "clothed with a public interest"; or (c) to extend the category even farther by analogy to other businesses that had for one reason or another "risen" to a "public" character because the owner had "devoted his business to a public use" or "to a use in which the public has an interest," whatever that meant;[22] or (d) to permit or to confine

---

"This is not regulation, but management, control, dictation—it amounts to the deprivation of the fundamental right which one has to conduct his own affairs honestly and along customary lines. . . . if it be now ruled that one dedicates his property to public use whenever he embarks on an enterprise which the Legislature may think is desirable to bring under control, this is but to declare that rights guaranteed by the Constitution exist only so long as supposed public interest does not require their extinction. To adopt such a view, of course, would put an end to liberty under the Constitution." McReynolds, dissenting in *Nebbia v. New York,* 291 U.S. 502, 554–555 (1934).

[20] *Adkins v. Children's Hospital*, 261 U.S. 525, 554 (1923), voiding a minimum wage law. See note 1, Chapter 2.

[21] "It is only where some right or privilege is conferred by the government or municipality upon the owner, which he can use in connection with his property, or by means of which the use of his property is rendered more valuable to him, or he thereby enjoys an advantage over others, that the compensation to be received by him becomes a legitimate matter of regulation. Submission to the regulation of compensation in such cases is an implied condition of the grant, and the State . . . only determines the conditions upon which its concession shall be enjoyed." Field, dissenting in *Munn v. Illinois*, 94 U.S. 113, 146–147 (1877).

"It is suggested that there is a monopoly, and that that justifies legislative interference. There are two kinds of monopoly; one of law, the other of fact. The one exists when exclusive privileges are granted. Such a monopoly, the law which creates alone can break; and being the creation of law, justifies legislative control. A monopoly of fact anyone can break, and there is no necessity for legislative interference. . . . If the business is profitable, anyone can build another; the field is open for all the elevators, and all the com-

petition that may be desired. If there be a monopoly, it is one of fact and not of law, and one which an individual can break."

Brewer, dissenting in *Budd v. New York*, 143 U.S. 517, 550–551 (1892), also involving grain elevators. Note that this view embodies not only a legal principle but an economic conclusion: that the only monopoly that can be great and enduring enough to justify regulation is one conferred or protected by governmental grant of exclusive privilege.

[22] These various rationalizations (listed as b and c) are so closely intertwined that it is awkward to document them separately.

"Businesses said to be clothed with a public interest justifying some public regulation may be divided into three classes:

(1) Those which are carried on under the authority of a public grant of privileges which either expressly or impliedly imposes the affirmative duty of rendering a public service demanded by any member of the public. Such are the railroads, other common carriers and public utilities.

(2) Certain occupations, regarded as exceptional, the public interest attaching to which, recognized from earliest times, has survived. . . . Such are those of the keepers of inns, cabs, and grist mills. . . .

(3) Businesses which though not public at their inception may be fairly said to have risen to be such and have become subject in consequence to some government regulation. . . . In the language of the cases, the owner by devoting his business to the public use, in effect grants the public an interest in that use and subjects himself to public regulation to the extent of that interest. . . .

"It has never been supposed, since the adoption of the Constitution, that the business of the butcher, or the baker, the tailor, the wood chopper, the mining operator, or the miner was clothed with such a public interest that the price of his product or his wages could be fixed by State regulation. . . .

"An ordinary producer, manufacturer or shopkeeper may sell or not sell as he likes. . . ." Chief Justice Taft, for the unanimous court in *Wolff Packing Company v. Kansas*, 262 U.S. 522, 535–537 (1923).

"Property does become clothed with a public interest when used in a manner to make it of public consequence, and affect the community at large. When, therefore, one devotes his property to a use in which the public has an interest, he, in effect, grants to the public an interest in that use, and must submit to be controlled by the public for the common good. . . ." C. J. Waite, for the majority, in *Munn v. Illinois*, 94 U.S. 113, 126 (1877).

"The public has no greater interest in the use of buildings for the storage of grain than it has in the use of buildings for the residences of families. . . . The public is interested in the manufacture of cotton, woolen, and silken fabrics, in the construction of machinery, in the printing and publication of books and periodicals, and in the making of utensils of every variety . . . indeed, there is hardly an enterprise or business . . . in which the public has not an interest in the sense in which the term is used by the court in its opinion. . . ." Field, dissenting *ibid.*, pp. 140–41.

"Is the business of insurance so far affected with a public interest as to justify legislative regulation of its rates? . . . We have shown that the business of insurance has very definite characteristics, with a reach of influence and consequence beyond and different from that of the ordinary business. . . ." McKenna, for the majority, in *German Alliance Insurance Co. v. Kansas*, 233 U.S. 389, 406, 414 (1914).

For majority opinions excluding from these categories businesses supplying various "ordinary commodities of trade" (*Williams v. Standard Oil*, 278 U.S. 235, 240, 1929) and services, see notes 10–15.

Holmes argued against the meaningfulness of these closed categories:

"The notion that a business is clothed with a public interest and has been devoted to the public use is little more than a fiction intended to beautify what is disagreeable to the sufferers. The truth seems to me to be that, subject to compensation when compensation is due, the legislature may forbid or restrict any business when it has a sufficient force of public opinion behind it. Lotteries were thought useful adjuncts of the State a century or so ago; now they are believed to be immoral and they have been stopped. Wine has been thought good for man from the time of the Apostles until recent years. . . . What has happened to lotteries and wine might happen to theatres in some moral storm of the future, not because theatres were devoted to a public use, but because people had come to think that way." Holmes, dissenting in *Tyson v. Banton*, 273 U.S. 418, 446 (1927).

"The phrase 'business affected with a public interest' seems to me to be too vague and illusory to carry us very far on the way to a solution. It tends in use to become only a convenient expression for describing those businesses, regulation of which has been permitted in the past. To say that only those businesses affected with a public interest may be regulated is but another way of stating that all those businesses which may be regulated are affected with a public interest." Stone, dissenting *ibid.*, p. 451.

"The business of supplying to others, for compensation, any article or service whatsoever may become a matter of public concern. Whether it is, or is not, depends upon the conditions existing in the community affected. If it is a matter of public concern, it may be regulated, whatever the business. . . .

"The notion of a distinct category of business 'affected with a public interest,' employing property 'devoted to a public use,' rests upon historical error. . . . In my opinion, the true principle is that the State's power extends to every regulation of any business reasonably required and appropriate for the public protection." Brandeis, dissenting in *New State Ice Company v. Liebmann*, 285 U.S. 262, 301–303 (1932).

It was these views, of Holmes, Stone, and Brandeis, that ultimately prevailed, in *Nebbia*:

"Obviously Munn and Scott had not voluntarily dedicated their business to a public use. They intended only to conduct it as private citizens, and they insisted that they had done nothing which gave the public an interest in their transactions or conferred any right of regulation. The statement that one has dedicated his property to a public use is, therefore, merely another way of saying that if one embarks in a business which public interest demands shall be regulated, he must know regulation will ensue." *Nebbia v. New York*, 291 U.S. 502, 533–534 (1934).

Although the latter decision eliminated the constitutional requirement, in some situations exposure to public utility regulation continues to turn in practice or under the governing statutes on whether the company "held itself out" to serve the general public. On the case of petroleum (and petroleum product) pipelines, for example, see George S. Wolbert, Jr., *American Pipe Lines* (Norman: University of Oklahoma Press, 1952), 111–132. The decision in 1969 by the public utilities commission of New Jersey to subject to regulation a business that had been set up to distribute fuel oil by pipeline from central storage to the individual residents in a real estate develop-

regulation to businesses enjoying "monopolies in fact," as contrasted with legally-conferred grants of exclusive privilege;[23] or, at the other extreme, (e) to permit legislatures to intervene in whatever manner required and in whatever situations a case could be made that the uncontrolled market worked badly. In principle this last view could prove to be just as restrictive as the first, depending on how its proponent answered the question: to whom did that sufficiently convincing case have to be made? But, of course, in practice proponents of that view were proponents also of judicial restraint or of more active state intervention in the economic field.

5. The extent to which they themselves believed in the efficacy of the unregulated market, competitive or otherwise.[24]

One view, which convinced the Court majority in *Munn v. Illinois*, in 1877, was that regulation might properly be introduced to protect customers from exploitation by private monopolists. Quite a different view, of which Brandeis was a leading exponent, was that unregulated competition could be excessively strong—injurious not just to the businessmen involved but to the public at large as well.[25]

In any event, it was over 36 years ago that the Supreme Court abandoned this historic distinction. In *Nebbia v. New York* it held, in effect, that there was no longer any constitutional barrier to legislatures imposing any type of economic regulation on any industries within their jurisdictions, where in their judgment it would serve the public interest, provided only that they did not do so in an utterly capricious or discriminatory manner:

"It is clear that there is no closed class or category of businesses affected with a public interest, and the function of courts in the application of the Fifth and Fourteenth Amendments is to determine in each case whether the circumstances vindicate the challenged regulation as a reasonable exertion of governmental authority or condemn it as arbitrary or discriminatory. . . . The phrase 'affected with a public interest' can, in the nature of things, mean no more than that an industry, for adequate reason, is subject to control for the public good. . . .

"So far as the requirement of due process is concerned, and in the absence of other constitutional restriction, a state is free to adopt whatever economic policy may reasonably be deemed to promote public welfare, and to enforce that policy by legislation adapted to its purpose. . . . If the laws passed are

---

ment project turned in part on the issue of whether the operation was a "service for public use," in part on whether they were operating under special grant of privilege from the state. *Public Utilities Fortnightly* (April 10, 1969), LXXXIII: 51–52. For other instances in which this criterion has been employed—for example in rejecting regulation over publication of the yellow pages of a telephone book—see A. J. G. Priest, *Principles of Public Utility Regulation* (Charlottesville: Michie Co. 1969), Chapter 1.

[23] This was one basis for the majority opinion upholding regulation of grain elevators in *Munn v. Illinois* and rejecting it for ice companies in *New State Ice*. See the opposing view of the dissenters in *Budd v. New York*, note 21, who refused to admit either the constitutional validity or the possible economic necessity of regulating

"monopolists in fact," on the one hand and, for a refusal to *confine* regulation to monopolies, see the famous dissenting opinion of Brandeis, in *New State Ice*, arguing that regulation was both permissible and desirable because competition frequently proved to be *excessive*. 285 U.S. 262, 280–311 (1932). The latter view prevailed in *Nebbia*.

[24] See note 23 contrasting the extreme views of Brewer, in the *Budd* dissent, and Brandeis, in *New State Ice*.

[25] Brandeis believed that competition was not just wasteful at the level of the individual industry but also responsible for the wide swings of the business cycle, for the succession of periods of speculative, overinvestment followed by long periods of excess capacity and deeply depressed prices and incomes. See *ibid*.

seen to have a reasonable relation to a proper legislative purpose, and are neither arbitrary nor discriminatory, the requirements of due process are satisfied. . . . With the wisdom of the policy adopted, with the adequacy or practicability of the law enacted to forward it, the courts are both incompetent and unauthorized to deal.''[26]

As far as the United States Constitution is concerned, there is no longer any distinction between the public utilities and other industries.

THE DISTINCTION IN PRACTICE

The distinction has become progressively blurred in practice as well. The government in one way or another regulates price and/or quality of product and/or entry in many industries that are not properly regarded as public utilities in most essential respects. Consider, for example, the application of the wage-price guideposts to particular pricing decisions by the steel and aluminum industries, among others, during the Kennedy and Johnson administrations;[27] the use of stockpiling of strategic materials (and releases from stockpiles), purportedly for national security but also, clearly, to raise (and, later, to hold in check) the prices and incomes of the producers;[28] the complicated government policies affecting the prices of agricultural products, the level of oil production, the quantity of sugar, oil and textile imports, the quality of drugs, and the number and identity of doctors, liquor stores, and tree surgeons permitted to practice their trades. The list could be extended almost indefinitely; the exercise would shed interesting light on the truly mixed character of the American economy.

In principle, as we have already suggested, many of these interventions are not intended to constitute economic regulation. The avowed purpose of licensing doctors, barbers, prize fighters and drugs is not usually to have the government substitute its judgment for that of the market in determining, on economic grounds, how many or who should be permitted to enter the market, but only to assure that those who do enter are qualified—on professional, scientific, or technical grounds.[29] But in point of fact, as we shall see, the licensure *is* often economic, in motivation or effect, and does effect-

[26] 291 U.S. 502, 536–537 (1934).

[27] John Sheahan, *The Wage-Price Guideposts* (Washington: Brookings Institution, 1967); George P. Shultz and Robert Z. Aliber, eds., *Guidelines, Informal Controls, and the Market Place* (Chicago: University of Chicago Press, 1966); Grant McConnell, *Steel and the Presidency* (New York: W. W. Norton & Co., 1962); Roy Hoopes, *The Steel Crisis* (New York: John Day Co., 1963); Gilbert Burck, "Aluminum: the Classic Rollback," *Fortune* (February 1966), LXXIII: 107–111 and ff.

[28] Walter Adams, "The Military-Industrial Complex and The New Industrial State," *Amer. Econ. Rev., Papers and Proceedings* (May 1968), LVIII: 659–661, summarizing U.S. Senate, Committee on Armed Services, National Stockpile and Naval Petroleum Reserves Subcommittee, 88th Cong., 1st Sess., *Inquiry into the Strategic and Critical Material Stockpiles of the United States, Draft Report*, Washington, 1963.

[29] Similarly, the encroachments that antitrust decisions in the 1950s and 1960s made on the right of businessmen outside the public utility industries to choose their customers did not in principle represent a substitution of economic regulation for competition. In principle it is only the public utilities that have an obligation to serve; other businessmen supposedly are free to refuse to sell, for reasons sufficient to themselves, unless that refusal is part of or incident to the imposition of an illegal restraint on price competition (for example, is a way of enforcing resale price maintenance) or to illegal monopolization. In practice, the result of the above-mentioned decisions has been to come much closer to imposing a positive obligation to sell (instead of, for example, exclusively to lease, as in *U.S. v. United Shoe Machinery Corp.*, 110 F. Supp. 295, 1953) on companies with market power. Still, the justification in these instances was the preservation of competition, not its replacement.

ively limit the force of the competitive market. Even in principle it is clear that many of the other instances of governmental intervention just mentioned represent policies of direct economic regulation, no more and no less, whatever their public rationalizations.

The period of the 1920s and 1930s, the very time when the constitutional issue was most strenuously contested and ultimately resolved, were especially propitious for this extension and blurring of the edges of the public utility concept, that is, of the boundaries between the industries appropriately regulated and those left to the regime of competition. Economists and lawmakers were pointing with increasing emphasis to the pervasiveness of monopoly elements throughout the economy,[30] and this suggested at least to some that direct regulation of performance might be required to protect the consumer over a far wider range of industry than the public utilities proper.[31] In other contexts, these and other observers were pointing out that some of the same factors that made competition infeasible and potentially destructive among public utility companies—notably economies of scale and heavy overhead costs—were widespread in unregulated industry as well.[32] This led some of them to call for the introduction of comprehensive regulation as a means of eliminating the wastes, instabilities, and social costs imposed by

See *U.S. v. Parke, Davis and Co.*, 362 U.S. 29 (1960); *U.S. v. General Motors Corp. et al.*, 384 U.S. 127 (1966); *U.S. v. Arnold, Schwinn & Co. et al.*, 388 U.S. 365 (1967); and *U.S. v. International Business Machines Corp.*, Civil Action No. 69, filed January 17, 1969, U.S. Dist. Ct., S.D.N.Y., *CCH Trade Regulation Reporter*, ¶ 45,069 (Case 2039).

[30] See, for example, Edward H. Chamberlin, *The Theory of Monopolistic Competition* (Cambridge: Harvard University Press, 1933), and Joan Robinson, *The Economics of Imperfect Competition* (London: Macmillan and Co., Ltd., 1933), both giving formal recognition in their theoretical models to the fact that all real markets lie somewhere between the polar extremes of perfect competition and pure monopoly.

[31] See Arthur Robert Burns, *The Decline of Competition* (New York: McGraw-Hill Book Co., 1936), especially Chapters 11 and 12. See also the dissenting opinions of Justice Stone in *Tyson v. Banton*, 273 U.S. 418, 447–454 (1927) and *Ribnik v. McBride*, 277 U.S. 350, 361–375 (1928), contending that the presence of substantial monopoly power and the necessity of protecting the unemployed from extreme exploitation justified these attempts by the states to regulate the fees of ticket brokers and employment exchanges. Of course, not all economists concluded that widespread imperfections of competition made it necessary to abandon antitrust policy generally and turn to regulation. See, for example, J. M. Clark, "Toward a Concept of Workable Competition," in American Economic Association, *Readings in the Social Control of Industry* (Philadelphia: The Blakiston Co., 1942), pp. 452–475.

[32] J. M. Clark was a leading and perhaps most profound exponent of this view:

"It soon became evident that railroads were not the only industry using large fixed capital and subject to the 'peculiarities' of constant and variable costs. It also became evident that discrimination was not the only untoward result. . . . It became evident that economic law did not insure prices that would yield 'normal' returns on invested capital. . . . The business cycle had become a recognized part of the order of things, with its recurrent periods of excess producing capacity, during which active competition tended to lower prices until even efficient concerns could make little or no return on their investment. . . .

"Here we have an array of problems, primarily relating to the economist's search for the laws governing normal and market price and to the question whether competition is natural and can endure. . . .

"Other important developments have occurred in connection with public utilities. . . . Here, for the first time, organized technical attention is paid to the recurrent ebb and flow of output and the daily and seasonal 'peaks' of demand. . . . [But] Restaurants, theaters, golf clubs, garment-making industries, railroads and street cars, building, and other trades—all have their peaks, daily or seasonal. And all industries suffer in common from the unpredictable irregularities of the business cycle." *Studies in the Economics of Overhead Costs* (Chicago: University of Chicago Press, 1923), 11–15. Copyright 1923 by the University of Chicago. All rights reserved.

competition,[33] an argument that reinforced the movement, increasingly popular among businessmen, for "rationalization" of industry by industry-wide cooperation and cartelization.[34] Not surprisingly, it was in the middle of the Great Depression that these views ultimately prevailed—in the *Nebbia* decision, which involved *minimum* price fixing for milk, and more generally in the National Recovery Program, which, in quest of general economic recovery, introduced industry-wide 'codes of fair competition.'"[35] That these codes were used to involve much more self-regulation of industry and cartelization than effective governmental controls does not alter the fact that the National Recovery Administration represented during its short lifetime a further blurring of the distinction between the competitive and public utility sectors; and many of its policies continue to be applied today.

And yet there *is* such a thing as a public utility. The line between these and other types of industries is a shadowy area; and it shifts over time. But there remains a core of industries, privately owned and operated in this country, in which, at least in principle, the primary guarantor of acceptable performance is *conceived* to be (whatever it is in truth) not competition or self-restraint but direct government controls—over entry (and in many instances exit), *and* price, *and* conditions of service—exercised by administrative commissions constituted for this specific purpose.[36] In this respect, the public utilities remain a fairly distinct group, comprising the same industries that 60 to 80 years ago would have been given essentially the same designation and regulatory treatment—the generation, transmission, and distribution of electric power; the manufacture and distribution of gas; telephone, telegraph, and cable communications; common-carrier transportation, urban and interurban, passenger and freight; local water and sewerage supply (to the extent at least that these continue to be provided by privately-owned companies); and, in a sense at the periphery, banking. The list could well embrace, also, warehouses, docks, wharves, stockyards, taxis, ticket brokers, employment exchanges, ice plants, steam heating companies, cotton gins, grist mills, irrigation companies, stock exchanges, and express

---

[33] See, for example, the analysis and proposals by Walton H. Hamilton and Helen R. Wright, *The Case of Bituminous Coal* (New York: The Macmillan Co., 1925), and Walton H. Hamilton, *A Way of Order for Bituminous Coal* (New York: The Macmillan Co., 1928); and A. R. Burns, *loc. cit.*

[34] See, for example, Robert A. Brady, *Business as a System of Power* (New York: Columbia University Press, 1943), Chapters 7 and 8; George W. Stocking and Myron W. Watkins, *Cartels or Competition?* (New York: Twentieth Century Fund, 1948), Chapter 2; and *Monopoly and Free Enterprise* (New York: Twentieth Century Fund, 1951), Chapter 8.

[35] See A. R. Burns, *op. cit.*, Chapter 10; and Clair Wilcox, *op. cit.*, 677–687.

[36] Every state, including the District of Columbia, Puerto Rico, and the Virgin Islands, has such a commission, although the powers vested in them vary. For example, the Minnesota and Nebraska state commissions do not regulate either the retail or the wholesale rates, and those of Texas and South Dakota control only the wholesale rates charged by private electric companies. But the Nebraska exception is easily explained: there are no private electric utilities in that state. In all four states the municipalities have jurisdiction over the retail rates. All the other state commissions regulate at least the retail rates. No less than nine states have not given their commissions authority to require certificates of convenience and necessity before companies may begin service in a new area or to control abandonments; but in many, if not all of them, the municipalities do have these powers. The situation in natural gas distribution is similar. All states except Texas regulate telephone rates. For a survey, see U.S. Senate, Committee on Government Operations, Subcommittee on Intergovernmental Relations, 90th Cong. 1st Sess., *State Utility Commissions: Summary and Tabulation of Information Submitted by the Commissions*, Washington, 1967. See also Federal Power Commission, *Federal and State Commission Jurisdiction and Regulation: Electric, Gas, and Telephone Utilities*, Washington, 1967.

companies.[37] There have been some new entrants that would have been recognized barely or not at all in, for example, 1900—the production and field sale of natural gas, common carrier pipeline transmission of hydrocarbons, commercial aviation and trucking. But the principles underlying the extension of direct regulation to most of them were the traditional ones: they were new common carriers, or required franchises or certifications carrying with them the right of eminent domain, or were conceived of as so intimately affecting the prices or service of the traditional utilities as to require regulation themselves (as in the case of trucking and the field sales of natural gas).

THE ECONOMIC RATIONALE

It would be tidy to include in this introduction an exposition of the economic logic of the institution of regulated monopoly. The list of economic justifications would have to involve the following:

1. The importance of these industries, as measured not merely by their own sizeable share in total national output, but also by their very great influence, as suppliers of essential inputs to other industries, on the size and growth of the entire economy. These industries constitute a large part of the "infrastructure" uniquely prerequisite to economic development. On the one hand they condition the possibilities of growth (as Adam Smith recognized, the division of labor is limited by the extent of the market, and the latter depends in turn on the availability and price of transportation).[38] On the other hand, because many of these industries are characterized by great economies of scale, their own costs and prices depend in turn on the rate at which the economy and its demand for their services grows. As general economic growth proceeds, the contribution of these industries to further expansion is thus enhanced by their own progressive realization of those economies of scale, in a cumulative and self-reinforcing process.

2. That many of them are "natural monopolies": their costs will be lower if they consist in a single supplier. This creates the efficiency case for monopolistic organization and, along with the importance of the service and the consequent inelasticity of demand, the need for regulation to protect the consuming public.

3. That for one or another of many possible reasons, competition simply does not work well.

But this would be a terribly superficial statement. And it will take many chapters to make it less so. The reason is that every part of the rationalization involves an issue or series of issues instead of a settled conclusion. For instance, the public utilities are important; but do they make a greater contribution to national product or economic growth than the provision of food, medical

---

[37] See, for example, Paul J. Garfield and Wallace F. Lovejoy, *Public Utility Economics* (Englewood Cliffs: Prentice-Hall, 1964), Chapters 1, 3, 13, and for specific industries *passim;* Martin G. Glaeser, *Public Utilities in American Capitalism* (New York: The Macmillan Co., 1957), Chapters 1–9. While entry into banking is restricted by the issuance of charters, and the operations of individual banks are subjected to complicated restrictions and detailed inspection and supervision, and certain restrictions are placed on their pricing—notably limitations on the interest charges they may pay to depositors—the rates banks actually pay and charge and the profits they may earn are not explicitly set by the regulatory authorities.

[38] Adam Smith, *op. cit.*, I: 19–22.

care, housing or education, none of which is regulated in the same fashion? Their importance, clearly, is not a sufficient explanation or economic justification for their subjection to regulation. Nor is it a *necessary* condition—one could find economic justification for regulating "unimportant" industries such as ticket brokers, except that since it uses resources to regulate, there would be no economic point in doing so for industries so unimportant that the benefits of regulation could not possibly outweigh the costs of administration.

There is no room for doubt that at least *some* of the public utility industries are in *some* respects "natural monopolies." But the interesting economic questions are: What makes them so? Is natural monopoly synonymous with long-run decreasing cost tendencies? If so, what about the public utilities, such as the supply of water, that *seem* to be characterized by long-run tendencies to increasing costs? Does a tendency for costs to decline over time constitute an evidence of natural monopoly?[39] What parts of these industries are natural monopolies, what parts not? Might they be natural monopolies in some static, efficiency sense but "unnatural" ones in terms of the prerequisites for innovation and growth? And how then do we handle, in theory and in practice, the growing competition between "natural monopolists," such as electric and gas distribution companies for the home heating and cooking market, or between international cable and satellite communications? And how do we cope with the historical fact that the prime historic exemplars of the extension of public utility regulation in the United States in the last quarter of the nineteenth century—railroads and grain elevators—were not really natural monopolists?[40]

As we have already suggested, part of the case for regulation and the inappropriateness of competition inheres in the heavy fixed costs that characterize most of these industries. But do heavy fixed costs make monopoly "natural"? Or competition unreliable? What then of agriculture or even the practice of medicine, most of whose costs are likewise fixed? Or trucking, whose fixed costs are only a small proportion of the total, yet which is regulated like a public utility? And does it make any difference whether the fixed costs that must be recovered from the sale of a number of services are mainly *common* to those various services, or *joint*?

In short, we have here not a description but a series of complicated analytical questions concerning the proper roles of competition and monopoly in these industries—questions that will concern us throughout this entire book, and especially in its second volume.

THE ECONOMICS OF REGULATION

In any event, the subject of this study is not the "economics of public utilities," but the "economics of regulation." Reflecting and encouraged by

---

[39] There is no reason to keep the reader in suspense or confusion on this point: the answer is "not necessarily." For an example of confusing decreasing costs *over time*, attributable to technological progress, with the "long-run decreasing costs" that are the condition of natural monopoly, see Charles F. Phillips, Jr., *op. cit.*, 23, note 8. The enormous decline of real costs in, for instance, agriculture over the last several decades obviously does not signify that this is a "natural monopoly." See on this point pp. 127–129, Chapter 5.

[40] See James R. Nelson, "The Role of Competition in the Regulated Industries," *Antitrust Bulletin* (January–April 1966), XI: 7–8, 17–21. The natural monopoly concept is the subject of Chapter 4 of our Volume 2.

the *Nebbia* decision, as we have already seen, the government regulates many industries that are not really public utilities. Conversely, even among the "public utility" industries or at least at their periphery the regulation is often incomplete—control over price but not entry (for example, in insurance), over entry but not price (for example, in radio and television) or quality of service (for example, in banking), and so on. And even over those industries most thoroughly regulated and most clearly identifiable as public utilities, issues abound concerning the appropriate definition and role of regulated monopoly as the principal institution of social control. These issues must of course be examined—but not in a first chapter, in *a priori* fashion, as though they represented settled and generally accepted principles. Instead we shall analyze them in detail *after* a detailed exposition of the relevant economic principles, in a series of chapters that examine this institution of regulated monopoly, its strengths, limitations, and the principles for delineating its proper scope.

This is not to deny that, even after *Nebbia*, there is a more or less distinctive core of public utility industries. It is to emphasize instead that it is the phenomenon of economic regulation itself, wherever practiced, whose economics we study here—not the public utility industries as such. Licensure of entry has certain implications and tendencies wherever it is practiced, whether over gas pipelines, radio and TV stations, community antenna television (CATV), doctors, or barbers. Government price-fixing has similar consequences whether it is for electricity, post office services, farm products, or air travel; and so has governmentally-enforced divisions of the market, whether by licensing motor carriers or assigning output quotas to individual oil wells. Private, collective price-fixing and market-sharing are subject to similar tensions and tendencies, whether by maritime shipping conferences, boards of fire insurance underwriters, stock exchange members, or real estate boards—although these implications and consequences will vary with the circumstances of the industry to which they are applied. Our purpose is to expose the unifying economic principles and tendencies, the common problems, rather than to describe or analyze the particular characteristics or regulatory problems of specific industries.

This purpose must not be interpreted as reflecting a belief that any simple set of rules can answer all problems of regulatory policy. On the contrary, each regulated industry (in fact, each unregulated one, too) is in essential respects unique and must be so treated.[41] This book springs from a conviction that valid scientific generalizations can be drawn and useful general guides to regulatory policies can be developed. Their intelligent application in particular situations, like the decision to regulate in the first place, can only be done on the basis of full consideration of the special characteristics of the industry in question—its technology and other conditions of supply, the nature of its market—and of the varying mix of public purposes, economic and

---

[41] Probably the outstanding proponent of this view was Walton H. Hamilton:

"an industry, like an individual, is part of all that it has met; it has a character, a structure, a system of habits of its own. Its pattern is out of accord with a normative design; its activities conform very imperfectly with a chartered course of industrial events." *Price and Price Policies* (New York: McGraw-Hill, 1938), 4.

"A policy for the operation of an economy is one thing; the ordering of the affairs of an industry quite another. . . . As the economy which fails to perform needs its general remedy, so the industry out of order requires its specific." "Coal and the Economy—A Demurrer," *Yale Law Journal* (February 1941), L: 595.

other, that regulation is supposed to serve. But the job is likely to be very badly done if it is not informed by a clear grasp of the common economic principles and considerations.

ECONOMICS AND NONECONOMICS, SCIENCE AND PRESCRIPTION

We have stated that we are interested in the principles that govern regulation and "the principles that ought to govern it." What policy *ought* to be is a topic about which the politician and political scientist, sociologist, philosopher and clergyman, and indeed, in a democracy, anyone who votes has important and relevant things to say. Public economic policies are not, cannot and should not be framed on the basis of "purely economic" considerations alone. Economic institutions and policies are in the last analysis only means to ultimately noneconomic ends—such ends as a good life, justice, the fuller development of the potentialities of the individual, national strength, or the glory of God. They can therefore be formulated and judged only in terms of some conception of the proper definition and weight to be placed on these various noneconomic goals. We shall try throughout our discussions to take into account the ways in which different social, political, and ethical considerations might and do properly influence the political process out of which public economic policies emerge.

At the same time, our main focus is on economic principles. Our central question is: What guidance can economics provide legislators, administrators, and judges in framing, applying, and enforcing policies involving the direct regulation of private industry?

The answer to this question combines the two quite distinct purposes of economics—science and prescription.[42] There is nothing unusual about this double motivation; it involves ambivalence only when we fail to keep clearly in mind which of the two purposes we are at any time serving, and in which of our two roles, physician or scientist, we are acting. As for the first, there must be very few professional economists who were not moved to enter that gloomy profession (no matter how far they may later have gone astray) by a belief that economic problems bulk large among the many vexations of human existence in society, and by a hope that the application of goodwill, intelligence, and professional expertise to the formulation of public policy could make an important contribution to the improvement of the human condition. The title of Adam Smith's master work, *An Inquiry Into the Nature and Causes of the Wealth of Nations*, suggests that his was essentially a scientific treatise. But Smith's work

"was, in fact as in intention, a system of political economy. . . . By a system of political economy I mean an exposition of a comprehensive set of economic *policies* that its author advocates on the strength of certain unifying (normative) principles such as the principles of economic liberalism, of socialism, and so on."[43]

The "principle of Natural Liberty" that Smith professed to have discovered was, as Schumpeter observed,

---

[42] The two currently fashionable adjectives for characterizing these two types of economics are "positive" and "normative," respectively.

[43] Stress supplied. Joseph A. Schumpeter, *History of Economic Analysis* (New York: Oxford University Press, 1954), 38.

"both a canon of policy—the removal of all restraints except those imposed by 'justice'—and the analytic proposition that free interaction of individuals produces not chaos but an orderly pattern that is logically determined: he never distinguishes the two quite clearly."[44]

This book is an essay in "political economy"—"the economic life of the nation and what we can do about it"[45]—which is what economics used to be called in the eighteenth and nineteenth centuries.

But if such an inquiry is to be conscientious, its scope and method must be rigidly scientific as well. The economist who asks a politician "Won't you let me advise you on your legislative program?" deserves only another question in response: "What do you *know*?" And only the economist who can answer "Well, I can tell you that if you pass a law that says such-and-such, these are the things that will probably happen," or, "If you do nothing about such-and-such, this is what will probably happen," deserves to have his offer taken seriously.

This is not to argue that economists have no other function in government than to serve as technical assistants to politicians. As we have already suggested, formulating public policy can never be a job for the scientist alone. In the last analysis, deciding what *should* be done can never be accomplished only with the help of the type of information that says "If you do A then B will follow." And if it follows from this truth that economists cannot, *as scientists*, presume to settle the ultimate issues of public policy, it also follows that there are no *other* scientists who can presume to do so either. If framing public policy requires in the last analysis the *art* of the politician or philosopher, this is an art that the economist may be better equipped than anyone else to acquire and to practice within his own domain: who can have given more thought than he to the ultimate ethical and political implications of alternative public economic policies?

Economists have a particular advantage when it comes to taking a direct role in the regulatory process. The job is an extremely technical one and becomes more so each year. It used to be done almost exclusively by lawyers and politicians, with accountants and engineers as assistants. But for decades there has been great and increasing dissatisfaction with their performance. One important criticism has been that they were behaving too much like lawyers and bookkeepers—excessively concerned with proper administrative procedures, the balancing of equities, and the measurement and covering of accounting costs—and too little like economists—paying practically no attention to things such as marginal cost, elasticities of demand, or to the dynamic conditions of innovation and growth. For these and other reasons that will appear later, economists have been drawn more and more into the process, bringing with them their own esoteric terminology and tools; the lawyers that have failed to seek their direct cooperation find they cannot understand what their opponents' witnesses are saying.

WHAT CAN ECONOMICS CONTRIBUTE? PRINCIPLES AND INSTITUTIONS

The unique set of tools that economics can contribute to the regulatory process is the familiar body of microeconomic theory, which purports to

---

[44] *Ibid.*, 185.
[45] Ben W. Lewis, "It's Political (Repeat Political) Economy," *The Antioch Review* (September 1949), IX: 372.

explain and predict the behavior of the individual consumer, investor, worker, firm, and industry under various circumstances.[46] Like all other scientific models and the generalizations that emerge from them, the models of microeconomic theory are simplified, describing causal relationships involving a limited number of variables. Therefore, the relationships it predicts will prevail only under the condition of *ceteris paribus*—"all other things remaining equal." Observations or predictions such as that under pure competition price will be set at marginal cost; that with monopoly and blocked entry, an industry will (tend to) earn supernormal profits; that customers will buy more of most products or services if their prices are reduced; that firms will continue to operate at subnormal or even negative profits so long as they cannot withdraw their capital and their revenues cover their variable costs; that prices will fluctuate more in response to changes in supply and demand if those functions are price-inelastic than if they are elastic—generalizations such as these are valid only subject to certain rather strict behavioral assumptions and only *ceteris paribus*.

The hypothesized causal relationships are based partly on deductive reasoning, partly on observation, partly on more rigorous empirical verification. The question of how relevant these traditional models are to the real world, and, therefore, how useful either as explanations of how the economy really works or as predictive tools is an open one. The belief underlying this

---

[46] Microeconomics is a study of the behavior of the *individual* decision-making unit, or, at succeeding levels of aggregation, the individual market, industry, or geographic region in an interdependent world of several regions. It is concerned with the way in which these transacting units or groupings make their economic decisions, and the way in which their several activities are coordinated by economic institutions to make the basic choices dictated by the universal economic problem of scarcity—what to produce, how and by whom to produce it, and how the product is to be distributed. In Western economies, the coordination is effected through the market system. Therefore microeconomics is concerned with the operation of individual markets—how prices, outputs, and distributive shares are determined—and their interrelationships. The criteria of effective performance consist in the desirability of the resulting allocation of resources, the physical efficiency (both statically and dynamically) with which scarce resources are used, and the acceptability of the resulting distribution of income.

Macroeconomics, in contrast, is concerned with the behavior of the major economic aggregates, not with prices in individual markets relative to prices elsewhere (affecting the allocation of resources and the distribution of benefits) but with the "general price level"; not with employment and output in this or that industry relative to others, but with total employment and output in the economy—its stability, adequacy, and growth.

The reason that two largely (and probably

excessively) distinct bodies of economic theory have been developed to explain and predict these separate types of phenomena is that their determinants are largely distinct. For example, the causes of the often unsatisfactory performance of aggregate employment are not to be sought principally in correctable decisions by individual householders, businessmen, investors or workers, or in the defective structure of individual markets (although one must emphasize the qualification "principally" in that statement). When the general price level or aggregate employment moves up or down, the pattern of changes in prices and employment in individual markets and industries exhibits two familiar characteristics: dispersion and central tendency. Microeconomics supplies the explanation of the first characteristic. It can explain why prices in individual markets rise or fall relative to those in other markets: something obviously has happened to demand or supply functions in individual markets relative to those in other markets that explains the divergent results. But it takes macroeconomics to explain the central tendency: the proximate cause must be found in a change in aggregate spending in the economy at large and the remedy must be found principally in public policies aimed at regulating the flow of aggregate demand. Individual transactors, markets, and industries are essentially powerless to react to deficiencies or excesses or instabilities in economy-wide demand in such a way as to prevent or remedy their unfortunate macroeconomic consequences, and public policies attempting to improve matters by regulating

book is that they are or can be useful in both ways; the reader will have to judge for himself whether that belief has proved justified.

As our earlier characterization of Adam Smith's grand design suggested, the elaboration of these theoretical models of a market or price system had a dual purpose: not just to describe and to explain, scientifically, but also to justify and to advocate. The main body of microeconomic theory can be interpreted as describing how, under proper conditions—for example, of economic rationality, competition, and laissez-faire—an unregulated market economy will produce optimum economic results. We will at a later point briefly examine the underlying value judgments on which this conclusion is based. We merely emphasize here that such a conclusion is meaningless except if stated in terms of specified political or ethical criteria or definitions of what constitutes a "good" or a "bad" result; and that the choice of criteria is not one that the economist as such is any more qualified to make than anyone else.[47]

It remains true that the particular standards or values that underlie this favorable appraisal of a market economy are still widely accepted in Western society; and that there is a wide consensus among liberals and conservatives alike that such an economy, regulated principally by the constraints of competition, would at least in some respects be ideal. (The major differences of political opinion in Western society therefore consist largely of differing judgments about the extent to which the conditions necessary for the market to work "ideally" do in fact prevail or can be made to prevail.) So that, for example, the single most widely accepted rule for the governance of the regulated industries is regulate them in such a way as to produce the same results as would be produced by effective competition, if it were feasible.

Microeconomic theory provides regulators with a set of principles that, if followed, will produce optimum results, by widely accepted criteria of optimality. The principles are at one and the same time *behavioral rules*, describing how prices should be set, investment decisions guided and so forth, and descriptions of the *ideal results* that these rules are supposed to produce—notably the use of society's limited resources in such a way as to maximize consumer satisfactions.

Part II of this volume is an attempt to expose those principles and to apply them to the task of regulation.

Even if we regarded the above body of economic theory as a complete and adequate description of the type of performance we would wish to elicit from the economy, its principles alone do not provide a sufficient set of policy rules

---

individual prices, businesses, or markets will be similarly ineffective.

[47] The economic historian could shed light, however, on why it was that Western economists chose to develop a scientific explanation of a market economy instead of another type—for example, one that was centrally planned; why it was that that specific economy emerged; and why the mainstream of Western economic thought chose to justify instead of to condemn that economy. The historical explanations would have to run in terms of (1) the configuration of economic groups, notably the emergent mercantile and industrial capitalists, that thought their interests would be best served by such an economy; (2) the emergent ideals of Western society—for example, of economic liberalism and improved material welfare instead of, for instance, of a more nearly equal distribution of income or the enhanced power of the national state or church; (3) the intellectual currents of the "Age of Reason," which looked in the social as well as the physical universe for the "natural laws" that maintained order without the need for human or governmental intervention; and (4) the scientific and technological developments that conditioned all the others.

for regulated industries. They do not answer the questions of *how* and *by what institutional arrangements* those ideal results are to be achieved. For unregulated industries, economic theory provides at least a large part of the answer: leave it to self-interest, constrained in turn by the "invisible hand" of competition. Competition will weed out the inefficient and concentrate production in the efficient; it will determine, by the objective test of market survival, who should be permitted to produce; it will force producers to be progressive and to offer customers the services they want and for which they are willing to pay; it will assure the allocation of labor and other inputs into the lines of production in which they will make the maximum contribution to total output.[48]

What institutional incentives, compulsions, and arrangements will play the same role where "the invisible hand" of competition is for one reason or another infeasible? "The visible hand of regulation" is not a sufficient answer. The reason, as we shall see more fully below, is that in a society that profoundly respects the institution of private property, the initiative, operating control, and responsibility for economic performance continue, even under regulation, to rest primarily with private management. The role of the government remains essentially negative—setting *maximum* prices, supervising expenditures, specifying *minimum* standards of service, in short, contravening the decisions of private persons only after the fact, only when their performance has been or would otherwise be obviously bad. In these circumstances regulation cannot supply the same assurances as competition that performance will be *positively good*—efficient, progressive, risk-taking, innovative. Its most important task is to define and develop institutional arrangements that will provide correspondingly powerful incentives and pressures on regulated monopolists.

Volume 2 is devoted to a survey and analysis of these critical institutional questions. In view of the historic controversies in economics between the "theorists" or, more precisely, "classical economists," on the one hand, and "institutionalists" on the other, it is important to emphasize that we intend to imply no such dichotomy by this distinction between these two major divisions of this study. On the contrary, the micro theory that is divorced from institutional realities is sterile. The essential task of useful theory is precisely to identify the important institutional determinants of economic behavior—such as number of sellers, barriers to entry, complexity of product, shape and character of the production cost function, or the presence of regulation—and to formulate hypotheses about their impacts on the various aspects of performance. Conversely, the "institutional economics" that is

---

[48] This is not to suggest that the ability of society to rely on competition to serve these ends solves all the institutional problems in the "unregulated" sectors of the economy. In a sense it merely restates the problem: there remain an almost unlimited number of difficult questions about the kinds of institutional arrangements and government policies best suited to preserve competition and make it most effective. What number of sellers best preserves the likelihood of strong interfirm rivalry consistent with achievement of economies of scale in production and innovation? What degree of patent protec-

tion strikes the optimum balance between the encouragement of competitive innovation and avoidance of excessive, patent-based monopoly? To what extent can government licensing or prescription of product standards make competition more effective by overcoming consumer ignorance? A student of the antitrust laws will recognize how difficult it is to determine either in general or in specific cases what types of policies respecting mergers, integration, various kinds of interfirm collaboration, price discrimination, or exclusive dealing will be best suited to preserve the most effective competition possible.

informed by no theory about which institutional variables are important and which unimportant, that begins with no testable hypotheses about how these variables are likely to operate, that attempts to develop no models of the relation between the various structural and performance variables is no science at all.

The distinction between our two volumes is, instead, that the first is essentially deductive and the second inductive. The former sets forth and develops the formal *rules* for achieving economic efficiency, rules inherent in the normative model of the competitive market system, and shows how they would apply to regulated industries. The latter analyzes the institutional arrangements in the regulated industries that determine how closely those norms are in fact achieved; it is a study of how regulated monopoly does in fact work and how it might be improved. Both make use of the main corpus of microeconomic theory to build the bridge between what we know or think we know and what we think policy ought to be.

CHAPTER 2

The Traditional Issues in the Pricing of Public Utility Services

The essence of regulation is the explicit replacement of competition with governmental orders as the principal institutional device for assuring good performance. The regulatory agency determines specifically who shall be permitted to serve; and when it licenses more than one supplier, it typically imposes rigid limitations on their freedom to compete. So the two prime requirements of competition as the governing market institution—freedom of entry and independence of action—are deliberately replaced. Instead the government determines price, quality and conditions of service, and imposes an obligation to serve.

The licensure of entry in most public utility industries tends to be an infrequent, once-and-for-all or almost-all determination. Franchises legally may have to be renewed, and new firms may seek to be licensed; in radio and television, and trucking this is a frequent occurrence. But even in those cases, and even more so in others, the tendency is to rely on the same chosen instruments, year after year and decade after decade; the structure of the market and identity of the firms selected to serve remain essentially unchanging. And what public utility commissions mainly *do* (though not in broadcasting) is to fix the prices the chosen instruments may charge—not just a ceiling, as in the case of permissible interest rates paid on time deposits or as prescribed in usury laws, or a floor, such as a minimum wage—but a set of specific prices. It is through the regulation of price that the limitation of profits is purportedly achieved; it is incident to the regulation of price that the levels and permissible kinds of cost are controlled, by allowing or disallowing payments for various inputs, by supervising methods of financing and controlling financial structures. Price regulation is the heart of public utility regulation.

This assertion might strike a constitutional lawyer or anyone who has read Chapter 1 as strangely old-fashioned. It sounds like something the United States Supreme Court would have said 40 to 50 years ago, when it was systematically striking down legislative attempts to regulate prices or wages outside the traditional "industries affected with a public interest" on the ground that the right to set prices free of public control was at the heart of the freedom of contract protected by the Fourteenth Amendment.[1] In 1934, in *Nebbia v. New York*, the Supreme Court finally rejected the notion that there was anything constitutionally sacrosanct about private price-determination, and declared that if any industry could, for good and sufficient reasons, be subjected to public regulation, there was no constitutional bar to its being subjected to price regulation in particular.[2]

Our assertion may seem irrational also to the economist. And to some extent it is. One purpose of regulation is to protect buyers from monopolistic exploitation—but buyers can be exploited just as effectively by giving them poor or unsafe service as by charging them excessive prices. Another purpose is to prevent destructive competition—but it would seem that sellers can compete just as destructively by offering better or more service for the same price as by offering the same service at lower prices. Price really has no meaning except in terms of an assumed quality of service; price is a ratio, with money in the numerator and some physical unit of given or assumed quantity and quality in the denominator. Price regulation alone is economically meaningless. Moreover, the nature of our dependence on public utility services is typically such that customers may correctly be *more* interested in the denominator than in the numerator—in the reliability, continuity, and safety of the service than in the price they have to pay.[3]

This relatively greater concentration on price than on quality of service is one reflection of the severe limitations of regulation as an institution of social control of industry. In this chapter we examine the major traditional components of that effort. In addition to laying the necessary factual foundation for our subsequent analysis, the purpose of this preliminary survey is to suggest (1) the limited resemblance between what regulation, as traditionally practiced, tries to do and the principles of normative microeconomic theory, thus providing the justification for our alternative approach, in Part II, and (2) the severe limitations of this institutional device for achieving optimal economic results, which provides the background for Volume 2.

THE LIMITED ATTENTION TO QUALITY OF SERVICE

The regulatory process devotes considerable attention to the denominator of the money-quantum-of-service ratio.[4] The governing statutes generally empower commissions to investigate and issue findings on whether the service offered under their jurisdiction is "unjust, unsafe, improper, inadequate or insufficient," and to promulgate rules for its improvement. The rules adopted

---

[1] See notes 11–20, Chapter 1. In *Adkins v. Children's Hospital*, the Court struck down a law fixing minimum wages for women in the District of Columbia in these terms:

"The essential characteristics of the statute now under consideration, which differentiate it from the laws fixing hours of labor. . . . [are] that the latter . . . deal with incidents of the employment having no necessary effect upon the heart of the contract; that is, the amount of wages. . . .

"If now, in the light furnished by the foregoing exceptions to the general rule forbidding legislative interference with freedom of contract, we examine and analyze the statute in question, we

shall see that it differs from them in every material respect. It is not a law dealing with any business charged with a public interest. . . . It has nothing to do with the character, methods, or periods of wage payments. It does not prescribe hours of labor or conditions under which labor is to be done. . . . It is simply and exclusively a price-fixing law. . . ." 261 U.S. 525, 553–554 (1923).

[2] 291 U.S. 502, 531–532, 536–537 (1934).

[3] See Irston R. Barnes, *The Economics of Public Utility Regulation* (New York: Appleton-Century-Crofts, 1942), 742–743.

[4] For a useful survey, see Charles F. Phillips, Jr., *op. cit.*, 400–438.

cover matters such as safety standards, minimum physical specifications (accuracy of meters, voltage of electricity, heating value of gas), the requirements of prompt meeting of customer demands, extension of service to new customers, controls on abandonment of service, provision of special facilities and arrangements, and certification of new entrants.[5]

But it is far more true of quality of service than of price that the primary responsibility remains with the supplying company instead of with the regulatory agency, and that the agencies, in turn, have devoted much more attention to the latter than to the former. The reasons for this are fairly clear. Service standards are often much more difficult to specify by the promulgation of rules. Where they can be specified, they are often essentially uncontroversial. Where they cannot—and this is particularly the case when it comes to innovations, to the dynamic improvement of service—in a system in which the private companies do the managing and the government the supervision, there is no choice but to leave the initiative with the company itself. The only role the regulatory commission can typically play is a negative one—formulating minimum standards and using periodic inspections to see that they are met; investigating customer complaints and issuing orders when service has been obviously poor, when management or subordinates have been blatantly inefficient or unfair, or when it wishes to insist that the companies take on or retain unremunerative business.[6]

This authority is by no means negligible. The aggressive commission has available to it the ability to penalize offending companies by holding permissible rates at less remunerative levels than it would otherwise be prepared to allow—subject to the constraint, however, that it would be self-defeating to punish them so severely as to impair their financial capacity to institute the desired improvements. And commissions frequently do use this weapon.[7]

Still, their role is essentially a negative one and this raises fundamental questions about the efficacy of the entire process. If, as far as quality of service is concerned, the principal responsibility rests with the private monopolist,

---

[5] "Public utility commissions are constantly passing upon questions of service. The determination of a rate without a determination of the quality of the service rendered would be similar to an individual's agreeing to pay a stipulated sum of money for a commodity without specifying the kind or grade of commodity he expects to receive in return for his outlay. A very large portion of the commissions' time is, then, necessarily devoted to the determination of the quality of service rendered by the utilities under their jurisdiction. Most states which have active commissions now have state-wide service standards. . . . Where there are departures from these standards the utility is obviously derelict in the performance of its duties, and unless excused by the commission because of unusual circumstances is subject to its disapproval." Charles Stillman Morgan, *Regulation and the Management of Public Utilities* (Boston: Houghton Mifflin, 1923), 270–271.

[6] The question of whether and in what circumstances a utility company may be required to extend service to new customers and areas, or be forbidden to discontinue services may of course be regarded as an aspect of the regulation of service and is usually so treated. But the issue here is usually quite explicitly one of price or of the relation of revenues to costs, present or prospective: to what extent may utilities be required to take on new, or continue to serve old markets that they think are or will be unremunerative; to what extent should profitable business subsidize unprofitable extensions or continuations? These issues are thus embraced (sometimes explicitly, sometimes implicitly) in our later discussions of cost-price relationships. Of course, as we have already suggested, all regulations of service quality are in economic effect also regulations of price.

[7] For example,

"The testimony given in the gas service case hearing at Neenah was conclusive that the quality of service rendered is totally inadequate. . . . The Commission finds therefore that no increase in rates for gas should be given consideration until the service rendered in the gas department shall conform in a reasonable manner to the standard laid down by the Commission. . . . That no increase in rates for the electric and street railway departments of this utility should be granted until the service in each of them shall be shown to be reasonably satisfactory, and the burden of proof of so doing shall be put on the company. . . ." Morgan, *op. cit.*, 272.

Or, to turn to more recent examples:

"We are receiving numerous complaints from portions of the territory served by Southern Bell. In some areas . . . installation intervals, or the time required to install service, fall well below a reasonable standard. Operator answering time consistently meets Bell's requirements but does not meet the standards recently adopted by this commission. By far the biggest complaint . . . is the length of time required to obtain service. . . . These are problems that can and must be resolved. We have recently adopted uniform standards for telephone service, and have prescribed administrative rules requiring periodic reports which, together with field inspections, will keep the commission fully advised concerning the quality and sufficiency of telephone service being provided. . . . Any rate adjustments, including the one in this docket, will be on a temporary basis for a reasonable period of time pending any necessary improvements in the quality and sufficiency of service. . . .

"Southern Bell will be required to furnish a good and sufficient surety bond conditioned on the prompt and full refund of the difference, if any, between the rates collected by it on a temporary basis pursuant to this order, and the rates ultimately prescribed or approved . . . . as a result of any further order that may be entered in this docket reducing such temporary rates because of service deficiencies."

Re Southern Bell Telephone and Telegraph Company, Florida Public Service Commission, Order No. 4462, November 26, 1968, 76 *Public Utility Reports* 3rd, 412–413.

"We make the following findings:

1. The present earnings of United Telephone Company of Florida are far below a reasonable level and said utility is entitled to some relief on a temporary and emergency basis.
2. United Telephone's present earnings of 3.15 per cent will not support the additional financing that is necessary to enable it to complete its improvement program.
3. The telephone service presently being rendered . . . by United Telephone has improved substantially during the past several months, but is not sufficiently adequate and efficient to justify the full increases requested. . . .

4. The company has virtually completed 64 per cent of its current 3-year (1967–1969) improvement program and, thus, has been able to bring about substantial improvement in service. On that basis, it is fair and reasonable to allow the utility 64 per cent of the requested increases in local exchange rates. . . .
5. The emergency increases authorized by this order will not result at this time in a fair and reasonable return for United Telephone Company, but will improve its financial position so that it should be able to finance the remainder of its improvement program. . . ."

Re United Telephone Company of Florida, Florida Public Service Commission, Order No. 4451, November 12, 1968, 76 PUR 3rd, 471. For other examples, see *ibid.*, 441–451 and 461.

"After years of deliberation, the Federal Communications Commission has decided to tackle the controversial question of how fast Western Union Telegraph Co. should be required to deliver telegrams. . . .

"Communications experts say the commission's involvement could lead to the first Government-mandated standards regulating speed of domestic telegram deliveries. . . .

"Western Union Telegraph has come under increasing fire in recent years from critics who complain that the cost of telegrams keeps going up while the quality of service declines. . . .

"The FCC's decision to consider the speed-of-service issue cropped up as a little-noticed part of the FCC's current investigation of telegram rate increases proposed by Western Union Telegraph. In announcing the inquiry, the FCC said it would consider not only the rate boosts, but also the 'speed, quality and adequacy' of the company's telegram service.

"FCC officials say this phrase means the commission probably will deal with a number of service-related telegram issues in its investigation, such as how many telegraph offices Western Union Telegraph should maintain, and whether it should be investing more money in its telegram service. But a key question, these sources maintain, is whether the FCC should force Western Union to meet certain speed requirements in its telegram deliveries. . . ." *Wall Street Journal*, October 18, 1968.

Again, in 1969 the New York State Public Service Commission ordered the Penn Central Company to take more than a dozen specific steps to provide "safe, adequate, just and reasonable service" on its Harlem and Hudson commuter lines, including the purchase or lease of at least 80 new cars and 24 new engines, assuring that each of its 340 weekday trains runs on time at lest 80% of the time each month, and providing enough telephone lines and employees and the government supervisor can intervene only where objective standards can be set or, after the event, when the monopolist's performance has been *obviously bad*,[8] do we have an adequate assurance—comparable to the assurance provided by competition in other sectors of the economy—that his performance will be *positively good* and continuously as good as possible? If poor service is economically the equivalent of high price, why is there not just as great a danger that monopoly power will involve the one as the other? If monopoly carries the danger of sluggishness with respect both to efficiency and to dynamic cost-reduction, is there not the danger of sluggishness as well in improving the quality and extending the scope of service?

These problems are real. Although, as we shall see later, they can never be wholly solved within the regulatory framework, they deserve more creative and active attention from commissions than they now receive.[9] But there is another reason why public utility commissions have been willing, and to some extent justified, to leave the quality of service, far more than price, to the companies themselves—the latter will typically have a strong interest in providing good, ample, and expanding service, as long as they can recoup its costs in the prices they charge. In this respect, far more than in the matter of price, the interest of the monopolist on the one hand and the consumer on the other are more nearly coincident than in conflict.[10] Why so?

1. Maintaining and improving the quality and quantity of service typically is costly. Any regulated monopolist who is prevented by regulation from fully exploiting the inelasticity of his demand but assured (albeit with a regulatory lag) of his ability to incorporate these additional costs in his cost-of-service and hence of recouping them in his price, will presumably be less hesitant than a nonregulated monopolist to incur them.[11]

2. Improvement and extension of service will often involve an expansion of the company's invested capital—that is, its "rate base"—on which it is entitled to a return. The regulated monopolist therefore will have some

---

so that passengers phoning to check on train schedules "receive a prompt response." *The New York Times*, June 6, 1969, 1. In response, the company petitioned for a rehearing. *Ibid.*, July 4, 1969, 1.

For a more general discussion of the way in which service standards and orders may be enforced and particularly of the authority of commissions to condition rate increases on specified improvements or extensions of service, see "The Duty of a Public Utility to Render Adequate Service: Its Scope and Enforcement," *Columbia Law Rev.* (Feb. 1962), LXII: 312, 327–331.

[8] See the astonishing intention of Senator Pastore, chairman of the U.S. Senate Subcommittee on Communications, explicitly to confine the powers of the Federal Communications Commission in precisely this manner in deciding whether or not to renew broadcasting station licenses. He would prohibit challenges to renewals unless the FCC first determines that the station has violated the "public interest." Daniel Zwerdling, "FCC Impropriety," *The New Republic*, June 21, 1969, 10–11. See also

note 134, Chapter 2, Volume 2.

[9] For the case of radio and television, and for a novel case involving the quality of passenger rail service, see Chapter 2 of Volume 2.

[10] Indeed, the greater danger might be that the companies place excessive instead of inadequate emphasis on providing high-quality service, at the expense of economy, for reasons that follow. See also the discussion in Chapter 5, Volume 2, of whether the public utilities reflect a general tendency for limitations on price competition to be associated with an intensification of quality competition.

[11] The unregulated monopolist also will have an incentive to improve his product or diversify his product offerings, to the extent that his demand is sufficiently responsive to offset the additional costs of his so doing. But if he is a profit maximizer presumably he will have set his price-quality combination at the profit-maximizing point, beyond which superior service will add more to costs than to revenues. A public utility, in contrast, if prevented from fixing its price at the profit-maximizing level, has a reserve of incompletely exploited monopoly power; in the

temptation to err in the direction of expanding and improving his services, and thus increasing his rate base beyond the point of economic optimality instead of the reverse.[12]

3. A public utility company is peculiarly exposed to public criticism if its service is inadequate. This exposure is increased by the possibility of customers complaining to regulatory commissions. Possibly associated with this consideration may be a tendency for managers of such companies to assume a quasi-professional responsibility for giving the best possible service, even at the expense of profit maximization.[13] Although customers may have very definite opinions about whether the prices they pay are too high, the determination of whether in fact they are doing so is a complicated matter, as we shall see. But they need no complex investigative and adjudicatory processes to tell them when they are suffering from a power failure, or a refusal of a railroad to make freight cars available to them, or when they keep getting busy signals or wrong numbers on the telephone.[14] Adequate levels of service can be guaranteed more satisfactorily than price by customer complaints, on the one hand, and the "conscience of the corporation," on the other.[15]

It is doubtful that these pressures are as reliable as those exerted by competition; and an unregulated monopolist will surely be subject to similar influences. Still, motivations such as these do to some extent take the place of competition in inducing the franchised monopolist to have a favorable attitude toward providing good and ever-improving service to his captive customers.

The customer may have a fair notion of whether the service he gets is satisfactory. He is likely to find it much more difficult to judge whether its quality and variety are *improving* at a satisfactory rate, because in making such a judgment it would not be pertinent to compare the quality of what he is receiving with what he has been accustomed to expect. But it is precisely these questions about dynamic performance, with respect not only to the quality of service but also to costs and price, that the regulatory commission also is least competent to answer decisively. Although it is in this respect that there may be the greatest danger of inadequate monopoly performance—or *excessive* performance, for the reason suggested under (2), above—this danger is not one to which the commissions have typically been able to devote effective attention.

REGULATING THE RATE LEVEL

Public utility commissions spend the major part of their time, by far, directly or indirectly regulating price. This task has two major aspects and the commissions have tended typically to treat them quite distinctly. The first has to do with the level of rates, taken as a group. The second has to do with the structure of rates—the specific charges on different categories of

---

same circumstances it will therefore have less disincentive to improve service, since any additional costs involved can serve as the justification for raising price correspondingly.

[12] On this particular distortion, see the section on the "A–J–W Effect," in Chapter 2, Volume 2.

[13] See, for example, Troxel, *Economics of Public Utilities*, 464–465, 557–560.

[14] See the flurry of complaints in New York City in July of 1969 over the annoying frequency of busy signals in the New York Telephone Company's Plaza 8 exchange. See, for instance, *New York Times*, July 14, 1969, 22.

[15] But see Glaeser, *op cit.*, 115, emphasizing the need for regulation, to overcome consumer ignorance and managerial inertia.

service and the relationship between them. Outside of the transportation field, the former task has claimed much the greater share of commission attention.

"The rate level," like "the general price level," is a statistical abstraction. It could be expressed only as some sort of index number, summarizing the numerous individual rates for the various classifications of service provided by each company: there are some 43 trillion railroad rates on file with the Interstate Commerce Commission![16] Its real economic meaning is disclosed when these separate prices are translated into total company revenues or into total profits expressed as a percent of owners' investments. Actually the regulatory process works the other way around. The commissions decide what total revenues the companies are entitled to take in, then adjust permitted "rate levels," either selectively or across the board, to yield these totals.

They typically do this by undertaking a thorough examination and appraisal of total company costs in a recent, "test" year.[17] In this way, item by item, they build up an estimate of total permissible "revenue requirements." On the basis of this total, adjusted as much as possible for known or readily predictable changes between the test year and the period for which rates are to be ascertained, the company is ordered or permitted to propose the required adjustments in its rate schedules. Therefore, discussions of rate levels are really discussions of total revenues.

The process of determining permissible revenues falls traditionally into the following three parts or steps, each of them involving an enormous variety of problems and boasting a correspondingly rich history of legal and economic controversy.

Supervision and Control of Operating Costs and Capital Outlays

Just as competition is supposed to hold prices down to the cost of production (ignore for a moment the question of precisely what that means) so regulation takes cost as its standard of the "revenue requirements" of public utility companies, hence the "just and reasonable" rates that the typical controlling statute enjoins them to maintain. It became clear that if the commissions were to be something more than rubber stamps they had to exercise their own judgment about the propriety of the items presented to them as the major components of the cost of service. To do so, first, they had to require the companies to keep uniform systems of accounts, according to procedures and rules stipulated by the commissions, and subject to their audit.[18] Then they needed to make determinations about which costs they were prepared

---

[16] C. F. Phillips, *op. cit.*, 314.

[17] They may do so regularly or only once in a long while, in a major general rate investigation, or never. If only occasionally, they may employ more limited checks in the intervening years, possibly permitting rate changes on the basis of estimates of cost changes since the "test year." For an illuminating case study of "The General Passenger Fare Investigation," the first undertaken by the Civil Aeronautics Board, about 15 years after passage of its enabling act (a delay for which it was criticized), see the case

study of that title by Emmette S. Redford, in Edwin A. Bock, ed., *Government Regulation of Business: A Casebook* (Englewood Cliffs: Prentice-Hall, 1962), 336–411. On the Federal Communications Commission's "continuous surveillance" over the telephone industry, see Chapter 2, Volume 2, at note 37.

[18] Commissions cannot review costs unless the regulated companies keep their records in some uniform and prescribed fashion. Accounting regulations become necessary also to prescribe those elements of outlay that are to be charged

to authorize for inclusion in the computed company cost-of-service; and, of these, which could be charged directly as operating expenses and thus included in annual revenue requirements dollar for dollar, and which capitalized, thus entering the cost of service in the form of annual allowances for depreciation and return on the undepreciated portion of the investment. Since mere disallowance of certain outlays after the fact could have the effect of reducing excessively the companies' rates of return, and hence of threatening their ability to attract additional capital, commissions came to insist also on the authority to control company expenditure in advance, supervising and passing on their budgets.

Why should it be necessary for commissions to involve themselves in passing on the operating costs of public utility companies? Presumably even an unregulated profit-maximizing monopolist would wish to hold his costs to a minimum, entirely on his own initiative. Could not the commissions then leave such matters to the self-interest of the company managers themselves? Answers can be framed at several levels.

First, there is the simple danger of concealment of profits by exaggeration of costs. Whatever his *actual* level of costs, it obviously pays a regulated monopolist to exaggerate his estimated cost of service. As long as regulation is effective in holding his profits lower than they otherwise could be, he can more completely exploit his monopoly power by fooling the commission into permitting him higher rates than his actual costs justify. Such exaggerations might be expected to show up, after the event, in excessive rates of earnings. But profits can be computed only from accounting records; if there are no understandings about how costs are to be computed and recorded, expenditures to be audited, and the capital value of the stockholders' investment to be measured, there is no way of appraising those records, and supernormal rates of profit can be concealed in padded expense figures and inflated capital accounts.

Second, the charge for depreciation represents not an objective datum but an imputation, an attribution to the production in any given accounting period of responsibility for the using up or obsolescence of capital assets. Similar to the cost of capital itself—that is, the requisite return on invested capital that must likewise be included in the cost of production—there is room for differences of judgment about its proper level. It is obviously in the interest of the regulated company to exaggerate its gross cost of capital—depreciation plus return on investment—and for the commission to hold it to the minimum, as we shall see more fully presently.

Third, it might be in the interest of the company—always assuming that regulation is effective in holding its profits below the levels that the market would otherwise permit—to incur actually greater costs than is in the best interest of the consumer, provided it is then permitted to incorporate those costs in the regulated price. One example would be heavy expenditures for advertising and public relations, since the companies might receive numerous

---

directly to income and those that are to be capitalized. The appropriate charges for depreciation cannot be determined and reviewed unless the depreciable property accounts are kept in some comprehensible fashion. Accounting rules are also necessary with respect to the valuation of property, which plays an extremely important role in determining the final cost of service, as we shall see. They are similarly necessary if the utility company itself or the commission is to use cost intelligently in the devising of rate structures.

benefits therefrom while passing the costs on to the consuming public. Public utility companies advertise in the hope of influencing regulatory commissions to treat them generously, and electric companies have financed expensive propaganda campaigns in opposition to competing public power projects.[19] Similar purposes might be served by large charitable contributions; with these, as with advertising outlays, commissions have had to decide how much, if any, is properly charged to the consumer and how much should be borne by the stockholders. A similar need for regulatory supervision could be created by the possible temptation of utility companies—to which we have already alluded, and which we will analyze more fully below—to use capital wastefully in order to inflate their rate bases and hence their total permissible profits.

Fourth, the regulated companies—even more, their promoters and managers—have extracted some of these potential monopoly profits by paying excessive prices to affiliated, unregulated companies for equipment, supplies, financial advice and underwriting, engineering, and managerial services—charges included in the cost of service and recovered from customers.[20]

Fifth, since the public utilities are typically not subject to intensive price competition, they are probably not under the same pressures as firms in more competitive industries to hold their costs down. It is understandable, therefore, that regulatory commissions, charged with taking the place of competition, should make some efforts in the same direction. The necessity for their doing so is accentuated, finally, by the unusually high degree of

---

[19] See Ernest Gruening, *The Public Pays: A Study of Power Propaganda*, rev. ed. (New York: Vanguard, 1964), *passim*. Gruening includes (xxix-xliii) the *Memorandum Opinion* of the Federal Power Commission, *In the Matter of Northwestern Electric Company et al.*, Docket No. IT–5647, Opinion No. 59, 1941, reporting on its investigation of the accounting disposition of expenditures for political purposes by five electric companies. Merle Fainsod and Lincoln Gordon report an estimate that the costs of the "educational" campaign by utility companies after World War I "to 'sell' their industry to the public and to convince the American people of the adequacy of existing regulatory techniques and of the dangers of further penetration of government into the utility business" ran $25–30 millions a year, "all charged off as proper advertising expenses . . . and computed in the rates which the public was required to pay." *Government and The American Economy* (New York: Norton, 1941), 308. And those were Coolidge and Hoover, not Nixon, dollars. The problem, although ancient, has not disappeared: "Five Manhattan State Senators protested yesterday what they called the Consolidated Edison Company's 'gigantic' advertising and promotion campaigns in connection with its request for higher electricity charges." According to the Company's own estimate, its expenditures for institutional advertising would have come to some $2.1

millions in 1965. *New York Times*, August 23, 1966, 27.

Utility companies engage in commercial as well as political and "institutional" advertising, and the former expenditures may well be economically legitimate (see, for example, note 16, Chapter 4). American Telephone and Telegraph (AT&T) and its affiliated companies ranked fourteenth among the nation's advertisers in 1965 with total expenditures of $70 million. But this was a relatively modest 0.6% of the system's total revenues, of $11.3 billion. *Advertising Age*, August 29, 1966, 44, 61.

For a summary of the regulatory treatment of such expenditures, see A. J. G. Priest, *Principles of Public Utility Regulation*, 59–65; also "Trends and Topics, Promotional Programs," *Public Utilities Fortnightly* (June 23, 1966), LXXVII: 65.

[20] See, for example, Louis D. Brandeis, *Other People's Money and How the Bankers Use It* (Washington: The McClure Publications, 1913); James C. Bonbright and Gardner C. Means, *The Holding Company: Its Public Significance and its Regulation* (New York: McGraw-Hill, 1932), esp. Chapter 6. The holding company in some ways has contributed to greater efficiency; but it was also used as a device for milking the (controlled) operating companies, and through them the rate-payers. The relation of the various Bell System companies to their parent, AT&T, and to its wholly-owned subsidiary and equipment

separation of ownership and managerial control in these companies.[21] This fact, taken in conjunction with the lesser pressures of price competition and the possibility of recouping higher costs in higher prices along an inelastic demand curve, creates a particular danger that, in the absence of regulatory scrutiny, managements may vote themselves unusually large salaries, expense accounts and other perquisites, as well as engage in other methods of exploiting their position for their own personal profit or nonpecuniary advantage, as in fact they have from time to time in the past.[22]

Manifestly, the operating expenses and capital outlays of public utility companies are by far the most important component of their rate levels, on the one hand, and the efficiency with which they make use of society's resources on the other. Therefore, in terms of their quantitative importance, it would be reasonable to expect regulatory commissions to give these costs the major part of their attention. But in fact they have not done so; they have given their principal attention instead to the limitation of profits.

The reasons for this perverse distribution of effort illustrate once again the inherent limitations of regulation as an institution of effective social control of industry. Effective regulation of operating expenses and capital outlays

---

supplier, Western Electric Company, has thus been a subject of continuing regulatory concern. In one of the landmark United States Supreme Court decisions in the 1920s the Court refused to permit the Public Service Commission of Missouri to disallow certain payments by the local Bell company to AT&T for rentals and services. *Southwestern Bell Telephone Company v. Public Service Commission of Missouri*, 262 U.S. 276, 288–289 (1923). The Court reversed itself on this matter in *Smith v. Illinois Bell Telephone Co.*, 282 U.S. 133, 152–153 (1930), and the general rule is that these charges must be justified in terms of the costs to AT&T of performing the services. Similarly, numerous state commissions check on the payments by their various Bell companies for Western Electric equipment and supplies, and the *Smith v. Illinois Bell* decision required that this scrutiny take into account Western's profits from these sales. The Michigan Commission has in the past scaled down the payments when it found that the rate of return on Western Electric's capital exceeded the rate of return that it permitted the Michigan Bell Company to earn. C. Emery Troxel, "Telephone Regulation in Michigan," in William G. Shepherd and Thomas G. Gies, ed., *Utility Regulation: New Directions in Theory and Policy* (New York: Random House, 1966), 168–169. But the overwhelming majority of commissions have found Western's charges reasonable and have permitted them to enter the operating companies' cost of service without adjustment. For a fuller discussion, see Chapter 6, Volume 2.

[21] Distribution of 176 large corporations, according to the proportion of voting stock owned by managements, September 30, 1939, by industrial classes:

Percent of Stock Outstanding	Industrial	Public Utility	Railroad
0–1	66	33	21
1–5	29	3	1
5–10	7	2	1
10–20	6	—	—
20–30	2	—	—
30–40	—	—	—
40–50	1	—	—
50 plus	4	—	—
Total	115	38	23

Source. Robert Aaron Gordon, *Business Leadership in the Large Corporation* (Washington: The Brookings Institution, 1945), 27.

A later study of the 200 largest nonfinancial corporations found that in 1963 18% of the industrial corporations were controlled by owners of more than 10% of their stock; the corresponding figures for public utility and railroad corporations were 2% and 4% respectively. At the other extreme, management-controlled companies were 78% of the industrial and 98% of the public utility group. In the case of railroads the percentage was 83, but if one adds in the corporations found to be controlled by a legal device such as pyramiding or the use of voting trusts, that figure rises to 97%, while the ratio for industrials rises only to 82%. Robert J. Larner, "Ownership and Control in the 200 Largest Nonfinancial Corporations, 1929 and 1963," *Amer. Econ. Rev.* (September 1966), LVI: 781.

[22] See Barnes, *Economics of Public Utility Regulation*, 618–619 and the cases cited there. Following up a finding by Gary S. Becker that monopolistic

would require a detailed, day-by-day, transaction-by-transaction, and decision-by-decision review of every aspect of the company's operation. Commissions could do so only if they were prepared completely to duplicate the role of management itself. This society has never been willing to have commissions fill the role of management and doubtless with good reason: it is difficult to see how any company could function under two separate, coequal managements, each with an equally pervasive role in its operations. Therefore, when the controlling decisions are made, they are made in the first instance by private management itself. Regulation can do little more than review the major decisions after the fact, permitting here and disallowing there. In these circumstances they have been unable as a general practice to substitute their judgments for those of management; and often when they have tried, the courts have denied them the authority to do so, except in cases of obvious and gross mismanagement.[23] Profits, in contrast, are merely a markup, something added to the sum total of expenses. This does not mean that profit control is noncontroversial—quite the contrary. But their regulation does not involve the same type of detailed and pervasive supervision as would a comparable control of the decisions that determine a company's efficiency.

---

enterprises discriminate against blacks more frequently than competitive ones, Armen A. Alchian and Reuben A. Kessel developed the more general hypothesis that the managements of companies whose pecuniary profits are limited by regulation (or similar pressures) will be under strong temptation to take out any possibilities of monopoly profit that remain unexploited in the form of "nonpecuniary gains," one category of which is "the indulgence of one's tastes in the kind of people with whom one prefers to associate. Specifically, this may take the form of pretty secretaries, pleasant, well-dressed congenial people who never say anything annoying, of lavish offices, of large expense accounts, of shorter working hours, of costly administrative procedures that reduce the wear and tear on executives . . . having secretaries available on a moment's notice . . . and of many others." "Competition, Monopoly, and the Pursuit of Pecuniary Gain," in Universities-National Bureau Committee for Economic Research, *Aspects of Labor Economics* (Princeton University Press: Princeton, 1962), 163. The likelihood of this managerial behavior may not be significantly greater for regulated public utility companies than in the case of unregulated companies with market power. See Oliver E. Williamson, "Managerial Discretion and Business Behavior," *Amer. Econ. Rev.* (December 1963), LIII: 1032–1057, and William G. Shepherd, "Market Power and Racial Discrimination in White-Collar Employment," *Antitrust Bulletin* (Spring 1969), XIV: 141–161 and, with particular reference to regulated companies, 155–157.

[23] See, for example, William K. Jones, *Cases and Materials on Regulated Industries* (Brooklyn: The Foundation Press, 1967), 175–186.

"Good faith is to be presumed on the part of the managers of a business. . . . In the absence of a showing of inefficiency or improvidence, a court will not substitute its judgment for theirs as to the measure of a prudent outlay." *West Ohio Gas Co. v. Public Utilities Commission* 294 U.S. 63, 72 (1935). See the exhaustive summary of the case law in Priest, *Principles of Public Utility Regulation*, I, Chapter 3.

On the other hand:

"The Alaska commission upheld disallowance of $50,000 of expenses to compensate for inefficiencies in an electric company's operation. Comparison of the company's expense with that of automated companies . . . showed the cost to be one and one-half to seven times that of the other companies designated as comparable. . . .

"[According to the hearing officer:] It was not out of place for the commission to disallow expenses claimed to be excessive because available advances in technology had been ignored and the capacity and efficiency of the plant had been eroded through years of inadequate maintenance. . . .

"It was not so much a matter of how the company stacked up in relation to the efficiency of other companies, but a measurement of how it operated at present compared to how it would have operated if suggested recommendations had been put into effect. . . .

"The company had adequate notice and opportunity to institute procedures recommended by engineers it had hired as consultants, which it had neglected to do."

"Expense Reduction to Compensate for Inefficiencies Upheld," *Public Utilities Fortnightly*, March 27, 1969, 60–61.

The process has focused primarily on profits, also, because these are politically the most visible—excessive profits the most obvious danger and sign of consumer exploitation, in the absence of effective competition, regulated profits the most obvious and comforting evidence that regulation can be "effective."[24]

And in those numerous, though comparatively unimportant instances in which commissions do in fact decide whether or not to disallow some item of expenditure, the governing consideration turns out to be what policy would be most "fair" to stockholders on the one hand and consumers on the other—a constantly recurring theme in the regulatory process.[25] It is certainly not suggested here that considerations such as these are irrelevant in what is, inescapably, a political determination—that is, a determination of who gets what and how much (and the "who" may include not just stockholders, managers, and customers but, for example, the colleges, churches, or minority groups that might benefit from contributions or other such expenditures that the corporation may be unable to justify on a purely economic basis).[26] But it is important to recognize that criteria such as these may or may not coincide with the type of results competition would produce, or with what would be economically optimal.[27]

---

[24] The analogous situation prevails with respect to weapons acquisition by the Department of Defense:

"a workable definition of efficiency requires considering all of the costs generated in a weapons program, profit . . . being just one special form of cost. Herein lies the second reason for the emphasis on minimum profits as an indicator of weapons acquisition efficiency. It is usually much easier for government negotiators or auditors to say that profits are too high than to claim that the cost of developing some technically complex item of equipment is excessive. Government personnel recognize that if any item in the weapons bill can be attacked and perhaps reduced, it is the profit item. However, this Machiavellian realism ignores the 90% or more of the bill in which a much greater potential for efficiency improvements typically exists." Merton J. Peck and Frederic M. Scherer, *The Weapons Acquisition Process: An Economic Analysis*, Division of Research, Graduate School of Business Administration (Boston: Harvard University, 1962), 509.

[25] It frequently recurs outside the regulatory area as well. A striking example is to be found in the field of antitrust policy, where precisely the same issues arise about the compatibility of "fair competition" and economic efficiency. See, for example, Joel B. Dirlam and Alfred E. Kahn, *Fair Competition, The Law and Economics of Antitrust Policy* (Ithaca: Cornell University Press, 1954), which is addressed to this issue.

[26] This means that the process, being essentially political, is capable of generating violent emotions or at least rhetoric, on the part both of the industry, in its efforts to reduce the load of regulation, to justify its managements' compensation and its own performance against the threat of government competition, and of its critics, who see regulation as ineffective and the consumer subjected to merciless gouging. For a fine example of the latter, see Lee Metcalf and Vic Reinemer, *Overcharge* (New York: David McKay Company, 1967), *passim*, and, specifically on cost items such as charitable contributions, managerial compensation, and political advertising, Chapters 6, 8, and 9. It is no condescension to point out that the book's economic analysis and appraisals are neither objective nor thorough; but its argument cannot be ignored.

[27] See, for example, the survey of the policies of regulatory commissions with respect to the allowance or disallowance of promotional, public relations, or charitable expenditures in C. F. Phillips, *op. cit.*, 186–188. Or see the very interesting conflicting majority, concurring, and dissenting opinions on the subject of contributions in *Pacific Telephone and Telegraph Co. v. Public Utilities Commission of the State of California et al.*, 401 P. 2d 353, 374–375, 379–382 (1965). It is very difficult to detect any consistent consideration, let alone application, of economic criteria, of the kind to be developed in Part II. Instead there is a mushy mixture of questions such as: Do these outlays benefit the company? Or the community at large? Or the stockholders, mainly? Are they properly part of the utility business? What would be fair? These observations are by no means intended to suggest that application of "strictly economic" criteria would provide any simple answers to these problems either.

Therefore, although efficient operation and continuous improvement therein are, quantitatively, the most important aspects of industrial performance, the principal reliance for securing these results cannot, in the nature of the case, be placed on the regulatory process itself. The major contribution that regulation can make, and it is a modest one, can only be the providing of incentives—or taking care not to remove incentives—for private managements to exert themselves continuously in this direction. Whether such incentives can ever be sufficient, once the spur of competition has been drastically attenuated, is the fundamental question with which we deal in Volume 2.

The allowance for depreciation expenses is of quite a different character. Operating expenses involve actual money outlays, which can be automatically recorded in company accounts and transferred into the computed cost of service. Depreciation, too, goes into cost of service and price; but it is not a money outlay in the year it is charged. It is an imputed cost, introduced to take account of the fact that the economic life of capital assets is limited; to distribute the decline in their value—which is a genuine cost of production— over their economic life, in order to assure its recoupment from customers. So the portion of total revenues it permits the company to earn does not, as is the case with normal operating expenses, go out in payments to outside parties—suppliers of raw materials, workers and so on. It belongs to the owners; it is part of the gross return they are permitted to earn on their investment.

The return to capital, in other words, has two parts: the return *of* the money capital invested over the estimated economic life of the investment and the return (interest and net profit) *on* the portion of investment that remains outstanding. The two are arithmetically linked, since according to the usual (but not universal) regulatory practice the size of the net investment, on which a return is permitted, depends at any given time on the aggregate amount of depreciation expense allowed in the previous years—that is, the amount of investment that remains depends on how much of it has been recouped by annual depreciation charges previously. And the two are linked economically, since the rate at which owners are permitted to get their capital out helps determine the true rate of return that they earn on their original investment. To the extent—as happens in some jurisdictions—that accrued depreciation is not fully deducted from the rate base, the regulated companies in effect are being permitted a higher rate of profit; and the same result could be achieved by allowing a higher nominal rate on original investment cost less full depreciation.

Any economic discussion of depreciation should really consider it along with the return on investment. In many contexts it must take into account also the changing provisions of the corporation income tax law concerning allowable rates of depreciation for tax purposes. Consider, for instance, the three-fold effect on the cost of service, hence on allowable rates of return, of provisions for accelerated depreciation in the income tax laws, such as were enacted in 1964, via (1) what it may do to the appropriate level of annual depreciation expense allowed by the regulatory commission, (2) the effect of different rates of annual depreciation on the net remaining investment, on which the net return is permitted, and (3) the amount of income taxes that ought to be included in the cost of service. That requires some explanation.

The effect of accelerated tax depreciation is not to reduce total taxes paid over the life of any particular piece of capital equipment, but only to change its timing. Only the original cost of the equipment can be charged off, in total, over its life. When a company charges a disproportionately large part of the total in the earlier years for tax purposes—which has the effect of reducing taxable income, hence taxes—this means it will be able to charge off correspondingly less, hence will be forced to pay equivalently higher taxes, in later years. Assuming no change in tax rates in the interim, the taxes saved in the early years have to be paid back in full in the later years. But the postponement is beneficial to the taxpayer; in effect, accelerated depreciation means the Treasury Department is giving him an interest-free loan, during the period of the postponement. It increases the real rate (after tax) of return on investment, if one is permitted to keep more of his profits for a while, before having to hand them over to the government.

So regulatory commissions have had to decide whether the taxes to be incorporated in price should be only those actually paid—in which event the benefits of accelerated depreciation are passed on entirely to customers in the years of tax saving—or "normalized" over the life of the investment (higher than actual taxes in the early years, lower in the later)—in which event the interest-free loan is retained by the company. If the latter is chosen, commissions have had to decide also what treatment should be given to the revenues recouped from consumers in excess of the taxes actually paid in the earlier years. These "phantom taxes" are typically segregated in a special reserve for deferred taxes, in recognition of the fact that taxes will in later years exceed these "normalized" recoupments from customers. But the controversial question is whether the amount of that reserve should be deducted from the company's net investment or rate base, on the ground that, as with depreciation, these monies have been retrieved from customers and that it would be double recoupment to permit the company also to earn a return on that portion of its undepreciated investment; or whether it should be left in the rate base, because Congress intended the tax savings to benefit investors and by so doing to encourage additional investment. The more frequent practice is to permit the company no return on the assets represented by the tax reserve; but many commissions permit a small return (for example, 1.5%, in contrast with 6.5% on the normal rate base), and some allow the full return—that is, they do not reduce the rate base by the accumulations of deferred taxes at all.[28]

Advocates of including in the cost of service only the taxes actually paid, which involves "flowing through" the benefits of accelerated depreciation to the customers, argue that the benefits are likely to be permanent—that is, that the amount of taxes saved is not really postponed but is, in effect, forgiven. And they are more right than wrong, *provided* the company's total investments grow over time at a sufficiently rapid rate. In that event, the tax postponements on its newer (and ever larger) investments will always exceed the higher taxes continually coming due on the older (and smaller) investments. Indeed, as long as total company assets grow at all, taxes will always be lower under accelerated amortization than they would be otherwise. Opponents of flow-through, assuming instead that the tax is merely postponed, maintain that this method confers a windfall of rate reductions on

---

[28] See Eugene F. Brigham, "Public Utility Depreciation Practices and Policies," *National Tax J.* (June 1966), XIX: 149.

current customers at the expense of future customers. And, indeed, under almost any assumption about future growth of the company, rates under flow-through *will* have to be increased at some time in the future—although, as long as growth is positive, not to the levels that would have to be charged all the way along by a company that failed to take advantage of this tax privilege.

Rate-payers benefit from normalization also, as long as the accumulated tax reserve is deducted in whole or in part from the rate base, since they no longer have to pay a return on that part of the company's total assets represented by those accumulated tax-savings. Flow-through gives them the greatest immediate benefit. Whether in the long run rates end up lower under flow-through than normalization depends, for the reasons already indicated, on how rapidly the company's total assets grow.[29]

Not surprisingly, there has been continuous controversy and litigation over which of these methods, if either, utility commissions ought to adopt; and, if they adopt flow-through, whether regulated companies can be required to avail themselves of the tax privileges, although they retain none of the benefits and run the risk of having to ask for rate increases in the future.[30] These are really questions of the appropriate return to be permitted on capital investment. When company spokesmen argue against flowing-through or deducting the deferred-tax reserves from their allowable rate base, they are in effect arguing for a larger return on investment. When consumer representatives argue on the other side, their contention, at least implicitly, is that regulation must in any case provide a sufficient rate of return—in which event these additional incentives are unnecessary and ought to be passed on in lower rates.

Another issue associated with the determination of depreciation expense is whether the number of dollars that investors are permitted in this fashion to recoup from customers should be the amounts originally invested, or whether that total should be adjusted over time to reflect the changing purchasing power of those dollars. Here, again, the question is really one of what type of return investors ought to be permitted; in economic essence, it is the same issue in another form as whether the rate base, on which the

[29] For a general survey of the issues, see Garfield and Lovejoy, *Public Utility Economics*, 109–114. For a very lucid account and analysis of the pattern of rates over time under the various possible systems and under different growth rate assumptions, see Eugene F. Brigham, "The Effects of Alternative Tax Depreciation Policies on Public Utility Rate Structures," *National Tax J*. (June 1967), XX: 204–218.

[30] A survey at the outset of 1970 showed that commissions in 20 states required normalization, in 17 flowing-through, and in 12 had taken no action at all. Both the Federal Power Commission and the Interstate Commerce Commission have ordered flow-through; the Civil Aeronautics Board, normalization; and the Federal Communications Commission has taken no stand, except to declare that the failure of a regulated company to take advantage of accelerated depreciation for tax purposes would be taken into account in fixing the rate of return. "States Split on Accelerated Depreciation," *Electrical World*, January 20, 1969, 73, and *ibid.*, January 12, 1970, 12. FPC decisions requiring flow-through and computing company costs of service *as though* the companies had availed themselves of the tax privileges even though they had ceased to do so, have been sustained in the courts. See *Alabama-Tennessee Natural Gas Co. v. Federal Power Commission*, 359 F. 2d 318 (1966), cert. denied, 385 U.S. 847 (1967); *Natural Gas Pipeline Co. of America v. Federal Power Commission*, 385 F. 2d 629 (1967); and *Midwestern Gas Transmission et al. v. Federal Power Commission*, 388 F. 2d 444 (1968), cert. denied 392 U.S. 928 (1968). But the ability of commissions to require flowing-through was severely curtailed by the 1969 income tax law revision. Public Law 91–172, 91st Congress, December 30, 1969, 83 Stat. 487, 625–628.

allowable return is to be computed, should be similarly adjusted—to which we turn shortly.

The treatment of depreciation expense under public utility regulation provides an early illustration of the respects in which pricing here departs from the norms of microeconomic theory. It is an elementary proposition of that model and one aspect of its central rule, as we shall see more fully in Chapter 3, that price ideally should be set at marginal cost—that is, at short-run marginal cost. But that marginal cost is a measure of changes in *variable* costs alone; it does not include (most of) depreciation, or any part of the net return on investment, as such. Nor do monopolists, who are supposed to equate marginal cost to marginal revenue, take depreciation into account either in their pricing decisions—again according to the traditional theory of the firm, which assumes continuous, short-run profit maximization. In both cases this means, roughly, that the businessman must cover his variable costs, if he is to continue to operate at all; and so far as gross return on investment is concerned, he takes as much as he can get, over and above the variable costs—sometimes much, sometimes little—whatever the market will bear. It is only in the long run, over the life of investments, that prices, thus set, are expected to be high enough on the average to cover fixed costs. Therefore, when regulatory commissions include fixed costs such as depreciation and return on investment in their cost of service computations, and hence in the permissible rates, they are in effect requiring not marginal-cost but average-cost or full-cost pricing—a practice widely followed in unregulated industries as well. How serious this departure from optimum pricing is in practice is a major topic of Part II.

Determination of the "Rate Base"

Since the production of public utility services typically is unusually capital-intensive,[31] the element of cost represented by the return on invested capital necessarily bulks larger in their final selling price than in unregulated

---

[31] Garfield and Lovejoy offer as typical the following capital turnover ratios (gross revenues divided by capital investment).

Electric utilities	0.30
Natural gas utilities	0.60
Natural gas pipelines	0.40
Bell Telephone System	0.40
Water utilities	0.20
Total manufacturing	2.00

Source. *Op. cit.*, 23.

A clearer impression of the unusually heavy utilization of capital in the public utility industries is provided by the following skeletal financial data taken from the Annual Reports of a public utility, a steel, and a grocery retailing company. Note the wide range in the ratios of their capital to sales, whether the former is measured by total assets, fixed assets —land, plant, and equipment—or, on the liability side, by total invested capital—that is, long-term debt and owners' equity. Or, to describe the same relationship by its reciprocal, note the differences in the number of times their capital "turns over" each year in the form of sales.

	Pacific Gas and Electric Co.	United States Steel Corp.	The Great Atlantic & Pacific Tea Co. (A&P)
Current assets	236	2,091	558
Land, plant, and equipment, net	3,551	3,446	326
Other assets	28	854	—
Total assets	3,815	6,391	884

industries generally.[32] And since it is this element in the cost of service that determines the size of the company's profit, it is not surprising that its determination has been by far the most hotly contested aspect of regulation,[33] consuming by far the greatest amount of time of both commissions and courts.

The number of dollars of investment return are, of course, a product of the aggregate investment, on which some return is to be allowed, and the percentage rate permitted. Arithmetically, the two factors are of equal importance; the result can be changed by increasing or decreasing one just as well as the other. But, largely for constitutional reasons, the traditional emphasis and focus of most of the litigation in the American regulatory experience has been on the former, the "rate base."

It was not always so. In its historic *Munn v. Illinois* decision, the Supreme Court addressed itself to the contention of the appellants that it was up to the courts to determine whether the rates prescribed—in this case by the legislature itself—were reasonable or unreasonable. It specifically declined to do so:

"It is insisted, however, that the owner of property is entitled to a reason-

	Pacific Gas and Electric Co.	United States Steel Corp.	The Great Atlantic & Pacific Tea Co. (A&P)
Long term debt	1,830	—	—
Owners equity	1,625	3,344	627
Total invested capital	3,456	3,344	627
Sales	1,005	4,609	5,459
Ratios to sales:			
Total assets	3.8	1.4	0.16
Fixed assets	3.5	0.7	0.06
Invested capital	3.4	0.7	0.11

Source. The P.G.&E. and U.S. Steel figures are for 1968, the A&P for the fiscal year 1967–68; balance sheet items are for the end of those years. From their *Annual Reports*.

[32] Capital costs as a percentage of sales, 1965.

	Net Income After Taxes Plus Interest Paid %[a]	Depreciation Plus Income Taxes %[b]
Transportation	5.9	9.7
Communications	13.4	18.6
Electric, gas, and sanitary services	15.4	19.3
Total manufacturing	5.1	6.3

Source. Computed from U.S. Treasury Department, Internal Revenue Service, *Statistics of Income, 1965, Corporation Income Tax Returns*, Washington, 1969, 17, 20.

[a] This column presents net return on investment (equity plus borrowed capital) as a percentage of total business receipts. Interest alone represented the following portions of the total return in the four industry groups: 41, 21, 38 and 14%, respectively.

[b] These are shown additionally in consideration of the fact, already noted, that they are also part of the gross costs of capital. The percentages in the two columns should therefore be added to obtain a fuller indication of the relative importance of all capital costs in these various industries.

[33] This generalization, along with the generalization that commissions have devoted their major attention to the general level of rates, does not apply to transportation, where, for more than four decades, profits (at least of railroads) have typically been below levels that regulatory commissions would have regarded as reasonable, and primary attention has gone instead to rate structures and the conditions of inter-carrier competition. See p. 170, below.

able compensation for its use, even though it be clothed with a public interest, and that what is reasonable is a judicial and not a legislative question.

". . . the practice has been otherwise. In countries where the common law prevails, it has been customary from time immemorial for the legislature to declare what shall be a reasonable compensation under such circumstances, or, perhaps more properly speaking, to fix a maximum beyond which any charge made would be unreasonable. . . .

"We know that this is a power which may be abused; but that is no argument against its existence. For protection against abuses by legislatures the people must resort to the polls, not to the courts."[34]

Thirteen years later, however, the Court took the opposite position:

"The question of the reasonableness of a rate of charge for transportation by a railroad company, involving as it does the element of reasonableness both as regards the company and as regards the public, is eminently a question for judicial investigation, requiring due process of law for its determination."[35]

Finally, in *Smyth v. Ames*, in 1898, the Court not only strongly reaffirmed its responsibility under the Fourteenth Amendment's due process clause to review the reasonableness of rates set by state commissions, but it proceeded to specify its criteria of reasonableness:

"We hold . . . that the basis of all calculations as to the reasonableness of rates to be charged by a corporation maintaining a highway under legislative sanction [the case in question involved a railroad] must be the *fair value* of the property being used by it for the convenience of the public. And in order to ascertain that value, the original cost of construction, the amount expended in permanent improvements, the amount and market value of its bonds and stock, *the present as compared with the original cost of construction*, the probable earning capacity of the property under particular rates prescribed by statute, and the sum required to meet operating expenses, are all matters for consideration, and are to be given such weight as may be just and right in each case. We do not say that there may not be other matters to be regarded in estimating the value of the property. What the company is entitled to ask is a fair return upon the value of that which it employs for the public convenience."[36]

The "specification" was hardly precise; several of the listed "matters for consideration" were distressingly vague, and the Court was also vague about how it wanted all of them, along with the "other matters," combined into a composite "fair value" figure. Nor were regulatory commissions thereafter much clearer about how they were following those instructions, as Ben W. Lewis has caustically observed:

"A word should be said at this point with reference to the hybrid 'fair value' ('trance') method. . . . The 'fair value' method consists of an examination by the commission of evidence relating to reproduction cost and prudent investment, together with evidence of intangible values and observed condition of the property, the application of judgment whose processes defy

---

[34] 94 U.S. 113, 133–134 (1877).
[35] *Chicago, Milwaukee & St. Paul Railway Company v. Minnesota*, 134 U.S. 418, 458 (1890). For a compendium of the leading cases concerning the

judicial review of utility regulation, see Barnes, *Cases on Public Utility Regulation*, Chapter 3.
[36] Stress supplied. 169 U.S. 466, 546–547 (1898).

analysis or description, and the selection of a final value figure which bears no derivative relation to any figures in evidence and no ascertainable relation to any functional purpose of rate making. The determination is typically accompanied by explicit denials that a formula was employed or that the result is a compromise, together with a statement that the commission is quite incapable of retracing and setting forth the processes by which the value figure was reached."[37]

It was not only its lack of precision that made *Smyth v. Ames* the bane of public utility regulation for the next 50 years, embroiling commissions and courts in endless controversies about the definition and measurement of fair value. It was also its specific insistence that stockholders were entitled to a return not on the dollars they had actually invested—a quantity easily recorded in the company accounts, hence readily ascertainable—or "prudently invested," but on the current value of their investment. The first thing wrong with such a standard is its possible circularity. As the Supreme Court pointed out 46 years later, in overturning *Smyth v. Ames*, "fair value" cannot serve as the basis for rate regulation if it is taken to mean market value, since the market value of any enterprise or of its common stock depends on its earnings or anticipated earnings, which in turn depend on the rates that are allowed it: "'fair value' is the end product of the process of rate-making not the starting point . . . . " [38]This objection is sound, however, only if "fair value" is to be measured in terms of the market value of the enterprise. It is incorrect if applied to the customary interpretation that measured fair value (at least in part) with reference to the cost of reproducing the company's assets, as *Smyth v. Ames* likewise instructed commissions to do. Whatever the problems of applying the reproduction cost standard, and they were great, circularity was not one of them. The current cost of duplicating the existing facilities or others capable of giving the same service does not move up or down so as to validate whatever levels of rates and earnings are permitted.[39]

---

[37] In Leverett S. Lyon and Victor Abramson, *Government and Economic Life: Development and Current Issues of American Public Policy* (Washington: The Brookings Institution, 1940), 2: 692.
[38] "The heart of the matter is that rates cannot be made to depend upon 'fair value' when the value of the going enterprise depends on earnings under whatever rates may be anticipated." *Federal Power Commission v. Hope Natural Gas Co.*, 320 U.S. 591, 601 (1944).

The "market value of its bonds and stock" was one of the considerations that the Supreme Court said had to go into the determination of "fair value" in *Smyth v. Ames*.
[39] There *is* some causal connection between rates and reproduction costs. Higher or lower rates will mean a greater or lesser volume of sales, hence a need for greater or lesser production capacity. To the extent that capacity is supplied under conditions of increasing or decreasing cost, its reproduction cost will vary depending on whether a greater or lesser volume is demanded, hence on the level of rates. In

principle, this relationship does not preclude a single determinate solution, with a level of rates set in order to permit the desired return on the current cost of producing the capacity required to satisfy the demand elicited by that rate level (and structure). In contrast, there are any number of possible rate levels compatible with earning that return on the *market value* of investment, since—if demand is sufficiently inelastic—higher rates will mean a correspondingly higher market value, low rates a lower market value. Indeed, in perfectly functioning capital markets the market value of the company will move up and down, whatever the level of rates set, sufficiently to keep the rate of return earned on that market value at a constant level. (If investors are satisfied with a 10% return on investment, the market value of any company or of its securities will be ten times its permitted earnings, no matter what the rates it is permitted to charge; so its earnings will always be equal to 10% on its "fair value," thus defined, no matter what their absolute level.)

As we shall see, a strong economic case can be made for basing rate levels on "the present as compared with the original cost of construction," as *Smyth v. Ames* suggested. But as it developed in practice it had a fatal flaw: it invited endless controversy over the proper valuation of sunk capital, in direct contradiction of the economic principle that sunk investment costs are prominent among the "bygones" that ought to be ignored in price making.[40]

"It is not too much to say that in terms of cost, delay, uncertainty, and the arousing of animosity and contention, the performance of the reproduction cost method falls little short of a public scandal; by far the greater part of the grotesque and costly ponderosity which characterizes modern rate regulation is to be attributed directly and solely to the reproduction cost approach. There is no occasion here to recite details of the maneuvering in a typical rate proceeding. The months and years spent by contending parties, commissions, and courts over such hypothetical factors as pricing, conditions of construction, labor performance, overheads, intangibles; the huge sums paid to engineers and accountants and other professional experts, directed in their claims and counter-claims by high-priced attorneys skilled in the art of rate case strategy; the highly charged, politico-legal-mystic character of the whole performance—this is all accepted practice under the reproduction cost method, yet it seems far removed from the essential business of setting the price of a single service in a single community under conditions of simple monopoly."[41]

It is ironic that when the Supreme Court insisted on the relevance of current or reproduction cost, in *Smyth v. Ames*, it did so in the interest of effective regulation, and specifically in order to preserve "the right of the public to be exempt from unreasonable exactions."[42] For obvious reasons, the respective enthusiasms for original and reproduction cost on the part of regulatory commissions and regulated companies has varied depending on the trend of prices and construction costs. *Smyth v. Ames* came at a time when the general price level had fallen to its secular low point as a result of the deflations following the Civil War and the extended Depressions of the 1870s and the 1890s. It was the state of Nebraska that argued for the use of present value, as measured by (the lower) reproduction cost, and the railroads that argued for book or historical cost. In supporting the position of the former, the Court had in mind not only the long-term decline of construction costs, hence of fair value relative to original investment, but also the common complaint that railroad capital structures, on the liability side, and property valuations, on the asset side, were vastly inflated because of excessive payments to contractors and promoters and inadequate accounting for depreciation.[43]

---

[40] This does not mean that the returns permitted on past investments are irrelevant to the optimal pricing of public utility services. It means that endless controversies over the proper valuation and continual revaluation of capital investments made in the past are a deplorably inefficient and indirect way of approaching the task of devising economically efficient rates. (See the discussion on pp. 109–117, Chapter 4).

[41] Lyon and Abramson, *op. cit.*, 2: 691. For a more recent appraisal, see Lewis' "Emphasis and Misemphasis in Regulatory Policy," in Shepherd and Gies, *op. cit.*, 229–236. A place of high honor in these evaluations must be accorded also to Justice Louis D. Brandeis, who made many of the same observations as long ago as 1923; see his famous dissenting opinion in the *Southwestern Bell Telephone* case, 262 U.S. 276, 289–312 (1923).

[42] 169 U.S. 466, 544 (1898).

[43] See *ibid.*, 544–545, and Justice Brandeis, in *Southwestern Bell Telephone, op. cit.*, 298.

During and after World Wars I and II, the positions of the contending agencies were reversed: inflation and the introduction of more effective controls over book (historical) property valuations and company capitalizations converted regulated companies into enthusiasts for reproduction cost, and most commissions and advocates of effective regulation the other way—into proponents of a rate or earnings base measured by "prudent investment"—the number of dollars originally, prudently invested in the property used and usable in public service, less accumulated depreciation.[44]

It was not until 1944, in the *Hope Natural Gas* case,[45] that the Supreme Court at last decided, in the immortal words of Lord Mountararat, to "withhold its legislative hand," when it explicitly declined to tie the Federal Power Commission to any particular prescribed formula for the fixing of reasonable public utility rates. Rejecting fair value on grounds of circularity, the Court asserted that it would no longer insist on commissions taking reproduction cost into account in fixing permissible rates, either.

"Under the statutory standard of 'just and reasonable' it is the result reached not the method employed which is controlling."[46]

What "end results" were relevant? The tests would henceforth be economic and pragmatic:

"Rates which enable the company to operate successfully, to maintain its financial integrity, to attract capital, and to compensate its investors for the risks assumed certainly cannot be condemned as invalid, even though they might produce only a meager return on the so-called 'fair value' rate base."[47]

As long as regulation treats investors sufficiently well, by the acid test of the competitive capital-market place, to enable the regulated companies to raise whatever funds they need to provide acceptable service, the Court seemed to say, it would pose no additional tests or obstacles.[48]

The Court has been true to its promise. Outside of the novel area of natural gas production, it has entertained no public-utility rate-level case of the traditional kind since *Hope.*[49] State regulatory commissions have responded,

---

[44] See, among others, John Bauer and Nathaniel Gold, *Public Utility Valuation for Purposes of Rate Control* (New York: The Macmillan Co., 1934), Chapter 3; Barnes, *The Economics of Public Utility Regulation*, Chapters 11–17, an especially thorough analysis; Troxel, *Economics of Public Utilities*, Chapter 13; Eli Winston Clemens, *Economics and Public Utilities* (New York: Appleton Century-Crofts, 1950), 157–158; Wilcox, *Public Policies Toward Business*, 311–314; James C. Bonbright, *Principles of Public Utility Rates* (New York: Columbia University Press, 1961), Chapters 11–12; C. F. Phillips, *op. cit.*, 231–240.

[45] *Federal Power Commission v. Hope Natural Gas Co.*, 320 U.S. 591 (1944).

[46] *Ibid.*, 602.

[47] *Ibid.*, 605.

[48] Even in applying that primary test, it indicated it would give heavy weight to the "expert judgment" of the regulatory commission:

"Moreover, the Commission's order. . . . is the

product of expert judgment which carries a presumption of validity." *Ibid.*, 602.

[49] Information by courtesy of Edward M. Barrett. In the natural gas cases, the Federal Power Commission was attempting to evolve some system for fixing the field prices of a commodity produced at widely varying costs by a large number of producers. The Supreme Court had to decide a number of issues, the most important of which was whether the Commission had to make the traditional type of cost of service determinations, company by company, or might instead shift, as it wished to do, to setting area-wide rates applicable to all companies regardless of their individual costs. In general, following the philosophy of *Hope*, the Court sustained the Commission's exercise of its own "expertise." See *Wisconsin v. Federal Power Commission*, 373 U.S. 294 (1962) and *Permian Basin Area Rate Cases*, 390 U.S. 747 (1968). For a similar decision in a case involving the ICC's use of multi-company costs in determining the proper division

in varying degree, by shifting their attention from a preoccupation with the rate base to the more manageable question of the appropriate rate of return.[50] In a sense, the change is completely insubstantial: the substantive question of how much return on investment should be incorporated in the total cost of service is the same whether it focuses on one or the other of the two factors by which it is determined. And, as for administrative practicability, since it is the aggregate of dollar profits that concerns the parties to regulatory proceedings, it would seem there would be just as much opportunity for controversy over the percentage rate as there was in the past over the principal sum to which that rate was to be applied. The battle has not abated but merely shifted ground. As regulatory attention has turned from the rate base to the rate of return, and the latter has become less and less an essentially conventional 6% or so, the litigants have become increasingly skilled and assiduous in developing prolonged, complex, and inconclusive testimony about its proper measurement.[51]

Nevertheless the transformation of the rate base by most state commissions from a hypothetical or imaginary to an actual book figure,[52] representing actual money outlays, introduced a strong element of stability and predictability into the regulatory process. While the question of what constitutes a "fair" rate of return, as an ethical or political matter, would seem to be just as potentially productive of controversy as the question of what constitutes "fair value," the economic question, though in a sense unchanged and no easier to solve than before, is at least subject to the pragmatic test suggested by the Supreme Court itself—are the regulated companies succeeding in attracting the capital they require?[53]

---

of revenues for multi-line freight service, see *Chicago & North Western Railway Co. et al. v. Atchison, Topeka & Santa Fe Railway Co. et al.,* 387 U.S. 326 (1966).

[50] This does not mean that they have been permitted to ignore the rate base. On the contrary, as long as the courts continue to review commission rate orders at all, it is difficult to see how they can avoid insisting on some evaluation of the property on which a reasonable return must be permitted. This has been the continuing practice of such courts as have spoken since *Hope.* See Francis X. Welch, "The Rate Base is Here to Stay!" *Public Utilities Fortnightly* (October 22, 1953), LII: 635–641.

[51] See, for example, the possibly jaundiced view of Ben Lewis:

"as we begin in sheer disgust to move away from the debacle of valuation, we will probably substitute a new form of Roman holiday—long-drawn-out, costly, confusing, expert-contrived presentations, in which the simple directions of the *Hope* and *Bluefield* cases are turned into veritable witches' brews of statistical elaboration and manipulation. . . . We do not need to do this sort of thing to regulation; we do not need to do it to ourselves. The behavior of investors will tell us, day by day, all we need to know about 'comparability.'" In Shepherd and Gies, *op. cit.,*

242–243. Copyright, 1966, by Random House, Inc.

[52] On the imaginary character of the reproduction cost calculation, see Wilcox, *op. cit.,* 317.

[53] Controversy over the rate base has by no means disappeared. With price levels increasing secularly since the *Hope* decision, it has paid regulated companies to argue for some incorporation of reproduction cost in their rate bases. The state commissions have to some extent acceded: as of 1967, 31 of them (including the District of Columbia) used original cost (or "prudent investment") in regulating electric and gas utilities, 12 used fair value—a compromise between original and reproduction cost—one called its method "average net investment," and one used reproduction cost specifically. Of the remaining six states, four had no state commissions to regulate gas and electric utilities (see note 36, chapter 1) and two commissions had no established procedures. U.S. Senate, Committee on Government Operations, Subcommittee on Inter-governmental Relations, *State Utility Commissions, op. cit.,* 37–40. See also Federal Power Commission, *Federal and State Commission Jurisdiction and Regulation: Electric, Gas, and Telephone Utilities, op. cit.,* 11–12, which gives a slightly different tabulation; and Joseph R. Rose on "Confusion in Valuation for Public Utility Rate Making," *Minnesota Law Review* (1962),

Selection of the Permitted Rate of Return

In essence, every part of the regulatory price making exercise involves determining the proper level of earnings to be permitted the regulated companies. This is obviously true of the explicit determination of return, whether concentrating, as it traditionally has, on the valuation of the property on which a more or less conventional rate of return is to be allowed, or, as has become the practice in the majority of jurisdictions, on the rate of return to be permitted on the dollars actually invested in the enterprise. It is also the consequence of a commission's deciding whether or not to include items such as public relations expenditures in the cost of service, or how to measure depreciation, or how to treat income tax costs when accelerated depreciation is available. The process has inevitably reflected a complex mixture of political and economic considerations. Governmental price-fixing is an act of political economy. And, it bears repeating, this means that it necessarily and quite properly involves the striking of a balance between conflicting economic interests, influenced by political considerations in both the crassest and the broadest possible senses, and informed by community standards of fairness. Therefore, from time to time, the courts and commissions have characterized the entire task of setting "just and reasonable rates," and particularly that portion representing return to shareholders, in terms of reaching an acceptable compromise between the interests of investors on the one hand and consumers on the other.[54] The conception is that there is no single, scientifically correct rate of return, but a "zone of reasonableness," within which judgment must be exercised.

What are the limits of this zone? The bottom limit is an economic one, set by the necessity of continuing to attract capital; but, as we shall see, even that limit is an elastic one, depending on how much capital is required and how well one wishes to treat the company's existing stockholders.[55] The upper

XLVII: 1, whose analysis demonstrates that the foregoing simple designations conceal considerable differences in application. In a few instances, for example, "original cost" states have applied the permissible rate of return to an *undepreciated* rate base. For a thorough survey of actual valuation practices and rates of return allowed, see *Return Allowed in Public Utility Rate Cases, 1915–54* and *1955–61*, 2 vols., Arthur Andersen & Co. (place and date of publication not indicated); also A. J. G. Priest, "The Public Utility Rate Base," *Iowa Law Review* (Winter 1966), LI: 283–303, yielding a count of 31 original cost, and 19 fair value jurisdictions.

This continued emphasis on the rate base might seem irrational: inflation can be taken into account just as effectively by varying the permissible rate of return as by continuing to fight the old valuation controversies. To some extent this is what has happened. State commissions continuing to employ original cost have tended to compensate by allowing higher rates of return than the states that have either continued to use or have turned to fair value. But the compensation has been only partial. There continues to be a strong element of convention

and tradition in the allowable rates of return; confined to something like a 5.5 to 8% interval, their variation has not been a complete substitute for alterations in the rate base as well. See C. F. Phillips, Jr., *op. cit.*, 268–271; Garfield and Lovejoy, *op. cit.*, 133–134, and the sources cited by both.

[54] See, for example, the words of Justice Douglas, speaking for the Supreme Court majority in the *Hope* case, 320 U.S. 591, 603 (1944).

[55] A firm can continue to attract outside capital, within limits, even though its overall rate of return is held well below the rate that new investors will require if they are to make funds available to it. If it does so, it will be at the expense of its present stockholders. See note 64, p. 46. Its managers will therefore be reluctant to do so in those circumstances, to the extent that they are interested in the welfare of their stockholders. The bottom limit can be lower if it is defined as how much the firm must be permitted to earn on its total investment in order for it to be *able* to pay new investors enough to have them willingly supply the firm with additional funds than if it is defined as the rate that will make a company *willing*, without

limit has been either what it was estimated capital was obtaining in investments of similar risk elsewhere or, even higher, at whatever it was deemed the traffic would bear. As Justice Holmes once commented, rate regulation

". . . has to steer between Scylla and Charybdis. On the one side, if the franchise is taken to mean that the most profitable return that could be got, free from competition, is protected by the Fourteenth Amendment, then the power to regulate is null. On the other hand, if the power to regulate withdraws the protection of the Amendment altogether, then the property is nought. *This is not a matter of economic theory, but of fair interpretation of a bargain.* Neither extreme can have been meant. A midway between them must be hit."[56]

Such a view of regulation, as a sort of collective bargaining process, with the commission mediating between investors and consumers, may be justified on two quite distinct bases. The first is that there really *is* such a thing as the correct rate of return, but that it is impossible to *measure* it precisely. The economist, taking as his model the equating of price and marginal cost, would ordinarily begin[57] by identifying as the "correct" return the one that covers the costs of (incremental) capital.[58] But as we shall see there is no objective, unequivocal method of ascertaining the cost of capital, even for a particular regulated company at a particular time and place; the process requires the exercise of a good deal of judgment, and judgments will inevitably differ as to the result.

---

coercion by the regulatory authorities, to seek outside capital. And it can be lower, still, if the company does not need *outside* capital. The point in either case is that, by virtue of their power to control the distribution of dividends and both to prohibit the discontinuance and to require extensions of service, commissions can compel public utility companies to reinvest internally generated funds or to seek outside funds despite the fact that allowed returns are less than sufficient to induce such investment on a voluntary basis. If the supply of capital thus obtained sufficed to provide the desired quantity and quality of service, it would not be necessary to give shareholders a return as high as would be demanded by suppliers of new capital. This is merely a recognition of the fact that capital irretrievably sunk in an enterprise has a lower opportunity cost than incremental capital. See pp. 70–73, 118.

This was one consideration underlying the decision of the Federal Power Commission in 1965 to introduce a two-price system for natural gas, with a lower price for gas discovered in the past and already committed under existing contracts, and a higher price for new, additional supplies of gas committed in new interstate contracts. The differentiation in this case took the form not of allowing different nominal rates of return but of using different cost computations for old and new gas, with the price for the latter being set at the estimated full current cost of new, additional supplies. The justification,

proffered by this writer and accepted by the Commission, was that it was both undesirable and unnecessary to extend that higher price to the old gas—undesirable because to do so would confer windfalls on the owners of reserves discovered and developed at lower costs in the past (a noneconomic argument), and unnecessary because the investments in the old gas had already been made (an economic consideration). *Area Rate Proceeding, Claude E. Aikman, et al.,* 34 FPC 159, 185–192 and *passim* (1965), sustained in *Permian Basin Area Rate Cases,* 390 U.S. 747 (1968).

[56] Stress supplied. *Cedar Rapids Gas Light Co. v. Cedar Rapids,* 223 U.S. 655, 669 (1912).

[57] On the reasons why he will not necessarily stop there, see pp. 44 and 69–70.

[58] This was one of the criteria listed by the Supreme Court in its leading decision in the *Bluefield* case, back in 1923:

"The return should be reasonably sufficient to assure confidence in the financial soundness of the utility and should be adequate, under efficient and economical management, to maintain and support its credit and enable it to raise the money necessary for the proper discharge of its public duties." *Bluefield Water Works & Improv. Co. v. Public Service Commission of West Virginia,* 262 U.S. 679, 693 (1923).

It was also one of the standards set forth by the Supreme Court majority in the *Hope* decision. See p. 40.

The other view would be that the proper return that the regulatory process seeks and should seek to ascertain is not itself an objective phenomenon: what is a "just" or "fair and reasonable" return is a political, not a scientific question. This view is certainly not incorrect, either as a description of the rate making process or as prescription. A model of the price system in the modern, impurely competitive economy constructed in terms of the interplay of various organized groups, each with some degree of market power, with the results determined by the equilibrium of power relations, on the one hand, and influenced by considerations of "just price," on the other, is in some ways more relevant than one in which the transacting parties are conceived of as individuals, each a pecuniary profit-maximizer whose actions are entirely dictated by the objective constraints of the impersonal market. In any event, the economist cannot claim that such a vision of regulation as an essentially political process is "wrong;" all he can do is point out the costs to society of departing from purely economic standards.

Economists could make such an argument with better grace and greater forcefulness if they could themselves declare unequivocally what rate of return those purely economic standards dictate. The problem is that even if we confine ourselves to economic criteria we find that the very *idea* of the "correct" rate is elusive. The cost of capital is only the beginning point, for two reasons, both of which we will be explaining and exploring at a later point. (1) If perfect competition does not prevail in the real world, non-regulated industries generally may earn more (or less) than that minimum return. If so, it would produce misallocation to hold the prices of regulated services down (or up) to that level: this is the problem of the so-called "second best."[59] (2) The microeconomic model that calls for equating all prices to (marginal) cost and profits to the (marginal) cost of capital, which we describe in Chapter 3, is a static one. It tells us how to make the most satisfactory use of our limited resources with given tastes and a given technology. But it does not necessarily tell us how best to promote economic progress. The provision of incentives and the wherewithal for dynamic improvements in efficiency and innovations in service may require allowing returns to exceed that level: this was the essence of Joseph A. Schumpeter's classic defense of monopoly.[60] Thus, the rate of return must fulfill what we may term an *institutional* function: it somehow must provide the incentives to private management that competition and profit-maximization are supposed to provide in the nonregulated private economy generally. We have already identified this as a central problem of regulation.[61] There is as yet no scientific way even of defining the rate of return arrangements that would achieve this more complex definition of economic optimality, not to mention measuring them.

In keeping with the purpose of this entire chapter, the following survey of

---

[59] See pp. 69–70, Chapter 3 and p. 195, Chapter 7.

[60] See his *Capitalism, Socialism and Democracy* (New York: Harper & Brothers, 1942), Chapters 7–9.

[61] This is not to suggest that it is only through the rate of return that the necessary incentives are best provided. Given the divorce between ownership and management, the rewards might better be offered to, and penalties assessed against, the managers themselves, for example, in the form of variable bonuses proportioned to some measure of performance. See the section on "Incentive Plans," Chapter 2, Volume 2.

the major problems and issues in determining the proper rate of return (we assume, for simplicity, that the investment to which it is to be applied is valued at original cost less depreciation) is intended principally to illustrate the foregoing observations. While summarizing the major traditional issues in price regulation, as background for our own, alternative approach in Part II, it should demonstrate also (1) the problems in measuring the minimum cost to which prices would be held by effective competition, which regulation is supposed to emulate; (2) the important influence of noneconomic considerations, and especially of conceptions of what is "fair;" and (3) the elusiveness of the proper economic standards, for the reasons just identified—the problem of "second best" and the institutional function of the rate of return.

Problems in Measuring the Cost of Capital. The public utility company competes with all other companies in the economy for the various inputs of its production process—for labor, materials, and capital. To the extent that these are supplied in open markets (instead of, for example, under negotiated bids), in principle there ought to be readily available objective measures of the prices of these inputs that have to be incorporated in the cost of service. This is clearly true of the capital input: since the regulated company must go to the open capital market and sell its securities in competition with every other would-be issuer, there clearly is a market price (a rate of interest on borrowed funds, an expected return on equity) that it must be permitted and enabled to pay for the capital it requires. Of course, the costs that go into its price (or rate levels) are a function not only of the unit prices of its inputs (for example, the price of a ton of coal, delivered to the generating plant, or the interest rate on its bonds) but also of the efficiency with which they are employed (for example, the number of tons of coal or the number of dollars of capital investment required to generate a kilowatt hour of electricity); and we have already alluded to the problem of assuring maximum efficiency under regulation and to the important role that the allowable rate of return may play in providing an incentive for managers to run their companies as efficiently as possible. But the proper starting point is clearly the competitive price—in this case, the so-called "cost of capital."

1. But whose cost of capital? Should it be the cost to the individual company under consideration? Or of a representative group of companies? If the latter, what constitutes a representative group? The concept of regulation as seeking to keep prices at the lowest possible level consistent with the company's supplying the amount and quality of service demanded at that price—which is surely the competitive ideal, also—would argue for measuring the actual cost of capital to that company alone. But suppose one company is so well run (or promises to become so much more so) that investors, having particularly great confidence in it (or in the stability or growth of its future earnings) are willing to make capital available to it at a price (for example, at current or promised rates of return) less than the average for other regulated companies? If the unusually efficient company's resultant lower cost of capital is automatically translated into lower permitted profits per dollar of invested capital—something that would *not* automatically happen under pure competition—will it not have been deprived of the incentive to be efficient, or to become more so? Its owners, and therefore conceivably its managers, would have been deprived

of the supernormal rewards (quasi-rents) that constitute in nonregulated markets a prime spur to efficiency.[62]

2. Should it be the cost of capital at a particular moment in time, or an average over some period in the past? If the former, what moment? If the latter, how long a period? Is what is sought the *historical* cost of capital, as of the time when it was raised? Or the current cost? The reader will recognize the relatedness of these questions to the question of whether the rate base and depreciation should likewise be measured at original or at current cost.[63] The usual practice is to combine the actual or historical interest cost, as far as debt capital and preferred stock are concerned, with the (estimated) current cost of raising money by sale of common stock. Does this make economic sense? Is it fair? How do these various possible approaches compare with the results that would be produced by competition? And, in such a comparison, *what* "competition" is relevant— "ideal" pure or perfect competition? Or the highly imperfect mixtures of competition and monopoly that actually prevail in unregulated markets?

3. The usual starting point for measuring the cost of equity capital is the ratio of earnings to market prices of the common stocks of the company or companies selected. The logic of this procedure—and it is persuasive— is that the price investors are willing to pay in the open securities markets for shares of stock with known levels of earnings provides an objective measure of the terms on which they are willing to make their money available to the companies in question. If, for example, the common stock sells at 10 times annual earnings, the earnings/price ratio is 10% and that may (subject to the very serious qualifications to be noted) be taken as the cost of capital—the rate of return that the companies must be able to earn on any additional dollars invested in them if they are going to be willing and able to raise those dollars in the capital markets.[64]

However, the principal difficulty is that what investors are capitalizing in the purchase price of the securities they buy is not current but antici-

---

[62] Of course, some diminution of the incentive to efficiency is inherent in any system of regulation that holds rates of return to some prescribed level, regardless of how or where that level is set. Still, if the more efficient and progressive company is permitted some sort of higher, industry-average rate of return, instead of its own, low cost of capital, it is on this account rewarded for its own, deserved, above-average attractiveness to investors, and retains an incentive to improve its efficiency in hope of increasing that reward.

[63] He is reminded, too, that we consider the economics of these interrelated choices in the following chapters—in particular, Chapter 4.

[64] As we have already suggested, a company *can* raise capital even if it is allowed a rate of return

below the cost of capital, but only at the expense of its existing stockholders. The common sense of this should be apparent: if a company sells its new stock on terms that give the new stockholders, for instance, a 10% return on their investment—the cost of capital being 10%, they will pay only ten times the prospective earnings for each share—and invests the funds in assets on which it is permitted to earn only 7 1/2%, clearly the other 2 1/2% must be coming out of earnings previously available to its existing stockholders. This is what is known as dilution—dilution of the share in equity (that is, in the claim on net assets of the firm) of existing stockholders.

Suppose, for example, the firm had the following skeleton balance sheet before the new stock issue:

Assets		Liabilities	
Net plant	$100	Net worth	
		Common stock (10 shares)	$50
		Surplus	50

And suppose its permitted rate of return (r) and cost of equity capital (k) were, as above, $7\frac{1}{2}\%$ and

10%, respectively. In this event, its permitted earnings would be $0.75 per share, and investors

pated earnings;[65] and there is no objective measure of what their antici-pations were or are. Thus, computed contemporaneous earnings/price ratios will either underestimate or overestimate the actual cost of capital, depending on the extent to which investors were expecting earnings to rise or fall from current levels when they paid those prices. From the late 1940s on, for example, security prices in the United States soared relative to earnings; this sharp drop in earnings/price ratios continued all through the 1950s, leveling off during 1960–1965 at the 5 to 6% level, which was well below the average of the preceding half-century.[66] There can be little doubt that these trends partly reflected the anticipation of increasing earnings and future appreciation of security values; those anticipations were an important consideration in the high and rising prices investors were willing to pay for each dollar of current earnings.[67] If so, the contemporaneous earnings/price ratios must have understated the true cost of equity capital: investors *thought* they were getting a better return

---

would pay only $7.50 for a share. (The market value would thus be below the book value of $10 per share, precisely because r is less than k; see note 69.) Now suppose the company sought to raise another $100 to invest in plant. It would be permitted to earn an additional $7.50 on this investment, or a total of $15. How many shares would it have to sell and at what price would they sell? Let x be the required additional number of shares. Then earnings per share will end at $15/(10 + x)$. These earnings would be capitalized at 10%—that is, investors would pay 10 times those earnings for each new share of stock, assuming they expected per share earnings to remain thenceforth at that level. So the price of each share would be $(10) ($15)/(10 + x)$ and x shares would have to be sold at that price to raise the required $100:

$$\frac{(10) \ (\$15)}{10 + x} \ x = \$100$$

$$x = 20$$

Therefore 20 additional shares would have to be sold to raise the added $100, at a price of $5. The price per share would thus have dropped from $7.50 to $5; the total permitted earnings of $15 would now be distributed among 30 shares, yielding $0.50 per share, capitalized at 10%. Assuming they predicted accurately the trend in earnings per share, the new investors would be in a position to demand the 10% k— they would pay only $5 for a share promising earnings of $0.50. But sale of the stock in these circumstances would *dilute* the share in ownership of the holders of the 10 original shares of stock: their share in book equity would decline from the original $10 per share to $6.67, the new total equity of $200 being distributed now among 30 shares. The $33\frac{1}{3}$% decline in the market value of their stock would reflect this corresponding dilution of their equity.

A company *can*, thus, raise more capital when r is below k (within limits—try to work out the above example if r is only 5%) but only at the expense of its existing stockholders. This is something its management would ordinarily be unwilling to do.

[65] It is uncertain to what extent and in what direction investors' appraisal of earnings is altered by variations of the proportions respectively distributed in dividends and reinvested in the business. The weight of informed opinion since the early 1950s seems to be that it is total earnings instead of dividends alone that investors value in purchasing securities; that pay-out ratios have little if any effect—that is, that investors are essentially indifferent to what percentage of earnings is distributed in dividends. See Fred P. Morrisey, "Current Aspects of the Cost of Capital to Utilities," *Public Utilities Fortnightly* (August 14, 1958), LXII: 217–227; Merton H. Miller and Franco Modigliani, "Some Estimates of the Cost of Capital to the Electric Utility Industry," *Amer. Econ. Rev.* (June 1966), LVI: 368–370; Irwin Friend and Marshall Puckett, "Dividends and Stock Prices," *ibid.* (September 1964), LIV: 656–682; cf. E. W. Clemens, "Some Aspects of the Rate-of-Return Problem," *Land Econ.* (February 1954), XXX: 32–43.

[66] Dividend/price ratios showed a similar trend, and between 1955 and 1965 were lower relative to levels of the preceding half-century than were earnings/price ratios. Board of Governors of the Federal Reserve System, *Historical Chart Book, 1967*, Washington, 37.

[67] It can be demonstrated that, under not un-reasonable assumptions, the market price of a share of stock (P) will be equal to current dividends (D) divided by (the cost of capital, k, minus the anticipated annual percentage growth in dividends, g): $P = D/(k - g)$. Or, in other words, that the cost of capital is equal to the

than would be indicated by that ratio.[68] Any successful effort by utility commissions to hold earnings on the companies' rate bases thereafter to the low rates suggested by those ratios would surely have resulted in a deflation of security prices, and, by thus increasing earnings/price ratios, have demonstrated that the true cost of capital was higher than they had originally inferred.[69] But how much higher, it is impossible to say with any precision.[70]

4. Is there need for consistency between the basis on which the cost of equity capital is determined and the rate base to which it is then applied? If the

---

current dividend/price ratio plus that anticipated percentage growth: $k = D/P + g$. For a fuller explanation, see the Appendix to this chapter, which reproduces a very lucid account by Herman G. Roseman.

To some extent, g results merely from the reinvestment of earnings. If a company earns 9% on book equity, distributes 2/3 and reinvests 1/3 (that is, 6% and 3% of book equity, respectively), the book value of each share of stock will grow 3% a year and dividends may therefore be expected to do the same on this account, *ceteris paribus*. If 9% is also the cost of capital, the market value of the stock will be equal to book (see footnote 69, below) and $(D/P) + g$ (in this case $6\% + 3\%$) will, as far as this source of growth is concerned, be the same as the earnings/price ratio, E/P (9%). The problem arises when g is expected to be greater or less than what would result merely from the reinvestment of earnings. See for example the estimates referred to in note 70.

[68] That certainly had been their experience during the preceding years. An investment of equal amounts in every stock traded on the New York Stock Exchange in December 1950 would have yielded an investor 15.0% compounded annually, in dividends and capital appreciation, by December 1960; a similar investment in December 1955 would have yielded 11.1% by

the later date. See L. Fisher and J. H. Lorie, "Rates of Return on Investments in Common Stocks," *Jour. of Bus.* (January 1964), XXXVII: 5. During the first period E/P ratios dropped continuously from over 15 to less than 5%, during the second its range was from about 8 to 5%. Board of Governors, *op. cit.*, note 66. Obviously what dropped E/P ratios was investor expectations that they would continue to see this kind of growth in earnings and market value of their investments.

[69] On the other hand, the sharp appreciation in the prices of public utility stocks, to one and a half and then two times their book value during this period, reflected also a growing recognition that the companies in question were in fact being permitted to earn considerably more than their cost of capital. Perhaps, indeed, the discrepancy was growing over time: as the data in note 76 demonstrate, the return on equity among the public utilities increased markedly relative to manufacturing in the two decades after World War II. See Miller and Modigliani, *op. cit.*, *Amer. Econ. Rev.* (June 1966), LVI: 386; David A. Kosh, "Recent Trends in the Cost of Capital," *Public Utilities Fortnightly* (September 26, 1963), LXXII: 19–26. Suppose, for example, the following skeletal balance sheet of a regulated company:

Net plant	100	Equity	
		Common stock (10 shares)	50
		Surplus	50

And suppose the true cost of capital is 10%. If the regulatory commission permits the company to earn 10% on its net plant, valued at original cost, the profits will be $1 a share, and, *ceteris paribus*, investors will buy those shares for $10: market value and book value will coincide. But the market value will exceed book value if the commission permits a return in excess of the cost of capital: if, for example, it allows 15%, this will yield $1.50 a share, for which investors will bid $15.

But suppose, to illustrate the point in the text, the commission had been allowing only the true cost of capital, 10% or $1 a share, but investors had bid share prices up to $15, yielding currently

only $6\frac{2}{3}\%$, because they expected to get the other $3\frac{1}{3}\%$ from future increases in earnings and appreciation of the securities' prices. If in this event the commission took the $6\frac{2}{3}\%$ earnings/price ratio to represent the cost of capital, it would permit earnings of ony $0.67 per share, and the market price of the securities would collapse either to the book value of $10, if investor confidence in future trends continued unshaken, or down to $6.67, if those favorable anticipations were now destroyed.

[70] Since the true cost of capital (k) may be taken as equal to $(D/P) + g$ (see note 67), some company witnesses in regulatory proceedings have attempted in various ways to make plausible

cost of equity capital is determined on the basis of the ratio of earnings to the *market price* of the company's common stock, is there not some inconsistency in applying that rate of return to a rate base as valued in the company's *books*—that is, at original or historic cost—when, as has been true for well over a decade, the market value of most public utility shares has far exceeded their book value? If, for example, earnings per share were $5, the market price $100, and the book value $50, the E/P ratio would suggest a 5% cost of capital; if that 5% were applied to the book value of (the equity portion of) the rate base, this would produce a return of only $2.50—thus eliminating the justification for the $100 market price.

The answer is that there would be an inconsistency in this case, but only because it involves inconsistent assumptions about regulatory policy.

---

estimates of the g investors had in mind in purchasing the company stock, in order to come up with an estimate of k (since D and P are of course known). See, for instance, the testimony of Irwin Friend, May 26, 1966, in Federal Communications Commission, *In the Matter of American Telephone and Telegraph Company*, Docket 16258, and of Roseman before the Pennsylvania Public Utility Commission, Re: *The Peoples Natural Gas Company*, Docket No. 18527, Exhibit No. 16, 1968. Roseman's basic approach, for example, is to determine statistically which measure of growth (average annual growth in earnings, in dividends, in book equity, in revenue, or in net plant, all over various time periods up to the present) correlates most closely with the current evaluation placed by the market on dividends—that is, with the D/P ratios—of 21 gas distribution companies. The correlation is negative: the higher the anticipated g, the higher the price investors will pay for a dollar of current dividends, so the lower is the D/P ratio. Then, having in this way identified the measure of actual past growth with the highest negative correlation with D/P, he proposes that for his measure of the (anticipated) g component of k. Applying this method for each of the 20 companies (in addition to the one for which he was testifying), he obtained an average estimate for k of 9.8%, compared with an *earnings*/price ratio of 7.6%. Roseman describes this method also in "Measuring the Cost of Equity Capital for Public Utilities," ABA, *Annual Report, Section of Public Utility Law*, 1969, 54–67.

Two other writers have suggested an alternative solution that would permit the use of E/P ratios alone as the measure of k. Their reasoning is that whenever regulated companies purchase their inputs in competitive markets, regulatory commissions correctly accept the prices thus determined for incorporation in the cost of service. Capital markets are highly competitive; they, too, therefore, should be able to provide

commissions with a very accurate measure of the competitive, minimum necessary cost of capital. The problem at present is that commissions have no way of telling what are the terms of the equity share contract. That is, when investors pay x dollars for a share of stock, they are buying not just current earnings but some unmeasurable amount of growth over and above the growth that occurs because of the mere reinvestment of earnings. (As we have already seen, if dividends are expected to grow only because of reinvestment of earnings, $(D/P)+g$ is the same as E/P, and the latter is a correct measure of k. See note 67, above. It is the expectation of greater— or lesser—growth than this that renders E/P an inaccurate measure of k.) The first key to a solution to this problem is to be found in the fact that when earnings are expected to grow over time merely because of reinvestment of earnings, the market and book values of a share of company stock will grow together; there is no reason for such growth to produce any discrepancy between them. It is the expectation of a capital gain resulting from a *discrepancy* between market and book values, thus, that makes E/P an inaccurate measure of k, and so makes the latter so difficult to measure. The second key to the solution is that if the allowed rate of return (r) is held at the cost of capital (k), market value will tend to equal book value (see note 69), and the possibility of a discrepancy between them is greatly diminished.

Therefore, the authors suggest, if regulatory commissions were to put investors on notice that henceforth they would allow a return equal only to whatever earnings/price ratio the securities markets set when the market value of the common stock equaled its book value (at which point presumably r equals k), they could greatly diminish, if not eradicate, the expectation of capital gains or losses arising from divergencies of market and book value and thereby cause the current earnings/price ratios to give them a much more accurate reflection of the true cost of

That is, it assumes at one and the same time that the commission allows returns on equity (r) in *excess* of and equal to the cost of capital (k). The source of the discrepancy between market and book value has been that commissions have been allowing r's in excess of k; if instead they had set r equal to k, or proceeded at some point to do so, both the discrepancy between market and book value and the inconsistency would have disappeared, or would never have arisen.[71] The fact that market value has remained above book value indicates that in most jurisdictions r has been high enough, relative to k, so that its application to the lower book value, in determining allowable earnings, has not destroyed the willingness of investors to continue to pay above book value for public utility company shares.[72]

5. To what extent does the cost of capital, which is a weighted average of the separate costs of obtaining funds by sale of bonds, preferred stock, and common stock, depend on the particular mixture of sources of financing selected? There is general agreement that up to a point the composite cost will be reduced by resorting to borrowing, because the interest costs of borrowed capital may be deducted from taxable income, whereas the return on equity capital—which is no less a genuine economic cost of production—is subject to the corporation income tax.[73] But some commentators have maintained that, apart from this tax aspect, the capital structure has no effect on the composite cost of capital; that the more a company resorts to borrowing, typically at lower contractual interest rates than the rates of return it has to promise to common stockholders, the correspondingly higher is its true cost of equity capital, in reflection of the greater risks to stockholders of having a larger and larger share of aggregate earnings subject to the prior, contractual claim of the bond holders.[74] The more traditional view is that up to some point

---

capital. Thereafter, when investors purchased the stock they would be buying only current earnings plus such anticipated growth as would result from reinvestment of profits, which would raise book and market value per share simultaneously. They would no longer be paying also for the expectation that the market value per share might rise relative to the number of stockholder dollars actually invested in the enterprise. Regulatory commissions could presumably obtain successive approximations to the true cost of capital by reducing permitted rates of return (r) sufficiently to bring market prices down to book value per share, and then adjusting r to the earnings/price ratios that emerged on announcement of the policy that destroyed anticipations of market price diverging from book.

In brief, what the commissions would be doing in this way would be specifying the terms of the equity share contract. If they succeeded in doing so, the capital market would then provide them with an accurate measure of the true competitive cost of capital. See Robert J. Gelhaus and Gary D. Wilson, "An Earnings-Price Approach to Fair Rate of Return in Regulated Industries," *Stanford Law Rev.* (January 1968),

XX: 287–317.

[71] In the foregoing example, once market value per share was reduced to book value—that is, to $50—because r was set at k, here assumed to be 5%, there would no longer be any inconsistency, provided, of course, the commission had correctly estimated k at 5%. Return per share would be $2.50, and this would be 5% of both market and book value.

[72] See note 69.

[73] If the cost of debt capital to a company is 5% and the cost of equity capital is 10%, and it raises $100 by borrowing, this will add $5 a year to its costs; if it raises it by issuing new stock, it will add not $10 but, with the corporation income tax rate at 48%, $19.23 a year to what it must recover in rates—$9.23 for the Internal Revenue Service, $10 for the new stockholders.

[74] Actually the cost of debt capital would likewise rise, reflecting growing risk to bond holders as well, as a larger and larger share of company income was pledged to them. The Grand Inquisitor's observation in *The Gondoliers*,

"When every one is somebodee,
   Then no one's anybody!"

clearly applies to bondholders: when everyone

trading on equity has the effect of reducing the average cost of capital, even apart from the tax advantage. Some commissions, in consequence, have based their allowances for rate of return not on the actual capital structure of the regulated company but on their conception of a preferable one, with a lower inferred composite cost.[75]

Should the Rate Be Adjusted for Changes in Prices? What allowance, if any, should be made for changes in the purchasing power of the investor's dollar, measured in terms of its changing ability either to buy consumer goods and services or to replace capital equipment? In particular, should the owners of the business be offered some sort of protection against inflation, whether by introducing some reflection of (presumably rising) replacement costs in the rate base and/or in allowable depreciation expenses, or in a higher rate of return? On grounds of fairness? Of economic efficiency? *Ought* or *need* the same protections be offered to existing shareholders as to future suppliers of capital? If to stockholders, why not also to creditors? We consider these questions at length in Chapter 4.

The Standard of Comparable Earnings. During the early 1960s, when price/earnings ratios ran around 5 to 6%, manufacturing corporations were earning 10 to 13% on their book equity.[76] *Ought* or *need* public utility

---

who supplies capital is at the head of the line in his claim on income, no one is at the head of the line—there is no line. See the considerably more complex argument of Modigliani and Miller, "The Cost of Capital, Corporation Finance and the Theory of Investment," *Amer. Econ. Rev.* (June 1958), XLVIII: 261–297, and "Some Estimates of the Cost of Capital," *Amer. Econ. Rev.* (June 1966), LVI: 338–343, 364–367; the comments on the former article by Joseph R. Rose and David Durand and the Modigliani-Miller reply, *ibid.* (September 1959), XLIX: 638–669; Haim Ben-Shahar, "The Capital Structure and the Cost of Capital: A Suggested Exposition," *Jour. of Finance* (September 1968), XXIII: 639–653.

[75] See C. F. Phillips, Jr., *op. cit.*, 169–171, 280–283; Troxel, in Shepherd and Gies, *op. cit.*, 166–168.

"On oral argument, Respondents' counsel stated:

'. . . I think the Commission's function here is to examine a debt policy that we follow . . . but unless you find that we have abused our discretion or have been imprudent, I don't believe you should disturb it. . . .'

"We agree that this Commission is not the manager of Respondents' business. It is neither our obligation or duty to dictate the business policies and practices to be followed by management. On the other hand, we have the statutory responsibility for the establishment and maintenance of just and reasonable rates. . . . If we are to discharge this responsibility . . . we must be free to examine fully all matters affecting the

future level of rates. . . . We are not limited to acting in situations in which we have first found abuse, imprudence or indiscretion on the part of management in the past. . . .

"At the 10-percent return on equity sought by respondents herein, each dollar of equity financing requires nearly five times as much gross revenue as a dollar of debt financing. Thus, the rate payer is penalized if more of the financing is by equity than is required. . . .

"We find, therefore, that a continuation by respondents of their past policies with respect to capital structure will not be conducive to the raising of future required capital in a reasonably economical fashion. . . .

"Accordingly, in fixing the rate of return to be allowed, we shall take into account this 'additional' and extraordinary amount of risk insurance respondents have given its [sic] stockholders by its low debt ratio policy. . . . respondents are in a position to improve equity earnings by increasing their debt ratio. . . ." FCC, *In the Matter of American Telephone and Telegraph Company*, Docket No. 16258, Interim Decision and Order, 9 FCC 2d. 30 (1967), sec. 86, 89, 216, 220, 222.

[76] See note 66, Chapter 2. During these same years (1960–1964, inclusive), the returns on book equity of the "electric power, gas, etc." companies surveyed by the First National City Bank of New York ranged between 10.0 and 11.0%, of telephone and telegraph companies between 9.7 and 10.3% and of transportation companies between 2.3 and 5.5%, as the following table shows. All returns are after tax.

companies be permitted earnings comparable to those received by companies in nonregulated industries, under conditions of comparable risk?[77] This question involves a number of issues, conceptual and factual.

1. Is the comparable earnings standard merely another measure of the cost of capital, reflecting what public utility companies themselves or purchasers of their stocks could obtain on their dollars elsewhere? Or may it be higher: may not returns in industry generally contain some monopoly component, for example? In point of fact, the owners or purchasers of public utility and industrial common stocks might well not be able to obtain that type of rate of return if they were to go into the market and buy those securities.[78] The cost of capital, which is what a utility company must match if it is to attract funds, is what investors could obtain by buying the *securities* of other companies in the open market—not what the companies themselves earn on a dollar of additional investment.[79]

2. If "comparable earnings" exceed the cost of capital, then, would an attempt to hold public utility earnings to the lower, competitive level reduce the prices of their services excessively, relative to the prices of other goods and services?[80]

Net Returns on Net Assets

Year	Total Mfg	Electric Power, Gas, etc.	Telephone and Telegraph	Total Transportation
1947–54	15.4	9.3	7.8	...
1959	11.7	10.1	9.9	3.9
1960	10.6	10.0	9.9	2.9
1961	9.9	10.0	9.9	2.3
1962	10.9	10.4	9.5	3.9
1963	11.6	10.6	9.7	4.6
1964	12.6	11.0	10.3	5.5
1965	13.9	11.3	9.9	6.9
1966	14.2	11.5	10.4	7.4
1967	12.6	11.6	10.2	5.4
1968	13.1	11.2	9.7	4.9
No. of Companies				
1968	2,250	237	19	176

Source. First National City Bank of New York, *Monthly Economic Letter*, April issues. 1947-54 compilation from Shepherd and Gies, *op. cit.*, 103.

[77] The Supreme Court specified such a comparable earnings standard in both its *Bluefield* and *Hope* decisions. 262 U.S. 679, 692 (1923); 320 U.S. 591, 603 (1944).

[78] See for example, Calvin B. Hoover, "On the Inequality of the Rate of Profit and the Rate of Interest," *The South. Econ. Jour.* (July 1961), XXVIII: 1–12; James Tobin, "Economic Growth as an Objective of Government Policy," *Amer. Econ. Rev., Papers and Proceedings* (May 1964), LIV: 13–14. This discrepancy is suggested by the far lower earnings to market price ratios of both industrial and public utility common stocks than those companies earn on book equity. However, as we have seen, investors have been earning more than the contemporaneous earnings/price ratios. (See note 68.) Whether what they have in fact earned in this way was the same as the cost of capital—that is, the rates

that they would have been *willing* to take to make their funds available—is highly uncertain.

[79] If the cost of capital is lower, any attempt of a regulatory commission, persuaded by the comparable earnings argument, to permit investors the higher return would only be self-defeating. Investors would respond to the higher earnings per share by bidding up the prices of the securities to the point at which new purchasers would earn only the old cost of capital on their investments. The only beneficiaries would be those who happened to own the stock at the time the policy change was announced or anticipated. There is no way of giving new purchasers of stock more than the cost of capital, except by changing the rules after they have made their purchases. See the same argument in another context, p. 116, Chapter 4.

[80] This is the "problem of the second best,"

3. In applying this standard, how does one select nonregulated industries of comparable risk? How *do* risks in public utilities compare with those of other industries, and to the extent they do differ how would this difference be allowed for in translating comparable earnings elsewhere into permissible rates of return here?[81]

The Problem of Rewards and Incentives. How, if at all, can rates of return be varied in order to reward, and hence to provide an incentive for efficiency and innovation? What standards of performance are available that will separate results attributable to good or bad management from those attributable to other factors? How can such rewards be related to performance, and how much in the way of rewards is required? In particular, is there any way of punishing poorly managed companies with a reduced rate of return without jeopardizing their ability to attract the very capital they may need to do a better job?

It has been urged by defenders of the comparable earnings standard and by others that public utilities be allowed returns markedly above the bare cost of capital, in order to provide them with both the financial means and the incentive to engage in risky innovation, both technological and commercial. That regulatory commissions have in fact allowed earnings well in excess of k is suggested not just by the behavior of the market prices of public utility securities but also by the apparent ease with which such companies have been able, since World War II, to raise the huge amounts of capital required to meet growing demands. It is suggested also by their aggressiveness in seeking such capital and expanding capacity, something that they would obviously have been reluctant to do if allowable returns were less than k.[82]

But this does not necessarily prove that these companies have been offered the optimum amount of incentive for undertaking risky investments.[83] The defining characteristic of such investments is that they offer a wide range of possible outcomes; those that are nevertheless economically worthwhile are so because the possibilities of very large pay-offs balance the possibilities of failure. Any restriction on aggregate earnings, by threatening to cut off the opportunities for the great successes, will therefore have some immeasurable effect of discouraging risky investments that otherwise would be made. How important this effect may be in public utility regulation is very difficult to determine, but it is probably slight. For one thing, there are mitigating or countervailing considerations, among them the slowness of regulation in

---

to which we have already referred. As Shepherd has observed, the problem of the second best is the core of economic validity in the comparable earnings standard. "Regulatory Constraints and Public Utility Investment," *Land Econ.* (August 1966), XLII: 353. See pp. 195–198, Chapter 7.

[81] See, for example, Shepherd, "Utility Growth and Profits Under Regulation," in Shepherd and Gies, *op. cit.*, 35–45. "if utility stocks are compared with those of non-utility corporations of comparable size, utilities which are protected from many forms of competition will be compared with the winners in other areas with no such . . . protection. . . . Somehow, in strict logic, the shadow losses of long defunct automobile companies would have to be subtracted from the profits of General Motors, after these

in turn had been adjusted downward for the hypothetical competition—and then, following this trip through the looking-glass, the result would be comparable earnings. . . ."

James R. Nelson, "Reassessment of Economic Standards for the Rate of Return Under Regulation," in Harry M. Trebing and R. Hayden Howard, *Rate of Return under Regulation: New Directions and Perspectives* (Institute of Public Utilities, Michigan State University: East Lansing, 1969), 16.

[82] See Troxel and Lewis, in Shepherd and Gies, *op. cit.*, 170–175 and 237–239 and note 64, above

[83] See Thomas G. Gies, "The Need for New Concepts in Public Utility Regulation," *ibid.*, 105–107.

reducing earnings that prove *ex post* to be "excessive"—this is the familiar "regulatory lag"—and the ability of regulated companies to seek any rate increases that may be required to keep their overall rates of return at satisfactory levels, and hence to compensate for some of their failures. More important is the fact that the regulatory restriction is on total earnings, not the returns from individual investments. It would only be if the latter were so overwhelmingly large as to threaten to push the total above permissible levels that regulation might discourage it. To the extent all these offsets and qualifications are insufficient, there is no easy solution to the incentive problem. Merely permitting all regulated companies as a matter of course to earn rates in excess of the cost of capital does not supply the answer; there has to be some means of seeing to it that those supernormal returns are *earned*, some means, for example, of identifying the companies that have been unusually enterprising or efficient and offering the higher profits to them while denying them to others. We return to these institutional problems in Chapter 2 of Volume 2.

REGULATING RATE STRUCTURES

With respect to the second major aspect of public utility price regulation—the regulation of rate patterns or structures—the typical statutory or judicial injunction is that rates be not "unduly discriminatory," that differences in the rates charged various customers or classes of service be likewise "just and reasonable." At this point we need make only two general observations about the way in which most regulatory commissions have carried out this mandate. First, outside of the transportation field, they have given far less attention to this subject than to determining general rate levels and especially the rate base and rate of return.[84] The height of particular rates and the differences between them have been from the very outset a very important consideration in the regulation of railroads: the feeling of different customers and localities that they were being subjected to unfair discrimination played a vital role

---

[84] The managements of public utility companies have been at least equally delinquent. See the following acid comments by the Public Utilities Commission of California on the apparent lack of interest of the Pacific Telephone Company in the various individual components of its aggregate cost of service and unwillingness to supply information about them:

"Pacific adheres to a concept of setting basic telephone rates in relation to the availability of main stations and on a statewide pattern. . . . By this scheme Pacific, as in all prior rate proposals, ignores the costs of providing service and from the present record it is apparent that it isn't even interested in knowing what its costs are for any given existing service. It is content to rely on broad and loosely-made estimates first put together at the time an initial or innovative service offering is proposed, no matter how long ago such estimates may have been made. . . . That the executives of Pacific have developed no means by which the actual costs of any of

Pacific's existing basic tariff offerings may be determined or measured seems incomprehensible but this record clearly establishes that such is the fact. Equally incomprehensible is the fact that Pacific does not even know, nor can it readily determine, what revenues its individual tariff offerings produce. . . . [F]or example, Pacific cannot even tell the Commission what revenues it actually receives from its charges for colored telephones without making a special 'study' of the situation."

"[I]t has been repeatedly pointed out that Pacific has not supplied actual revenue, cost or plant data in support of its tariffs. When specifically requested to do so . . . its Counsel argued in opposition to the request. . . .

"The arguments of Pacific's counsel and the comments of its witnesses make it abundantly clear that the whole subject is distasteful to Pacific. It desires, apparently, to forever rely on estimates made prior to the setting of rates on

in the passage and enforcement of the Interstate Commerce Act, from the very beginning.[85] In the other utilities, the major issue has usually revolved around the adequacy of total or net revenues; and the solution has usually been a more or less across-the-board increase or decrease of the entire structure.[86] Second, to the extent regulatory laws and commissions have considered the pattern of prices set, they have been guided by the same sort of mixture of essentially economic and political-social considerations as have influenced their determinations of the proper returns on investment.

The relative neglect of individual prices most clearly epitomizes the difference between the traditional approach to public utility price regulation and the one the economist would recommend. In this area, the commissions typically proceed only in response to specific complaints: businessmen in locality A complain that the freight rates charged them are higher than those charged their competitors; railroads point out that they are losing particular classes of business to trucks or barges and ask permission to reduce the relevant rates to meet competition; the affected trucking and navigation companies intervene to prevent the proposed reductions. Commercial customers assert that they are paying a higher price than residential users for electricity; local utility commissions complain that high rates for local service are subsidizing unduly low rates on long-distance calls; oil jobbers argue that gas distribution companies are offering uneconomically low promotional rates on home heating; the latter maintain that too large a proportion of the capacity costs of the interstate pipelines that supply them are incorporated in the demand charges that they pay and too little is imposed on the lines' direct industrial customers; and representatives of the bituminous coal industry join in these protestations, because the low-priced gas sold for use as boiler fuel for electricity generation takes business away from them. And all too often, from the economist's standpoint, the commissions resolve such controversies on bases other than economic efficiency, seeking to protect offended competitors from excessive losses of business, to preserve a "fair share" of the

---

new services as justification for continuing rate forms and relative rate levels whether or not the services are in reality today properly priced. One of its witnesses is 'hopeful' that the original estimates will so price new services that they will not be a burden on basic service. While this Commission may share or even applaud such 'hopes,' it has the duty to see to it that rates are fair and reasonable. . . ." *In the Matter of . . . the Pacific Telephone and Telegraph Company et al.*, Decision No. 74917, November 6, 1968, mimeo., 30–31, 60–61.

[85] In describing what was to become the Act to Regulate Commerce, in 1887, the Cullom Committee said: "the provisions of the bill are based upon the theory that the paramount evil chargeable against the operation of the transportation system of the United States as now conducted is unjust discrimination between persons, places, commodities, or particular descriptions of traffic." U.S. Senate, Select Committee on Interstate Commerce, 49th Cong., 1st Sess., Sen. Report 46, Part I, Washington,

1886, 215. Correspondingly, "it would be possible to write an extensive history of railroad regulation without mentioning cost of capital or rate of return." James R. Nelson, "Pricing and Resource Allocation: The Public Utility Sector," in Shepherd and Gies, *op. cit.*, 83. Since 1922, the Interstate Commerce Commission "has not found it necessary to specify a fair rate of return for the roads." Phillips, *op. cit.*, 271.

[86] See, for example, Troxel, in Shepherd and Gies, *op. cit.*, 150–151, 175–176. Regulatory commissions and courts alike have tended to leave the designing of rate structures to the discretion of managements. Even in transportation, both company managements and the Interstate Commerce Commission for much too long neglected the much-needed reconsideration of common-carrier rate structures in the light of the intensified competition of newer transport media and of private and contract carriers. See the section on "Transportation," Chapter 1, Volume 2.

market for each, to strike some equitable or politically acceptable distribution of common costs among the various classes of patrons. We will see numerous illustrations of this kind of behavior in Chapters 1 and 2 of Volume 2.

Microeconomics, in contrast, is interested first and foremost in the determination of individual prices. Its normative models also include certain notions about the appropriate relation between an industry's average prices or total revenues on the one hand and its average or total costs on the other; but that optimum is conceived to be the result or *end product* of a competitive process that operates directly and in the first instance in individual markets, in the fixing of individual prices.[87]

With respect to those individual markets, the rules of microeconomics are in principle simple and grounded in objective facts: subject to important qualifications that we shall elaborate at a later point, prices should be equated to marginal costs. In this scheme, there is no room for separate considerations of "fairness." Or, to put it another way, fairness is defined in strictly economic terms: those prices are fair that are equal to marginal costs, those unfair that are not equal.

"As in so many other policy areas, the lawyers and engineers (and increasingly the accountants)—*not* the economists—have largely dominated regulatory policy."[88] This does not mean that economists have not written at length and incisively about public utility regulation. But until recently, their analyses have been directed mainly toward the traditional issues, and organized within the framework formulated by administrative commissions and courts and by *Smyth v. Ames* in particular. Our next chapters, following

---

[87] These comments may seem arbitrarily to suggest that short-run equilibrium is somehow more important than long-run, and in so doing to reflect the essentially static character of traditional economic theory, or its tendency simply to assume mobility of resources sufficient to ensure the achievement of long-run equilibrium. In a dynamic world and in the presence of resource immobilities, competition sufficiently pure to hold prices constantly at short-run marginal cost may prove destructive and violently unstable; and much of the pricing in impurely competitive or oligopolistic markets can often be understood as seeking to achieve the long-run competitive result—which in a perfectly competitive market could safely be left to instantaneous inflows and outflows of labor and capital—at the possible expense of the constant equation of price with short-run marginal cost. The student of industrial organization may be as much concerned with the process that holds an industry's total profits, averaged over some period of time, at the competitive level as that its individual prices be instantaneously equated with short-term marginal cost.

The fact remains that the welfare ideal is constructed on the basis of the equation of price to marginal cost in individual markets and in the short-run. That is where the process starts. Departures from that standard must be individually justified. The mere control of overall rates of return does not in itself ensure that the pattern of individual prices is economically efficient:

"A great many *different* patterns, efficient and inefficient, within the firm may be perfectly consistent with a *given* over-all rate of return. So, whatever the rates of return may actually have been, they cannot by themselves demonstrate whether resource allocation (to and within the utilities) has been efficient." Shepherd, in Shepherd and Gies, *op. cit.*, 20. See also Nelson, *ibid.*, 66.

Moreover—and this is a point critically important with respect to the public utility industries—even long-run equilibrium price is not the same thing as a price that covers current operating expenses plus some acceptable average rate of return on investment, which is what has principally concerned regulatory commissions. On the contrary, it involves the equation of price with long-run marginal cost. Correspondingly, the investment policy that produces long-run equilibrium in the competitive ideal is one that equates with the cost of capital the rate of return on incremental investment, not the *average* rate of return on historical investment, however the latter is valued. We shall explore these similarities and differences in the ensuing chapters.

[88] Shepherd, "Conclusion," in Shepherd and Gies, *op. cit.*, 266.

the lead of some of the recent economic literature[89] and accepting the implied invitation of the *Hope Natural Gas* decision, returns to the economic principles and attempts to apply them to the problems of public utility regulation. In so doing we will try not to neglect the traditional regulatory issues set forth in this chapter, but will instead analyze them in economic terms, while continuing, as throughout this study, to assess the limitations as well as the possible contributions of economics to their resolution.[90]

---

[89] See, for example, the works cited *ibid.*, 267 and throughout this chapter and those that follow.

[90] There is no intention here to exaggerate the novelty of this approach, as compared with current regulatory thinking and practice. On the contrary, the traditional approaches that we have been describing in this chapter have certainly been modified in recent years.

Regulated companies and commissions alike have been paying increasing attention to the design of economically efficient rate structures; and, in this task and in others, as we have already observed, they have made dramatically increasing use of the tools and perspectives of the economist. This book is in a sense a survey, summary, and critique of this emergent practice.

Explanation of Mathematical Derivation of Cost of Capital Formula

The price the investor will be willing to pay for a stock will be equal to what he estimates to be its present worth. This present worth is the discounted value of what he expects to receive as a result of being a stockholder, namely the dividends he will be paid plus the price at which he will eventually sell the stock. As we shall see, this boils down to the present worth of all expected future dividend payments.

Let us suppose that the investor buys the stock at the beginning of Year 0. He expects to receive dividends of D_0 at the end of Year 0, D_1 at the end of Year 1, D_2 at the end of Year 2, etc. He expects to sell the stock at the price P_n at the end of Year n. If the investor is using a discount rate of 10%, then the present worth of a dividend D_0 received one year from now is:

$$P.W. = \frac{D_0}{1.10}$$

For any discount rate, k,

$$P.W. = \frac{D_0}{1+k}$$

The present worth of a dividend D_1 received *two* years from now is:

$$P.W. = \frac{D_1}{(1+k)^2}$$

Thus, if the investor has a discount rate of k, the present worth of all the expected future receipts will be:

$$P.W. = \frac{D_0}{1+k} + \frac{D_1}{(1+k)^2} + \frac{D_2}{(1+k)^3} + \cdots \frac{P_n}{(1+k)^{n+1}}$$

The following numerical example may be helpful in understanding this formula.

Year	Receipts	Discount Factor	Present Worth of Receipts
1	1.00	1.100	0.91
2	1.05	1.210	0.87
3	1.10	1.332	0.83
4	1.15	1.464	0.79
5	1.20	1.610	0.75
5	$25.00	1.610	15.53
			$19.68

In this example, the investor expects to receive dividends of $1.00, $1.05, $1.10, $1.15, and $1.20 at the end of each of the first five years and also to seel the stock for $25.00 at the end of the fifth year. The second column shows the applicable discount factor for each of the years; the discount rate is 0.10, or 10%, and the discounting gets progressively greater by the law of compound interest, with each year. The final column is derived by dividing the receipts in each year by the discount factor for that year. This column represents the present worth of these future receipts; for example, the present worth of a $1.05 dividend received two years from now is $0.87. The total present worth of these receipts, including the price at which the stock is later sold, is $19.68. Thus, the investor will only be willing to pay $19.68 for this stock.

Let us now consider what basis the investor might have for estimating the future price at which he will be able to sell the stock. Obviously, some other investor at that future date will be willing to buy the stock at a price based on *his* estimate of dividends to be received at a still later date and the price at which *he* will be able to sell the stock. The third buyer must envisage still a later buyer, etc. Thus, as we push the analysis further and further into the future, we find that the value of the stock is equal to the present worth of all the dividends to be paid to stockholders over the entire future. This makes a certain amount of ordinary sense, once you brush away the technicalities, because all that the stockholders as a group will ever be able to get out of the company are dividends, so that the true value of a company to its stockholders must depend on the value of the dividends it will pay out over its life.

The present worth of a stream of annual dividends extending indefinitely into the future is:

$$P.W. = \frac{D_0}{1+k} + \frac{D_1}{(1+k)^2} + \frac{D_2}{(1+k)^3} + \cdots \frac{D_n}{(1+k)^{n+1}}$$

Now, if we suppose that the dividends grow at a constant annual percentage rate of growth, g per cent per year, the equation becomes:

$$P.W. = \frac{D_0}{1+k} + \frac{D_0(1+g)}{(1+k)^2} + \frac{D_0(1+g)^2}{(1+k)^3} + \cdots \frac{D_0(1+g)^n}{(1+k)^{n+1}}$$

As is shown in the Mathematical Appendix,* if the current price, P_0, is equal to the present worth of the stock, then it follows that:

$$P_0 = \frac{D_0}{k - g}$$

That is, the price the investor is willing to pay for the stock will depend on (1) D_0, the first year's dividend, (2) g, the expected long-term growth rate, and (3) k, the investor's discount rate, which is the company's cost of equity capital. Thus, if we know what the current price and dividend are, and if we can make a reasonable estimate of growth, we can infer what k, the cost of equity capital must be. By simple algebra,

$$k = \frac{D}{P} + g$$

This is the basic formula for measuring the company's cost of equity capital.

---

*This is Appendix A of Roseman's testimony. It explains the solution of the preceding equation, which can (like the familiar multiplier in macro-economics) be reduced to a constant term $(D_0/1+k)$ times the sum of an infinite geometric progression

$$\left(1/1 - \frac{1+g}{1+k}\right),$$

the latter term of which can be reduced to $1 + k/k - g$. So

$$P_0 = \frac{D_0}{1+k} \cdot \frac{1+k}{k-g} = \frac{D_0}{k-g}$$

This solution is possible only if k exceeds g; but actually any persistent excess of g over k is economically inconceivable.

PART II

Economic Principles of Rate Making

CHAPTER 3

Marginal Cost Pricing

The traditional legal criteria of proper public utility rates have always borne a strong resemblance to the criteria of the competitive market in long-run equilibrium. The principal benchmark for "just and reasonable" rate levels has been cost of production, including, as the economist would include, the necessary return to capital. The rule that individual rates not be unduly discriminatory similarly has been defined in terms of the respective costs of the various services. Rates that produce widely divergent profits on different parts of the business are suspect.[1] The famous prohibition of "long versus short haul" discrimination in the original Interstate Commerce Commission Act of 1887 was grounded in a recognition that it could not cost more to transport passengers or the same commodity "for a shorter than for a longer distance over the same line or route in the same direction, the shorter being included within the longer distance. . . ."[2] Correspondingly, rates may differ if costs differ: this is the justification of higher monthly charges for one-party than for multi-party line telephone service or for basing railroad rates for carload shipments partially on weight.[3]

Actually, from the very beginning, regulated companies have also been permitted to discriminate in the economic sense, charging different rates for various services even when the costs were not correspondingly different. In particular, rates have been adjusted to the respective "value of service" to different classes of customers; what this means, in effect, is that they have in

---

[1] In its comprehensive examination of the reasonableness of the rates charged by the American Telephone & Telegraph Company (and its associated companies), initiated in 1965 —the first in 33 years—the Federal Communications Commission instructed AT&T as follows:

"In connection with respondents' presentations as to the appropriate ratemaking principles and factors which should govern the proper relationships among the rate levels for each of their principal services, respondents shall take into consideration the wide variations in levels of earnings revealed by the . . . seven-way cost study." *In the Matter of American Telephone and*

Telegraph Company and the Associated Bell System Companies, Docket No. 16258, Memorandum Opinion and Order, 2 FCC 2d 143 (1965).

See also *Atlantic Coast Line Railroad Co. v. North Carolina Corporation Commission*, 206 U.S. 1 (1907), at 25–26, and Isaak B. Lake, *Discrimination by Railroads and Other Public Utilities* (Raleigh: Edwards and Broughton), 153–188.

[2] *U.S. Code*, 1964 ed. (Washington, 1965), Title 49, Sec. 4.

[3] C. F. Phillips, Jr., *The Economics of Regulation*, 311–312, 358; D. Philip Locklin, *Economics of Transportation*, 6th ed. (Homewood: Richard D. Irwin, 1966), 159.

part been patterned on the basis of the respective elasticities of demand. The railroads have been the leading practitioners of this type of pricing, typically charging higher rates for more valuable than for less valuable commodities, on the assumption (not always justified, as we shall see) that these differences reflect what the respective traffics will bear. A similar justification underlies the typically higher monthly flat-rate telephone service charges for commercial than for residential customers. Of course, price discrimination would be impossible under pure competition. But the traditional rationalization—not typically stated in these terms, to be sure—was that it could permit a closer approximation to optimum use of resources in situations in which pure competition was infeasible.[4] In principle this argument is correct, as we shall see.

Various developments of recent decades have encouraged an even more explicitly economic approach to public utility pricing. One was the open invitation of the *Hope* decision to regulatory commissions to break out of the fair return on fair value of property box within which *Smyth v. Ames* had them confined for so long. A second has been the tendency of business management to adopt increasingly sophisticated economic criteria and techniques in formulating investment and price policies.

Finally, the march of technology has made most of the traditional public utilities, even the most "naturally monopolistic" among them, increasingly subject to competition. The share of total intercity ton-miles of the nation's freight traffic carried by the railroads dropped from 74.9% in 1929 to 61.3% in 1940 and to 41.6% by 1967.[5] The decline in their share of total freight *revenues* was even greater, as competitive carriers made deep inroads into their higher-priced business (whose demand the railroads for too long continued to assume was inelastic), leaving them with the carriage of bulky, heavy commodities, at comparatively low-ton mile rates.[6] The rapid spread throughout the country of interstate natural gas transmission lines since World War II has enormously accentuated the competition of local natural gas distribution companies with the unregulated distributors of distillate oils and coal in the home heating market, of residual fuel oils and coal for industrial uses such as boiler fuel, with electric companies in the fields of residential and hot water heating, cooking, and air-conditioning.[7] Electric companies responded with special promotional rates for the all-electric home, using electricity for air-conditioning in the summer and home heating in the

[4] See, for example, Arthur T. Hadley, *Railroad Transportation, Its History and Its Laws* (New York: Putnam's, 1895), Chapter 6.

[5] James C. Nelson, *Railroad Transportation and Public Policy* (Brookings: Washington, 1959), 10, and Interstate Commerce Commission, *82nd Annual Report, 1968* (Washington, 1968), 86. The rate of decline slowed down considerably after 1960.

[6] For example, the participation of the railroads in the combined tonnage of intercity freight carried by them and by trucks dropped only from 86 to 74% between 1940 and 1955; but the share of Class I railroads in the estimated freight revenues of themselves and all intercity motor carriers of property fell from 67.4 to 38.7% in

the same period. Partially computed from J. C. Nelson, *op. cit.*, 10, 439, and 445.

[7] There were 218,000 miles of natural gas pipelines and utility main in the United States in 1945 and 816,000 in 1967. *Statistical Abstract of the United States, 1968*, 521. Approximately 10% of the occupied dwelling units in the United States were heated by utility-supplied gas in 1940; in 1960 the figure was 43%. The proportion of those heated by fuel oils and kerosene also rose in this period from 10 to 32%, while the share heated by coal dropped from 55 to 12%. U.S. Department of Commerce, Bureau of the Census, *Census of Housing, 1960*, Washington, U.S. Government Printing Office, 1963, Vol. I, Part 1, XL.

winter;[8] and oil and gas companies have in turn made major efforts to develop and market the fuel cell, which enables large users to generate their own electric power, while using the by-product heat for heating purposes.[9] In the communications field, reduced long-distance telephone rates have made sharp inroads into Western Union's telegraph business; and the spreading use of private microwave systems by businesses and governments has offered growing direct competition with the regulated common carriers. The latter have in turn responded by offering their own special communication and data-transmission services, in competition with both the private systems and each other. And communications satellite systems compete with overland wire and microwave communications and undersea cables.

This intensification of competition has forced these companies into fundamental reexaminations of their pricing policies. Both they and their regulators have found themselves groping for criteria by which to develop and to test competitive rates, where the regulated company itself is interested in knowing to what extent it is in its own interest to reduce prices in order to compete for business, and commissions have to decide under what circumstances these competitive rates maybe unduly or destructively discriminatory. Among the most important and challenging developments in utility rate-making in recent decades have been the efforts of railroads to free themselves from their own conservative pricing practices and regulatory restrictions, in order to regain some of their lost business; the increasing attention paid by electricity and gas distributors to the possibilities of promotional rates and by regulatory commissions to the complaints that such rates have elicited from competitors; and the various investigations by the Federal Communications Commission of the rate structures of the Bell System and of the proper method of integrating the costs of transmission-by-satellite into communications rates.[10]

These various developments have compelled a reexamination of the economics of public utility pricemaking. They make particularly appropriate the attempt to develop and apply economic standards to the assessment of both the private and the public interests in that process.

THE CENTRAL ECONOMIC PRINCIPLE: MARGINAL COST PRICING

The central policy prescription of microeconomics is the equation of price and marginal cost. If economic theory is to have any relevance to public utility pricing, that is the point at which the inquiry must begin.

As almost any student of elementary economics will recall, marginal cost is the cost of producing one more unit; it can equally be envisaged as the cost that would be saved by producing one less unit. Looked at the first way, it

---

[8] In 1965, over 20% of new houses were equipped with electric heating, thus cutting into a market long dominated by gas and oil. Lee C. White, "Growth Prospects for the Natural Gas Industry," *Public Utilities Fortnightly* (October 13, 1966), LXXVIII: 38.

[9] See Irwin M. Stelzer and Bruce C. Netschert, "Hot War in the Energy Industry," *Harv. Bus. Rev.* (November–December, 1967), XLV: 14–19.

[10] We will be discussing these various developments below. Another similar development, this one stimulated in part by financial adversity, was the economic analysis of the airline fare structure by the staff of the Civil Aeronautics Board, published in 1968, and the Board's proposals for revising that structure so as to relate individual fares much more closely to their respective costs. See *Wall Street Journal*, June 16, 1969, 34.

may be termed incremental cost—the added cost of (a small amount of) incremental output. Observed in the second way, it is synonymous with avoidable cost—the cost that would be saved by (slightly) reducing output. (Although these three terms are often used synonymously, marginal cost, strictly speaking, refers to the additional cost of supplying a single, infinitesimally small additional unit, while "incremental" and "avoidable" are sometimes used to refer to the *average* additional cost of a finite and possibly a large change in production or sales.) Why does the economist argue that, ideally, *every buyer* ought to pay a price equal to the cost of supplying one incremental unit?

At any given time, every economy has a fixed bundle of productive resources, a finite total potential productive capacity. Of course, that total can grow over time; but at any given time the basic economic problem is to make the best or most efficient use of that limited capacity. The basic economic problem, in short, is the problem of choice. A decision to produce more of any one good or service is, in these circumstances, *ipso facto* a decision to produce less of all other goods and services taken as a bunch. It follows that the cost to society of producing anything consists, really, in the other things that must be sacrificed in order to produce it: in the last analysis, "cost" is opportunity cost—the alternatives that must be foregone. In our economy, we leave the final decision about what shall be produced and what not to the voluntary decisions of purchasers,[11] guided by prices on the one hand and their own wants or preferences on the other.

If consumers are to make the choices that will yield them the greatest possible satisfaction from society's limited aggregate productive capacity, the prices that they pay for the various goods and services available to them must accurately reflect their respective opportunity costs; only then will buyers be judging, in deciding what to buy and what not, whether the satisfaction they get from the purchase of any particular product is worth the sacrifice of other goods and services that its production entails. If their judgments are correctly informed in this way, they will, by their independent purchase decisions, guide our scarce resources into those lines of production that yield more satisfaction than all available alternatives—which means that total satisfaction will be maximized.

But why does economic efficiency require prices equal to marginal, instead of, for example, average total costs? The reason is that the demand for all goods and services is in some degree, at some point, responsive to price. Then, if consumers are to decide intelligently whether to take somewhat *more* or somewhat *less* of any particular item, the price they have to pay for it (and the prices of all other goods and services with which they compare it) must reflect the cost of supplying somewhat more or somewhat less—in short, *marginal* opportunity cost. If buyers are charged more than marginal cost for a particular commodity, for example because the seller has monopoly power, they will buy less than the optimum quantity; consumers who would willingly have had society allocate to its production the incremental resources

[11] We briefly summarize the familiar rationalization of a market system, in which the consumer is supposed to be sovereign. How "voluntary," or "free" consumer decisions actually are in any such economy is an interesting and important question. To the extent that an economic system influences consumer tastes, it is no longer possible for an economist to describe its functioning as "optimal" or "efficient" on the ground that it gives consumers what they want, since the system itself helps determine what they want. See note 1, Chapter 1, and pp. 67–69, below.

required, willingly sacrificing the alternative goods and services that those resources could have produced, will refrain from making those additional purchases because the price to them exaggerates the sacrifices. Conversely, if price is below incremental costs, perhaps because the suppliers are being subsidized, production of the products in question will be higher (and of all other products taken together lower) than it ought to be: society is sacrificing more of other goods and services to produce the additional quantities of the subsidized service than customers would willingly have authorized, had the price to them fully reflected that marginal opportunity cost.

The corollary of the social rule that price should equal marginal cost is the rule of thumb for the businessman—it pays him to continue to produce and sell as long as his incremental revenues cover his incremental costs. Since under pure competition incremental revenues to the businessman are simply the market price times the additional quantities sold, we have the elementary proposition that under pure competition businessmen will increase production and sales up to the point where their marginal costs are equated to price. Therefore, competitive behavior assures the equation of price and marginal cost that is required if free consumer choices are to result in the optimum allocation of resources.

It is impossible here to provide an adequate survey of all the assumptions, definitions, and value judgments implicit in the foregoing sketchy summary, or of all qualifications to which the marginal cost equals price rule must be subjected. Many will be introduced, where appropriate, as we go along: recall out initial statement that marginal cost is (only) the place to *begin*.[12] But we must point out at once that the allocation of resources that the rule produces can be described as "optimal" only on the basis of two essentially unprovable assumptions or value judgments: that the "best" economy is the one that gives consumers what they individually want; and that income is either distributed optimally or can best be redistributed without departing from marginal cost pricing.

1. One need accept the allocation of resources the rule produces in a market economy only to the extent that one approves of the choices consumers make or would make. The economist has no scientific basis for objecting if, instead, society decides to improve on the result, either by trying to influence consumer choices (for example by education or by taxing or prohibiting sale of goods whose consumption it wishes to discourage) or by subsidizing the production of goods it thinks would otherwise be consumed in inadequate quantities. The question of what is the best measure or definition of social welfare, which it is the function of the economy to serve, is a political or philosophical, not an economic, one. Economics as such is the science of means, not ends.

2. One need accept the result as optimal only if one is willing to place a similar evaluation on the distribution of income—either the preexisting distribution of income, which decides how many dollar votes each buyer has in deciding what to order the economy to produce,[13] or the

---

[12] The reader will recognize that we have already raised such questions (see pp. 25, 29–31, 44–45, 53), about which the rule is silent, as the proper level of cost, to which price is to be equated, the proper rate of service or process innovation, and

the problems of achieving these ends in the public utility industries. We return to these extremely important questions in Volume 2.

[13] It reasonably could be argued that satisfactions are not being maximized in an economy

distribution of income that results from equating price to marginal cost.[14] This, too, is an ethical judgment, not an economic one.

The pricing rule does suggest that if one disapproves of the distribution of income, one might better correct it by lump-sum taxes (for example, on rents, income, or inheritance) and money transfers than by departing from the requirements of economically efficient pricing: equating price to marginal cost remains a necessary condition if the best choices are to be made, *however* income is distributed or redistributed. Unfortunately, however, there are few taxes that are completely neutral—that is, that may not themselves distort marginal choices and thereby thwart the maximizing of satisfactions.[15] In practice, as Graaff puts it, "tinkering with the price mechanism is one of the more feasible and generally satisfactory ways of securing whatever distribution of wealth is desired."[16]

For example, the government may feel that a particular service is so

---

that produces yachts for some while providing inadequate food and medical care for others. The quarrel here would be with the distribution of income, about which the economic rules for the efficient making of choices are silent. The assumption underlying such a criticism is that a dollar spent by a poor man yields more satisfaction than one spent by a rich man (or simply that some noneconomic value such as justice requires a reordering of our economic priorities in the suggested direction). See, for example, A. C. Pigou, *The Economics of Welfare* (London: Macmillan and Co., 1920), Chapter 8, and Abba P. Lerner, *The Economics of Control* (New York: The Macmillan Co., 1944), Chapter 2. Economists have been typically unwilling, *as economists*, to make judgments involving interpersonal utility comparisons.

[14] For example, equating price to marginal cost produces economic rents—scarcity returns to nonreproducible factors of production of supermarginal quality, such as well situated land or some scarce natural resources. One may object to the earning of such "unearned income," and be prepared to sacrifice some of the benefits of an efficient price system for what one conceives to be a better distribution of income. This was an important consideration underlying the decision by the Federal Power Commission to adopt a two-price system for regulating the field price of natural gas, in which only newly committed gas would receive the higher price corresponding to (current) marginal cost. The reason for departing from the economic rule that the price of *all* units sold be set at marginal cost was a reluctance to permit the consequent large transfer of income from consumers to companies that had discovered their gas many years earlier, at far lower cost, and committed it under longterm contracts at much lower prices. Area Rate Proceeding, Claude E. Aikman, *et. al.*, 34 FPC 159, 185–194 (1965), sustained, 390 U.S. 747 (1968). Compare Joel B. Dirlam, "Natural Gas: Cost, Conserva-

tion and Pricing," *Amer. Econ. Rev., Papers and Proceedings* (May 1958), XLVIII: 491–495 and Kahn, "Economic Issues in Regulating the Field Price of Natural Gas," *ibid.* (May 1960), L: 506–510, with Paul W. MacAvoy, *Price Formation in Natural Gas Fields* (New Haven: Yale University Press, 1962), 252–263. Or, like Henry George (and most other economists), one may prefer to keep prices equal to marginal costs, and tax away the unearned increment. *Progress and Poverty* (San Francisco: W. M. Hinton & Company, 1879). See also note 55, Chapter 2; James C. Laughlin, "The Case Against Dual Pricing in Southern Louisiana," *Land Econ.* (February 1967), XLIII: 56—64; Kahn, "Comment" on that article and Laughlin, "Reply," *ibid.*, forthcoming.

Again, equating price to marginal cost under conditions of decreasing costs would require public subsidies to make up the difference between marginal and average total costs. (See pp. 130.) This means an income transfer from taxpayers to consumers of the service in question. For a strong statement that economists are incompetent to evaluate such results of marginal cost pricing, with particular application to public utilities, see J. Wiseman, "The Theory of Public Utility Price—An Empty Box," *Oxford Economic Papers*, (February 1957), n.s. IX: 58–59, 62–68.

[15] Excise taxes obviously cause relative prices to diverge from marginal costs. But opportunity the income tax also *may* distort the choice between work and leisure, by reducing the individual's return from marginal effort below the social value of his product. (See note 15 Chapter 5.)

[16] J. de V. Graaff, *Theoretical Welfare Economics* (Cambridge: Cambridge University Press, 1957), 171. Graaff's point here is that the economist cannot say that such tinkering is "wrong"; all he can do is "make clear . . . the probable consequences of setting it [price] at various different

important to welfare generally that it may wish to subsidize its consumption by holding its price below marginal cost, either generally or selectively (for instance, for poor families); and it may be unwilling to achieve this purpose instead by merely making cash grants to poor families, for fear they may spend the cash instead for other, less socially approved purposes.

There are two corollaries of the marginal cost pricing principle:

1. Prices must reflect all the (marginal) costs of production and consumption—not only those borne directly by the transacting parties but also those that may be foisted on outsiders. (A familiar case of an external cost is the air or stream pollution that may be caused by a particular production process or a particular act of consumption. If it is not borne by the responsible party, his marginal cost will understate the true opportunity cost of the transaction in question—the true sacrifice involved in making it possible—and the result will be overproduction of the good or service in question.) All the social benefits of particular acts of production or consumption must similarly accrue to or otherwise be brought to bear in (positively) influencing the decisions of the buyers, who alone will determine whether the production is undertaken. (If, for example, I would benefit if my neighbor undertook the expense of keeping mosquitoes from breeding on his land, that benefit must somehow be added into his calculus of costs and satisfactions if the proper amount of resources is to be devoted to this endeavor: I might, for instance, offer to pay part of the costs. Where external benefits of a particular economic activity are not appropriated by or do not accrue to the transacting parties, the effect will be an underallocation of resources to that activity.)

2. The rule does not necessarily produce optimal results if it is applied only partially: it does not necessarily provide a correct guide for pricing in individual markets or industries if it is not being followed uniformly throughout the economy. If, for example, the price of good A is held above marginal cost, perhaps by monopoly or by disproportionately heavy taxation, then it may produce a worse instead of a better allocation of resources to push the price of its substitute, B, down to marginal cost. This "problem of the second best" is obviously a very serious one in an economy shot through with imperfections of competition, monopoly power, and government taxes and subsidies, causing all prices to diverge in varying directions and degrees from marginal costs. The "first best" solution, in the foregoing example, would be to reduce the prices of both A and B (and of all other goods and services in the economy) to marginal costs; the "second best" *might* be to keep the price of B above its marginal cost, perhaps by means of an excise tax, in order to avoid distorting buyers' choices between it and A.[17]

---

levels." *Ibid.* For a general argument against "tinkering with price" for such purposes, see Bonbright, *Principles of Public Utility Rates,* 58–62 and chapter 7.

[17] On the other hand one cannot be certain, strictly speaking, that this is the proper solution without taking into account all other distortions in the economy as well. The pioneering demonstration of this is by R. G. Lipsey and Kelvin Lancaster, "The General Theory of Second Best," *Rev. Econ. Studies* (1956), XXIV: 11–32; they in turn cite the earlier analyses of J. E. Meade. Lipsey and Lancaster show that

". . . in general, nothing can be said about the direction or the magnitude of the secondary departures from optimum conditions made necessary by the original non-fulfillment of one condition. . . . In particular it is *not* true that a situation in which all departures from the

The existence of pervasive imperfections in the economy greatly complicates the problem of efficient pricing. In the author's view in principle it does not make solution impossible in specific situations, nor does it make it practically impossible in such instances to make the type of informed piecemeal decisions policymakers must inevitably make about how far and in what directions to qualify the basic rule of marginal-cost pricing:

"Over the whole of the discussions . . . there looms most menacingly the injunction of the theorem of the second best: Thou shalt not optimize piecemeal. But I would argue that in practice this admonition must be softened lest otherwise all effective policy be stultified. I would propose, instead, that one should shun piecemeal ameliorative measures that have not been sanctioned by careful analysis and the liberal use of common sense. Many policies may plausibly be expected to yield improvements even though things elsewhere are not organized optimally."[18]

PROBLEMS OF DEFINING MARGINAL COST

It is no simple matter to measure marginal costs—that is probably the understatement of the year. But even before one turns to that task, a number of difficult questions have to be answered about what it is, precisely, that one is trying to measure.

Specifying the Time Perspective

It is a familiar and elementary proposition in economics that sunk costs are and should be irrelevant to short-run pricing and output decisions. The only costs relevant in deciding how much to produce in plants already constructed, with production capacity already installed, are the variable costs of operating that plant, farm, or service establishment already equipped.

The longer the time perspective of the costing process, the greater the proportion of costs that become variable. As existing plant and equipment continue to be operated over time, they will ordinarily involve higher and

optimum conditions are of the same direction and magnitude is necessarily superior to one in which the deviations vary in direction and magnitude. For example, there is no reason to believe that a situation in which there is the same degree of monopoly in all industries will necessarily be in any sense superior to a situation in which the degree of monopoly varies as between industries." *Ibid.*, 12.

Their article has stimulated extensive discussion in literature about whether and under what circumstances the problem they elucidate means that it is impossible to tell *even in individual instances* whether efficiency is served by bringing a *particular* price closer to marginal cost. See M. J. Farrell, "In Defense of Public-Utility Price Theory," *Oxford Econ. Papers* (February 1958), n.s. X: 112–113; J. Wiseman, "The Theory of Public Utility Price: A Further Note," *Ibid.* (February 1959), XI: 92–93; Otto A. Davis and Andrew B. Whinston, "Welfare Economics and the Theory of Second Best," *Rev. Econ. Studies* (January 1965), XXXII: 1–14; and the articles by P. Bohm, Takashi Negishi,

M. McManus, and Davis and Whinston, *Ibid.* (July 1967), XXXIV: 301–331.

[18] William J. Baumol, *Welfare Economics and the Theory of the State*, 2d ed. (Cambridge: Harvard University Press, 1965), 30. As Baumol points out elsewhere, the problem of piecemeal solutions demonstrated by the theory of second-best is one of interdependencies: the proper price for *A* depends on the price-to-marginal-cost relationships of all other commodities the production of which is in any way, however remotely, related to that of *A*. But some interrelationships are more remote and therefore more safely ignored than others. "It may, then, be possible to partition the economy more effectively than some might have expected." "Informed Judgment, Rigorous Theory and Public Policy," *South Econ. Jour.* (October 1965), XXXII: 144. Similarly I.M.D. Little, who regards the general P = MC rule as both useless and wrong in an imperfect economy, nonetheless urges not only the possibility but the necessity for making informed judgments in individual cases about the proper relationship of prices and marginal cost. *A*

higher variable costs—of shutdowns, repair and maintenance, and wastage of labor and materials. Meanwhile, the progress of technology will ordinarily make increasingly attractive alternatives available. Eventually, therefore, the question of replacement will arise. At some time, the businessman, in determining whether or not to continue to produce and if so on what scale, will be able to decide once again whether to incur some or all of the capital costs of production. He will find, that is, that these costs—fixed in the short run—are variable in the long-run. The doctor can and should ignore the costs he incurred in the past for his training, in deciding whether it is worthwhile for him to keep practicing; but each prospective medical student makes the calculation afresh in deciding whether to embark on that profession. When the competitive model prescribes prices equated to marginal costs, does it mean the incremental short-run, variable cost of operating existing capacity, or intermediate-run cost, which will include also the prospectively mounting costs of repair, maintenance and operation, or the long-run costs of ultimately renewing, replacing, or adding to capacity? Are the optimum medical fees what it takes to induce doctors already trained to continue offering their services, or what it takes to bring in a fresh supply of new doctors?

When we turn to the practical problems of price making we will find that there is no single answer to these questions. But the economic principles are clear-cut. They are two. First, the essential criterion of what belongs in marginal cost and what not, and of which marginal costs should be reflected in price, is causal responsibility. All the purchasers of any commodity or service should be made to bear such additional costs—*only* such, but also *all* such—as are imposed on the economy by the provision of one additional unit.[19] And second, it is short-run marginal cost to which price should at any given time—*hence always*—be equated, because it is short-run marginal cost that reflects the social opportunity cost of providing the additional unit that buyers are at any given time trying to decide whether to buy.

It might appear that these two principles are in conflict. The first one surely implies that price must include *all* the costs that production of an additional unit imposes, regardless of when those costs are actually realized. If, for example, taking on additional business will for a time involve only the hiring of additional workers, the use of additional raw materials and fuels, but in time will necessitate also higher expenditures than otherwise for maintenance and repairs; if it will cause capital equipment to wear out faster and therefore need to be replaced sooner than otherwise—then the principle of causal responsibility would clearly require that these longer-run marginal costs be reflected in price. The second rule would seem to state, in contrast, that if some of these additional costs, for which present production is causally responsible, will in fact be felt only at some time in the future, then present purchasers should not have to bear them. But this latter interpretation would be incorrect. Variable costs include any sacrifice of future value or any future realization of higher costs that are causally attributable to present production.[20] Short-run marginal cost is simply the change in total variable cost

Critique of Welfare Economics, 2d ed. (Oxford: Clarendon Press, 1957), compare 161, 194 and 201–202.

[19] We set aside the possibility that different purchasers of the same service may be charged different prices. Economic efficiency calls for a uniform price to all buyers of an identical service at any given time (unless there can be perfect price discrimination: see pp. 131–132).

[20] This element in variable cost is called user cost: it is the loss in the net value of a firm's assets attributable to its having engaged in

caused by producing an additional unit: to the extent wear and tear of equipment varies with use—and it certainly does—depreciation *is* a variable cost, although it is typically most convenient for accounting purposes to lump physical wear-and-tear together with provision for obsolescence, label the package "depreciation," and charge it off per unit of time instead of output.[21] If price does not cover such variable costs, it is not doing its job, which is to reflect the marginal opportunity costs to society of providing the service. The second principle remains valid: ideally, price should reflect *only* those ("short-run") costs that do vary with output (regardless of when they are actually felt or give rise to additional cash outlays), because production of an additional unit is causally responsible for only those costs.

It then follows that to the extent that maintenance, depreciation, cost of capital, and various other overhead expenses are *not* a function of use, they do not belong in short-run marginal cost or, *as such*, in the ideal price. (Whether the ideal price will nevertheless cover these fixed costs is a question we shall consider presently.) Depreciation, for example, is in large measure a provision for obsolescence and not just for physical deterioration as a result of production; to this extent, it, along with the minimum necessary return on capital, is a function of time instead of the rate of utilization. To the extent that such costs are truly fixed, so far as the continued provision of service is concerned, they do not belong in the computation of marginal cost, for purposes of economically efficient pricing.[22] Moreover, even to the extent

---

production instead of not engaging in production at any particular time period. See John Maynard Keynes, *The General Theory of Employment Interest and Money* (New York: Harcourt Brace & Co., 1936), 52–55, 66–73. It may be measured as the discounted, present value of the additional prospective yield that could be obtained from the facilities if they were not used now. We encounter it most frequently as an important determinant of the proper rate of producing stock natural resources: part of the social cost of producing a ton of copper today is the (discounted) future value of that copper if it were instead sold next year; but the concept of user cost applies equally to any depreciation of capital equipment attributable to current use. Or it could be conceived as the (discounted) additional future costs of repair or earlier replacement attributable to current use.

[21] The source of confusion is the economist's use of the unfortunate terms "short-run" and "long-run." They seem to correspond to time in some chronological sense—short-run to costs that are incurred today and long-run to those incurred next year, or some such. But in fact they do not. Most firms are at any given time making both short-run and long-run decisions—determining the daily level of output, on the one hand, buying new equipment or hiring a new office secretary, on the other—and incurring the corresponding costs. The difference is that the former relates to output decisions with given capacity and to costs that vary with such decisions, while the latter relates to investment

decisions, broadly defined—to the acquisition of fixed factors of production—and give rise to costs that will not then vary as the capacity thus created is more or less fully utilized. Thus, the distinction is between costs that are fixed and those that are variable with output during some arbitrary period of time.

These variable costs, which is what we mean by short-run costs, may be not only incurred but realized instantly (for instance, the cost of the power required to turn a lathe, or the materials on which it operates) or only eventually (for example, the additional wear and tear, hence higher maintenance expense or earlier scrapping, of equipment). P. J. D. Wiles, on whose *Price, Cost and Output*, 2d. ed. (Oxford: Blackwell, 1961), 8–11, this discussion draws heavily, suggests we abandon the short- and long-run distinction, and substitute two others: partial vs. total adaptation (which corresponds to what economists mean by the rejected terms) and immediate vs. ultimate costs (depending on when the costs are actually realized). So there could be both immediate and ultimate marginal costs under "partial adaptation" (that is, in the short-run). User cost belongs in the category "ultimate marginal cost under partial adaptation."

[22] If the capacity can be used to provide other services, its use for any particular service does involve an opportunity cost—the value of the other services foregone. Therefore, that cost should be reflected in price. Also, if it has scrap or salvage value, the variable costs of continued

that depreciation does vary with use, what belongs in the marginal cost calculation is not the book cost, the writing off of investment costs historically incurred, but the amount by which this and other capital costs will be higher than they would otherwise be *in the future* by virtue of the incremental production in question. It is for the higher future costs or the decline in future values—not for fixed, historically sunk costs—that the marginal production is causally responsible; it is only the future, not the past, costs that will be saved if the production is not undertaken. Notice how, at once, the traditional practices of public utility price regulation diverge from economic principles.

It follows also that these additional repair and replacement costs belong in marginal cost and in price only if (there is a likelihood that) they will in fact be incurred; and this will depend, in turn, on whether there is likely to be sufficient demand to justify those additional expenditures. Suppose, as is probably true of much railway plant,[23] production of the additional service is the only possible use of the equipment in question, present or future, and that output cannot now or in the foreseeable future be sold for a price that covers the additional depreciation, or the cost of the eventual additional repairs, attributable to operating instead of not operating.[24] As long as users *will* pay a price covering the immediate, variable costs of operation— including the current value equivalent of whatever salvage value the equipment may have—it would be better from the standpoint both of society and the stockholders to charge them such a price (the stockholders will be indifferent unless the price includes something extra for them, however little) and continue to operate, than to refuse the business. Operations should continue until the time when either higher operating costs on the increasingly dilapidated equipment or the impossibility of further postponing the required repair, maintenance, or replacement expenditures finally drive immediate, short-run marginal costs above price and force a shutdown. In this case, the buyers will have been subsidized by the stockholders who made the mistake of financing the capacity in the first place. But from the point of view both of society and the stockholder, those costs are bygones and best forgotten as far as efficient pricing is concerned. For a continuing or expanding operation, in contrast, no business should be taken on that does not cover all the costs causally attributable to it, immediate and ultimate.

The second principle of efficient pricing might seem to raise yet another difficulty. If the ideal is to set price at marginal short-run variable cost, and if only a part of the firm's costs is variable in the short run, it would seem that these ideal prices would never cover fixed costs—notably the minimum gross return on invested capital (depreciation and return and income taxes) that must be earned if internally generated funds are to continue to be reinvested in the business and outside capital to be attracted. It is important to see clearly that this is not necessarily the case. As a glance at the familiar Figure 1 will quickly disclose, while short-run variable costs per unit of output

---

operation must include a return above direct costs equivalent to what the owners could earn on their investment if they scrapped the plant and invested the money elsewhere: this is also a marginal opportunity cost of continued production. This is a variant of the principle that we shall encounter below, that when the absolute limits of capacity are reached, price should be equated to marginal social opportunity cost. But this is still not the same as incorporating capital costs like depreciation, as such, in price.

[23] See James R. Nelson, *op. cit.*, *The Antitrust Bulletin* (January–April 1966), XI: 23.

[24] In this event, to use the concept of note 20, the marginal user cost—which should always be incorporated in price—is zero.

(AVC) can never be as large as total costs (ATC), short-run marginal costs $(SRMC)$ can be lower, equal to (at Pe), or higher than average total costs, depending on the relation of market demand to plant or industry capacity. As that diagram demonstrates there will usually be some point, with any given plant, beyond which the rate of output can be expanded only at rising unit variable costs. If the average total cost curve turns up at any point along the output scale, it will be because marginal costs beyond that point exceed total unit costs. Marginal-cost pricing at or beyond this point will therefore cover or more than cover average total costs as well. Therefore pricing at short-run marginal cost need not be unremunerative in the long run or inconsistent with long-run equilibrium: the price need never explicitly be formulated to cover long-run or fixed costs, yet at certain times, when demand is sufficient, it will do so or more than do so.[25]

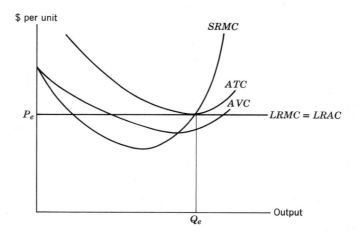

Figure 1. The unit costs of the firm under long-run constant returns.

Whether in fact prices set at SRMC will cover ATC with sufficient reliability and without involving intolerably great fluctuation over time, is a question we consider below (pp. 84–86, 103–109).

---

[25] In long-run competitive equilibrium, as Figure 1 shows, price will be at precisely the point (P_e) where short-run marginal costs $(SRMC)$ and average total costs (ATC) are equal. This demonstration is simplified by the assumption in Figure 1 that the industry operates under conditions of long-run constant costs— that is, if a firm were to plan to produce much more or much less than Q_e, it could best do so in plants with the same lowest cost (P_e) as the one shown. So the long-run marginal cost $(LRMC)$—that is, the total additional costs per unit of additional blocks of output, when capacity is altered so as to produce the larger output at minimum cost—is at P_e, and coincides with long-run average costs. A similar coincidence of $SRMC$, $LRMC$, and ATC would be achieved by perfect competition in industries subject to increasing costs as well. But if the industry were instead subject to long-run decreasing costs, as some public utilities are in important respects, pricing at the ideal point where both $SRMC$ and $LRMC$ were equal would be inconsistent with long-run equilibrium, because ATC would not be covered (as we shall see, pp. 130–133). On these matters, see F. H. Knight, "Some Fallacies in the Interpretation of Social Cost," *Q. Jour. Econ.* (1924), XXXVIII: 582–606; Jacob Viner, "Cost Curves and Supply Curves," *Zeitschrift Für Nationalökonomie* (1931), III: 23–46; Howard S. Ellis and William Fellner, "External Economies and Diseconomies," *The Amer. Econ. Rev.* (1943), XXXIII: 493–511, all three as reproduced in the American Economic Association, *Readings in Price Theory* (Selection Committee, George J. Stigler and Kenneth E. Boulding) (Chicago: Richard D. Irwin, 1952), 160–179, 198–232, and 242–263, respectively.

In sum: the economic ideal would be to set all public utility rates at short-run marginal costs (with appropriate adjustments for problems of second-best);[26] and these must cover all sacrifices, present or future[27] and external as well as internal to the company, for which production is at the margin causally responsible. The ideal is worth emphasizing, because in certain circumstances it can and should be embodied in rates. But, in the real world, it is not usually feasible or even desirable to do so, for a variety of reasons that will become clear as we consider two other related aspects of the problem of defining marginal costs.

Specifying the Incremental Block of Output

The level of incremental cost per unit depends, also, on the size of the increment. Consider the passenger airplane flight already scheduled, with the plane on the runway, fueled up and ready to depart, but with its seats not completely filled. The incremental unit of service in this case might be defined as the carrying of an extra passenger on that flight—in which case, the marginal cost would be practically zero. It was just such a marginal cost calculation, involving the smallest possible number of additional units and the shortest-possible run, that underlay the introduction of standby youth-fares by some American airlines in 1966—half-price for young people willing to come out to the airport and take their chances of finding an empty seat on their flight ten minutes before departure time.

Or is the incremental unit in question the particular scheduled flight, taken as a whole, involving the carrying of 50 or 100 passengers between a particular pair of cities at a particular time? If the plane must fly anyhow, as long as the flight is scheduled, the additional cost of taking on all the passengers is still practically zero. But schedules can be changed in the comparatively short run, in which event the relevant marginal costs of a particular flight include all the costs of flying the plane as compared with not flying it. Or is the incremental unit of sales the provision of regular service between a pair of cities, involving an entire schedule of flights? In this case, still more costs enter into the marginal calculation—airport rentals, ticket offices, the cost of advertising in local newspapers, indeed the cost of the planes themselves, which need not be acquired or can be used in other service. The larger the incremental unit of service under consideration, the more costs become variable.

As in the choice between short- and long-run marginal cost, so the choice of the proper unit of sale for purposes of pricing necessarily involves a balancing of the practicable and the economic ideal. This topic is the subject of the concluding section of this chapter. The nature of the possible conflict between these two considerations and the need for compromise should already be clear.

Ideally, if the flight is going anyhow, it is economically inefficient to turn away any passenger willing to pay the marginal opportunity cost of his trip —which is virtually zero as long as there are empty seats. In short, the ideal remains pricing at the shortest-run marginal cost for the smallest possible

---

[26] We shall ignore the second-best qualification during the subsequent discussions, returning to it at a later point—though only briefly, because it is impossible to set forth general rules, in *a priori* terms, about how and to what extent to take it into account.

[27] Strictly speaking, any postponed cost incurrences should be incorporated in price only at present, discounted value.

increment of output. That is why the youth fare plan was an inspiration, at least for the (young) flying public: it offered them the option of traveling at greatly reduced fares on seats that would otherwise go unused. But the airlines were able to move closer to short-run marginal cost pricing in this instance only because and to the extent that (1) they could offer a genuinely inferior service—the travelers had to take the risk that any particular flights for which they might stand by would have no space for them and (2) they could do so selectively—the youth fare was an ingenious form of price discrimination, the principles of which we discuss more fully in Chapter 5. In fact, the airlines found it difficult to preserve the necessary separation of the two markets.[28] Moreover, being discriminatory, the plan was still not economically "ideal": that would have required offering a zero price to all potential customers, as long as there were empty seats—something that would have been very difficult for an airline company to arrange, while still collecting fares high enough to cover the common costs of the entire flight.

In fact, as we shall see, the ideal would be for the airlines to determine the proper level of capacity—number and scheduling of flights—and then to auction off the seats on each flight nondiscriminately, at prices down to marginal cost, in such a way as to assure that as many seats as possible were sold. Such a procedure would indeed produce prices for each flight equal to the marginal opportunity cost of a single passage, that is, to short-run marginal cost, while also enabling the airlines to cover total costs, provided their decisions with respect to capacity were correct.[29]

Of course, the proper size of the incremental unit of output depends on the perspective of the decision under consideration. From the standpoint of the supplier, the decision to add an extra section to a flight already scheduled will involve a different marginal cost, which is to be compared with marginal revenues, than the decision to add another flight or route to its schedules. When the decision is one to extend or withdraw an entire service to some particular block of customers—as in the abandonments of railroad passenger service that have become increasingly frequent since 1958—the relevant unit

---

[28] This experience also illustrates both the necessity and the difficulty, familiar in the economics of price discrimination, of keeping the various markets or classes of customers separate. The differentiation was on the basis of (1) age and (2) willingness to take a service that was inferior because it carried no assurance of space on any particular flight. However, the airlines found that youths were telephoning and making reservations under fictitious names—thus foreclosing the sale of those spaces at full fare to regular customers—which they then neglected to claim at the regular price. In this way, they increased their assurance that there would be an empty seat available for them at half-fare, while causing the airlines to lose full-fare business. For example, Braniff Airways pointed out that during the period the youth fare was in effect, the ratio of its cancellations to boardings rose from 1.8 to 4.8%. *Brief* in Civil Aeronautics Board, *Standby Youth Fares Young Adult Fares*, Docket 18936, Exhibit BI-10, November 14, 1968. Several companies found that the marginal

costs of the program were well above zero: they encountered a greater demand on the time of agents in answering questions about the possibilities of finding standby space, greater congestion at ticket counters, and increased annoyance to regular passengers, who were often offended by the dress, hirsute and ablutional state, and the comportment of some of their new fellow travelers.

[29] See notes 49, 51, this chapter, and pp. 87–93, 103–104. The market for seats on each flight could be further differentiated, without discrimination, by letting passengers bid and pay varying prices, depending on the amount of advance assurance they required with respect to their having a reserved seat. See the ingenious proposal along these lines by William Vickrey for transoceanic flights, with tickets going at varying prices as the time of departure approaches, "Some Objections to Marginal-Cost Pricing," *Jour. Pol. Econ.* (June 1948), LVI: 232–234.

of output is clearly the entire service in question. And the relevant economic question is: What additional costs would be imposed if that service were to be extended, what total costs saved or avoided by its withdrawal?[30]

Identifying Marginal Cost When a Large Proportion of Costs are Common

The problem of specifying the size of the incremental block of output, the unit cost of which is to determine the ideal price, is itself a reflection of a more general phenomenon, that of common costs. The costs of carrying 50 passengers on a scheduled plane flight constitute a single lump of common costs: they are incurred not on a passenger-by-passenger basis but all together or not at all. Another way of saying this is that the unit of production (the single flight), which is the basis of cost incurrence, is larger than the unit of sale (a single ticket to a single passenger).[31] In consequence, the marginal cost of each sale, considered alone, is practically zero; whereas the cost of the unit of production comes to very much more than zero per passenger.

No public utility company (and precious few others) sells a single product or service to all customers. A single railroad company carries passengers for trips of varied lengths, and an enormous variety of freight for equally varied distances. Virtually no part of its plant provides only a single one of these services, at a single price. The gas company sells fuel during the day and at night, in winter and in summer; to some customers it guarantees a firm supply at all times; to others it sells on an interruptible basis, which means that it can decline to meet the buyer's needs when its capacity is being fully employed in meeting the demands of its firm customers; the same mains carry gas to numerous customers for heating, cooking, clothes-drying, and suicide. River valley development projects supply electric power, water for irrigation, flood control, and navigation services, largely with the same facilities. By far the largest part of the interstate plant of the Bell System is used to furnish message toll telephone, day and night, telephotograph, teletypewriter services, television program transmission, and various business data transmission services.[32]

To the extent that multiple products or services are supplied by the same plant or productive operation, their costs are either common or joint (we will distinguish the two presently). Individual services or sales do of course typically have their own clearly identifiable specific costs: the turbines employed in a multiple-purpose river development project serve only to generate electricity; and every purchaser of a thousand cubic feet of natural gas at the terminus of a pipeline specifically imposes on that line the necessity for buying one thousand cubic feet of gas in the field. But most costs are common: the same interstate pipeline carries gas for sale to customers A, B . . . Z under different conditions and at various times during the year. Since costs must be recovered over periods of time instead of instantaneously —even wages are paid on a weekly basis—the costs of serving customer A

---

[30] See pp. 154–155.

[31] See George W. Wilson, *Essays on Some Unsettled Questions in the Economics of Transportation*, Foundation for Economic and Business Studies (Indiana Univ., 1962), 14–20, 69–78. This would be even more clear if one regarded the unit of production as the provision of regular service between two cities.

[32] For an interesting illustration of the pervasiveness of common costs in satellite communications, see Leland L. Johnson, "Joint Cost and Price Discrimination: The Case of Communications Satellites," in Shepherd and Gies, *op. cit.*, 118–121.

today and customer A tomorrow are likewise in a sense common, even if the service is physically the same. The same theatrical performance may be witnessed from row B or row Z, on Wednesday afternoon or Saturday night; the services are different, most of the costs are joint. Indeed, what constitutes a separate product or service depends in a sense on what it pays the businessman to price or to cost separately.[33]

The fact that most services are typically provided in combinations, using the same facilities, does not mean that definable shares of the common costs can not in principle be causally attributed to each. When the same equipment may be used to make products A and B, and when producing A uses capacity that could otherwise be used to supply B, then we may speak of their costs as common instead of joint: and in this event, the marginal cost of A *may* include an identifiable part of these common costs. This situation is widespread in the public utilities, and in industry generally. The same railway plant can be used for passenger or freight service, and for any number of kinds of freight, over any number of routes.[34] The same coaxial cable may transmit telephone messages, business data, or TV programs. The same warehouse may be used to store a variety of products. If any one of these products or services uses freight cars, circuits, or warehouse space that would in fact otherwise be used for one of the others, or if it requires the construction of greater capacity than would otherwise be necessary, then it *does* bear a causal responsibility for a share of the common capacity costs.[35] The cost allocation formulae actually employed may achieve only a rough, rule-of-thumb approximation to the actual costs for which each product or service is responsible, but those costs have objective reality.[36]

---

[33] The producer of a play may sell each seat for a separate price, or may differentiate them by blocks. He may vary his prices from day to day, depending on what the traffic will bear. The airline may have a single per passenger charge between any two points, or may sell separately the carriage of infants, wives, adults, with or without free champagne, with wider or narrower spacing between seats, and with varying charges from one day to the next.

[34] See the reference, note 11, Chapter 4, to the famous Taussig-Pigou controversy, which hinged on the question of whether rail costs were mainly joint or common, and whether therefore individual rail services might be said to have separate costs.

[35] Whether A's marginal cost includes a portion of the capacity costs (for example, depreciation and return on investment) *as such*, depends, strictly speaking, on whether one is thinking of short-run or long-run marginal costs. As we have already seen (see pp. 71–74, above), short-run marginal cost does not include them. But if as a matter of economic (that is, not merely technological) fact, the capacity could indeed be used to make either A or B, then even short-run marginal cost of A includes as an opportunity cost the value of B that has been sacrificed. See note 22, and pp. 83, 85.

Here again we see the relevance of the other

dimensions of costing already mentioned. If the plant or warehouse has excess capacity sufficient to produce or store A without cutting down service B—and this will depend, too, on how much equipment or room A takes, and that will depend in turn on how the incremental service "A" is defined—the relevant marginal costs of A could be zero or considerably more, depending on whether it is long- or short-run costs that are being measured, and whether the excess capacity is short-lived or permanent.

[36] Companies often allocate various common overhead costs in proportion to the variable costs that can be directly attributed to the individual products. The assumption presumably is that the greater the quantity and the higher the cost of labor and materials used in fabricating a product, the greater also will be the quantity and value of equipment employed in its production, the draft on the time and attention of inspectors, superintendents, purchasing agents, salesmen, and so forth. Less tenuous would be the practice of distributing the expenses of a personnel department among operating divisions on the basis of the relative number of employees; or the practice of sawmills allocating the joint costs of production among the numerous grades of lumber on the basis of the relative number of board feet of the various types and grades—on the assumption that a board-foot of low-grade

If services produced in common are to have separate marginal production costs it must be possible to vary their proportions. At least in the long run, this is true of almost all such products. As Marshall pointed out, sheep can be bred to give more or less mutton per pound of wool;[37] crude oil, which used to be subjected only to a physical separation of its components in whatever proportions they were found in the original state, is now cracked in order to increase the yields of the higher-value and decrease those of the lower-value fractions. A system of dams can be constructed or, once constructed, operated to yield varying proportions of electric power, flood control, water for irrigation, navigation benefits, and so on. But for this possibility to yield economically relevant, separate costs, the physical variability must fall within the range of economic feasibility—and this depends on the respective demands for the individual services. If, for example, it is physically possible to increase the production of A, while holding the quantities of B constant, but the cost of doing so is more than buyers are willing to pay, or need pay as long as the output produced in invariant proportions meets their requirements, then the services are still being produced in fixed proportions, and have no separate economic costs.[38] If then the proportions are effectively (that is, economically) variable, one can unequivocally identify as the marginal cost of any one product the addition to the total cost of the joint production process occasioned by increasing the output of that one product, while leaving the output of the others unchanged.[39]

When instead the products are truly joint, in that they can be economically produced only in fixed proportions, neither of them has a genuine, separate incremental cost function, as far as the joint part of their production process is concerned. (They will each typically have separate additional costs of processing, shipping, and marketing, but these need not concern us here.) If producing a bale of cotton fiber invariably involves producing also the seeds from which can be extracted ten gallons of cottonseed oil, there is no objective way—if one looks at the cost of production alone—of attributing causal responsibility for some part of the joint production costs to one of the products and the remainder to the other. The economic product is the composite unit; the only economically definable cost of production, marginal or average, and "price" or "marginal revenue" are those of the composite unit.

However, each of a number of joint products does have a competitive supply function. The intersection of these with the respective demand functions yields an economically optimal set of separate prices for the joint products—a set that would be achieved by perfect competition—that will not only equate the total of their prices with their composite marginal *production* cost but will also equate the price of *each* with its own separate

lumber has fabricating, handling and storage costs comparable to a board-foot of high quality lumber. On the use of this technique, see Theodore Lang, ed., *Cost Accountants' Handbook* (New York: Ronald, 1947), 526.

[37] *Principles of Economics*, 9th ed., I: 389–390; see also his discussion of this entire subject in *Industry and Trade* (London: Macmillan, 1932), 190–194.

[38] See National Bureau of Economic Research, Committee on Price Determination, *Cost Behavior and Price Policy* (New York: N.B.E.R., 1943),

177–179. Also J. M. Clark, *Studies in the Economics of Overhead Costs*, 99.

[39] Such a calculation can then be made not only for the short run—what would it add to total costs to increase the output of product A, holding the output of the other products constant, with existing capacity?—but also for the long run—what will it add to total costs to build additional capacity to produce A, while holding constant the capacity available to produce B?

marginal *opportunity* cost. These separate marginal opportunity costs can not be determined from production costs alone; what makes them determinate is the joint supply function, on the one hand, and the separate demand functions on the other. Since joint supply is pervasive in the public utility industries, it is important to explain these propositions in some detail.

In Figures 2 and 3, we posit the joint production of cotton fiber and cotton seeds in any fixed proportion—the ratio of one bale to enough seeds to make ten gallons of cottonseed oil is purely illustrative. The relevant marginal production costs are the same in the two figures. They are assumed for simplicity to be constant (that is, horizontal) within the relevant range, and may be taken to stand for either short- or long-run marginal costs. MC_{c+cso} is the joint cost of producing the combination; MC_{cso} is the cost for the separate production process of extracting cottonseed oil from the seeds. (In reality the fiber will also have its own processing costs, but here we assume it has none; introducing them would add nothing to the demonstration.)

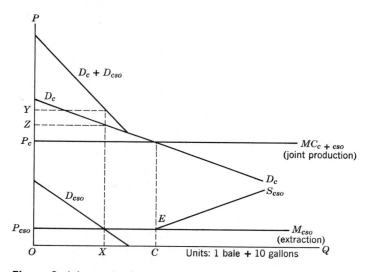

Figure 2. Joint production, cotton and cottonseed oil; cotton seeds a free good.

The only difference between the two figures is the relationship between the separate demands for fiber and oil (D_c and D_{cso}). For simplicity, D_c is held the same; only D_{cso} is altered. The demands can be summed vertically to show the combined "prices" or average revenues at which various quantities of the composite unit of fiber and oil can be sold ($D_c + D_{cso}$). For example, OX composite units in Figure 2 (for example, 2 million bales of fiber plus 20 million gallons of oil) would bring in an average revenue of OY, composed of a price of OP_{cso} for each 10 gallons of oil and OZ for each bale of fiber.

There is no way of defining individual production costs for the separate products, except for MC_{cso}, which is distinct from the joint production process. But note that it *is* possible to define a competitive supply function for each, given the cost data and demand *for the other*. For simplicity we do it in Figure 2 only for the oil; since the demand for cotton *fiber* is the same in both figures, the supply curve for *oil* is likewise the same in both. Producers of the oil must always obtain a price at least as high as MC_{cso}. How much more will they require? Up to the quantity OC, nothing more; the demand for cotton is so strong that quantities of fiber offered up to OC will bring a price (P_c or better) that covers all the joint costs. However, beyond OC additional offerings of fiber will force prices below MC_{c+cso}; for additional supplies of oil to be forthcoming, its price will have to make a contribution to the joint costs sufficient to fill the gap. Therefore, the separate processing costs, the joint costs, and the demand for cotton fiber together define a competitive supply curve for oil (S_{cso}) that runs along the MC_{cso} curve to E, then rises, as indicated in both figures. The supply function for cotton fiber (S_c) in Figure 3 is constructed in the same way, by determining from the demand for oil how much of a contribution purchasers of that product would make (over and above MC_{cso}) to the joint costs (MC_{c+cso}) when different quantities are offered for sale: when OC is offered, for example, the price of (10 gallons of) oil will contribute only EF to the joint costs; therefore, if OC bales of fiber are to be forthcoming, buyers will have to pay CG (CG plus EF equals CH).[40]

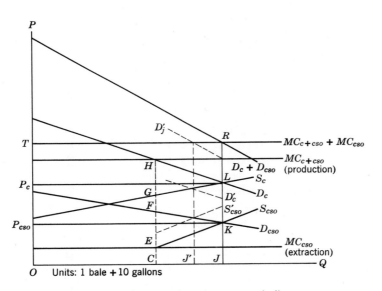

Figure 3. Joint production, cotton and cottonseed oil.

We are now in a position to determine how much of each product would be produced and at what price they would sell under perfect competition. The equilibrium outcome requires that the combined prices cover joint marginal cost, that the price of each cover any separate marginal costs, and that prices clear the market—that is, that all who are willing to buy and sell at the price are in fact able to do so. In Figure 2, the demand for cotton alone is so strong relative to the demand for oil that it alone determines how much fiber and seeds are produced: adding the demand for oil to the demand for cotton does not change the equilibrium output, OC bales. Each bale will sell

---

[40] The derivation may be easier to see if the reader will look to the top cost curve in Figure 3, $MC_{c+cso} + MC_{cso}$, which tells for how much the composite units must sell if they are to cover all relevant costs—the costs both of joint production and of extracting the oil. OJ units of oil will bring a price that contributes JK to this total; cotton will have to pay JL: the supply curve for cotton, S_c, is derived as the difference between the composite cost and the contribution made by purchasers of oil, D_{cso}, so that $RL = JK$, and JL plus $JK = JR$.

at OP_c; fiber will bear all the joint costs. Only OX gallons of oil will in fact be extracted—that is where D_{cso} intersects the supply curve—and they will sell at OP_{cso}. Any additional quantities of oil offered would only depress the price below the marginal costs of extracting the oil. If their only use is as a source of oil, oil *seeds* are a free good in this case; they will sell for a zero price and some of them will still go unsold and unused.[41]

In Figure 3, the solution is easier to see when we introduce the cost function $MC_{c+cso} + MC_{cso}$, because in this case the relation of the demands is such that all components of the composite unit produced will be sold, and each such unit will have to return a price sufficient to cover both the marginal joint production cost and MC_{cso}. Here the perfectly competitive output will be OJ for both end products, produced in the fixed ratio of one bale to ten gallons. The fiber will sell at OP_c, the oil at OP_{cso}; together these prices will cover total costs, and at those prices the quantities of each product demanded and supplied will be equated.

This result could be read off Figure 3 merely by noting that the intersection of the combined demands $(D_c + D_{cso})$ and the combined marginal cost $(MC_{c+cso} + MC_{cso})$ establishes the equilibrium output OJ, and the separate demands then indicate the separate prices at which OJ cotton and OJ cottonseed oil will sell. Or the separate results could be read directly as determined by the intersection of the individual demand *with their respective individual supply functions*. As far as the joint production process is concerned, joint products do not have separate production cost functions. Each does have a definite competitive supply function, indicating how much of the joint costs its purchasers must pay for various quantities.

Are these respective supply curves true cost functions? Little purpose would be served by semantic argument. But the Figure 2 situation definitely embodies objectively separate marginal costs of production, in the only economically important sense—which is that they reflect incremental, causal cost responsibility. For all outputs beyond OX—that is to say, *within the range in which the sales ratios will in fact vary*—all the joint costs are unequivocally attributable to cotton fiber. Any joint costs that society incurs for production beyond OX are incurred solely in order to serve the fiber customers; added costs of MC_{c+cso} will be incurred if they ask for more, and saved if they ask for less. Increases in the demand for cottonseed oil will, up to OC, impose no additional joint production costs on society; decreases in the demand for oil will reduce joint production outlays not one whit. Therefore, economic efficiency requires that the price of cotton reflect 100% of the joint costs, in the Figure 2 situation.

In the Figure 3 situation, it is not true in the same sense that each product has a separate production cost function. Within its entire range, sales will be in fixed proportions. An increase or decrease in the demand for one of the

---

[41] In the case of joint products it might appear that if either product is produced at all, the cost of the other is in a sense zero—and conversely. But actually this will be true only if the "one" (this would be the cotton, in Figure 2) is produced in sufficient quantities to supply all of the "other" that will be demanded at a zero price. In that event, the marginal cost of the latter (cotton seeds, in Figure 2) is zero. Consumption of an additional cotton seed would impose no additional production cost on society and would deprive no one of desired cotton seeds. But whether that condition prevails will depend, then, on the respective levels of demand for the two products; it does *not* prevail in the circumstances depicted in Figure 3; and it cannot be true of both products simultaneously.

joint products will *not*, unless that range is exceeded,[42] increase or decrease society's production costs by the amount of the competitive price it had been paying (or by the area under its competitive supply curve). It will change the distribution of the joint burden borne by itself and the other product, and how much of society's resources will be drawn into additional output or saved will depend on the elasticity of the two demands.[43]

Whether the separate supply functions do represent corresponding marginal *production* costs, the equilibrium prices of the several joint products, derived as indicated in Figure 3, do equal their respective marginal opportunity costs. What is the measure of the marginal opportunity cost of supplying some customer the OJth unit of cotton and cottonseed oil? It is what the next customer, the first one *not* served, would have been willing to pay for that last bale or gallon, auctioned off at their respective market-clearing prices: and in Figure 3, that would be (infinitesimally less than) OP_c and OP_{cso}. Therefore, the economically efficient solution does involve equating the price of each joint product to its marginal opportunity cost.[44]

TEMPERING PRINCIPLE WITH PRACTICALITY— OR ONE PRINCIPLE WITH ANOTHER

The outcome of this entire discussion about the problems of defining (as contrasted with actually measuring and applying) marginal cost is that neither the choice between short and long-run, nor the problem of defining the incremental unit of sale, nor the prevalence of common and joint costs raises any difficulties in principle about the economically efficient price. It is set at the short-run marginal cost of the smallest possible additional unit of sale. Common costs do not preclude separable marginal production costs, and joint products have separate marginal opportunity costs.

But, as we have already suggested, short-run marginal costs (SRMC) are the place to begin. There are situations in which it is both efficient and practical to base rates on them, as we shall see. Typically, this is not the case; principle must be compromised in various ways in the interest of practicality, for a number of interrelated reasons:

1. It is often infeasible, or prohibitively expensive, for businesses to make the

---

[42] If either demand shifted far enough relative to the other to restore a Figure 2 situation, we would once again have separate production costs. This would be so in Figure 3 if, for example, D_{cso} shifted sufficiently to the left to intersect S_{cso} short of point E.

[43] A change of this type is depicted in Figure 3, in dashed lines. D_c declines to D'_c. This means that the combined demand (D_{c+cso}) falls by the same amount, to D'_j. (It is unnecessary, but perhaps helpful, to draw in the new supply curve for oil, S'_{cso}, reflecting the diminished contributions fiber purchasers are now prepared to make toward joint costs at various levels of output.) Joint output falls to OJ'. Society's resource savings are not measured by the area between J and J' under the cotton fiber supply curve, S_c, as they would be if this were a true marginal production cost curve; instead they are measured by the entire area between J and J' under the

combined cost curve $(MC_{c+cso} + MC_{cso})$.

[44] See Jack Hirshleifer, "Peak Loads and Efficient Pricing: Comment," *Q. Jour. Econ.* (August 1958), LXXII: 458–459. On the application of this reasoning to public utility pricing, see pp. 87–88 and pp. 91–93, Chapter 4.

On the general theory of joint products, their costing and pricing under competitive and monopolistic conditions, see the very lucid discussion in Mary Jean Bowman and George Leland Bach, *Economic Analysis and Public Policy: An Introduction* (New York: Prentice-Hall, 1943), Chapter 18. Also see Kenneth E. Boulding, *Economic Analysis, Microeconomics* (New York: Harper & Row, 1966), I: 579–584; Joel Dean, *Managerial Economics* (New York: Prentice-Hall, 1951), 317–319; T. J. Kreps, "Joint Costs in the Chemical Industry," *Q. Jour. Econ.* (May 1930), XLIV: 416–461.

necessary fine calculations of marginal cost for each of their numerous categories of service.

2. Marginal costs will vary from one moment to the next, in a world of perpetually changing demand, as firms operate at perpetually changing points on their SRMC functions (unless marginal costs happen to be constant, that is, horizontal), and between far wider extremes than either average variable or average total costs (see Figure 1). It will vary also because cost functions themselves are constantly shifting. Thus, it would be prohibitively costly to the seller to put into effect the highly refined and constantly changing pricing schedules, reflecting in minute detail the different short-run marginal costs of different sales. It would also be highly vexatious to buyers, who would be quick to find discrimination in departures from uniform prices, who would be put to great expense to be informed about prices that were constantly changing, and whose ability to make rational choices and plan intelligently for the future would be seriously impaired.

3. For these reasons the practically-achievable version of SRMC pricing is often likely to be pricing at *average* variable costs (AVC), themselves averaged over some period of time in the past and assumed to remain constant over some period in the future—until there occurs some clear, discrete shift caused by an event such as a change in wage rates. But since short-term AVC (in contrast with SRMC) are never as large as average total costs (see Figure 1), universal adoption of this type of pricing is infeasible if sellers are to cover total costs, including (as always) a minimum required return on investment. This in turn produces a strong tendency in industry to price on a "full cost" basis—usually computed at AVC (really *average* AVC over some period of time) plus some percentage mark-up judged sufficient to cover total costs on the average over some time period[45]—a far cry, indeed, from marginal cost pricing.[46]

4. SRMC can be above or below ATC, as we have seen; but whether it is above often enough for businesses pricing on that basis to cover total costs on the average depends on the average relationship over time between demand and production capacity. As J. M. Clark has often pointed out, excess capacity is the typical condition of modern industry;[47] and we would probably want this to be the case in public utilities, which we tend to insist be perpetually in a position to supply whatever demands are placed on them. In these circumstances, firms could far more often be operating at the point where SRMC is less than ATC than the reverse,[48] and if they based their prices exclusively on the former they would have to find some other means of making up the difference. Partly for this reason, and partly because of the infeasibility of

---

[45] See the survey article by Richard B. Heflebower, "Full Costs, Cost Changes, and Prices," in National Bureau of Economic Research, *Business Concentration and Price Policy* (Princeton: Princeton Univ. Press, 1955), 361–392.

[46] Recall that to the extent that depreciation, taxes, and return on capital are a function not of use but of time—as is preponderantly the case—they do not belong in SRMC, hence in price, at all.

[47] *Overhead Costs*, 437–439, 448–449; *Competition as a Dynamic Process* (Washington: Brookings Institution, 1961), 59, 81, 120–121, 133, 140.

[48] This does not follow inevitably from the perpetual presence of surplus capacity. Most of the standby capacity probably has high variable costs—that, indeed, is why it is selected for the standby function. In consequence, even if an industry operates on the average at, for example, 80% of physical capacity, it might find its

permitting prices to fluctuate widely along the SRMC function, depending on the immediate relation of demand to capacity,[49] the practically achievable benchmark for efficient pricing is more likely to be a type of average long-run incremental cost, computed for a large, expected incremental block of sales, instead of SRMC, estimated for a single additional sale. This long-run incremental cost (which we shall loosely refer to as long-run marginal cost as well) would be based on (1) the average incremental variable costs of those added sales and (2) estimated additional capital costs per unit, for the additional capacity that will have to be constructed if sales at that price are expected to continue over time or to grow.[50] Both of these components would be estimated as averages over some period of years extending into the future.

5. The prevalence of common costs has similar implications. Service A bears a causal responsibility for a share of common costs only if there is an economically realistic alternative use of the capacity now used to provide it, or if production of A requires the building of additional capacity. The marginal opportunity cost of serving A depends on how much the alternative users would be willing to pay for devoting the capacity to serving them instead. The sum of the separable marginal costs will therefore cover the common costs only if at separate prices less than this the claims on the capacity exceed the available supply.[51]

6. Long-run marginal costs are likely to be the preferred criterion also in competitive situations. Permitting rate reductions to a lower level of SRMC, which would prove to be unremunerative if the business thus attracted were to continue over time, might constitute predatory competition—driving out of business rivals whose *long-run* costs of production might well be lower than those of the price-cutter.

SRMC on the average equal to its composite ATC—running far above ATC when operations exceeded the 80% level and correspondingly below at other times. See pp. 94–97, Chapter 4, below.

[49] If SRMC pricing did not cover ATC over time, capital would eventually be withdrawn and new capital, needed to meet the rising demand, repelled, until a recovering demand, moving up along a steeply rising MC curve, pushed prices up high enough and held them there long enough to attract new capital into the industry—with the possibility of a return of depressed prices with any temporary reemergence of excess capacity. In the case of the partly-empty airplane (see pp. 75–76), the "efficient price" would be zero as long as the response of travelers remained insufficient to fill the plane; then it would have to jump the moment the empty spaces fell one short of demand, possibly to the full cost of an added flight but in any case to whatever level necessary to equate the number of available seats with the number of would-be passengers. On each flight, the available seats would have to be auctioned, with the uniform price settling at the point required to clear the market.

[50] See W. Arthur Lewis, *Overhead Costs* (New

York: Rinehart, 1949), 15–20; Marcel Boiteux, "Peak-Load Pricing" in James R. Nelson, *Marginal Cost Pricing in Practice* (Englewood Cliffs: Prentice-Hall, 1964), 70–72.

[51] As we have just seen in another connection (pp. 82–83), the marginal opportunity cost of providing a cubic foot of warehouse space to any particular user, A, is the most valuable alternative use of that space excluded by serving A— what the most insistent excluded customer would have been willing to pay for it. If at any price per foot less than the proportionate share of the common costs (that is, less than ATC) of the warehouse, there are or would be unsatisfied customers—that is, more cubic feet demanded than were available—then clearly the marginal opportunity cost of each cubic foot would be at least equal to average total costs, and prices correctly set at SRMC would cover total costs. If, instead, at a price equal to ATC there is excess capacity, this demonstrates that price exceeds marginal opportunity costs: serving A is not preventing anyone else willing to pay that much from getting all the space he wants. In this circumstance, prices set lower, at true SRMC, would not provide enough revenue to cover total costs.

It is important to recognize that all these reasons for compromising principle with practicality make sense even in purely economic terms—hence the equivocal subtitle of this section. Consider the fact, for example, that it is costly—that is, it uses resources—to measure and base prices on SRMC. (This will be easier to see at a later point: see pp. 182–187.) If these costs exceed the efficiency advantages of moving to such a pricing system, clearly considerations of economic efficiency alone would dictate refraining from doing so. Therefore, it is not a matter merely of compromising an economic principle; it is a question of correctly applying the relevant principle or of balancing one principle with another.

The limitations of trying to base prices solely on SRMC may be stated more generally. The theory of efficient pricing that we sketched earlier in this chapter is a static theory. It describes the conditions for optimum choosing, given some preexisting technology and pattern of consumer desires. It describes the optimum, equilibrium outcome that will prevail after all adjustments have been made to those two fundamental determinants of supply and demand functions. It makes no calculation of the costs or likelihood of achieving that result in a dynamic economy, in which demand and costs are constantly changing. Or, alternatively, it may be said to describe how that result will be achieved effortlessly, costlessly, and instantaneously under perfect competition—where buyers and sellers of every good and service are infinitely numerous, have perfect knowledge and foresight and act rationally on it, and where resources are perfectly mobile and fully employed. But obviously these conditions do not and cannot prevail in the real world. Only, then, if we can compare the efficiency gains of each proposed movement toward SRMC pricing, on the one hand, with its possible costs and drawbacks in a world of imperfect competition, knowledge, rationality, and resource mobility can we decide whether that move is indeed optimal even in purely economic terms. We have just suggested several reasons why it might not always be optimal.

This list of considerations is by no means exhaustive. Since the best probable compromise of offsetting considerations will clearly vary from one pricing context to another, it is impossible to set forth an integrated, general set of conclusions. Instead what we have is really a set of hypotheses, of relevant considerations. We proceed now to apply them to the most important public utility pricing problems: to the proper distribution of capacity costs; to the optimum pattern of rates over time (these two in Chapter 4); to decreasing cost situations, where MC is less than ATC, and the proper design of a rate structure in these circumstances (Chapter 5); and to situations in which competition is involved—competition involving public utility companies themselves and competition among their customers (Chapter 6).

The Application of Long- and Short-Run Marginal Costs

Having established in Chapter 3 that economically efficient prices of public utility services would be based on some *a priori* unspecifiable mixture of short and long-run marginal costs, in this chapter we consider two major contexts in which the best mixture needs to be discovered and applied: in determining which customers should pay the capital costs, and in deciding how and to what extent rates ought to be changed over time, as marginal costs change.

THE DISTRIBUTION OF CAPACITY COSTS

In industries as capital-intensive as public utilities, the costs of providing the capacity to serve—depreciation, property, income taxes, and return on investment—are very large. Yet, we have asserted, capacity costs are not part of SRMC and therefore, in principle, should not be reflected in price (except to the limited extent that they are in fact variable).

However, what if a price that covers only the variable operating costs elicits a demand for the service so great that it cannot be supplied with existing capacity? Economists have long been bemused by Dupuit's and Hotelling's historic example of the bridge and the strong case they made against charging tolls, on the ground that operating, maintenance, and capital costs do not vary significantly with the rate of utilization.[1] But what if charging a zero toll would, at least at certain hours of the day, produce such an increase in traffic that cars lined up for miles at the bridge entrance and a crossing took an hour instead of a few minutes? In that event, the SRMC of bridge crossings, at those times, is not zero. It can be envisaged in terms of congestion: the cost of every bridge crossing at the peak hour is the cost of the delays it imposes on all other crossers. Or it can be defined in terms of opportunity cost: if A uses the bridge at that time, he is taking up

---

[1] Jules Dupuit, "On The Measurement of the Utility of Public Works," *Annales des Ponts et Chaussées*, 2nd series, VIII (1844), and reprinted in *International Economic Papers*, No. 2 (New York: Macmillan, 1952), 83–110; Harold Hotelling, "The General Welfare in Relation to Problems of Taxation and of Railway and Utility Rates," *Econometrica* (July 1938), VI: 242–269.

space that someone else could use; therefore, the cost of serving him is the value of that space or capacity to others who would use it if he did not.[2]

The Shift to Long-Run Marginal Costs

Suppose now that for any one or more of the following reasons, we decide that it is either infeasible or undesirable to base tolls on SRMC

1. It would mean an unacceptable fluctuation in rates over time, depending on the changing relation of demand to capacity;
2. It would be too difficult, annoying, or expensive to compute the changing marginal congestion or opportunity costs just described and to base price on them;
3. Pricing on this basis might not cover ATC over the life of the bridge, and therefore might require public subsidy.[3]

Suppose, therefore, we decided to base tolls on long-run marginal costs. Then we would have to recognize that satisfying additional demand at times of congestion may sooner or later call for construction of additional capacity. In these circumstances, LRMC includes capital or capacity costs: and efficiency (of a kind of "second-best," however[4]) requires that each potential bridge-crosser be confronted with the price that reflects those marginal opportunity costs of serving him.

But notice that a shift from SRMC to LRMC does *not* mean that prices should be set on the basis of current variable costs plus a gross return (including depreciation) on past investment, however valued. Marginal costs look to the future, not to the past: it is only future costs for which additional production can be causally responsible; it is only future costs that can be saved if that production is not undertaken. If capital costs are to be included in price, the capital costs in question are those that will have to be covered over time in the future if service is to continue to be rendered. These would be the depreciation and return (including taxes) of the future investments that will have to be made. These incremental capital costs per unit of output will be the same as average capital costs of *existing* plant only in a completely static world and under conditions of long-run constant cost. As for the former and by far the more important qualification, in a dynamic economy, with changing technology as well as changing factor prices, there is every reason to believe that future capital costs per unit of output will not be the same as the capital costs historically incurred in installing present capacity.

Here, then, we encounter a major discrepancy between the economist's

---

[2] See our discussion for the separability of joint costs on this basis, pp. 79–83, above. For an interesting example in the case of communications satellites, see Johnson, in Shepherd and Gies, *Utility Regulation*, 119, note 5 and 120. And for a strong demonstration of the inefficiencies caused by our failure to impose charges for the use of the radio spectrum reflecting these opportunity costs—measured by the value of any particular allotted channel to the next-excluded potential user—see Harvey J. Levin, "The Radio Spectrum Resource," *Jour. Law & Econ.* (October 1968), XI: 433–501.

[3] On the first two problems see pp. 83–86 and

103–109; the third is the subject of Chapter 5.

[4] "First-best" rates would equal LRMC only by chance at some instant of time: at certain times (when capacity is ample—for example, right after the new or additional bridge has been built) they would be far below, then (as demand grew) they would rise gradually to and above it, as congestion increased, to whatever point necessary to cover congestion costs and ration the limited capacity, until construction of yet more facilities was justified. LRMC would instead represent an average over time of estimated total additional costs. (See pp. 107–108.)

prescription for optimal pricing and the traditional and still generally followed approach of public utility regulation. The latter, preoccupied with assuring a reasonable gross return on the existing investment, cannot possibly, except by accident, be basing its permitted rates on marginal costs, long-run or short-run.[5] The one conceptual merit—in contrast with its crippling administrative infeasibility—of the use of the reproduction cost instead of the original cost rate base was that it sought to bring the computation of capital costs closer to current, and away from historic costs. But, as we shall see later in this chapter, its manner of doing so was defective.

Does the shift to LRMC mean that all users of the bridge should pay a price that includes capacity costs? No. The off-peak users impose no such costs on society, *provided* their demand is sufficiently slight and inelastic that even at a zero toll no congestion occurs at the time they cross over. The incremental costs of serving them—in the long-run, not just the short—are still zero, and may remain so indefinitely. This is the case even if the off-peak demand grows over time and continues to be satisfied without congestion only because the bridge's capacity is being expanded. The necessity for expansion is imposed by the customers at the peak hours. It remains true that if one or all of the off-peak users ceased to cross the bridge, briefly or permanently, society would be saved no costs whatever.

Notice how the intensity and elasticity of demand help determine the level of marginal costs. For those hours of the day at which demand is insufficiently strong or responsive to a toll covering only operating expenses, long-run marginal costs include only those operating expenses; for those times of day at which demand is strong or so responsive to a lower toll as to cause congestion, LRMC necessarily includes capital costs as well.[6]

Peak Responsibility

The economic principle here is absolutely clear: if the same type of capacity serves all users, capacity costs *as such* should be levied only on utilization at the peak. Every purchase at that time makes its proportionate contribution in the long-run to the incurrence of those capacity costs and should therefore have that responsibility reflected in its price. No part of those costs as such should be levied on off-peak users.

The principle is clear, but it is more complicated than might appear at first reading. Notice, first, the qualification: "if the same type of capacity serves all users." In fact it does not always; in consequence, as we shall see, off-peak users may properly be charged explicitly for some capacity costs. Second, the principle applies to the explicit charging of capacity costs, "as such." Off-peak users, properly paying *short-run* marginal costs, will be making a contribution to the covering of capital costs also, if and when SRMC exceeds average variable costs. Third, the principle is framed on the assumption that all rates will be set at marginal cost (including marginal capacity costs). Under conditions of decreasing costs, uniform marginal-cost

---

[5] See, for example, Troxel, *Economics of Public Utilities*, 305–306, and in Shepherd and Gies, *op. cit.*, 150:

"Like other state commissions, the Michigan Commission relies mainly on legal and accounting ways of thought. In a general-rate case, for instance, attention is focused primarily on past revenues, past costs, and the value of an existing plant."

[6] This should not be surprising. Except when marginal costs are constant, it has to be the intersection of the demand and the cost functions that determines the equilibrium level of MC.

pricing will not cover total costs. Lacking a government subsidy to make up the difference, privately owned utilities have to charge more than MC on some of their business. In these "second-best" circumstances, some (of the difference between average and marginal) capacity costs might better be recovered from off-peak than from peak users. We will illustrate all these facets of the principle presently though reserving systematic consideration of the decreasing costs situation for Chapter 5.

First, to establish the basic principle, it is wisest to simplify. Consider only a uniform type of capacity, serving both peak and off-peak users; assume that marginal costs, both short- and long-run, are constant, so that SRMC cannot ever exceed AVC and there can be no difference between marginal and average capacity cost; and assume, finally, that the peak is fixed—that is, that demand at one fixed time or period always presses hard on capacity (after making allowance for reserve capacity held in standby for emergency)[7] and at "the" other period never does so even if the former bears all and the latter none of the capacity costs.

The problem of apportioning capacity costs between these two classes of customers is, precisely, the problem of costing joint products—the solution for which we have already described, using the example of cotton fiber and cottonseed oil. In the present instance, the same production capacity is available to provide two separate services, in fixed proportions: every kilowatt of electricity capacity, every cubic inch of natural gas pipeline space, every telephone circuit available for service in January is available also in July. As we have already seen, the respective supply prices of the joint services (as far as the joint portion of the production process—in this case, the provision of capacity—is concerned) depend on the relative elasticities and intensities of the two demands. The competitive solution requires, first, that the combined prices of the two services add up to no more than the marginal cost of producing the two together, and, second, that the price of each be set at a level at which the quantities demanded and the quantities supplied will be equated.

The case of the fixed and unchanging peak is the case illustrated in our Figure 2. The peak demand there is for cotton; the demand for cottonseed oil is irrevocably "off-peak" and must bear none of the capacity costs. Any attempt to shift capacity costs to the off-peak demands, by raising prices for that service above its own separate, incremental cost (MC_{cso}), will cause available production capacity at that time (cottonseeds) to be wasted, and would cut off purchasers willing to pay the additional cost of serving them. Any reduction of the peak (cotton) price below the full joint cost, P_c, would stimulate additional purchases at the peak, requiring additions to capacity that would not be made if buyers had to pay the full opportunity costs of the additional resources required to supply them. Similar to the cotton seeds in Figure 2, the capacity available off-peak is a free good and should be priced that way: it has a zero marginal cost at the point of intersection of competitive supply and demand.

---

[7] Actually a utility has some discretion about the times and seasons when it will close down various units of capacity for repair and maintenance, and will try to concentrate those shutdowns in off-peak periods. It will have identifiable peak and off-peak uses, then, only if the fluctuations of demand are wider than the fluctuations in plant availability due to maintenance. See Ralph Turvey, "Peak-Load Pricing," *Jour. Pol. Econ.* (January–February 1968), LXXVI: 103.

In the real world, demand peaks do not necessarily stay fixed: their location may shift for two reasons. First, if the elasticities of the separate demands are great enough, imposing all of the capacity costs on the peak customers and none on the off-peak may give rise to excess capacity at the former time (the previous peak) and congestion or shortages at the latter. And, second, the pattern of demand may change over time. The first phenomenon is static: it exists because the relationship between the demand functions is such that the proportion of total capacity costs imposed on each will determine at which time demand presses on capacity. An example would be the way in which public utility promotion of residential air-conditioning has apparently contributed in some areas to a shift in the peak demand for electricity from winter to summer. The second source of the shift is dynamic: it occurs as a result of changes over time in the respective demand functions. The increased use of electricity for summer air-conditioning has almost certainly reflected, above all else, dynamic factors such as the general rise in incomes, the perfection and reduced prices of air-conditioning equipment and the inclusion of air-conditioned summer comfort in the American standard of living. We confine our attention in this section to the static phenomenon; the second clearly belongs in our discussion, below, of what utility companies should do if long-run marginal costs change over time.

The demand situation in Figure 3 is the one that corresponds to the shifting peak. We reproduce it in Figure 4 with captions relevant to a public utility situation—for example, the demand and supply of natural gas in January and in July[8]—with the added complications of (1) recognizing that each of these services will have its own, separate set of variable costs (AVC), (2) introducing (in a dashed line, $SRMC_b$) an alternative short-term marginal cost, embodying the assumption of short-run increasing costs (for simplicity, we do so for a plant designed to produce OB units at lowest possible cost), (3) adding a line (AQ) that enables us to show how the competitive norm would apply in a situation of long-run disequilibrium, and (4) introducing a third, much weaker demand—for April.[9] Let us begin with the assumption that the variable costs are constant—that is, that the $SRMC_b$ does not apply. In this event we can ignore the April customers: their demand is unchangeably off-peak; they should pay MC_1, consume OM, and contribute nothing to the joint costs.

Suppose, initially, that capacity is OA. Clearly, it would be wrong at this point to levy all the capacity costs on the January customers: at such a price (LRMC separate), which includes the total joint capacity costs plus the

[8] In this event the x-axis would represent cubic feet, the y-axis cents per cubic foot; MC and $LRMC$ would be the marginal costs of supplying various quantities of cubic feet *per month*. The assumption here is that those costs would not differ from one month to another; it is not a necessary assumption but it simplifies the presentation. And it is assumed that only January and July are potential peaks, depending on the allocation of the joint capacity costs between them.

[9] The figure and exposition are based on Hirschleifer, *op. cit.*, *Q. Jour. Econ.* (August 1958), LXXII: 452, slightly reformulating those of

Peter O. Steiner, "Peak Loads and Efficient Pricing," *Q. Jour. Econ.* (November 1957), LXXI: 588. For a slightly different presentation of these same solutions see Ronald L. Meek, "An Application of Marginal Cost Pricing: The 'Green Tariff' in Theory and Practice," Part I, *Jour. Ind. Econ.* (July 1963), XI: 224–230 and the famous article by Marcel Boiteux, *op. cit.*, in Nelson, *Marginal Cost Pricing in Practice*. For an elegant, more generalized statement of the solution, see Oliver E. Williamson, "Peak-Load Pricing and Optimal Capacity under Indivisibility Constraints," *Amer. Econ. Rev.* (September 1966), LVI: 810–827.

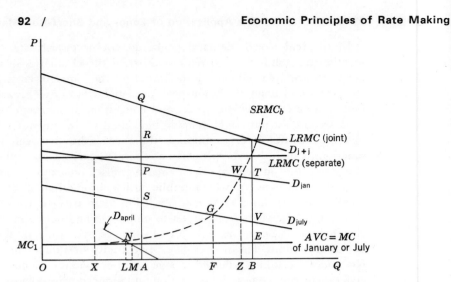

LRMC (joint) includes long-run capacity costs plus two long-run variable costs, one for January, one for July. Both are assumed constant. This is the amount that the sum of January and July prices must cover, in long-run equilibrium.

LRMC (separate) includes long-run capacity cost plus one long-term variable cost, representing the long-run costs of serving January or July.

AVC: the long-run variable costs of serving January or April or July.

$SRMC_b$: an alternative short-run marginal cost of producing from a plant of OB capacity.

Figure 4. Allocation of capacity costs, shifting peak.

variable costs of serving the January customers, they would demand only the quantity OX; XA capacity would remain idle in January. And the July users, being charged only their own separate variable costs (MC_1), would experience shortages. For the limited available supplies to be effectively rationed, while fullest economic use is made of capacity, the July users would have to be charged AS and the January customers AP. At such prices, the supplier would be earning excess profits: a combined price of AQ for one unit of sales in each month (remember that the demand curve D_{j+j} represents a summation of D_{july} and $D_{january}$)[10] compared with a combined unit cost of AR. The long-run competitive solution would be to increase capacity to OB, which is at the juncture of the combined demands and the joint long-run marginal costs of supplying both (capacity costs plus one set of long-run average variable

---

[10] The addition of the two demands (and the entire discussion in the text) assumes that they are independent of one another. This was a reasonable assumption for cotton fiber and cottonseed oil. But as between peak and off-peak power, gas or telephone service, there is likely to be some cross-elasticity of demand: a reduction in the rate on night long-distance telephone calls, for example, is likely to induce some users to shift their telephoning from day to night. To this extent, adding together the separate demand curves as though they were independent will exaggerate the elasticity of the joint demand curve. (In Figure 4, for example, $D_{january}$ shows how the quantities of power purchased in

January would vary if the January price *alone* were changed and correspondingly for D_{july}. But if their prices were reduced simultaneously, from AP to BT and AS to BV, respectively, and if the elasticity of each was in part a reflection of cross-elasticity, the combined quantities purchased would not increase by the full AB indicated.) Rate cuts on either of the two services would take some business away from the other, and would therefore not increase total sales by the amount indicated by the separate curves. (An attempt to sell the additional quantities AB both in January and July would thus depress the respective prices below BT and BV.)

In practice, public utility companies will, of

costs for each), charging the January users BT, the July users BV. At this point, both efficiency requirements are met: the combined prices do not exceed the marginal cost of producing the two services, and the price of each is set at a level that clears the market. There is no other set of prices at which these equilibrium conditions would be satisfied.

The introduction of the shifting peak does not alter the fundamental principle of peak-responsibility. The point is, simply, the January and July users both represent the peak, and they must therefore share the costs. On what basis? On the basis of the respective intensities and elasticities of the two demands.[11] It remains true that the long-run marginal cost of supplying purchasers in, for example, April and October includes no capacity costs as such; nor, ideally, should their prices.

Whether confronting a fixed or a shifting peak, the principle of peak responsibility is a relatively simple one in the presence of simplifying assumptions. One of these assumptions is that variable costs are constant to

---

course, have to take into account the impact of changes in some of their rates on revenues from other parts of their business in planning both their price structures and their decisions with respect to capacity. But this consideration in no way vitiates the conclusions we have reached with respect to socially optimal pricing; it merely suggests that in our Figure 4, the presence of cross-elasticities of demand will produce a long-run equilibrium capacity of something less than OB and rates for January and July sales somewhat higher than BT and BV, respectively.

[11] Steiner concluded for this reason that his solution to the problem of apportioning capacity costs in the case of the shifting peak involved price discrimination: the separate marginal costs of serving the January and the July customers are the same (AVC in Figure 4), yet the prices charged them differ. Hirschleifer contends, correctly I believe, that the solution is not discriminatory. His exposition follows two alternative lines.

1. The fact that the correct solution would involve the nondiscriminatory result of carrying on production in each market to the point where short-run marginal cost equaled price is obscured, in Figure 4, by the convenient, simplifying assumption of constant short-run marginal costs up to the limit of physical capacity. If the more conventional costs were assumed, increasing before the limit of producing capacity is reached (as in $SRMC_b$), it would be clear, as we point out in the text immediately following, that the efficient solution would involve producing in each market up to the point (F and Z respectively) where that short-run marginal cost was equated with demand price.

2. But even if the short-run marginal cost were indeed horizontal, then discontinuous, as at EVT, in Figure 4, so that in both January and

July production was carried on to the physical limit of capacity, the efficient prices would still be equated with the respective marginal opportunity costs. As we have already pointed out in discussing the separate costing of joint products (pp. 82–83), the economic cost of supplying an additional unit to any single customer in each of the two markets is measured by what the next customer, the first one not served, would have been willing to pay for that service: and, in Figure 4, that would be (infinitesimally less than) BV and BT in the respective markets. Therefore, according to this conception of cost as well, the correct solution involves equating price in each market to $SRMC$, and hence no discrimination.

This second line of argument, as Steiner points out, does seem to obscure the difference between the demand function and the cost function, which are supposedly equated at the margin in each market if there is to be no discrimination: the "marginal opportunity *cost*" is defined as equal to the market price at *whatever* level the latter happens to be set. It might seem therefore to define away the possibility of discrimination. "Reply," *Q. Jour. Econ.* (August 1958), LXXII: 467–468. But in fact it does not. The critical consideration, Hirschleifer responds, is that when markets are artificially separated, in the familiar price discrimination model, the marginal opportunity costs in the two markets are really the same—namely the price that the next-unsatisfied customer *in the higher price market* would be willing to pay: so, since their MC's are the same and their prices differ, genuine discrimination is practiced in that case. In the January–July model, instead, the joint products are not the same; the marginal cost of supplying the July customer is the lost opportunity of supplying the next-unsatisfied purchaser in *July*, not in

the physical limit of capacity, as in the horizontal AVC of Figure 4.[12] But in point of fact the production of public utility services is at times subject to short-run increasing costs. This is particularly clear of the generation of electricity. At any given time, generating plant will vary widely in age, type, location, and efficiency—hence in the level and slope of its $SRMC$. The common—and entirely rational—practice of electric companies, therefore, is to hold the less efficient generating units in reserve and phase them into operation from one moment to the next, according to the level of demand, in ascending order of their marginal costs.[13]

In this event some such alternative as $SRMC_b$ of Figure 4 becomes the relevant marginal cost function. How does its introduction alter the solution? Now, ideally, production in July should not exceed OF, and July users should pay not BV but FG.[14] Clearly the July users, though charged only the $SRMC$ of serving them, will end up paying a much larger contribution to joint costs than before in each MCF of gas they buy. Even more interesting, note what happens to the April customers. They ought now to be charged LN. But this price exceeds the average variable costs. Therefore, although they pay only $SRMC$, consume far less gas than the January and July customers, and their purchases are certainly off-peak, they make some contribution (over and above AVC) to joint capacity costs—and correctly so.[15]

January; and correspondingly for the January customer. So *their* marginal opportunity costs do differ, and, if so, their prices *should*; and, if they do, there need be no price discrimination. *Ibid.*, 459. The classic discussion of this very issue was that of Frank W. Taussig and A. C. Pigou, on the subject of "Railway Rates and Joint Costs", *Q. Jour. Econ.* (February, May, and August 1913), XXVII: 378–384, 535–538, and 687–694. A central issue in their debate was whether railway services to different customers are in fact homogeneous, in which event it would be proper to characterize rate differences as discriminatory. Their underlying difference of opinion was whether the costs of serving different railroad customers may properly be regarded as joint, as we have used the term (in which event the rate differences, they agreed, would not be discriminatory), or common.

However, in practice, for reasons we have already suggested, it has usually been infeasible for utility companies to differentiate and to vary their rates with the ever-shifting balances of capacity and demand at various times of day, year, and planning period in such a way as to equate price at each moment to short-run marginal opportunity costs. Therefore, they typically—in wholesale and large industrial sales—charge separately for variable and for capacity costs (as in the two-part tariff, discussed below), and do engage in considerable price discrimination in distributing the latter burden among various classes of customers on the basis of their respective elasticities of demand (see pp. 95–98, on the 2-part tariff, and Chapter 5).

[12] Another simplifying assumption that we make in this chapter is that LRMC are constant. We turn to the decreasing cost situation in Chapter 5. For the solution to the problem of apportioning capacity costs in the case of the shifting peak under conditions of decreasing costs, a case that unequivocally requires price discrimination if revenues are to cover total costs, see Johnson, in Shepherd and Gies, *op. cit.*, 131–132.

[13] For a more precise statement see the discussion of integration and power pooling, at note 51, Chapter 2, Volume 2. Also Meek, *op. cit.*, Part II, *Jour. Ind. Econ.* (November 1963), XII: 46–47; Bonbright, *Principles of Public Utility Rates*, 320–322.

[14] January users would now pay ZW, instead of BT, and consume correspondingly less. We make no effort here to relate the case of rising SRMC to determining the correct size of plant or ascertaining at what level of capacity total revenues collected at the new January and July prices (equated to the $SRMC$ of that plant) would cover total costs. See the sources cited in note 9. It might appear that OB was still the proper size, since the combined demand prices just suffice to cover total $LRMC$ at that point. But the $LRMC$ curves represent the costs *per unit* of output, on the assumption that whatever plants are built are operated to capacity in January and July. If in fact, with rising $SRMC$, only OF and OZ are now consumed, the $LRMC$ per unit for a plant of OB capacity will be higher than those shown on the diagram.

[15] See, for example, Meek, *op. cit.*, Part II, *Jour. Ind. Econ.* (November 1963), XII: 47–48.

Public utility companies do employ peak-responsibility pricing to some degree. The telephone companies charge lower rates for night than for daytime long-distance calls; electric companies frequently have low night rates for hot-water heating; both they and natural gas companies—local distributors and interstate pipelines alike—offer at lower rates service that the customer will agree may be interrupted if capacity is being taxed by other users and try to promote off-peak sales in numerous ways;[16] railroads charge lower rates for return-hauls of freight, when the greater flow is in the opposite direction; airlines offer special discount fares—family plans, youth fares, and so forth—for travel on unfilled planes or in slack seasons or days of the week.[17]

The two-part tariff, generally credited to John Hopkinson, an English engineer, and almost universally used by electric and gas utilities for large-volume sales at wholesale and to industrial users, represents an effort to apply just such a principle. The first part—the energy, commodity or "running" charge—embodies the variable costs, properly charged to all customers, and is levied on a per unit of consumption basis (per kwh or per MCF of gas). The second part—the demand or capacity charge—is a charge for the utility's readiness to serve, on demand. This readiness to serve is made possible by the installation of *capacity*: the demand charge, therefore, distributes the costs of providing the capacity—the fixed, capital costs—on the basis of the respective causal responsibilities of various buyers for them. And the proper measure of that responsibility is the proportionate share of each customer in the total demand placed on the system at its peak. (Sometimes the tariff will have three instead of two parts—the third, "customer" charge reflecting the costs of services such as meter-reading and billing that vary on a per customer basis instead of with different amounts purchased.)[18]

Unfortunately, the principle has usually been badly applied, in several important ways. First, if the demand charge were correctly to reflect peak responsibility it would impose on each customer a share of capacity costs equivalent to his share of total purchases at the time coinciding with the

---

[16] A particularly illuminating example is provided by the case of a combination company—that is, one distributing both electricity and gas—the two major portions of whose business had noncoincident peaks. The Chairman of the Board of Directors of the Public Service Electric and Gas Co. reported to his stockholders:

"In our sales promotion programs we are stressing the selling of 'off-peak loads', such as electric heating, to increase the winter use of electricity, thus helping to offset the summer air-conditioning peak; and gas air-conditioning and interruptible gas service to induce greater use of gas in the off-peak summer period." Annual Meeting of Stockholders, April 18, 1966.

Note that the company was competing with itself—pushing the off-peak sales of each product in competition with the other in periods of the latter's peak demand.

Our discussion of peak-responsibility has run entirely in terms of pricing policies. As the Public Service example suggests, the same considerations would justify public utility companies using various other sales promotional devices, such as intensive advertising or the sale of the relevant appliances at cost, or less, to increase off-peak sales. On the general question of the proper treatment of selective promotional expenditures, see p. 149, Chapter 6, note 10.

[17] For a decision sustaining reduced railroad rates for coal shipped during the slack season, provided those rates were available nondiscriminatorily to all shippers, see *ICC v. Louisville & N.R. Co.*, 73 F. 409 (1896) and another disallowing a similar seasonal reduction by a motor carrier on household goods because it did not meet the condition of nondiscrimination, ICC, *Reduced Seasonal Household Goods Rates*, Report and Order, 332 ICC 512 (1968).

[18] More often the customer costs will be recovered by specifying a minimum bill, or in sufficiently high per unit charges for the first block of electricity or gas purchased.

system's peak (a "coincident peak" demand charge). Instead, the typical two-part tariff bases that rate on each customer's *own* peak consumption over some measured time period, regardless of whether *his* peak coincides with that of the system (hence the designation "noncoincident" demand charge). That is, the peak (for example, half-hour) consumption of all customers, regardless of the time of day or year in which each falls, is added up, and each then is charged a share of total system capital costs equivalent to the percentage share that his peak consumption constitutes of that total. The noncoincident demand method does have some virtue: it encourages customers to level out their consumption over time, in order to minimize their peak taking, hence their share of capacity costs. This, in turn, tends to improve the system's load factor—the ratio of average sales over the year to capacity—that is, the degree of capacity utilization. But it is basically illogical. It is each user's proportion of consumption at the *system's* peak that measures the share of capacity costs for which each is causally responsible:[19] it is consumption at *that* time that determines how much capacity the utility must have available. The system's load factor might well be improved by inducing individual customers to cut down their consumption to a deep trough at the *system* peak and enormously increase *their* peak utilization at the system's off-peak time: yet the noncoincident demand system would discourage them from doing so.[20]

Second, the charges have typically been based on average instead of marginal costs. Therefore, the energy charge has generally ignored the fact that electricity is produced under conditions of short-run increasing cost; and the demand charge has tended to embody the opposite error.

Third, the two-part tariff has applied only to bulk sales. Retail sales of gas and electricity to households typically contain no such differentials based on time of consumption (with specific exceptions such as special night rates for water-heating). Instead, they usually carry block rates, with diminishing charges for larger blocks of consumption: for instance, 6¢ for the first 30 kwh, 4¢ for the next 50, 3¢ for the next 100, 2¢ for the next 570 and 1½¢ for anything above 750 kwh—regardless of the time of taking.[21] Since household utilization typically has a marked peak that coincides roughly with that of the system (whether because of air-conditioning on hot summer days, or for home heating, lighting, and cooking in the early evenings of short and cold winter days), the use of diminishing block rates has a strong perverse tendency to underprice marginal sales at the peak.[22] Against this distortion, however, one must weigh the tendency of such declining block rates correctly to reflect the declining unit costs of electricity and gas distribution with increased intensity of use.

---

[19] This entire discussion continues under the assumption that capacity costs are constant, so that *average* capacity costs (which is what are measured by both coincident and noncoincident demand methods) are the same as marginal capacity costs. If instead the system is subject to decreasing costs (see Chapter 5), each user will be *marginally* responsible for less than his percentage of coincident peak demands multiplied by total capacity costs, because marginal cost is less than average.

[20] See W. Arthur Lewis, *op. cit.*, 50–53; Ralph

K. Davidson, *Price Discrimination in Selling Gas and Electricity* (Baltimore: Johns Hopkins Press, 1955), 84–88, 133–134, 192–193.

[21] This schedule is taken from C. F. Phillips, *op. cit.*, 352, who identifies the preponderant uses of the successive blocks as lighting; refrigeration, washer, and dryer; cooking; water-heating and air-conditioning; and electric house heating, respectively.

[22] See Shepherd, "Marginal-Cost Pricing in American Utilities," *South. Econ. Jour.* (July 1966), XXXIII: 62.

In recent years, both England and France have taken important steps toward remedying some of these deficiencies of the Hopkinson tariff. The famous French "Tarif Vert," put into effect in 1956 (only for bulk and industrial sales), instituted rates varying with the time of day and season of the year in order to base demand charges on the system peak. The change recognized that energy charges too should vary with the level of demand because variable costs are not constant.[23] The British Central Electricity Generating Board (CEGB) went over in 1962–63 to the coincident peak for determining demand charges on its (wholesale) sales to the regional Area Boards and introduced a differential day-night "running" (that is, energy) charge.[24] In 1967–68, explicitly recognizing that the latter charges were erroneously based on average (day and night) instead of marginal operating costs, it introduced differential time-of-day, -week and -year energy charges reflecting the increasing SRMC function.[25]

The 1967–68 reforms reacted to another, even more interesting problem already alluded to briefly above: how should the principle of peak responsibility be applied if the same capacity does not serve all users? If capacity is not interchangeable, so that the same type of plant or equipment does not necessarily serve both peak and off-peak users, it is no longer true that peak consumption alone should bear all capacity costs. In electricity generation, it is economical for short periods of time to use gas turbine generating units, which have low capital costs but high operating costs. These are inefficient for continuous utilization, but are less costly than installing regular capacity for just the extreme peak demands.[26] In consequence, when the CEGB tried to incorporate the entire capacity costs in the demand charges, at about £10 a year per kw, it found that some of its Area Board customers began to install their own gas turbines, at a cost of about £4 per kw, and therefore cut down their peak purchases. The Board correctly recognized that the true incremental or avoidable costs of supplying capacity that would be used for peaks of comparatively short duration (it estimated this type of capacity would be economic if operated no longer than 250 hours of the year) were not £10 but £4 per kw, and that the £11 now estimated to be the capital costs per kw of basic capacity, such as would be economic for longer periods of operation (because of its far lower variable costs) should therefore be borne by

---

[23] The demand charge to industrial customers in the Paris region provides discounts ranging from 0% in winter peak hours to 98% in summer "empty" hours. Eli W. Clemens, "Marginal Cost Pricing: A Comparison of French and American Industrial Power Rates," *Land Econ.* (November 1964), XL: 391. See also Meek, *op. cit.*, Part II, *Jour. Ind. Econ.* (November 1963), XII: 45–63, and the articles by Marcel Boiteux and Pierre Massé in J. R. Nelson, *Marginal Cost Pricing in Practice*, 134–156.

[24] R. L. Meek, "The Bulk Supply for Electricity," *Oxford Econ. Papers* (July 1963), n.s. XV: 107–123.

[25] The Board settled for three running or energy rates:

". . . one for *peak units*—now defined as those used between 8 and 12 A.M. and for 4:30 and

6:30 P.M. from Mondays to Fridays in December and January, except for Christmas and Boxing Days . . .;

". . . a second rate for *day units* used between 7:30 A.M. and 11 P.M. daily, but outside the peak . . .;

". . . a third rate for *night units* used between 11 P.M. and 7.30 A.M. . . ." "Puncturing the Power Peak," *The Economist*, May 14, 1966, 734.

The consequence of moving to increasing marginal charges for operating costs was to cause the operating charges to make some contribution to capacity costs as in our model, p. 94, above; the French Green Tariff has the same effect.

[26] For a general, diagrammatic statement of the conditions for such a choice, see M. A. Crew, "Peak Load Pricing and Optimal Capacity: Comment," *Amer. Econ. Rev.* (March 1968), LVIII: 168–170.

consumption during the longer-period, "winter plateau" of demand.[27] Similar qualifications of simple-minded peak responsibility pricing would clearly be appropriate to the extent storage capacity instead of basic pipeline capacity served the peak needs of natural gas consumers.[28]

Although most public utility executives and regulators recognize that peak responsibility pricing has some validity, probably most would also vigorously resist its wholehearted acceptance. William G. Shepherd's survey disclosed that the majority of American electric utilities practice little or no explicit marginal cost pricing, and among those that do, the main emphasis is on raising off-peak sales, by charging them something less than average capacity costs, instead of purposefully imposing all the capacity charges on the peak users.[29] He found, moreover, that publicly-owned companies, if anything, follow marginalist and peak responsibility principles even less than private;[30] and that electric utilities in states with "tough" regulatory commissions, such as New York and California, similarly incorporate little marginalism in their rate structures.

An outstanding illustration of the resistance of strong regulatory commissions is provided by the Federal Power Commission's formula for natural gas pipeline rate-making specified in its famous *Atlantic Seaboard* decision of 1952.[31] The distinctive feature of the Atlantic Seaboard formula is that it requires that capacity costs be distributed 50–50 between the demand and commodity charges instead of incorporated exclusively in the former. Since the demand costs are distributed among customers in proportion to their shares in the volume of sales at the system's (three-day) peak, while the commodity costs are borne in proportion to their annual volume of purchases, the consequence of the 50–50 formula is to shift a large proportion[32] of capacity costs to off-peak users. This produces an uneconomic encouragement to sales at the peak (whose price falls short of the true marginal costs of peak

---

[27] Accordingly, it introduced two demand rates: an £11 "basic capacity charge" for consumption during the winter plateau, when it estimated that demand would be on the average no more than 90% of the maximum system demand, and a "peaking capacity charge" of £4 for the period, estimated not to exceed 250 hours a year, when demand would exceed the 90% plateau. See R. L. Meek, "The New Bulk Supply Tariff for Electricity," *Econ. Jour.* (March 1968), LXXVIII: 48–53 and *passim;* "Puncturing the Power Peak," *The Economist*, May 14, 1966, 734.

This complicating factor in peak responsibility pricing was pointed out by Melvin G. de Chazeau, "Reply," *Q. Jour. Econ.* (February 1938), LII: 357 and recognized—along with most other problems—by Bonbright, *op. cit.*, 354 note.

[28] For an analysis of the ways in which the introduction of gas storage requires a modification of the simple charging of all capacity costs to peak users, see R. K. Davidson, *op. cit.*, 138–147.

[29] *Op. cit., South Econ. Jour.* (July 1966), XXXIII: 61–65. Effective earlier critics of the failure of

electricity as well as gas distribution companies to employ marginal costing, in particular with respect to the allocation of capacity costs, were I. M. D. Little, *The Price of Fuel* (Oxford: Clarendon Press, 1953), 54–76 and R. K. Davidson, *op. cit.*, especially 81–97, 111–147.

[30] See also Richard L. Wallace, "Cost and Revenue Associated with Increased Sales of TVA Power," *South. Econ. Jour.* (April 1967), XXIII: 526–534; and, for an Australian example, H. M. Kolsen, "The Economics of Electricity Pricing in N. S. W.," *Economic Record* (December 1966), XLII: 564–565.

[31] *In the Matters of Atlantic Seaboard Corporation and Virginia Gas Transmission Corporation*, Opinion No. 225, 11 FPC 43 (1952).

[32] This is not wholly 50%, because peak users also pay their proportionate share of the commodity charge, which includes half of the capacity costs. But the point is that in deciding to what extent to cut their purchases at the peak relative to off-peak, peak customers are influenced by only the 50% of capacity costs incorporated in the demand charge; the other 50% does not affect that calculation because they pay it equally whenever they take the gas.

service[33]) and an uneconomic discouragement of off-peak.[34] (In fairness, it should be pointed out that the FPC has permitted departures from this strict formula when it appeared that the pipelines would suffer large losses of interruptible, off-peak sales at the inflated commodity charges it produced—permitting them instead to "tilt" the rate schedule downward on the commodity side of the balance.[35] Among other alleged harmful consequences of *Atlantic Seaboard* has been a tendency to discourage distribution companies from installing storage capacity: demand and commodity charges more fully reflecting the true respective marginal costs of peak and off-peak purchases would have increased their incentive to "shave" their purchases at the former

---

[33] This is so, as we have already pointed out, only to the extent that the pipeline function is subject to constant costs. Since pipelines do have some tendencies to long-run decreasing costs (see the section on "Natural Gas Transmission, Economies of Scale," Chapter 4, Volume 2), so that LRMC may be lower than ATC, the arbitrary 50–50 allocation tends to produce a less harmful result, that is, less of an understatement of the true *marginal* costs of peak service, than would otherwise be the case. Laurence C. Rosenberg concludes, however, that some considerable distortion remains. See his *Natural Gas Pipeline Rate-Making Problems*, unpublished Ph.D. dissertation, Cornell University, June 1963, 176–184 and *passim*. See also Stanislaw H. Wellisz, "Regulation of Natural Gas Pipeline Companies: An Economic Analysis," *Jour. Pol. Econ.* (February 1963), LXXI: 33, who contends that the constant cost assumption is not unreasonable.

It should be reemphasized, too, that the fact of gas storage may justify imposition of some capacity costs on off-peak customers—to the extent that, by using pipeline space that could otherwise be used to pump gas into storage, they create a need for more capacity than would otherwise be required. (See p. 98.)

[34] The formula discourages off-peak sales not only by the pipeline companies but also by their distribution company-customers, since *their* variable costs are inescapably inflated by the 50% allotment of fixed costs to the commodity charge. Wellisz demonstrates that the pipeline companies would in any event have an incentive to exploit their off-peak customers, charging them a monopoly price and using the super-normal profits thereby earned to subsidize peak sales, in this way "justifying" an uneconomic expansion of capacity. See *op. cit.*, 35–36. This tendency is discussed at greater length in Chapter 2, Volume 2.

[35] See, for example, C. F. Phillips, *op. cit.*, 624–628 on this and for a description of the Atlantic Seaboard formula; also Garfield and Lovejoy, *Public Utility Economics*, 181–185 and Wellicz, *op. cit.*, 30–43. The difference between the two rates is large: in 1968 the demand

charges of one pipeline company on one schedule ranged between $2.79 and $4.28 per MCF, while its commodity charges ran from 22.1¢ to 26.2¢.

A later decision, interestingly enough involving the Atlantic Seaboard Company itself, demonstrates how far the "tilting" process has gone, under the pressures of competitive necessity. The case involved a protest by the Lynchburg Gas Company against special "partial requirements" rates that the FPC had permitted Atlantic Seaboard and other subsidiaries of the Columbia Gas Company to institute—higher, penalty rates imposed on those customers that purchased their supplies in part from suppliers other than the Columbia companies. In justification of these rates, the Commission had accepted the pipeline companies' justification that any losses of sales that they suffered by virtue of such diversions made it necessary for them to raise the rates that they charged their more loyal, full requirements customers. The Circuit Court of Appeals sent the case back to the Federal Power Commission, holding that these special rates had been inadequately supported in the record. See *Lynchburg Gas Co. v. FPC*, 336 F. 2d. 942 (1964). Upon rehearing, the FPC Presiding Examiner found that the Columbia System companies had so drastically departed from the original Atlantic Seaboard formula as to undermine their previous justification of the partial requirements rates. As the Circuit Court of Appeals explained in 1968, after the case had returned to it for a decision, one reason for the alleged necessity of protecting the full requirements customers from any loss of sales by their suppliers was that "not all of Columbia's fixed costs are recovered by the demand charges." At the time of the original *Lynchburg* decision, roughly half of Seaboard's fixed costs were recovered by the commodity rate. Thereafter, the Columbia companies had departed drastically from the original formula, in order to be better able to compete for off-peak business, with the result that only 6% of the company's fixed costs were now being recovered in the commodity rate. *Atlantic Seaboard Corporation et al. v. Federal Power Commission et al.*, 404 F. 2d. 1268, at 1270–1271 (1968).

by installing storage, which they could fill by low-cost purchases off-peak and draw on at the peak.[36]

We present two last examples of the pervasive uneconomic departure from peak responsibility pricing. First, commutation books and other such devices that give commuters quantity discounts on passenger trains and toll bridges have the consequence that occasional travelers, who usually travel off-peak, pay a higher rate than commuters, who concentrate their traveling in the rush hours.[37] Second, airplane landing fees do not reflect the enormous variations in airport congestion, from one time of day, day of the week, or one airport to another. These variations themselves doubtless tend to induce air travelers and airplane companies to rearrange their traveling plans and schedules to avoid peak hours and locations and make fuller use of off-peak time; equivalently varying landing fees could make a further contribution.[38]

There are often very good reasons of expediency and practicality for these widespread departures from economically efficient pricing, to some of which we shall allude below. But objections are sometimes made to the principle itself. Prominent among these are:

1. It is unfair and discriminatory to charge peak-utilization alone with the fixed costs, since the capacity obviously serves all users at all times;[39]
2. The utilities or regulators have a special responsibility to protect the ordinary, unorganized householder, and should try to keep down his rates;

---

[36] See Homer Ross, "How Practical Is The Seaboard Formula?" *Public Utilities Fortnightly* (January 3, 1963), LXXI: 32 and Wellisz, *op. cit.*, 41. For (1) a reminder that the Commission's methods are defective also because the capital charges they allocate are historic instead of future costs, (2) an interesting and persuasive application of the peak responsibility principle to the problem of allocating the demand costs among customers located in different geographic markets, and (3) a clear demonstration that the Commission's methods of doing so fail by a wide margin to reflect customers' respective marginal responsibilities for the capacity of the various segments of the pipeline, see Laurence C. Rosenberg, "Natural-Gas-Pipeline Rate Regulation," *Jour. Pol. Econ.* (April 1967), LXXV: 159–168.

[37] See William Vickrey, "Some Implications of Marginal Cost Pricing for Public Utilities," *Amer. Econ. Rev., Papers and Proceedings* (May 1955), XLV: 619.

[38] See William D. Grampp, "An Economic Remedy for Airport Congestion: the Case For Flexible Pricing," *Business Horizons* (October 1968), XI: 21–30.

[39] As Garfield and Lovejoy state, "The fact that the [Atlantic Seaboard] formula permits no free ride on the line is its greatest strength. . . ." *Op. cit.*, 183. Here is the Commission's justification, in that decision:

"A pipeline would not normally be built to

supply peak service, that is to say, service on the peak days only. We know . . . that pipelines are built to supply service not only on the few peak days but on all days throughout the year. In proving the economic feasibility of the project in certificate proceedings, reliance is placed upon the annual as well as the peak deliveries. Stated another way, the capital outlay for the pipeline facility is made—and justified—not only for service on the peak days but for service throughout the year. Both capacity and annual use are important considerations in the conception of the project and in the issuance of certificates of public convenience and necessity. Both capacity and volume, therefore, are what are known as cost factors or incidences in respect to the capital outlay for a pipeline project. It follows that reasonably accurate results can be achieved only by allocating the fixed expenses flowing from the capital outlay to both operating functions, viz., capacity and volume " *Atlantic Seaboard*, Opinion No. 225, 11 FPC 43, (1952).

A similar, further illuminating example of this argument was offered by the National Association of Railroad and Utilities Commissioners (NARUC) in support of a procedure, adopted by the Federal Communications Commission in 1967, for allocating the interexchange plant of the Bell System between interstate and intrastate service—a necessary procedure for FCC rate regulation since it has jurisdiction only over the former. The issue was whether it was appropriate

3. The utilities should promote the maximum extension of their services, subject only to the condition that aggregate revenues cover aggregate costs—goals that may well conflict with peak responsibility pricing.[40]

Justifications such as these are for the most part not susceptible to scientific refutation, since basically they involve nonscientific value judgments.[41] An economist can only cite the following counterconsiderations:

1. In economic terms, peak-responsibility pricing is not discriminatory between peak and off-peak users. Discrimination consists in price differences not corresponding to cost differences. It is an objective fact that it costs more to supply users at the peak than off-peak, and the proposal is to reflect that cost difference in the respective prices. Every peak user actually *imposes* on society, in the long run, the incremental cost of the capacity on which he draws. There is no such causal connection between off-peak utilization and capacity costs: the capacity would be there whether or not the off-peak user made demands on it. It would be discriminatory to levy any of these costs on the off-peak user.[42]

to lump together plant of AT&T's Long Lines Department, which is used exclusively for interstate service, with other facilities used for both inter- and intrastate service, before allocating the total between the two services on the basis of the number of message-minute-miles of each type. NARUC argued for lumping the two on the ground that "The toll network has been designed as an entity and every portion benefits every other portion. . . ." *In the Matter of American Telephone and Telegraph Co.*, Interim Decision and Order, 9 FCC 2d 30, 71 (1967). AT&T argued, correctly, that the costs of any facilities used exclusively by one of the services (in this case the Long Lines plant) should be assigned directly to that service, and only the common plant be allocated between the services. It also pointed out that combining the two discriminated against long-distance messages, since it obscured the fact that the (average) investment cost (per circuit mile) of the Long Lines Department is markedly less than that of the Associated Company plant (*Ibid.*, 96–97). Indeed, since it is the Long Lines Department that has the greater tendency to long-run decreasing costs, the marginal costs diverge even more than the average. Here again, an argument that all users *benefit* from the presence of capacity was used to obscure the markedly different *costs* of the two services, which should have been reflected in their respective rates. NARUC and the Commission were later persuaded to accept the AT&T position. *In the Matter of Prescription of procedures for separating and allocating plant investment etc.*, Docket No. 17975, Report and Order, January 29, 1969, pars. 6–19. For further discussion of these separations procedures, see pp. 152–153, Chapter 5.

[40] This is the implicit assumption of G. J. Ponsonby, when he seems willing to see off-peak

users of city buses charged more than the LRMC of serving them, in order to permit a greater improvement of service at the peak than what that traffic would itself be willing to pay for. "The Problem of the Peak, with Special Reference to Road Passenger Transport," *Econ. Jour.* (March 1958), LXVIII: 78–82, 87. For a suggestion that these goals may also be in the interest of the public utility companies themselves, see note 34.

[41] However, Wellisz does point out that the *Atlantic Seaboard* formula is of dubious efficacy even as a means of achieving the goal of subsidizing household consumption (much of which is at the peak). The householder buys his gas from the distribution company. The latter, he points out, will have an incentive, for the reason just suggested (note 34), to maximize profits on its off-peak sales, because this will enable it to subsidize peak sales. But when its own marginal costs of supplying off-peak gas are inflated by the incorporation of capital costs in the commodity charge, it will be forced in turn to price such sales above the point that would maximize their contribution to the overhead costs of the system as a whole, hence to the subsidization of on-peak sales. *Op. cit.*, 37–38. When seller B buys some of his inputs from producer A at prices in excess of marginal costs, B's own profit-maximizing price will in turn exceed the price that would maximize the profits of A and B together. On the reason for this, see the section "Financial Integration," Chapter 6, Volume 2.

[42] It might be argued that peak-responsibility pricing involves no discrimination, also, because peak and off-peak power are not the same service, in economic terms, any more than are Tuesday and Saturday evening tickets to the same theatrical performance; and price discrimination occurs only when different prices are charged for

2. In this sense, it is inequitable to make off-peak users pay some share of capacity costs, for which they are not themselves causally responsible.[43]

3. Moreover, such a policy would be economically inefficient. To the extent that off-peak demand has any elasticity at all, a charge to these users that incorporates any capacity costs will cause them to give up satisfactions, the true social costs of which they would be perfectly willing to pay. And some productive capacity is left wastefully idle. Conversely, and subject to the same condition, if peak users do not have to pay the full (marginal) costs of being supplied, they will induce society to provide them with a capacity that uses resources that would have given greater satisfaction if directed to other employments.

4. In these circumstances, off-peak users would be subsidizing peak users. Now this may be something that society is willing to do; but such a policy will make sense only if the membership of each group is clearly identified, so that the decision in effect to transfer income from the one to the other is a conscious one. The mere identification of the subsidizing group as consisting of commercial and industrial customers and of the subsidized group as householders, for example, does not in itself demonstrate that the abandonment of economically efficient pricing is justified as a means of promoting a more equal distribution of income. The higher-than-marginal costs imposed on business and industrial customers must ultimately be paid by *their* customers or the customers of their customers: and these, too, are people, who may or may not, on the average, have higher incomes than the direct household customers of the utilities.[44]

---

the same service. As students of the Robinson-Patman Act will recognize, this argument is a treacherous one. What makes the Tuesday and the Saturday evening tickets of "unlike grade and quality," in the terms of that Act, is not just the physical difference in the service, but also the fact that buyers are willing to pay more for the latter than for the former. Since discrimination always requires that some customers be willing to pay more than others, if that difference in willingness to pay is then used in turn to prove that the services are economically different, there never can be any discrimination. However, the fact remains that the two services are in this case objectively separate: the use of capacity to supply gas in July for cooking could not be transferred to January and used instead to cut the costs of home-heating; the two markets are not artificially, but physically and inescapably separate. See note 11.

[43] It might appear that peak users are responsible not for the entire capacity, but only for that portion by which their consumption exceeds off-peak consumption—that is, that efficiency requires that they pay the entire costs only of the "peak" or protuberance of the mountain above the surrounding plateau, not of the entire mountain. The answer is to be found in the case for equating price to *marginal* cost. *Every* peak kilowatt hour consumed is marginal in the sense that capacity costs would be less in its absence.

The purchaser of every kilowatt hour at the peak must therefore be confronted with a price that, by including its share of incremental capacity cost, makes him decide whether it is worthwhile to him to impose on society the cost of constructing his share of the entire mountain. *No* off-peak use is marginal in this sense.

[44] The *Atlantic Seaboard* formula, for example, has the effect of imposing higher-than-marginal cost rates on, among others, electricity generating companies that purchase natural gas on an interruptible basis for their steam generating plants; in effect, therefore, it tends to impose lower-than-economic costs on residential purchasers of natural gas (who buy heavily at the peak) and higher-than-economic costs on residential purchasers of electricity. It would be difficult to demonstrate that the formula produces a more acceptable distribution of income than would full peak-responsibility pricing. Again, the Federal Communications Commission is often urged to exercise its regulatory authority over interstate telephone rates to give particular protection to the householder instead of the business subscriber. But the average income of the (weighted) average household user of interstate (that is, long distance) telephone service could well be considerably higher than that of the customers of most of the commercial and industrial users of Bell System services.

5. Even if society were to make a conscious decision to transfer income from off-peak to peak users, such a policy would not be an intelligent one if it did not take into account the fact that departures from efficient pricing are an economically inefficient way of effecting such a transfer. The "proof" of this, which depends only on peak demand having some elasticity, is that if the transfer were made as a money grant to those users, instead of in the form of prices below cost, they would not use all that money to purchase the public utility service in question, but would spend some of it for a variety of other goods and services.[45]

THE APPROPRIATE TIME PATTERN OF RATES

Efficient pricing of public utility services calls for as fine a differentiation as practical of rates for the various services provided, in various locations, so as to reflect the different marginal costs of each. To the extent that differences in marginal cost can be ascribed also to the particular times at which service is taken, rate schedules should incorporate time-differentials as well. All this would be true even in a purely static situation, with unchanging cost and demand functions.

In the real world, costs and demands are constantly changing over time. These dynamic changes give rise to at least three major types of problems of efficient pricing. First, the ever-changing relationship of capacity to demand raises the question of whether it is feasible to price on the basis of short-run marginal cost, and what mixture of SRMC and LRMC would provide the optimum combination of feasibility and efficiency. Second, how should prices be varied over time in reflection of the changes in cost functions, because of ever-changing input prices, productivity, and technology? Third, if one departs from pricing on the basis of SRMC, what is the proper time pattern for the recovery of fixed costs such as depreciation, in the face of fluctuating demand on the one hand and unpredictably changing technology on the other?

Changing Relationship of Capacity to Demand

System demand peaks shift not merely because the quantities demanded respond to different prices—a static, elasticity phenomenon; they shift also because demands at any given price change over time. Promotional pricing of air-conditioning equipment by electric companies, like the pusher's free distribution of addictive drugs, may have played a role in spreading the habit; but the habit spread for other reasons as well, moving demand sufficiently to the right and making it sufficiently price-inelastic to give rise in some areas to a fixed, summer peak. If the peak shifts, or becomes shiftable, or *may* shift five, ten, or fifteen years in the future, how should that shift or shiftability be reflected in peak responsibility pricing today?

---

[45] For a more formal demonstration, see pp. 190–191, Chapter 7. This "proof" is of course no better than the assumptions underlying the economic model whose conclusions it adopts: notably that the subsidized purchasers would be the best judges of what most satisfies them and that society *ought* therefore to be more willing to give them cash grants than, for example, cheap electricity. See pp. 67–69, Chapter 3. Even if a governmental body rejects the second precept, the economist could still observe that the social decision is more likely to be rational and the economic costs less if the subsidized service is paid for openly by appropriation of taxpayer funds instead of covertly in charges levied on off-peak users.

Apart from peak shifts, changes in demand from one moment, month, or year to the next will involve movements along existing SRMC functions—and unless those costs are constant (horizontal), this will mean corresponding changes in marginal costs. We have already seen how volatile the SRMC of individual airplane trips must be—ranging between zero and levels far in excess of average total costs, depending on what price it takes to ration the fixed number of places—that is, to fill the plane while turning away no traveler willing to pay the price.

Similarly, on the supply side, capacity is constantly changing. Typically, public utility companies must build in advance of demand in order to be in a position to meet unexpected peak requirements and simply because the investment process is a lumpy one: additions to capacity are most economically made in large units. Therefore, at any given time, there is almost certain to be excess capacity,[46] which will remain idle if customers are charged long-run marginal costs. What, in these circumstances, is the proper measure of marginal costs? Or, to put the question another way, how far into the future should the calculation of long-run marginal costs extend?

As we have already seen, there is a strong economic case for letting price rise and fall as demand shifts along the rising SRMC curve. If SRMC is at times zero and at other times discontinuous (because an absolute physical limit of capacity has been reached), the price should fluctuate—down to zero, if necessary, because in the presence of excess capacity, no matter how temporary, no business should be turned away that covers the SRMC of supplying it; and up in periods of shortage to whatever level is necessary to ration limited supplies among customers. Once the new bridge is built, it is wasteful to keep people from crossing it; the time to charge for crossings is when congestion sets in.[47]

But, we have also pointed out, this is a counsel of perfection. It may well require modification in a world where (1) buyers and sellers make mistakes, (2) perpetual price fluctuation can be expensive for sellers to administer and buyers to keep track of and respond to intelligently, (3) capital and labor are incompletely mobile, (4) many other prices are highly inflexible, and (5) there is a business cycle.[48]

---

[46] For a demonstration that economies of scale make it rational to have excess capacity see Hollis B. Chenery, "Overcapacity and the Acceleration Principle," *Econometrica* (January 1952), XX: 1–10. Chenery shows that the optimum amount of the excess is comparatively insensitive to the interest rate, which determines how costly it is to build capacity in advance of the time it is utilized.

[47] It might appear that no customer whose continued patronage would eventually require additions to capacity should ever be charged a price that completely excludes those capital costs; the economic ideal, it might appear, would be to include them, but discounted back to present value, to reflect the fact that continued service of the customer in question would require their incurrence only sometime in the future. Such a prescription ignores the fact that buyers whose continued patronage *could* require the

incurrence of additional capacity costs are not in fact responsible for them if they drop out of the market when the time comes for the supplying company to make the decision whether to make the additional investment. It is only at *that* time, when there is a possibility of resources being used to expand capacity, that *all* (peak) customers should be confronted with a price that once again incorporates those costs, forcing them (as before) to decide whether the benefit to them of continued service justifies society's incurring the marginal opportunity costs of serving them.

[48] See pp. 83–86, Chapter 3. Consider how vexatious it would be to price each airplane flight at *SRMC* by auctioning seats off at whatever price it takes to clear the market—how difficult and costly to administer, how much time of passengers and airplane employees (and computers) would be used in the auctioning process itself, how difficult it would make it for

Consider what it means, for example, about the proper method of recovering the gross cost of capital—depreciation, interest, profits, income and property taxes—over the business cycle.

Except for the portion of depreciation that varies with the extent to which the facilities are used (that is, that represents user cost), these costs are a function of time—so much per dollar of investment per year—instead of a function of the rate of output from given facilities. There are three possible ways in which they might be recovered from customers:

1. In equal amounts for equal periods of time—for example, a certain amount per year. This method would seem to be recommended by the fact that these costs are a function of time. This means they would be recovered in prices that fluctuated inversely with the fluctuations in demand—capital charges per unit being low in years of large sales and high in years of low sales.

2. In equal amounts per unit of sales, on the theory that no purchase or purchaser should pay more than any other, per unit of purchase, over the life of the investment. This would mean recovery in constant prices over the cycle, which is the tendency under regulation. Depreciation, taxes, and return are calculated at a particular amount of money per year.[49] Usually, the companies are then instructed to propose a schedule of rates that will cover the total charges on the average over some period of years in the future. This means that in practice the capital costs will be recovered unequally over the cycle—in larger amounts when sales exceed the average, in smaller amounts when they fall below the average.[50]

3. In prices that fluctuate directly with the business cycle. This would be the tendency of pricing at SRMC: prices would be low and revenues would tend to cover only variable costs in periods of weak demand in recognition of the fact that the demand at such times puts no burden on capacity. Price would have to move up far enough above that level and remain there long enough in periods of recovering and strong demand not only to cover ATC at that time but to make good the losses of previous periods.

There is no settled economic theory of the ideal behavior of the general price level over the cycle. (Indeed, cyclical fluctuations have become so much more modest since World War II that the subject itself is of reduced interest.) Economists would almost certainly reject the first as a general rule. In view of the general tendency of prices in the economy to move up and down with the cycle (although the latter tendency especially has become faint in recent

---

passengers to plan their travel. Or suppose the same free pricing system were used for taxicabs: consider how their rates would have to fluctuate from sunny to rainy days, from one time of day and from one section of the city to another, and with what costs of time and annoyance to passengers and drivers.

[49] Straight-line depreciation—writing off an investment in equal amounts over its estimated life—remains the usual procedure. When accelerated depreciation is taken for purposes of calculating income tax liability, the taxes incorporated in the cost of service are often "normalized," that is, set at a stable annual figure over the life of the asset, although actual taxes will be below that normalized level in the earlier years and above it in later years. See pp. 32–34.

[50] This is only a tendency. It may be offset by a tendency of *variable* costs to fluctuate directly with the level of operations—for example, because the utility puts inefficient plant into service only when necessary—while the variable component of the cost of service is an average estimated for a period of years.

decades), it would probably result in uneconomic distortions to have public utility prices going the other way. Moreover, it would tend to have precisely the wrong effect in rationing consumption—discouraging utilization when demand is low relative to capacity and encouraging it when marginal (congestion) costs are high.[51] Economists would be less clear in their response to the third way of recovering costs. It would probably be fair to say that most believe it serves no useful purpose to have the general price level fluctuate widely with the cycle, either. In view of the comparative rigidity of the general price level it would probably do more harm than good to have the prices of public utility services alone fluctuate as widely as the third rule would dictate.[52]

Therefore, the usual practice of charging capital costs on a per unit of sales basis and recouping them *on the average* over the cycle—that is, the second rule—is probably the best available general rule as far as the determination of general rate *levels* is concerned.[53] The rate stability that it provides is not just a pragmatic compromise between the extremes produced by rules 1 and 3: it also has the positive virtue of making it easier for customers to make the type of long-run commitments that consumption of a utility service usually involves (to install a certain furnace, to locate industry in a particular area), on the basis of reasonably stable expectations about the prices they are likely to have to pay.

This does not mean that SRMC, or fluctuations in the relationship of demand to capacity, should be ignored. The key is the necessity for reasonable predictability on the part of supplier or customer. Where not only *differences* but *changes* in the SRMC of supply at different times can be predicted with reasonable assurance, it is economically efficient to embody corresponding differentials in rate *structures*. In the presence of excess capacity, utility companies ought to make every effort to design rates, down to SRMC, to put it to use. We have recognized that the "ideal" of rates fluctuating with SRMC could have highly inefficient consequences on the buyers' side of the market. Household customers induced to shift to electricity or natural gas or industrial users persuaded to locate somewhere by rates approximating short-term marginal costs in periods of excess capacity would have a legitimate complaint if, having made the switch, they were then faced unpredictably with steadily rising rates as SRMC came increasingly to cover capacity costs as well. Therefore, the essential proviso would have to be attached that the proffer of any such temporarily low rates be accompanied with the warning that service would be interrupted as demand caught up, or rates increased to whatever extent necessary to ration demand until additional capacity was once again constructed.

[51] See the same observation in an analogous context, by Seymour Smidt, "Flexible Pricing of Computer Services," *Management Science* (June 1968), XIV: B–582.

[52] However, see the reference to J. R. Nelson, note 67. Additionally, Bonbright points out that if public utility rates were free to fluctuate like purely competitive prices over the cycle, it would in principle be necessary for regulatory commissions to play a much more active role than they now need to in the investment decision process—specifically, to compel companies to expand capacity when necessary. Private managements would have a strong temptation to delay capacity expansion in time of strong demand, hoping instead to enjoy the high profits resulting from the high prices required to ration customers. *Op. cit.*, 99.

[53] The Civil Aeronautics Board has explicitly recognized that it would be futile to try to iron out year-by-year fluctuations in rate of return in an industry so subject to fluctuation in its financial fortunes. See its *General Passenger Fare Investigation*, 32 CAB 291, 294–309 (1960).

Such a notice would protect the utility against charging customers less than the true and full eventual MC of serving them, while also giving the latter the predictability of future rates necessary if they are to avoid making irrational commitments.

The same sort of warnings are necessary with peak responsibility pricing. The ideal, once again, would be to price on the basis of *current* MC: this means that currently off-peak users would pay zero capacity costs today and full capacity costs in the event of a shift to a new fixed peak at their time of consumption tomorrow. But fluctuations of this kind would be impractical, for the reasons already given. The key once again must be reasonable predictability. Therefore, capacity costs ought to be shared in varying proportions, from 100% down to zero, by purchasers in periods that have correspondingly varying likelihoods of being or becoming peaks in the foreseeable future. The farther ahead the utility can see with reasonable assurance that certain sales will remain off-peak, the greater is the justification for offering this service on a firm (noninterruptible) basis at rates that incorporate no capacity costs. Conversely, if there is a strong possibility that within a very few years the service that is now off-peak will in fact put a strain on capacity, the off-peak tariffs are justified only if they are inter-ruptible[54] and/or the buyers are put clearly on notice that the rates may in time have to be sharply increased.[55]

On the other hand, customers have no absolute right to perpetual protection against drastic rate changes if cost changes counsel such measures. Consider-ations of fairness will join with considerations of efficiency in calling for reasonable compromises between the interests of different classes of cus-tomers: offering moderate assurances of rate stability in the face of unantici-pated cost changes unfavorable to certain customers, yet refusing indefinitely to burden other customers with the necessity of paying prices disproportion-ately *above* the MC of serving them in order to shelter the former group per-manently against the consequences of change or of errors, their own or the company's.[56]

We return to some of these practical considerations in Chapter 7. But there is no simple solution available. The proper balance will ordinarily have to make very large concessions in the direction of rate stability: the efficiency advantages of having rates vary over the life-cycles of particular increments to capacity are typically outweighed by the numerous disadvantages.[57] And even the advantages are probably diminishing over time: as the elec-tricity generating industry and natural gas pipelines (the latter far more slowly than the former) approach participation in regional or national grid systems, in which additions to capacity in the various regions of the country are synchronized over time, the problem of temporary excesses of capacity on the one hand, and the efficiency advantages of varying prices over time because of them, will become correspondingly less important.

For these various reasons, growing public utility industries that are constantly adding to capacity generally must attempt to set their rates, as

---

[54] Standby, no-reservation airplane service, to which the youth fares apply, is by definition this type of service.

[55] On most of these problems, see Bonbright, *op. cit.*, 360–366.

[56] See *ibid.*, 129.

[57] For examples of electricity rates remaining absolutely unchanged for 10 and 15 year periods and a consideration of the reasons for this, see Raymond Jackson, "What Others Think, Rigidity in Electric Rates," *Pub. Util. Fort.* (June 20, 1968), LXXXI: 42–44.

stably as possible, on the basis of some estimated average cost level over some more or less arbitrarily selected planning period—of perhaps five years.[58] In this event, the appropriate benchmark must be some estimated average level of long-run, not short-run marginal costs[59]—and closer approximations to SRMC must be confined largely to (1) incorporation in rate schedules, insofar as prediction is possible,[60] (2) the offer of special rates for interruptible service, and (3) exemption of clearly off-peak pricing from capacity charges.[61]

Yet there all sorts of possible situations in which stability and predictability may be less important than the efficiency advantages of flexible SRMC pricing. With sufficient ingenuity, it is often possible to find ways of practicing it. For example, Smidt has proposed that computers be programmed so as to vary the price of their own service from one five-minute interval to the next, as well as over the life of the equipment, depending on the balance of demand and capacity, with users given considerable choice in specifying in advance

---

[58] An indirect confirmation of the reasonableness of an offer of stability over a more or less arbitrary planning period is provided by the special, short-term arrangements under which the Tennessee Valley Authority and the Bonneville Power Commission sold surplus power to private utilities, in one case under a five-year contract, in the other subject to cancellation on five-year notice if the power were required by municipal distributors and co-ops. See Glaeser, *Public Utilities in American Capitalism*, 499–500, 557. According to officials of AT&T's Long Lines Department, they build capacity when and where needed in the expectation that it will come to be fully used within four to six years. They base prices on average estimated costs for such a period, and on a nationwide basis, because they feel it is entirely infeasible to price flexibly within that period or with reference to local differences in excess capacity. Their system is national in the sense that communications are automatically switched from one route to another depending on which circuits are busy and where there is excess capacity. (See the section on "the national telecommunications network," Chapter 4, Volume 2.) For a finding of ten- and twenty-year (or more) planning horizons for capital budgeting by electric power companies—projections over which are "not . . . taken very seriously"—with five years being "the standard long-term forecast in the industry," and three years "the point at which important practical consequences follow from projections of demand," see Michael Gort, "The Planning of Investment: A Study of Capital Budgeting in the Electric-Power Industry," Part I, *Jour. of Bus.* (April 1951), XXIV: 81–82.

Vickrey defines the proper planning period for which marginal costs are appropriately measured as being determined by the period during which it is anticipated rates will be stable: "The proper time horizon for the cost determination is the

probable interval between rate adjustments." And he would solve the question of the proper size of the incremental block of output, for which LRMC are to be estimated, in a similarly pragmatic way:

"The increment in traffic for which the cost increment is to be estimated should have a composition similar to the increment induced by the rate change under consideration. . . . Thus unless a policy is being contemplated of suppressing a class of service entirely, the traffic increment for which the cost is being ascertained should never be an entire class of traffic, but only a final increment in that traffic corresponding to a realistically contemplated rate change." Testimony in FCC Dockets 16258 and 15011, *In the Matter of American Telephone and Telegraph Company*, Networks Exhibit No. 5, July 22, 1968, mimeo., 23–24.

[59] See Bonbright, *op. cit.*, 331–336.

[60] See some of the challenging suggestions of William Vickrey in Lyle Fitch and Associates, *Urban Transportation and Public Policy* (San Francisco: Chandler Publishing Co., 1964), esp. pp. 146–156; "Pricing in Urban and Suburban Transport," *Amer. Econ. Rev., Papers and Proceedings* (May 1963), LIII: 452–460; and "Pricing Policies," *International Encyclopedia of the Social Sciences* (New York: The Macmillan Co. and The Free Press, 1968), XII: 457–463.

[61] The second and third examples are really only one illustration of the first. Moreover, they are equally examples of LR as of SRMC pricing: the LRMC of definitely off-peak business (and interruptible service is by definition off-peak) includes no capacity costs either. And, it should be noted, (2) and (3) both are aspects of given rate schedules instead of examples of rate *changes* over time. (It is not really the long-distance telephone rate that "changes" at 6:00 P.M.: it is time that changes, moving subscribers from one prescribed rate schedule to another.)

the priority they wish assigned to their jobs and for which they are willing to pay.[62] William Vickrey, one of the most assiduous and ingenious proponents of "reactive pricing," has suggested it could feasibly be applied to long-distance telephoning, tickets for theatrical performances, sporting events, long-distance airplane travel, and electricity. For the first, he would have computers programmed to inform subscribers, immediately on dialing, how much—depending upon the availability of circuits—it would cost them to place that particular call at that particular time, giving them the opportunity then to decide whether the call should be completed. He has proposed that the prices of the theater and airplane tickets might be gradually reduced as the time of performance or departure nears, depending on how much of the space has been sold to customers willing to pay the premium for advance reservation. For electricity, he observes,

". . . the same load signal used by Électricité de France to switch rates according to time of day could be used to vary rates on a reactive basis, simultaneously encouraging the switching on and off of deferrable demands such as water heaters and refrigerators."[63]

He is certainly correct in pointing out that there is no reason in logic or fairness for public authorities to impose tolls on bridges immediately on their completion and take them off when the investment is fully paid off— a practice likely to produce a time pattern of rates just the opposite of what the relation of demand to capacity requires.[64]

Changing Cost Levels: Reproduction Versus Original Capital Costs

Most of the time and energy expended in regulatory proceedings is taken up with recomputing aggregate company revenue requirements, with a view toward adjusting the general rate level to changes in total costs.[65] There is no question of economic principle about the necessity for these efforts: ideally, prices should reflect marginal cost at the time of sale—not at some time in the past.

This consideration constitutes the strongest economic argument for the use of reproduction instead of original cost as the basis for computing capital charges. As proponents of that method of valuation point out, prices in competitive markets will tend to be set at the level that covers current, not past, capital costs. This is a statement of long-run tendency only, to be sure; in periods of rising reproduction costs, it will be achieved only as demand presses to the limits of existing capacity and new investments need to be attracted or old capacity replaced. Still, it represents the competitive ideal, and departures from it in periods of long-run inflation or deflation involve inefficiencies, to the extent that there is any elasticity in demand. These

---

[62] *Op. cit.*, B–581–600.

[63] *Op. cit.*, *International Encyclopedia of the Social Sciences*, XII: 460. See also his "The Pricing of Tomorrow's Utility Services," paper presented at Occidental College, June 1966, processed, and note 29, Chapter 3.

[64] As a result, he observes, in New York City a great deal of traffic over the East River is diverted from the new toll bridges, with comparatively large capacities and ample access facilities, to the clogged, ancient bridges that no longer carry tolls, and dump traffic right in the middle of the most congested areas of the city. *Op. cit.*, *Amer. Econ. Rev., Papers and Proceedings* (May 1963), LIII: 455.

[65] To some extent this is accomplished automatically, as in the purchased-gas and fuel-adjustment clauses incorporated in the tariffs of many distributors of gas and electricity. See Garfield and Lovejoy, *op. cit.*, 146.

distortions may take various possible forms (for simplicity, we assume the situation is one in which reproduction costs exceed book costs):

1. Current costs reflect marginal social opportunity costs. Since under original cost valuation the buyers pay not these, but some lower average as the cost of new, increasingly expensive plant is blended in with that of the old, the result is excessively large purchases of the public utility service and correspondingly excessive flow of resources into its supply.

   This tendency is accentuated when the service competes with unregulated commodities whose prices may behave more nearly according to the competitive norm—railroads with trucks, buses, and private cars, electricity and gas with oil, common carrier transportation and communication with private microwave. Since the competition of these substitutes increases the elasticity of demand for the regulated services, this is only another way of saying that the greater the elasticity of demand, the greater the waste consequent on holding price below marginal cost.

   It might appear that basing prices on historic capital costs would cause offsetting distortions in investment incentives—for example, in periods of rising capital costs discouraging capital expenditures that would otherwise be made. If this were true there would be an underallocation instead of overallocation of resources into regulated industries in periods of inflation. But, as long as the permitted rate of return covers the cost of capital, neither management nor investors need be deterred from making whatever additional investments are required to satisfy the artificially inflated demand. Whatever current dollars are required for the incremental investment enter the original cost rate base, on which the required rate of return is then permitted: as long as additional investments bring in enough additional net revenue to cover the cost of capital, it is in the interest of the company and of its existing stockholders to make the additional investments.[66] The distortion is on the demand, not the supply side.

2. When customers have a choice to buy from one utility company or another, that choice will be determined not solely, as it should be, by their respective marginal costs, but, quixotically, by differences in the average age of their plants, which will produce different average rates. Thus, industry may be impelled to locate where the suppliers of electricity or transportation have a rate base of comparatively old vintage, even though long-run marginal supply costs may actually be higher there than elsewhere.

3. Original rate-base costing tends to produce a perverse cyclical behavior of prices, holding down the charges for utility services when commodity prices generally are rising, and holding them up in periods of general

---

[66] Walter A. Morton, who supports reproduction cost valuation on grounds of fairness, concedes that an original cost earning base need not involve economic inefficiency on this score. "Rate of Return and the Value of Money in Public Utilities," *Land Econ.* (May 1952), XXVIII: 117–118. The statements by M. J. Peck and J. R. Meyer to the contrary in "The Determination of a Fair Return on Investment for Regulated Industries," in *Transportation Economics,* A Conference of the Universities—National Bureau Committee for Economic Research (New York: National Bureau of Economic Research, 1965), 202–203 seem to be incorrect. Actually a company could raise additional capital, within limits, even if the permitted rate of return were below the cost of capital. But since this would dilute the equity of existing stockholders, the company presumably would be reluctant to do so. See note 64, Chapter 2.

price decline. In addition to the inefficient substitution effects of the resulting relative price movements already mentioned, there are adverse macroeconomic consequences because of the high capital-intensity of these industries: holding down their prices and encouraging consumption of their services in periods of general inflation forces them to expand their disproportionately large investment outlays, thus contributing to the excessive levels of aggregate demand. The opposite happens on the downturn.[67]

Although arguments such as these have traditionally been directed toward the question of the proper valuation of the rate base, the same economic principles apply to the computation of depreciation expense and rate of return. What gross cost of capital (depreciation plus return) should be entered into the economically efficient price? Is it the historic cost of the dollars invested in the enterprise at various times in the past? Or the current or future cost of capital? Setting aside the consideration that capital costs as such do not enter at all into the computation of short-run marginal costs, clearly, it is an average of future costs of capital over the planning period that properly belongs in LRMC. Yet the usual formula for capital cost calls for a heterogeneous mixture—composed of depreciation computed by applying some conventional length of time based roughly on past experience to historic investment; a current cost of equity capital, usually estimated over some period in the recent past, and applied to an original-cost rate base; and an actual, historic cost of debt capital, as embodied in existing bond obligations, adjusted to include the cost of any debt planned for incurrence in the near future—all of these plus an inescapable element of "judgment."

This practice is rationalized essentially on the ground that it is the function of regulation to permit companies simply to cover their revenue requirements—to recover the money capital actually invested in the service of the public, to earn a return on investment sufficient to meet their actual debt service obligations, and to attract new equity capital. And it does do these things. It avoids conferring windfall gains on stockholders, such as they would earn in a period of inflation and high interest rates under a system that incorporated in the cost of service the current instead of the (lower) historic cost of debt capital; and it protects them in turn from the windfall losses they would otherwise suffer when interest rates turn down. In so doing, it also protects the credit standing of the company and its ability therefore to serve the public, both of which could be impaired under a reproduction cost system, when current interest rates were much lower than those the company had actually incurred in the past.[68]

But it is precisely the characteristic of competitive markets that they expose stockholders to the possibilities of earning unanticipated, windfall gains and losses, of getting back much more or much less than the dollars they originally invested, or earning much more and much less than the cost of capital on

---

[67] See James R. Nelson, in Shepherd and Gies, *op. cit.*, 71–76. See the classic statement of these various arguments by Harry Gunnison Brown, "Railroad Valuation and Rate Regulation," *Jour. Pol. Econ.* (October 1925), XXXIII: 505–530 and "Railroad Valuation Again: A Reply," *ibid* (August 1926), XXXIV: 500–508; also Willard J. Graham, *Public Utility Valuation,*

Studies in Business Administration, Vol. 4 (Chicago: Univ. of Chicago Press, 1934).
[68] See Bonbright, *op. cit.*, 186–187, 245, 248–249, 278–280. We consider below the opposing argument that such a system does not really treat stockholders fairly for the very opposite reason: that it fails to take into account the changing purchasing power of the dollar.

those dollars. Such markets necessarily expose buyers to prices that vary and fluctuate correspondingly.

These arguments against the use of historic costs can be appraised at various levels. Some of the opposing considerations concede the theoretical validity of the criticisms but deprecate their practical importance; others strike at their theoretical validity as well. Some responses (in addition to the very important considerations of administrative feasibility, already suggested in Chapter 2) argue for the superiority of an original-cost rate base; others emphasize that to fix prices principally by applying a gross cost of capital to a rate base, however valued, is economically unsound and in any case constitutes the minor part of the task of efficient rate making:

1. The actual importance of the case for reproduction costs depends not on principle but on fact. How serious a distortion is created by the lag of prices behind reproduction costs depends on (a) the size of the lag and (b) the elasticity of the demand for public utility services. As for the first, all utility company rate bases are a mixture of vintages; all of them, in growing industies, are heavily weighted by recent expenditures.[69] The difference between the prices produced by original and reproduction cost valuation therefore can easily be exaggerated. As for the second, defenders of original costing have tended to argue that demand is comparatively price-inelastic.[70]

2. The seriousness of the distorting effect also depends on how promptly prices in unregulated markets, and particularly of substitute services, adjust to the long-run competitive equilibrium level. The pervasiveness of market imperfections in the nonpublic utility sectors of the economy (consider for example the cyclical price behavior of such competitors as trucks, cars, buses, and petroleum) suggests that any attempt to fix public utility rates at the purely competitive equilibrium level would produce distortions in the opposite direction. This observation, the reader will recognize, raises once more the problem of the "second best." It suggests the necessity of looking to the prices of specific public utility services in the light of the elasticities of their particular demands, which necessitates in turn a consideration of the price of substitutes and the relationship of those prices to *their* costs, before deciding whether to try to move any of the former closer to the purely competitive level. Since this is an argument as much against marginal-cost pricing in general as against reproduction cost rate bases, we return to it briefly in Chapter 7. But most economists would almost certainly reject any general attempt to make prices in only one sector of the economy highly flexible cyclically.

3. As Justice Brandeis pointed out decades ago, the "reproduction cost" to which prices in purely competitive markets tend to correspond is not the current cost of reproducing the existing plant, brick by brick, but the current cost of producing the *service* with the most modern technology available. It has been the former, not the latter, that public utility

---

[69] See B. W. Lewis, in Lyon, Abramson and Associates, *op. cit.*, II: 689, including the reference in note 134 to Bernstein, *Public Utility Rate Making.*

"For instance, the 1963 A.T.&T. Annual Report shows a net telephone plant investment

of more than 23½ billion dollars in 1963 . . . as against a mere 7¼ billion in 1950. All of the difference, as well as a considerable part of the 7¼ billions, consists of warm *new* dollars. . . ." Lewis, in Shepherd and Gies, *op. cit.*, 237.

[70] See Bauer and Gold, *op. cit.*, 405–413.

commissions have typically been involved in laboriously estimating in reproduction-cost proceedings.[71] In view of the rapid technological progress that has characterized some public utility industries and their tendencies toward long-run decreasing costs (see pp. 124–130), it is by no means clear that reproduction costs correctly defined are typically higher than original costs in periods of moderate inflation.

4. If the reproduction-cost rate base were correctly defined to embody the most recent technology, it would still be anomalous to add together, as is the typical regulatory procedure, capital costs for such a hypothetical new plant and operating expenses actually incurred in some test year in the plant that actually did the producing. If the competitive norm is conceived to be the average total cost of a new plant, using new technology, it is the operating cost of *that* plant that would have to be incorporated in the cost of service.[72]

5. Of course, the proper economic standard is not current average total cost but either short- or long-run marginal cost. The entire concept of determining rates by incorporating some average necessary rate of return on *total investment*, however valued, is a misleading one except in the circumstance that the industry operates under conditions of long-run constant cost. Under any other conditions, the level of cost depends on the level of output, and the latter in turn depends on the price that is set, if demand has any elasticity at all. In these circumstances, the typical method of basing average prices on average current *or* past costs of producing current or past levels of output in some test year[73] becomes

---

[71] See, for example, the listing of the typical methods of estimating reproduction costs in C. F. Phillips, *op. cit.*, 241–242, all of which ,it will be noted, ignore technological progress. For the Brandeis observation, see his famous dissent in *Southwestern Bell Telephone Company of Missouri v. Public Service Commission*, 262 U. S. 276, at 312 (1923); see also J. M. Clark, *Social Control of Business*, 2d ed. (Chicago: Univ. of Chicago Press, 1939), 306–308; and compare H. G. Brown, *op. cit.*, *Jour. Pol. Econ.* (October 1925), XXXIII: 505–530 with John Bauer, "Rate Base for Effective and Non-Speculative Railroad and Utility Regulation," *Jour. Pol. Econ.* (1926), XXXIV: 494–495. As J. R. Nelson aptly observes, "if particular assets are really to be replaced in kind, there must be something wrong with allowing for *any* obsolescence in the annual depreciation charge." Shepherd and Gies, *op. cit.*, 72.

[72] See Charles W. Smith, "Public Utility Depreciation," *Pub. Util. Fort.* (October 23, 1952), L: 630. However, this defect in the application of reproduction cost would disappear if the allowance for depreciation deducted were just sufficient to reflect the obsolescence of the old plant and hence to offset its excessive (by new plant standards) operating costs. See Bonbright, *op. cit.*, 229 and our fuller discussion in the next section of this chapter.

[73] An interesting departure from reliance on a single past test-year has been the informal acceptance by the Federal Communications Commission staff of an accounting system for the Communications Satellite Corporation in which revenue requirements are estimated on the basis of *anticipated* cost experience over a five-year period in the future. This innovation was dictated by the fact that Comsat's rate schedules had to be developed before the company had accumulated any operating experience with its revolutionary new method of communication, and—of particular significance at this point— the elasticities of demand and the prospective future behavior of unit costs made it evident that the company would suffer high operating losses during its initial period of operations under any conceivable system of rates. Congress had instructed the FCC to develop a global system of space communications as rapidly as possible. Had Comsat attempted to set rates high enough to cover the high initial costs of doing so, it would have found itself without customers. Therefore, it and the Commission properly decided that some of these high initial costs were chargeable to later users. (On this principle, see pp. 121–122.) They agreed to amortize some of the developmental costs and preoperating expenses over a ten-year period, using the *reverse* sum-of-the-digits method—that is to say, with heavier depreciation allowances taken in later years than in earlier—in order better to match

hopelessly circular: it offers no indication of what average costs *would be* if some other level of rates were set, leading to some other volume of sales.[74]

Of course, competitive prices do move up and down in correspondence with costs. But they are not determined solely by costs, and certainly not by average total costs, reproduction or historic.[75]

depreciation expenses with the anticipated sharply rising flow of revenues. They envisaged, similarly, that the annual rate of return would be substantially below the ordinary range of reasonableness in the early years of service, and substantially above it in later years. These various understandings, they believed, would permit Comsat to charge rates low enough to induce a rapidly increasing utilization of its large initially installed capacity, thus drastically reducing unit costs over the life of the satellite. See the interesting paper by A. Bruce Matthews, "Problems Posed by Current Regulatory Practices to the Rapid Introduction of Communications Satellite Technology," delivered at a Symposium on the Rate Base Approach to Regulation at the Brookings Institution, June 7, 1968. [74] In a survey of 90 public utility commission decisions over the period from 1937 to 1946, Troxel found that only two indicated any allowance for buyer responses to price changes. "Demand Elasticity and Control of Public Utility Earnings," *Amer. Econ. Rev.* (June 1948), XXXVIII: 372–373. "To achieve better regulatory effects, commissions need studies of demand behavior—any studies." *Ibid.*, 382.

Troxel and, following him, Phillips both argue that regulation should pay closer attention to the marginal instead of the average return on investment—pointing out that efficiency requires firms to invest up to the point at which the return on *incremental*, not average, investment is equated with the cost of capital (k). See Troxel, *Economics of Public Utilities*, 391–395 and C. R. Phillips, *op. cit.*, 300–302. (On the possibility of firms being faced with an increasing cost of capital, where the MC of capital exceeds the average, and the implications of profit-maximizers equating the marginal return with the former instead of the latter, see note 30, Chapter 2, Volume 2. I confess to great difficulty in following their argument.

I can think of three tendencies (in addition to those suggested in the text, above) to which they may be referring when they imply, as they seem to do, that the concentration of regulatory attention on the average return on total investment (however valued) may produce inefficiencies. First, there are times when permitting regulated companies to earn an average return equal at least to k may result in excessively high prices and underutilization of capacity. This would be so in a period of inadequate demand,

when the prospective marginal return on investment is in any event below k, so that the companies would not be making any investments anyhow and would therefore have no economic need or justification (on SRMC-grounds) for earning such returns. This may be what Troxel has in mind when he says:

". . . the marginal rate of return is not the same thing as the cost of capital. Yet utility commissions use current costs of capital to determine the fair rate of return. Either the utility companies pay these borrowing costs, the commissioners say, or no borrowing can be done. True; but the utility company does not borrow unless the marginal rate of return is above the market rates of interest." *loc. cit.*, 392.

The second possible resulting distortion is that regulated companies may undertake investments the marginal return on which is *less* than k—investments that are, therefore, socially undesirable—where they have reason to believe regulation will permit them to recoup the difference in other markets, in order to keep their average rate of return at the legally permissible level. To prevent such investments, regulatory commissions might have to investigate the return on each investment, in order to disallow those that fell short of k. (We discuss this "A–J–W" tendency at length in Chapter 2, Volume 2.)

The third possibility is that the traditional policy may discourage regulated companies from undertaking very risky investments—risky because they offer a strong possibility of heavy losses, but worth undertaking because they offer the possibility also of very high returns—by threatening to take away the gains from a successful venture if it raises the company-wide average return too high. (See pp. 53–54.)

Apart from these three possibilities (and it is by no means clear that these are what they intend) I do not see what the authors have in mind. It is certainly *not* true that regulation prevents companies from attracting whatever additional capital they need for investments on which the marginal return exceeds the cost of capital. See our discussion of this point, p. 110. [75] For an argument that rate base calculations are irrelevant to efficient pricing in the cases of railroads, natural gas, and urban transport, as well as an excellent analysis of the entire reproduction cost rate base issue, see Bonbright, *op. cit.*, 224–237.

Quasi-competitive pricing can be achieved for public utilities only by an explicit and separate consideration of the short- and long-run marginal costs on the one hand, and the intensities and elasticities of demand on the other for each one of their services in each of their markets. The economic and constitutional requirement that investors be given some assurances of a sufficient average return on their investment must, to be sure, exert some influence on these individual pricing decisions, and especially on the level of the entire structure. But, as Melvin de Chazeau has eloquently argued, the valuation of property, which is an essential part of the process of determining an *"earnings* base" for purposes of regulating the return to investors, is of very little use as a *"rate* base"—that is, for the determination of rational individual prices.[76]

This much remains valid in the economic case for a reproduction cost rate base and gross rate of return as an approach to price making: that unless second-best considerations dictate otherwise, and to the extent that prices are to be based on LR instead of SRMC, it is definitely the current and future—not the historic—capital costs that are relevant. But the use of reproduction cost valuation itself makes small contribution to efficient pricing compared with the immense resources that have gone into its support and application. Indeed, to the extent that LRMC are below ATC, because of economies of scale, its contribution could well be negative, even in a period of long-run inflation. The reason for this is that both original and reproduction cost rate base valuation are relevant only to average-cost pricing. If average costs are higher on the latter than on the former rate base, because of inflation, moving to reproduction costs may compound the inefficiency inherent in such pricing, and prices based on average historic costs may therefore come closer to the proper level.[77]

It should be emphasized that the case for reproduction cost does not rest on economic considerations alone. At least equally influential, particularly as a result of the general inflation since 1940, has been the noneconomic argument that reproduction cost valuation is much fairer to utility company stockholders than original cost. To base depreciation charges and return on investment on historic costs during or after a period of inflation is to return to the investors dollars of much lower purchasing power (measured in terms of the cost either of consumer goods and services or of replacing the old capital goods with new, that is, of keeping their capital investment intact in real terms) than the dollars they originally invested.[78]

The concensus of most economists in this matter would seem to be the following:

1. As Ben Lewis has put it, "any scheme of compensation is fair provided only that it was reasonably anticipated at the time of investment."[79] The

---

[76] *Op. cit. Q. Econ. Jour.* (February 1938), LII: 346–359; see, also, essentially in agreement, Bryan and Lewis, *ibid.*, 342–345.

[77] That is, efficiency could require two corrections of prices based on average historic costs in these circumstances—upward because of inflation and downward because LRMC are below ATC. Reproduction cost valuation does only the first of these. In so doing it may push prices far above LRMC; whereas prices based on

average historic costs may come much closer to that level.

[78] See the excellent survey of the arguments on both sides of this issue in Glaeser, *op. cit.*, 315–331, 393–402; and for a strong presentation of the view just summarized, see Morton, *op. cit.*, pp. 91–131.

[79] In Lyon, Abramson and Associates, *op. cit.*, II: 688.

argument here is that as long as investors are informed in advance of whether they will be explicitly protected against inflation (or, by use of an original cost rate base, against deflation), they can in fairness be left to take that fact into account in the prices they pay for the stock at the time of purchase. If, for example, they anticipate inflation, they will presumably pay a lower price per dollar of current earnings for the stock of company A, which promises them no protection, than for company B, whose rate base and/or depreciation are determined on the basis of reproduction cost. In this way they will demand—and get—a percentage yield on their actual investment in A sufficiently higher to compensate for their poorer treatment.

2. By this reasoning, it is *impossible* to compensate *future* stock purchasers for past inflation—they will simply bid up the price of the stock and thereby offset that compensation; or to protect them against future inflation: they will simply compete to pay a higher price for the stock when they buy it, in reflection of this better treatment. And to change the regulatory rules in order to give such compensation to *existing* stockholders would be simply to confer on them a windfall, a higher return on their investment than they had reason to expect when they made it.[80]

3. If the desire is, rather, to compensate existing stockholders because such inflation as has occurred or may occur in the future has exceeded or may exceed their expectations—protecting them against their mistakes—what ethical reason is there to do so for stockholders and not for bondholders? It is only the former who would benefit by increasing the total number of dollars allowed for depreciation or included in the rate base. This seems particularly anomalous when it is stockholders who typically demand and receive the higher return, precisely in order to compensate them for the greater risks they are supposed to bear.

4. If, nonetheless, the government does want to adjust stockholder returns, in the interest of fairness, it can do so just as well and with far less damage to the efficiency of the regulatory process by varying (their part of) the permissible rate of return, or by applying some sort of price index number to the total dollars of permitted net income.[81]

5. Finally, to return to our main theme of whether revaluation of property or investment is necessary in order to assure fair *earnings* to existing stockholders, it makes economic sense as the basis for fixing *prices* only as some sort of average for all services taken together and over a number of years.[82]

---

[80] "The yield on securities cannot be determined [that is, fixed or set] by regulatory fiat in the same manner as the rate of return on invested capital or equity. The best commissions can do with the market is arbitrarily influence the prices of the securities by altering investor expectations and generating windfall gains or losses to those who hold the stock coincidentally with the effectuation of those influences." Morris Mendelson, "The Comparable Earnings Standard: A New Approach," paper presented to the Bell Telephone Co. of Pennsylvania Seminar on the Economics of Public Utilities, June 9, 1967, mimeo., 4–5.

[81] It is difficult to quarrel with Bonbright's observation that employing a reproduction cost rate base is "an absurdly crude device" for remedying this situation, if indeed it calls for a remedy. *Op. cit.*, 189–191.

[82] See de Chazeau, "The Nature of the 'Rate Base' in the Regulation of Public Utilities," *Q. Jour. Econ.* (February 1937), LI: 298–316, the illuminating comment by Robert F. Bryan and Ben W. Lewis, "The 'Earning Base' as a 'Rate Base,'" and the "Reply" by de Chazeau, *ibid.* (February 1938), LII: 335–359. Also see Bonbright, *op. cit.*, 266–276.

Depreciation Policy and Technological Progress

One of the most difficult and interesting problems of rate making in the face of cost changes over time has to do with the appropriate reflection of technological change in determining the depreciation component of cost of service.[83] In view of the immense importance of technological progress for economic welfare it becomes especially important to see to it that cost-of-service determinations are compatible with the optimum adoption of new technology.

The purpose of including an allowance for depreciation in price is to ensure recovery of invested funds over the economic life of the physical capital in which they have been embodied; and of course to see to it that price reflects this authentic economic cost. (We assume, as is the case in most jurisdictions, that the original vs. reproduction cost issue has been resolved in favor of returning the dollars originally invested, no more and no less.) The principal limits on that economic life are wear-and-tear (a user cost) and obsolescence; we confine our attention here to the latter, since, in principle, the former obviously should be included among the other variable costs of production.[84]

It is equally correct to say that the *total* of depreciation charges is supposed to reflect the total decline in the value of the physical asset, from original cost to scrap value—that is to the point where it is just as valuable in the form of scrap as installed production capacity. A familiar question in the public utility literature has been whether the *periodic*—for example, annual—depreciation charges should have the same function—that is, whether they should also reflect as closely as possible the year-by-year decline in that economic value; or whether, instead, they can be nothing more than a conventional and arbitrary mechanism for prorating the total amount to be recovered over the total estimated economic life. We make no effort to resolve that controversy, although it is clear that the latter is surely more accurate than the former as a description of actual practice, considering that (1) rate bases are now typically stated in original costs instead of "fair value,"[85] (2) straight-line depreciation is the method almost universally used,[86] and (3) the rate of decline in economic or market value depends primarily on trends in replacement cost[87] and technological change, whose year-by-year rates are surely irregular and unpredictable. However, some of the most interesting economic questions arise when the rate of decline in market value differs significantly from the depreciation rate actually employed.

What happens if technological change has been unexpectedly rapid? (It is

---

[83] Is it unbearably repetitious to remind the reader again that rate making on the basis of SRMC can ignore the depreciation that is not part of variable cost, but that pricing on the basis of LRMC or ATC must take it explicitly into account?

[84] See pp. 71–73, Chapter 3.

[85] As Bonbright points out, it is anomalous to think of depreciation as measuring decline in market value when one uses an original cost rate base, making no effort to adjust it up or down with the current value of the asset. *Principles of Public Utility Rates*, 194–201.

[86] Eugene F. Brigham, *op cit.*, *National Tax J.* (June 1967), XX: 210.

[87] In a period of inflation the market value of the asset may remain stable or actually rise, despite wear and tear and obsolescence: presumably "economic depreciation" would have to take this offsetting factor into account, so that the book value of the asset (original value less depreciation) would correctly reflect market value at the end of each accounting period. For simplicity we assume constant price levels in this discussion.

this possibility instead of the opposite one that most troubles economists and public utility companies, partly because regulatory commissions have typically been very conservative in the depreciation rates they allow[88] and partly because the discrepancy of inadequate depreciation can have a more seriously distorting effect on pricing and replacement policy.) There is a real danger in this event that replacement of old plant and equipment with new will be uneconomically discouraged. To understand this danger, we must have a brief and simplified look at the economics of replacement.

The way for a company to decide whether to replace a piece of machinery (or plant or other equipment) is to compare the average *variable* cost of producing with it (AVC_0) with the average *total* cost of production with new equipment (ATC_n). Only the variable costs of the old can be saved by turning to the new; the choice therefore is between continuing to incur those AVC, on the one hand, or incurring the ATC—including the capital costs as well—involved in purchasing a new machine. If the AVC_0 are smaller than the ATC_n it is economical to continue to use the old capital goods. But if, *regardless* of the fixed costs on the old, the AVC_0 are the greater, it is foolish not to scrap; every moment of continued production with the old means a greater drain on the company's resources, a greater avoidable cost of production, than would be involved in replacement.[89]

In either event, the continuing, fixed costs on the old equipment—the depreciation that may not yet have been fully recovered, the return on the net investment not yet fully written off, interest on the debt already incurred —are irrelevant to the decision. Sunk costs such as these are bygones, unchangeable past history, and best forgotten. The way to maximize profit is to minimize the variable, or incremental, or avoidable costs of production (since the others are fixed anyway); and that means the variable costs for existing plant and the total costs for new. This is just as true for a monopolist as for a firm operating under pure competition.

But it need not be true for a regulated company. That company cannot ignore the fixed costs on existing assets, because the regulatory commission may or may not choose to include them in its cost of service once the assets have been replaced. Suppose, for example, that the average variable costs under the old process are a constant $7 per unit, the average fixed costs (depreciation and return on the unamortized part of the investment) $3, and the regulated price is $10. Suppose then a new process becomes available with the same capacity as the old, with average variable costs of $4.50 and average fixed costs of $2. Such an investment would be economically efficient; every unit that continued to be produced under the old process (at an avoidable cost of $7) would be involving society as well as the firm in the unnecessary expenditure of 50 cents worth of resources (since the *total* unit

---

[88] In 1964, depreciation expense for large privately owned electric utilities seems to have run at 2 to $2\frac{1}{2}\%$ of gross book investment. Federal Power Commission, *Statistics of Electric Utilities in The U. S., 1964, Privately Owned*, March 1966. The typical depreciation rate for interstate gas pipelines is 3 to $3\frac{1}{2}\%$. Richard W. Hooley, *Financing the Natural Gas Industry* (New York: Columbia Univ. Press, 1961), 66. The FCC prescribed an increase in the rate for the telephone industry from 5.1 to 5.4% effective

January 1, 1968.
[89] This statement ignores the effect on these calculations of the expectation that in the future some even more efficient plant or machine may become available. Such an expectation might justify a company practicing what Fellner has termed "anticipatory retardation"—stalling the replacement of an old machine with a new, in order to await the next, even lower ATC_n that will be available. See note 91.

costs under the new are only $6.50). In an unregulated industry, even a monopolist would make the investment: at the very least, he could produce at the same rate and sell his product at the same price as before, and simply pocket the 50-cent per unit cost saving. Suppose, however, that the company was a regulated utility and that its regulatory commission insisted that the cost savings be more or less promptly translated into price reductions. A price cut to $9.50 would raise no difficulty, apart from possible considerations of risk: the company could continue to obtain the $3 of capital costs on the old equipment plus the $6.50 full unit cost of the new. But the commission might well insist that the old assets be removed from the rate base, once they had been replaced, even though depreciation on them had not yet been fully recovered. It might insist, that is, that the price be reduced to $6.50, the new unit cost of service, thus forcing the stockholders to bear the loss of the unamortized portion of their investment in the old equipment. In this event the company would find itself in a position of having incurred *additional* capital costs of $2 a unit, and yet had its gross return on capital (depreciation and profit) reduced from $3 a unit to $2 a unit. It obviously would have been better for the company to postpone the new investment and continue to take in the $3 per unit of depreciation and return on the old assets until the latter had been completely written off.

What happened in this example was that technological progress had outrun the allowances for depreciation: it reduced the economic value of the old plant to zero (or to its value as scrap) before those assets were wholly written off in the books and the original investment fully recovered from customers. And the moral would seem to be that when this occurs, a regulated company will be deterred from replacing old assets with economically more efficient new ones unless it is permitted to continue to charge customers the capital costs of the unamortized portion of previous investments.[90] These customers may complain, with justice, that they are being made to pay more than the marginal, or indeed the total cost of serving them; that the company is being permitted to recoup from them sunk costs that should have been charged against customers in the past. But they are still better off than if the company refused to install the new, lower-cost equipment for serving them.[91]

---

[90] See Troxel, *Economics of Public Utilities*, 356–369.

[91] There is no well-developed "economics of error"; in the present instance there is no perfect solution of a problem that arises because mistakes have been made in the past. But it should also be emphasized that price will not instantaneously fall to the ATC of the newest and lowest-cost available processes even under perfect competition. As William Fellner has pointed out, rational firms will practice "anticipatory retardation" in the face of a continuous flow of cost-reducing innovations over time. Even pure competitors will not instantly adopt a new technology as soon as the ATC of the latest available process falls below market price. With correct anticipations they will recognize that, since technological progress is continuous, such an investment policy would produce continual disappointment; with further improvements in technology, price would be perpetually slipping below (or, to the extent that the gains of improved productivity are passed on in higher incomes to the factors of production, costs would be perpetually rising above) the levels at which the calculations were made, and investors would therefore continuously fail to make the anticipated return on investment incorporated in the ATC_n. They will therefore systematically delay the introduction of new processes, introducing not the first improvement whose ATC is below current market price but one later on in the flow of improvements, waiting until the return from cost savings promises to be sufficiently high in the early years of life of the new equipment to offset the eroding away of those gains as still later techniques become available—until, that is, it appears they will be able to earn the anticipated depreciation and return over the life of the new plant. So purely competitive price remains on

It could be argued, instead, that the costs of mistakes such as these ought to be borne by the stockholders. It is their function, not that of consumers, to bear the risks of unanticipatedly rapid obsolescence; their rate of return ought to be high enough to compensate for such risks. The argument would not be wrong, in principle. But by the same reasoning the allowable rate of return of public utilities is kept typically below that in industry generally precisely because stockholders share these risks with consumers; what consumers would gain by a different treatment of depreciation in these circumstances they would lose by having to pay a higher return.[92] Moreover, allowable depreciation is usually determined by the regulatory authorities: if it proves *ex post* to have been inadequate, it is not clear that the burden is properly borne by stockholders.[93] Here again is reflected the conception that regulation should in the face of change and uncertainty permit public utility companies to cover their authorized revenue requirements—not more and not less—rather than treat them as they would be treated by a competitive market. Finally, there remains the basic problem that putting the burden on stockholders would discourage economically efficient replacement of obsolete assets.[94]

---

the average sufficiently above the total unit costs under the latest available technique to permit investors on the average to write off old plant and earn the required return on its undepreciated portion. William Fellner, "The Influence of Market Structure on Technological Progress," in Amer. Econ. Ass'n, *Readings in Industrial Organization and Public Policy* (Homewood: Richard D. Irwin, 1958), 287–291. This is precisely what the recommended public utility commission treatment of depreciation and return on undepreciated, replaced equipment would accomplish: by holding price above ATC_n it would permit recovery of the fixed costs of the old. The danger, then, would not be that utility companies would be unduly discouraged from introducing new techniques but that they would be encouraged in this manner to inflate their rate bases, being permitted by their commissions to recover investment in the old and to earn a return on the new even though the latter was unneeded. On this "A–J–W" danger, see Chapter 2, Volume 2.

[92] This consideration does not fully dispose of the argument. It might still be that efficiency would be better served by having risks of this kind borne in the overall rate of return than in continued amortizations of incompletely depreciated, obsolete assets: the incidence of these two methods would almost certainly differ, depending on how precisely the amortization was effected.

[93] But see note 94. "In a non-regulated competitive industry, market forces will punish those investors who select managers who have incorrectly foreseen the rate of technological advance. . . .

"In a regulated industry with only one or two suppliers, however, society can not afford the disruptive effects on supply which the market discipline enforces for inevitable errors of foresight. . . .

"Regulation should not, of course, provide an umbrella for all errors of managerial judgment; however, it appears to me that a consistently used current cost base might reduce the willingness of investors to provide capital funds . . . *unless* management slows down the rate of technological change to one that is more readily predictable and is in line with past investment decisions embedded in existing durable equipment." Testimony of Paul Davidson, in FCC, *In the Matter of American Telephone and Telegraph Co.*, Docket 16258, Western Union Exhibit 4, 1968, mimeo., 71–76.

[94] It is very largely the fear of unanticipatedly rapid technological obsolescence that apparently explains the recent tendency of regulated companies to press for higher allowable rates of depreciation—a tendency that might otherwise be difficult to understand, since higher depreciation expense means a more rapid diminution of the rate base. (See note 32, Chapter 2, Volume 2.) This fear is intensified where the utility companies face the competition of companies that have access to the newer technology and are unencumbered by the costs of older, incompletely amortized plant—a situation that has prevailed in communications in recent years. See the discussion in Chapter 4 of Volume 2, especially around notes 94–96.

On the other hand, the utilities are themselves responsible in part for these difficulties. Many of them have resisted the adoption of more rapid depreciation, with its attendant income tax advantages, precisely in order to avoid the more rapid decline in rate base that this would have

Therefore, if technological progress outstrips depreciation, and regulated companies are permitted to recover their as-yet unamortized investment in obsolete facilities, prices will exceed LRMC. This will be true even under conditions of constant costs, when LRMC equals ATC_n. The source of the discrepancy is the difference between ATC computed so as to include gross return on a historic rate base and ATC_n. If the rate of depreciation accurately reflects the year-by-year decline in the economic value of existing assets no such discrepancy can occur: ATC on a historic rate base will be the same as ATC_n. The reason for this is that the economic value of existing assets at any given time is, precisely, the current value of the differences between AVC_0 and ATC_n over their remaining life (or their value as scrap, whichever is larger). As long as AVC_0 is less than ATC_n, the plant clearly has positive value, measured by the cost-saving that continued use makes possible. Once those two are equal, the old plant has zero value (for purposes of production; it may have positive scrap value). If the economic value were correctly stated on the books, the addition of gross return on that net book value to the variable costs of operating the old plant would produce a cost of service exactly equal to that of a new plant.[95]

The same end would be achieved by using a true current value rate base. But it is not the calculation of a reproduction cost rate base, as such—with all the administrative travail and expense that this has traditionally involved—that is the goal. Instead the goal is to estimate the cost of reproducing the service, with current technology. In principle, this can be achieved just as well by following an economically realistic depreciation policy, applied to original cost. In practice, the task of predicting obsolescence is likely to be a difficult one: but so has been the use of reproduction cost.

Clearly the charging of depreciation raises interesting and difficult questions of who should pay what share of capital costs over time. We have already posed the question of the proper rate when a plant is built far in advance of total need—perhaps because there are great economies of scale. To charge depreciation in equal annual installments would be to impose a disproportionately heavy burden on customers in earlier years, when much of the capacity lies idle. Considerations of fairness—the idle capacity is really for the benefit of future, not present customers—and economic efficiency present a case for something similar to SRMC pricing, which would have the effect of concentrating the capital charges in later years.[96]

Precisely the opposite course is suggested with respect to an investment required to meet current needs, but which may be expected to become rapidly

---

entailed. They did so feeling secure in their monopoly positions and their ability to continue earning an acceptable return on the larger investment. They have resisted also for fear of being forced by regulatory commissions to flow through the resulting tax benefits in the form of lower rates—a practice that does expose them to the possibility of higher tax liabilities and consequently reduced earnings in the future, and the necessity of asking for rate increases at that time. See pp. 32–34, above, and the excellent "Comment" by William H. Melody in Trebing and Howard, *op. cit.*, pp. 164–175,

which concludes: "The long-run viability of utilities in some markets that are subject to external competitive pressures may well depend upon the maintenance of a depreciation policy that properly reflects the rate of economic depreciation in an environment of rapid technological change."

[95] The preceding discussion draws heavily on the testimony of Vickrey in FCC, *In the Matter of American Telephone and Telegraph Co.*, Docket 16258, mimeo., esp. 53–56.

[96] See the example of Comsat, note 73, p. 113, note 4, p. 88, and p. 104.

outmoded by new technology already on the horizon.[97] In this instance, the investment should be written off rapidly, however long its physical life is likely to be, in reflection of the early anticipated decline in its economic value. The effect would be to put the heaviest capital charges on customers now and in the immediate future—and properly so, since it is for their benefit that the capacity is being built now instead of later, when it could embody the lower cost technology. Such higher charges might well restrict demand sufficiently to demonstrate that the investment in question would better be postponed until the new technology was perfected. The opposite course—to charge depreciation only at the modest rate dictated by average historic experience—would result in charging future users much more than LRMC: they would be stuck with the costs of writing off the inadequately depreciated and obsolete older equipment. And the effect in this event would be to discourage the introduction of the new technology, because demand at that later time would be restrained by the inefficiently high price for the services, "rolling-in" the excessive ATC of the old, inadequately depreciated assets with the much lower ATC of the new.[98]

Manifestly, the rate at which depreciation is charged can have important effects on technological progress. And although it is an impossible task to estimate the proper rate in advance, as Vickrey states,

". . . even a rough approximation to the inclusion of such an analysis in the rate making process is to be preferred to sticking to a fundamentally erroneous approach."[99]

---

[97] This example also depends heavily on the Vickrey testimony, *ibid.*, 27 and 56–60.

[98] Considerations of this type were apparently central to the controversy within the FCC that eventuated in 1968 in its authorizing AT&T to lay a submarine cable between the United States and Spain. In the dissenting opinion of Commissioner Johnson the cable project played the role of supplying the additional capacity (questionably) required in the near future, with current technology, and the satellite the role of the superior technology of the future (indeed, he felt, of the present). Commissioners Cox and Loevinger asserted, in support of the FCC decision, that:

". . . satellites are not now, and will not for at least the next 5 to 7 years be, the most economic means of providing international communications service."

But, Johnson asserted:

"Of course, by depreciating the cable over *twenty* years it appears that the per-year cost of the cable is lower than the per-year additional satellite cost over its projected *five*-year life. The point is that . . . neither will be needed as insurance for more than five years." FCC 68–212, 12514, letter from Rosel H. Hyde, Chairman, to Richard R. Hough, Vice President, American Telephone and Telegraph Company, and accompanying Concurring Statement of Commissioners Cox and Loevinger and Dissenting Opinion of Commissioner Johnson, February 16, 1968.

[99] *Op. cit.*, FCC Docket 16258, 59.

CHAPTER 5

Decreasing Costs and Price Discrimination

The marginal cost pricing principle justifies, at the extreme, a separate price for every sale. The marginal costs of serving no two customers are identical, except by chance; and those costs will fluctuate from one instant to the next as output moves up and down along the SRMC production curve and as the price necessary to clear the market fluctuates similarly with the changing balance of demand and capacity. Or, tempering that principle with the others we have already discussed, it justifies an elaborate system of rate *differentials* for the various categories of service, corresponding to their different (approximate) marginal costs, even if the entire structure is held constant for substantial periods of time. But it does not justify rate *discrimination*—that is, charging different purchasers prices that differ by varying proportions from the respective marginal costs of serving them. On the contrary, charging any customer more or less than the marginal cost of serving him violates the dictates of economic efficiency, for reasons we have already set forth.

THE OCCASIONS FOR DISCRIMINATION

One of the virtues of pure competition is that it eliminates the possibility of price discrimination. The more necessitous buyer does not have to pay more than the less, the rich more or less than the poor; no one, however inelastic his demand, can be exploited by sellers with monopoly power—which is, precisely, the power to hold price above marginal cost. And in long-run equilibrium, the seller can have no *need* to discriminate in price, although he would find it profitable to do so if he could: when capacity is properly adjusted to the level of demand, the price to all buyers can be at SRMC and at the same time cover ATC, as our Figure 1 (p. 74) illustrates.

But this coincidence of SRMC and ATC is possible only if the firm is not operating on the declining portion of its ATC curve. Only when ATC is at its lowest point are the two equal. In fact, the public utility industries are preeminently characterized in important respects by decreasing unit costs— or increasing returns—with increasing levels of output. That is indeed one important reason why they are organized as regulated monopolies: a "natural monopoly" is an industry in which the economies of scale—that is, the tendency for average costs to decrease the larger the producing firm—are continuous up to the point that one company supplies the entire demand. It is a reason, also, why competition is not supposed to work well in these industries.[1]

The Nature and Prevalence of Decreasing Costs

The phenomenon of decreasing costs, or increasing returns, has three possible aspects that must be kept quite distinct, in principle. The first is short-run decreasing costs, which reflects the familiar fact that once an investment has been made to provide a productive capacity (recall our definition of the short run as the period in which the firm operates with a given capacity already in being), total unit costs of production decline as output increases up to or almost up to the physical limits of capacity operation. Any plant and equipment will be designed for some level of production at which total unit costs will be at their lowest point. As output increases to that point, the fixed costs are spread over a larger and larger number of units. (Up to a point variable costs per unit will probably decline also, as the number of workers and the amount of raw material and other variable inputs approximate the level for which the operation was designed.) In view of the heavy fixed costs of most public utility operations and the tendency for companies to build capacity in advance of demand—partly because of the economies of building in large units and partly because of their obligation to supply a service that cannot in most cases be stored but can only be produced on demand—excess capacity and short-run decreasing costs as output expands, at least in certain dimensions,[2] are pervasive.

The second is long-run decreasing costs (LRDC). In many aspects of public utility operations, there are great economies of scale, in the sense that the larger the plant constructed or the larger the unit of additional capacity put into operation, the lower will be its unit costs if operated to the capacity for which it has been designed. Long-run, like short-run decreasing costs, as the economist uses the term, is a static phenomenon: with *given* technology, at any *given* point in time, the utility has before it the possibility of constructing larger or smaller capacities or additions thereto;[3] and, at least in certain aspects of production or distribution, its engineers will tell it that the unit costs of the larger capacities will be less than of the smaller, if operated at optimum rates. It is LRDC that constitute the justification for considering some public utility operations "natural monopolies."

We make no effort here to summarize the evidence of the extent to which the various public utility industries do operate under long-run decreasing

---

[1] See the fuller analysis of these two rationalizations of the public utility institution in Chapters 4 and 5, Volume 2.

[2] One source of confusion in characterizing the cost tendencies in any industry is that "output" is not unidimensional. As we shall see, increased sales of electricity, gas, and telephone services to existing customers will almost certainly be subject to at least short-run decreasing costs, whereas extension of service to additional customers (another possible "expansion of output") might well exhibit the opposite tendency. See the discussion along the same lines with respect to long-run costs, immediately following.

[3] The purest case of LRDC prevails when a firm begins with an absolutely clean slate and faces a "planning curve" demonstrating the unit costs of different planned levels of output, each in a plant constructed in order to produce *that* output at minimum cost. But most firms carry with them into new investment decisions the consequences of investment decisions made in the past. They also will face an LRDC situation when and if additional output would reduce ATC (entirely apart from changes in technology) or involve lower unit costs the greater the addition to output.

costs, other than to observe that the phenomenon is widespread and important. It should be emphasized that they may in certain respects but not in others. For example, the telephone business is said to be subject to long-run increasing costs, when the dimension of output is taken to be the number of subscribers, because as that number increases the number of required connections in the central exchange increases more than proportionately.[4]

On the other hand, telephone capacity costs *per message* almost certainly decline within very wide limits as the number of messages per subscriber are increased. In the same way electricity distribution costs per customer may well increase with increased urban sprawl, that is, with increased average distance between customers; the same is probably true of the distribution of gas and water and the supply of urban transit. But electric generating costs, and electric and gas distribution costs and the costs per passenger over existing routes decline sharply per customer and per unit of sales in any given area.[5] The distribution cost of serving an all-electric house is said to be probably no more than 10 to 15% higher than for the average residence, though its average electricity consumption may run five or six times as much.

The long-distance telephone business provides striking illustrations of these static economies of scale. Table 1 summarizes the estimated costs of providing

table 1 Illustrative Costs for TD2 Radio Relay Systems per Repeater Station

Voice Grade Circuit Capacity	Total Costs	Average Costs per Circuit	Additional Circuits	Incremental Costs per Circuit
600	$368,000	614	600	614
3,600	$492,000	137	3,000	41
6,000	$574,000	96	2,400	34

Source. Testimony of Albert M. Froggatt, FCC Docket No. 16258, *op. cit.*, Bell Exhibit 24. May 31, 1966, Table I.

a particular facility for transmitting various types of messages via microwave radio, with varying alternative capacities, supplied by an AT&T vice-president testifying before the FCC. There are certain common, starting-up costs totaling $368,000 that must be incurred whether the planned capacity is 600 or 6,000 circuits—the costs of the land, tower, building and access roads, maintenance equipment, and so forth. If capacity is planned for only the 600 channels, the average cost per circuit is $614; if 6,000 circuits, the average cost falls to $96. If the average cost falls in this fashion, it must be that the incremental costs of adding circuits fall even more sharply, or at least remain below the average within this range of output. The first increment of 600 costs $614. The cost is only $124,000 to add the next 3,000 circuits: this gives an incremental cost of $41 per circuit. To move from 3,600 to 6,000 circuits adds another $82,000, for an incremental cost of $34.

---

[4] David G. Tyndall, "The Relative Merits of Average Cost Pricing, Marginal Cost Pricing and Price Discrimination," *Q. Jour. Econ.* (August 1951), LXV: 369. But see the section "Cases of apparently increasing costs," in Chapter 4, Volume 2.

[5] See, for example, Ralph Turvey, *Optimal Pricing and Investment in Electricity Supply* (London: George Allen and Unwin, Ltd., 1968), 70–72.

William Iulo finds that consumption per residential customer is the single most important determinant of intercompany cost differences. Its sign is negative: the greater the former the lower the costs per unit. *Electric Utilities—Costs and Performance* (Pullman: Washington State Univ. School of Economics and Business, 1961), 102–107.

This example illustrates also some of the ambiguities of the concept of long-run decreasing costs. Although what it describes is a long-run, planning phenomenon—the costs of supplying varying capacities—the increasing returns within the 600 to 6,000 range may be construed instead as illustrating only short-run decreasing costs. ATC declines because certain investment outlays have to be made merely to provide the 600 circuits. These outlays create capacity that can then be spread over the next 5,400. Since the average utilization of these repeater stations was said to be only 3,500 circuits or so, as of 1967, do we not have here a mere illustration of the (short-run) tendency of ATC to decline in the presence of excess capacity? The point is that tendencies to increasing returns, of both varieties, are created basically by the presence of indivisibilities. The cost of clearing land, digging trenches (for gas or water mains and oil or gas pipelines), putting up telephone and electric poles, putting a telephone and a gas, electricity, or telephone line and a meter into a customer's home or place of business are an inescapable, indivisible burden of installing any capacity at all. What creates economies of scale is that these indivisible outlays then can be used to provide greater or lesser capacities and a greater amount of service by supplementary investments and variable expenses that will increase total cost less than proportionately. That is what makes it inefficient to have more than one supplier. As long as the market demand is less than the ultimate total that can be provided in this way, the firm is operating on the declining portion of its long-run as well as its short-run average cost curve; LRMC are below LRAC.[6]

---

[6] Moreover, according to Froggatt, the economies of scale are not exhausted at the 6,000-circuit capacity. If it became necessary to add successive increments of circuits, the average total cost would rise as the company passed each multiple of 6,000, but each time to a level below the ATC of the preceding 6,000, because, once again, some of the same facilities could be used for the larger number of messages.

For other attempts to determine over how wide a range of plant or firm size static economies of scale prevail in various regulated industries, see George H. Borts, "The Estimation of Rail Cost Functions," *Econometrica* (January 1960), XXVIII: 108–131 (LRAC increasing in the Eastern U.S., decreasing or constant in the West and South); Kent T. Healy, *The Effects of Scale in the Railroad Industry*, Committee on Transportation (New Haven: Yale Univ. Press, 1961), 3 (costs turn up beyond a range of 10,000–19,000 employees); Zvi Griliches, "Notes on Railroad Cost Studies," University of Chicago, Center for Mathematical Studies in Business and Economics, Report 6918, June 1969 (few economies of scale once the very small roads are eliminated); J. Johnston, *Statistical Cost Analysis* (New York: McGraw-Hill, 1960), 44–73 (LRAC for electricity generation in U.K. plants in 1946–1947 was L-shaped—that is, beyond a point, there were no more economies of scale); Marc Nerlove, "Returns to Scale in Electricity Supply," in Carl

Christ et al., *Measurement in Economics* (Stanford: Stanford Univ. Press, 1963), 167–198 (LRAC for the firm first declines, then shows a mixed picture at the upper reaches of firm size); Ryutano Komiya, "Technical Progress and the Production Function in the U.S. Steam Power Industry," *Rev. Econ. Stat.* (May 1962), XLIV: 156–166 (continuously increasing returns to scale within the observed range); Yoram Barzel, "Productivity in the Electric Power Industry," *ibid.* (November 1963), XLV: 401–403 (strong economies of scale in generating plant size and consumption per customer); Phoebus J. Dhrymes and Mordecai Kurz, "Technology and Scale in Electricity Generation," *Econometrica* (June 1964), XXXII: 287–315 (LRAC decreasing); Leslie Cookenboo, Jr., *Crude Oil Pipelines and Competition in the Oil Industry* (Cambridge: Harvard Univ. Press, 1955), 8–32 (LRAC declining up to pipelines carrying 400,000 barrels per day); Johnson in Shepherd and Gies, *op. cit.*, 121–124 (economies of scale in communications satellites); and, on natural gas pipelines, see note 33, Chapter 4. The statistical findings are inevitably dependent on the particular dimension of output selected. As Griliches points out, his negative findings do not exclude the likelihood of decreasing average costs

". . . for some types of traffic, at some times, in some areas. But all the studies examined ask the

The third aspect of decreasing costs in public utilities must be handled with special care because as usually conceived it is not a phenomenon of decreasing costs at all. This is the decline in ATC *over time* as a result of technological progress. Most public utilities can be sure that unit costs will decline over time, unless the tendency is offset by inflation in the economy at large; a plant constructed ten years from now will be much more efficient than a plant constructed today. In most utility operations, the technology is so dynamic that it is highly probable real costs fall more rapidly than in most other sectors of the economy.[7]

In principle, dynamically decreasing costs, in consequence of technological progress, are clearly distinguishable from statically decreasing costs, both long- and short-run. Technological progress does not in itself mean that a larger output can be produced at lower ATC than a smaller output; that there are economies of scale; or, therefore, that MC are less than ATC. It could simply lower the ATC function at all levels of output, for all sizes of firm, and still leave the relation of MC to ATC unchanged. But in practice, the two phenomena may be causally intertwined.[8] Technological progress may either *involve* or *reflect* genuine increasing returns in one of two possible ways. First, the technological advance may be of a type that embodies or gives rise to static economies of scale. (Or it may do the opposite.) Second, the technological advance may itself be *induced* by the higher levels of demand or output—that is, it may not be truly independent of the increase in output. If the need for higher levels of output either *calls forth* or makes it economical *to put into practice* technological advances *that would not otherwise be induced or feasible*, then it is reasonable to consider that the reduction in cost (over time) was in fact a consequence of the higher level of output, hence reflected increasing returns in the strict sense of the term.

Because the relationship of technological change to the level of output is far more difficult to specify, predict, or prove than static relationships of cost to different levels of planned output with a given, known technology or set of technical alternatives, this type of "economy of scale" is not usually embraced within the economist's conception of increasing returns. But it is in principle identical, and in the real, dynamic world may be even more important than the others.

Two illustrations will dramatically demonstrate the possible gains from rapid technological progress in the public utilities and indicate its possible

---

question what will happen to average costs if total traffic is expanded on the *average* in the same proportions and having exactly the same distribution over the various commodities, types, routes and seasons as the previously handled traffic. There may be very little return to scale from a *proportionate* increase in all kinds of traffic." *Op. cit.*, 30.

For a strong argument that the railroad cost studies measure economies of scale "in a manner that is totally irrelevant to the special economics of the transportation industry," and in no sense undermine the presence of substantial economies of scale for increases in "the volume of traffic in a given area or along a given corridor," see William Vickrey, "Current Issues in Trans-

portation," unpublished manuscript, undated. See also note 87, Chapter 6, Volume 2.

[7] See Chapter 3, Volume 2. This means that if input prices rise only in proportion to the rise in average productivity in the economy at large—a general condition of average price-level stability implied in the wage-price guidelines (note 27, Chapter 1)—money unit costs in public utilities would be expected to fall over time.

[8] The classic statement on the difficulty (he would have said meaninglessness) of distinguishing the two is J. H. Clapham, "Of Empty Economic Boxes," *Econ. Jour.* (1922), XXXII: 305–314, reprinted in American Economic Association, *Readings in Price Theory*, 119–130.

causal connection with decreasing costs, strictly defined. The size of electrical generating units commissioned in Great Britain rose from 30 megawatts in 1950 to 550 megawatts in 1963. And the capital costs per kilowatt sent out declined from £67 to £37 in the same period—and this in the face of a very substantial increase in the general price level.[9] In the United States, the largest generating unit in operation in 1930 had a capacity of 208,000 kw; in 1956, the largest was 260,000 kw; and by 1965, only nine years later, a 1,000,000 kw unit was placed in service. Transmission voltages have shown a similar growth curve, with correspondingly dramatic effects on the distances over which it is feasible to transport power and on the opportunities for economies from large-scale generation and power pooling.[10] A reflection of these developments has been the decline in annual operating expenses of privately owned companies from a peak of 8.95 mills per kwh in 1948 to 6.56 in 1966—in the face of a 17% increase in the wholesale price index.[11] The electricity case seems clearly to be one in which dramatic technological advances have greatly increased the economies of large and geographically coordinated operations.[12]

A different example, in which the expansion of demand has clearly played an important causal role in inducing technological advance, is provided by long-distance communication in the last few decades. The same AT&T testimony that provided the basis for Table 1 supplied a chart showing the book costs per circuit route mile of the company's Long Lines Department between 1930 and 1965: the figure starts at $217 and drops continuously—to $158 in 1940, $78 in 1945, $40 in 1955 and $25 in 1965.[13] These unit cost figures, observed as the circuit route mile capacity of the system grew, almost certainly do not reflect simply a static, unchanging $LRAC_{\text{'30--'65?}}$ curve as shown in our purely illustrative Figure 5—in which event plants built at any time during that period would have had ATC's like $SRAC_1$ and $SRAC_2$, depending solely on their size. All we have is a series of observations, at different points in time, of various book costs associated with various levels of capacity and output (marked with X's). This historical experience reflected a mixture of causal influences.

1. To some extent the decline in costs could have had nothing to do with the scale of operations. That is, costs might have declined whatever the level of output: the 1930 observation might have been a point on the $LRAC_{\text{'30?}}$ indicated in the figure, the 1940 observation on a lower $LRAC_{\text{'40?}}$ and so on. If this horizontal set of hypothetical cost curves is the true one, the net book cost could have been $25 per circuit route mile in 1965 for a company $\frac{1}{2}$, $\frac{1}{10}$, or $\frac{1}{100}$ the size of AT&T, as suggested by the alternative $SRAC_a$ and $SRAC_b$.

[9] Andrew Shonfield, *Modern Capitalism: The Changing Balance of Public and Private Power* (New York: Oxford Univ. Press, 1965), 49 note.
[10] Federal Power Commission, *National Power Survey*, Washington, 1964, Part I, 14, and *Steam Electric Plant Construction Costs and Annual Production Expenses* (annual).
[11] The expenses are for all departments combined —production, transmission and distribution, customer accounting and collecting, sales and administrative. Derived from Edison Electric Institute, *Historical Statistics of the Electric Utility Industry* (New York, 1963) and id., *Statistical Yearbook of the Elec'ric Utility Industry* for 1966 (New York, 1967); and (for the WPI) *Statistical Abstract of the United States, 1968* (Washington, 1968), 341.
[12] See also the studies referred to in note 6, and, for a discussion of the institutional implications of these developments, the section "The imperfect adaptation of business structure: electric power," in Chapter 2, Volume 2.
[13] A. M. Froggatt, *op. cit.*, Chart 4. The backup table provided by the company.

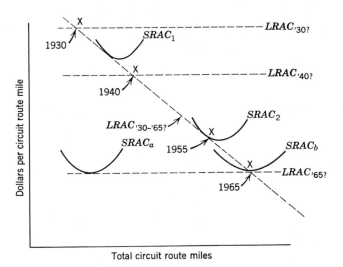

Figure 5. Alternative hypothetical explanations of the decline in book costs of circuit route miles.

2. To some extent it probably reflected *SRDC*—simply a fuller use of capacity, particularly in the first 15 years. During World War II this fuller use also involved some degradation of the quality of service, so that the decline in money costs shown for that period is in some degree misleading.

3. To an important extent it also reflected genuine static economies of scale of the familiar kind: that is, the static *LRAC* functions in 1930, 1945, and 1965 all were undoubtedly negatively sloped, for reasons we have already suggested, though certainly not over the entire range suggested by the *LRAC* $_{30-'65?}$ curve depicted in Figure 5. The 1930 system used poles with open wire: once the poles were up, added wires could be attached with a less than proportionate increase in costs. Then the company used cables; the cost of a cable with 100 pairs of wires is less than twice as much as one with 50. Similar economies of scale were available in the subsequent systems, using successively coaxial cable, microwave radio, and larger coaxial cables.

4. It involved static economies of scale in yet another sense: with higher levels of demand, it became economically feasible to use preexisting technology whose *ATC* would be lower only if the market were large enough to justify its emplacement.

5. The preceding aspect merges with the dynamic one: higher levels of demand *stimulated* the company to develop the new technologies in order to meet the burgeoning needs. When telephone company officials point out that coaxial cable, costing $100,000 a mile, would have been prohibitively expensive in the past and became economical only when hundreds of thousands of circuits were required, they are talking about a mixture of 4 and 5, probably more the latter than the former. But in any event they are describing a genuine phenomenon of decreasing cost—a larger output involving lower unit costs than a smaller one.

Therefore, we have three types of decreasing cost situations in the public utility industries: SRDC, in the presence of excess capacity; LRDC, or static economies of scale; and that part of technological progress that is causally attributable to the increase in volume. All three mean that the more rapidly output expands, the lower unit costs will be. And this means in turn that incremental or marginal costs, both short- and long-run, to the extent that these tendencies prevail, will be less than average total costs. (See, for example, Figure 1, in which this condition prevails at all outputs less than Q_e. Or see Figure 6.)

Implications and Solutions

The consequence is that in all such situations we encounter a flat contradiction between these two fundamental rules: one, that price *to all buyers* be equated with marginal costs and two, that total revenues cover total costs. (If marginal cost is less than the average total cost per unit, and prices are set at the former level, total revenues will be less than total costs.)

Some economists have resolved this conflict by preferring the first to the second principle. If following the rule of equating price to marginal cost means that total revenues fall short of total costs, their solution would be to make up the difference out of taxpayer-financed subsidies. Governments have in fact adopted this solution with respect to numerous "public goods" —the technical definition of which is that the marginal cost of making them available to an additional user is zero.[14] They have also subsidized the provision of public utility services in various ways. But these subsidies are not usually explicitly justified or justifiable by, or systematically related to, the discrepancy between marginal and average costs. Consider, for example, the fact that commercial barge and shipping lines are not charged for the costs of maintaining the inland waterways or that large, diesel-burning trucks apparently do not pay the *marginal* highway costs for which they are causally responsible. On the other hand, the subsidized interest rate for rural electricity cooperatives might have some such justification, in whole or in part. But since governments do not usually follow this practice with respect to privately owned utilities, we devote no more attention to this way out of the conflict.[15]

---

[14] See note 102, Chapter 1, Volume 2.

[15] Economists have long been arguing the theoretical correctness and the practicability of marginal-cost pricing plus public subsidies in circumstances such as these, a debate we make no effort to summarize or resolve here. Our failure to pursue this possibility is grounded mainly on the practical considerations that governments in the United States at least do not follow it with respect to privately owned utilities and that there would be considerable political objection to having taxpayers subsidize users of the service as a general practice. This latter consideration illustrates the limited qualifications of economists for advocating schemes of this sort; the resort to taxpayer-financed subsidies inevitably involves in practice some redistribution of income, from taxpayers to users of the services. As we have already indicated, economic theory alone cannot state in such circumstances that the one result is

"better" than the other. (And this of course raises also the noneconomic consideration that it may strike voters and legislators as unfair.)

Even if we confine our attention to considerations of economic efficiency, our advocacy of tax-financed subsidies to permit marginal-cost pricing must confront the anomaly of

"reliance on the tax system to adjust divergences between average cost and marginal cost despite the fact that the tax system itself is the greatest example of nonmarginal cost pricing." Eli W. Clemens, "Discussion," *Amer. Econ. Rev., Papers and Proceedings* (May 1963), LIII: 482.

Except for levies on pure economic rents, there are practically no neutral taxes, no taxes, that is, that do not in one way or another distort the functioning of a price system. Individual excise taxes alter the relationship between price and cost, hence artificially discourage the con-

There is another solution, even more acceptable in principle (for the reasons indicated in note 15) that comes closer to the one that is feasible for unsubsidized, privately owned utility companies: perfect price discrimination. The entire justification for marginal cost pricing lies in the elasticity of demand—the fact that customers will buy more or less than the optimum amount if price is lower or higher than marginal cost. More satisfactions are conferred on buyers than are taken away from sellers when prices are reduced to marginal cost; producers can be spared losses greater than the buyer satisfactions sacrificed if prices that are below marginal costs are raised to that level.[16] What if, then, the seller could segregate each purchase by each customer, charging him for that particular purchase as much as he is willing to pay, charging less and less as necessary to bring in additional purchasers or to induce existing buyers to take additional units, finally down to marginal costs for those purchases that will not be made at any higher

---

sumption of the taxed commodities compared with others; and general excise taxes affect the decisions of households to spend on consumption or to save. Income taxes are taxes on work, saving, and investing; so they too introduce an extraneous consideration into those decisions.

See Richard A. Musgrave, *The Theory of Public Finance, A Study In Public Economy* (New York: McGraw-Hill, 1959), 140–159, and for a survey of some of the literature, Nancy Ruggles, "Recent Developments in the Theory of Marginal Cost Pricing," *Rev. Econ. Studies* (1949–1950), XVII: 110–111, 119; also Robert W. Harbeson, "A Critique of Marginal Cost Pricing," *Land Econ.* (February 1955), XXXI: 54–74. In short, the problem would be one of weighing the benefits of a closer approach to economically efficient pricing made possible by these subsidies against the possible departure therefrom involved in the taxes required to finance them.

This consideration obviously weakens the *general* economic case for marginal-cost pricing plus tax-financed subsidy of utility services, but it does not destroy it, as many economic theorists sometimes suggest. It calls instead for a factual judgment of benefits and costs in each individual case. See, for example, the very useful survey in Little, *A Critique of Welfare Economics*, Chapter 11, which begins with a general rejection of marginal-cost pricing and then proceeds to indicate a wide range of services for which it may be desirable. It has yet to be shown, for example, that income or inheritance taxes do, *in fact*, significantly affect the choice between work and leisure (see George F. Break, "The Effect of Taxation on Work Incentives," in Edmund S. Phelps (ed.), *Private Wants and Public Needs, Issues Surrounding the Size and Scope of Government Expenditure*, rev. ed. (W. W. Norton and Company, Inc., 1965), 55–65 and the Brookings study by Robin Barlow, et al., *Economic Behavior of the Affluent* (Washington: The Brookings Institution, 1966). Where economic rents have been inflated by the subsidized

investment (for instance, property values around a newly constructed bridge) they could well be tapped to finance the subsidies without involving either economic distortion or unfairness.

[16] In other words, both moves would maximize total "transactions surplus"—the sum of consumer surplus and producer (or seller) surplus. Consumer surplus is the difference between what buyers would be willing to pay for any given quantity of output and what they actually do pay: so it is represented by the entire area under the demand curve above price. Seller surplus is the difference between the revenues necessary to elicit any given quantity of output (that is, the sum total of marginal costs) and the revenues actually received: so it is represented by the entire area between the marginal cost curve and price. Consider the following simple example:

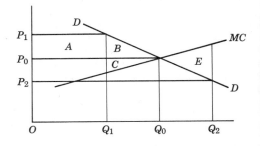

A reduction of price to *MC*, from P_1 to P_0, will increase consumer surplus by the sum of areas *A* and *B*. Area *A* will not represent a net increase in transaction surplus, since it is a mere transfer from seller surplus to buyers. But area *B* represents a net addition to both consumer and transaction surplus, since it reflects the difference between what buyers would have been willing to pay for the additional output, $Q_1 Q_0$, and what they actually have to pay, and does not come out of the pockets of producers. Similarly, area *C* represents a net addition to both seller and transactions surplus, since that added output

price? Suppose, for example, that the toll-collector on the (zero marginal-cost) bridge that we referred to at the beginning of Chapter 4 were omniscient and could charge for each crossing just what the traffic would bear—$1.50, perhaps, to those for whom the particular crossing was very important, down to zero to those who would be deterred by any toll at all. The correct number of crossings would take place; no one would be deterred from buying as much as he would if price were at marginal cost; and no crossing would occur whose value was less than the additional cost to society of making it possible. If production were justified in the first place, total revenue could be made to cover total costs. Instead of collecting only the price equal to marginal cost on the total volume of sales, the seller would collect that low price only on the marginal ones, and take in progressively more on the intramarginal sales.[17]

Perfect price discrimination involves fashioning charges according to what each unit of traffic will bear. Its basis is differences not in cost but in demand, in the value of each unit of service to each purchaser. Of course, it is not achievable in actual practice. In rough approximation, it is how private businesses, natural monopolies and others, determine their differential

---

costs them only the area under the MC curve between Q_1 and Q_0 whereas they receive a price of P_0 for those added sales. Therefore, total transaction surplus is increased by B plus C.

By the same reasoning, raising the price *to MC* from P_2 (which is below MC for the output OQ_2) would produce a net increase in seller plus buyer surplus measured by area E—the difference between what supplying Q_0Q_2 adds to producer costs and consumer satisfaction (the areas under the MC and DD curves, respectively, between Q_0 and Q_2).

[17] See the articles by Dupuit and Hotelling, cited in note 1, Chapter 4; also H. T. Koplin, "A Note on Price Discrimination," *Land Econ.* (February 1958), XXXIV: 92–95. In the extreme case, price discrimination might make it economical for a private firm to construct facilities that would not otherwise be feasible because, as illustrated by the accompanying diagram, at no single price (AR) would revenues be large enough to cover total costs. The socially

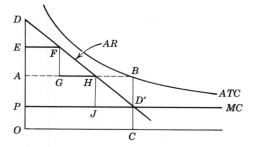

optimum price would be OP, output OC, but the resulting revenue, $OPD'C$ would fall short of total cost. Perfect discrimination could achieve the same output but capture revenues equal to the entire area under the demand curve $ODD'C$. As

long as this exceeded total costs, $OABC$, the investment would be justified in private terms. Pricing successive blocks of sales at lower prices —for example, $EFGHJD'$ in the diagram— could approximate the same result. A take-it-or-leave-it offer of OC quantity at an OA unit price would work also but would be feasible only if there were a single buyer or buying group.

Would the investment be socially justified? Since the total benefits, as measured by the total amount consumers would be willing to pay, would exceed the total costs, the proximate answer is yes. It must be qualified by a recognition that there are many alternative uses to which society's resources might be put that would be equally justified in terms of the size of the consumers' surplus but are not because of the impracticality of sufficient price discrimination; to apply this more generous test in some areas and not in others could therefore lead to misallocation. See Bonbright, *Principles of Public Utility Rates*, 397–398; and J. R. Meyer, J. F. Kain, and M. Wohl, *The Urban Transportation Problem* (Cambridge: Harvard Univ. Press, 1965), 344–345. For an analogous argument see Robert M. Dunn, "A Problem of Bias in Benefit-Cost Analysis: Consumer Surplus Reconsidered," *South. Econ. Jour.* (January 1967), XXXIII: 337–342.

There is special justification in decreasing cost situations that does not apply in others: under conditions of constant or increasing cost, price can be equated to marginal cost and also cover total costs without the need for discrimination. The welfare loss from failing to discriminate and failing to take advantage of the possibilities of increasing returns to scale are therefore greater in the former than in the latter situation. See on this also p. 197, below.

charges—on the basis of the respective elasticities of demand in their various markets, where they can be separated.

The practice of price discrimination is to some extent suspect in industry generally. Charging customers on the basis of value of service, ability to pay or benefits derived instead of on the basis of cost is like levying taxes; these criteria are in fact familiar principles or rationalizations of taxation. Therefore, in private industry the practice can serve as an effective method of monopolistic exploitation, as we have already suggested. Nor is it as frequently necessary for economic efficiency in competitive industries, where the phenomenon of decreasing costs is in normal times less pervasive, and where, therefore, price can be at marginal and average cost at one and the same time.[18] But in public utility situations, where the possibilities of monopolistic exploitation are subject to stringent controls, price discrimination is an often essential way of dealing with the pervasive phenomenon of marginal cost below average total cost.[19]

Price discrimination then becomes the means by which public utility companies can (1) cover (or come closer to covering) average total costs, while (2) making fuller use of existing capacity and/or (3) taking fuller advantage of long-run decreasing costs, by (4) permitting as many purchases as possible to be made as long as buyers are willing to pay the incremental costs of supplying them.[20]

---

[18] This is an oversimplification, to be sure. Imperfectly competitive industries are frequently burdened by excess capacity, hence subject to SRDC; and all in varying degree have economies of scale or LRDC, within limits. *Given* pervasive monopoly pricing in unregulated markets, price discrimination (in particular, reducing price closer to MC in markets with greater elasticity of demand) may more often than not bring output closer to the optimum level. See J. Robinson, *The Economics of Imperfect Competition*, 188–195. The fact remains that in industries in which competition is feasible—that is, in which internal economies of scale are exhausted well before the point at which a single firm supplies the entire market—price discrimination is less necessary for achieving optimal results.

The welfare case for price discrimination is that by enabling a firm, in the presence of short- or long-run decreasing costs, to charge some buyers something closer to marginal costs than would be possible if charges to all buyers had to be uniform, it permits either a fuller use of capacity or a fuller achievement of economies of scale. In the competitive situation, any additional sales that a firm obtains in this way are likely to be obtained mainly by taking customers away from other sellers or by buying off potential buyer-entrants. This fact inevitably raises the question of the possible deleterious effects on the preservation of effective competition, a question of less significance in the public utility area outside of transportation. (See our Chapter 6.) Moreover, in this case the "marginal-cost pricing" is far less

likely to lead to fuller utilization of *total industry* capacity than in the case of a public utility company—which is more likely to *be* the entire industry in itself. Similarly, to the extent public utilities are more "naturally monopolistic," with long-run marginal cost below average total cost throughout the entire relevant range, the justification in terms of the fuller achievement of economies of scale is more persuasive for these companies than in the competitive sector. With respect to the latter, it is proper to pose the question: if there are economies of scale to be achieved, why do they require *selective* price cuts?

[19] This does not deny that *inadequately regulated* price discrimination is probably more dangerous in public utility than in unregulated industries, precisely because of the greater monopoly power of the former. There is always the possibility of customers shifting to other suppliers and of competitive entry, outside the public utility arena. The subscriber hooked up to the only gas, electric, water or telephone company in the area typically has no such alternatives. It was mainly because competition in the public utility industries, and particularly in transportation, tended to be highly selective and discriminatory that they were subjected to regulation.

[20] See especially E. W. Clemens, "Price Discrimination in Decreasing Cost Industries," *Amer. Econ. Rev.* (December 1941), XXXI: 794–802; also the extremely clear graphical presentation by D. A. Worcester, Jr., "Justifiable Price 'Discrimination' Under Conditions of National Monopoly: A Diagrammatic Representation," *ibid.* (June 1948), XXXVIII: 382–388.

Technological Progress and Overhead Costs

There are two other possible occasions for price discrimination that remain to be considered. One is decreasing cost in the popular—not the economic—sense: that is, the tendency of costs to decline over time, without reference to economies of scale. As long as the capital component of average total costs —depreciation, return, income and property taxes—is computed in part on the basis of historic, book values, the average total cost of producing with new plant and equipment (ATC_n) may fall below the utility's unit cost of service (ATC_o). This will occur, we saw in Chapter 4, only if the rate of technological progress outruns the effects both of price inflation (which tends to inflate ATC_n) and the gradual erosion of the historical rate base by the application of (in this case unrealistically low) depreciation allowances. We have already discussed the merits of permitting utilities in these circumstances to recover their uneconomically high ATC_o, when economically efficient prices should be based on ATC_n: marginal cost looks to future instead of past cost responsibility. The fact remains that if utilities *are* permitted to do so, marginal costs will on this account be below ATC, and price discrimination; it is only the fact that joint output may be subject to increasing panies to recover these fixed, sunk costs from some markets while pricing closer to marginal costs in others.

The other is the pervasive joint and common costs described in Chapter 3. May not price discrimination be justified or necessary as a means of distributing and recovering these overhead costs among the various services jointly produced? In principle, no, except in the presence of decreasing costs. The presence of common or joint costs does not itself justify or necessitate price discrimination; it is only the fact that joint output may be subject to increasing returns that does so, for reasons we have already fully explored. But in practice (as our "in principle" qualification suggests) discrimination may indeed be the only, or the most, feasible method of recovering some part of the costs.

Consider, first, the case of joint costs, that is, where the proportions of the several services cannot be varied. In public utilities the same capacity is available to produce the same volume of service at different times of the day, week, or year, or because every trip of a railroad train in one direction inevitably creates the equivalent capacity for a return haul. Joint services do not have separable production costs. And, as Figure 4 in Chapter 4 illustrates, the joint costs *must* be distributed between them in a manner *akin* to price discrimination—that is, on the basis of the relative intensities and elasticities of the separate demands. But such pricing is *not* discriminatory. The markets are not artificially but physically and inevitably separate and distinct. There is no way of selling more in the high-price market by diverting capacity or product from the low-price market, as would be the competitive solution in the case of genuine discrimination. The capacity is in each market being rationed among the only customers who could possibly compete for it, in such a way as to clear that market; and each customer that continues to be served is in fact forced to pay the marginal opportunity cost of doing so— which is what the first-excluded customer in that market would have been willing to pay.[21]

---

[21] See pp. 87–88 and esp. note 11, Chapter 4,   380–381.
and Bonbright, *Principles of Public Utility Rates,*

Consider next the case of common costs. As long as the proportions of the common services and the capacity planned or used for each can be varied, the marginal cost of each can be determined. The marginal cost would be either the cost of producing an additional unit of the one while holding output of the others constant or the value of the other that could be produced with common facilities, or for whose production the facilities could otherwise have been designed. And there is no reason why these marginal costs (multiplied by their respective quantities) should not add up to total costs—unless, that is, production is subject to increasing returns.[22] In these circumstances price discrimination is in principle not necessarily justified: no service should sell at less than its marginal costs, and none need sell for more, since the sum total of marginal costs could well cover total revenue requirements.[23]

Common costs might well be subject to increasing returns, of the two familiar varieties. Every board-foot of lumber has a proportional cost responsibility for its share of the total warehouse space. But the marginal cost of storing it will be equal to the average total cost only: (1) if the warehouse is full or would be filled even if the particular board-feet being costed were not there and (2) if there are no economies of scale in the provision of additional cubic feet of warehouse space. As for the first, if excess capacity prevails, the short-run marginal opportunity cost of storing the lumber could be anything down to zero, depending on what price it would take to fill the warehouse.[24] That would be the value of the space to the first-excluded user. In reference to the second possibility, if the cost of providing an additional cubic foot is less than the average, here again there arises the problem that the sum total of marginal costs will fall short of total costs. If either SRDC (1) or LRDC (2) prevails, discrimination becomes possibly justifiable as a way of more closely approaching economically efficient pricing while covering total costs.[25]

---

[22] Bonbright's discussion of the reasons for the "failure of the sum of differential costs to equate with total costs" seems at one point to suggest that such a failure is inevitable in all common cost situations:

"These differential or incremental or marginal costs are nonadditive except under special conditions. For the determination of the cost of any particular type and amount of output assumes the continued production of the rest of the output, an assumption which is shifted when the costs of other types and amounts of output are under inquiry," *Ibid.* 297, 299.

However, at other times Bonbright attributes this failure only to one of the following circumstances: (1) decreasing costs, in the static sense, (2) differences between historical and current costs, or (3) the enormous practical difficulties of making the fine distinction necessary to break down all the common costs among all the categories of services and customers, taking into account the enormous variety of independent factors determining the variation in cost from one unit of sale to another, and incorporating all these variations in differential rates. The third

set of considerations, which Bonbright lucidly and persuasively expounds, does not conflict in principle with the statement in the text, above, but constitutes a powerful practical reason for price discrimination to recover a large portion of the common costs. See *ibid.* 296–301, 346 note, 348 note, 351 note (to miss Bonbright's footnotes is to miss some of the most interesting parts of the book), 355–356, 361–362, 383.

[23] For a strong statement of this position, see Donald H. Wallace, "Joint and Overhead Cost and Railway Rate Policy," *Q. Jour. Econ.* (August 1934), XLVIII: 583–619.

[24] Wallace's conclusions are subject always to the proviso "when the state of demands is such that best utilization can be obtained with uniform rates to all customers," *ibid.*, 585. That is to say, when there is excess capacity, he points out, the situation will resemble that of joint costs, in which rates may appropriately be varied in relation to the different elasticities and intensities of demand for the various services.

[25] Apart from the true joint-cost case (the solution to which he improperly terms discriminatory, *ibid.*), Wallace maintains that price discrimination is not economically justified

Finally, there are the practical considerations. In the presence of pervasive common costs, it is simply infeasible to make exhaustive computations of the ever-changing and infinitely differing marginal costs of each unit of service and to embody them in charges. To this extent, it is impossible for public utility companies to escape basing charges first on ascertainable, separate

---

except in the presence of excess capacity, a situation that is ordinarily only temporary. Since this view denies that the presence of *long-run* decreasing costs justifies continuing discrimination, the argument must be set forth and confronted.

The (static) concept of long-run costs refers to a planning situation, one in which a firm is in a position to build new or additional capacity of various possible sizes. If these potential plant

sizes fall within the range of decreasing long-run costs, a situation described in the accompanying figure, the long-run marginal cost curve will fall below the long-run average cost curve, reflecting the fact that output can be expanded with a less than proportionate increase in total cost. Now, whatever the slope of its planning curve ($LRAC$), the firm sooner or later must construct a particular plant. If it is planning for some particular output—setting aside expectations that demand

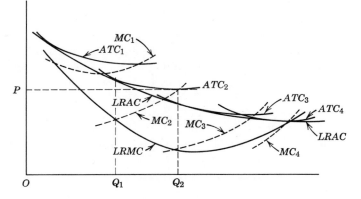

$LRAC$, $LRMC$, ATC, and $SRMC$ for four different plants, under conditions of long-run increasing returns. Taken from E. W. Clemens, *op. cit.*, *Amer. Econ. Rev.* (December 1941), XXXI: 799.

---

may change over time—it would pick the lowest-cost plant for that level of output. In the figure, the appropriate plant for output OQ_1, for example, would be the one with the ATC denoted by the subscript 2. There are three things to note about that choice. First, at that level of output the $SRMC$ of the particular plant selected (MC_2) and the $LRMC$ are equal. If they were not equal, the firm must have built the wrong-sized plant: it could have achieved its output at lower cost by operating farther along whichever of the two marginal cost curves was the lower—the short- or the long-run. See E. W. Clemens, *op. cit.*, *Amer. Econ. Rev.* (December 1941), XXXI: 799–800, and *Economics and Public Utilities*, 262–265. It is precisely the comparison between the costs of producing at a higher rate in a given plant with the costs of producing with an expanded plant that plays an important role in the decision to build additional capacity. The

point of indifference is where $SRMC$ and $LRMC$ are equal. See Fellner, *op. cit.*, 277–287. Another way of seeing this necessary equality is to recognize that when a firm is producing its output in the lowest-cost plant for that level of production, it is operating at the point at which the ATC of that plant is tangent to the long-run average cost or envelope curve; their slopes are equal, and so are the slopes of the total cost curves of which they represent the respective averages. Since $SRMC$ *is* the slope of the former total cost function, and $LRMC$ of the latter, $SRMC$ and $LRMC$ must likewise be equal at this point.

The second observation is that the plant selected is not necessarily the one with the lowest of all possible costs. Larger plants (for example, ATC_3 and ATC_4 in the figure) might have potentially lower average total costs but not be justified by the level of demand. Finally, the plant selected will not itself be operated at its

average variable costs and using price discrimination to recoup from their customers the additional revenues needed to cover unassignable common costs.[26]

PRINCIPLES OF DISCRIMINATION

The various possible occasions for price discrimination all involve the same common elements: (1) the relevant, ascertainable, or chargeable marginal costs are below average total costs, (2) there may or may not be a single, uniform price at which total costs could be covered by total revenues;

---

lowest cost point (that is, where its $SRMC$ and ATC are equal), which would be at an output of OQ_2 instead of OQ_1. Whatever the planned level of output (in this illustration OQ_1), the rational firm would have selected the particular plant to build whose short-run ATC was tangent to $LRAC$ at that output: that would give it the OQ_1 production at the lowest possible cost. The firm would have *planned* to have some excess capacity (Q_1Q_2, in the figure). Actually, to the extent that public utility companies expect that demand for their services will increase over time, they will typically construct plants (perhaps ATC_3 in the figure) that will be lowest-cost for an output that they expect to achieve not instantly but several years in the future. In either event, as long as these plants, once constructed, are operating short of their lowest-cost point (for example, at Q_1), their short-run marginal costs will be below their average total costs and price discrimination may be justified, as long as the incremental business taken on covers those marginal costs. But *if and as demand expands* over time, the excess capacity will disappear, the plant will come closer and closer to operating at its optimum point (Q_2 in our example), where marginal costs and average total costs are equal (at P). At this point, Wallace observes, *price discrimination is no longer necessary or desirable*: no class of service *should* pay less than its marginal costs and none *need* pay more than average total costs for total costs to be covered out of total revenues; and MC and ATC are equal. Therefore, although price discrimination might initially have been justified by the discrepancy between both marginal costs and ATC_2, the range of permissible price differences should thereafter be narrowed, as the quantities demanded increase toward OQ_2 and the firm moves up along the $SRMC_2$ curve until, finally, all customers are served at a uniform P.

According to this model, price discrimination depends on the presence, size, and duration of discontinuities in additions to capacity. And against this must be weighed the degree to which it is impractical to vary rates over time to reflect changing levels of capacity utilization. To justify discrimination, there are classic examples of building ahead in large lumps such as the case of

a railroad shifting from a single to a double track and examples of chronic excess capacity such as persist in that industry. On the other hand, there is argument to the contrary, that even for railroads, once the basic line has been constructed, "investment in railroad plant is for all intents and purposes continuous . . . ," and that railroad average costs probably do not decrease over the normal operating range. Merton H. Miller, "Decreasing Average Cost and the Theory of Railroad Rates," *South. Econ. Jour.* (April 1955), XXI: 395 note, also the studies cited at 390 note; Wallace, *op. cit.*, 608. See, on the other hand, the estimate of Vickrey that long-run marginal costs for railroad freight transport are on the order of only 80% of average costs. *Op. cit.*, *Amer. Econ. Rev., Papers and Proceedings* (May 1955), XLV: 614. This demonstration seems to minimize unduly the role of long-run decreasing costs in justifying continuing price discrimination. First it slights the fact that public utility firms may be more or less constantly "facing their planning curves," that is, almost constantly making decisions with respect to expansions of capacity. Although this fact may reduce the significance of the discontinuities and short-term excess capacities, it confronts them constantly with the discrepancy between their long-run marginal and long-run average costs. Instead of being confronted, principally, with a steady upward creep of production along a rising $SRMC$, requiring the gradual elimination of rate differentials, their principal decisions would in these circumstances be relating to what size of plant to build—and such a decision must perpetually evoke the possible contributions of price differentiation in enabling them to build the more instead of the less efficient plant. Second, it ignores the possible discrepancy between long-run average and long-run marginal costs consequent on technological progress, inadequately reflected in depreciation allowances. Third, the practical difficulties of pricing constantly at a changing $SRMC$ level, which Wallace cites as arguing against discrimination, typically cuts the other way, as we point out in the text immediately following.

[26] See the references to Bonbright, note 22.

but (3) the latter condition could still be met while permitting a level of output closer to the optimum by charging different prices to different classes of customers. In Figure 6 we have chosen to use the case of static, long-run decreasing costs as our example for illustrating the principles common to all. The choice seems appropriate in light of the general case for basing utility prices on long-run instead of short-run marginal cost.[27]

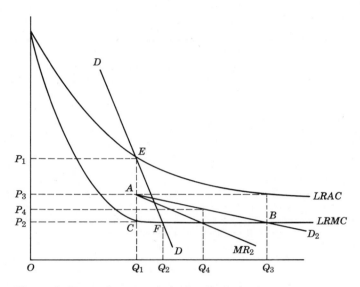

Figure 6. Decreasing costs and price discrimination.

So we assume, in Figure 6, that the firm is in the planning stage, attempting to choose between the various possible sizes of plants tangent to the *LRAC* curve, each with its own *MC* function, as in the figure in note 25. There are assumed to be two potentially separable classes of customers, with the respective demands D_1 and D_2. The D_1 customers could be served alone at a uniform price. That price would be P_1, and their demand would justify the construction of the size of plant appropriate for producing an output of Q_1.[28] But such a uniform price would fall considerably short of optimality. There are some D_1 buyers and an entire class of D_2 willing to buy a great deal more, $Q_1 Q_2$ and $Q_1 Q_3$, respectively, at prices covering the long-run

---

[27] To use Figure 6, instead, to exemplify the case of short-run decreasing costs, we would need only to interpret *LRAC* and *LRMC* as representing the short-run functions with existing capacity.

The model is simplified in that it excludes the possibility of separate, identifiable marginal costs of serving the different classes of customers; in effect, it assumes the provision of a uniform service. Separable marginal costs could easily be incorporated, by interpreting the respective demand curves D_1 and D_2 as representing the demands not for the separate final products or services but only for the common or joint portion of the production process—derived by subtracting from each of the demands for the final

services its separate marginal costs. In this way, the diagram could be modified also to illustrate the third possible case for discrimination, the presence of common or overhead costs that cannot practically be either identified or charged to the separate classes of service. Steiner uses this device in treating the problem of the proper distribution of (joint) capacity costs. *Op. cit.*, *Q. Jour. Econ.* (November 1957), LXXI: 585–610.

[28] Since in note 25 we have already illustrated the process of choosing the right size of plant, we omit from Figure 6 the *SRAC* functions for the individual plants of various sizes.

incremental costs of that additional output, Q_3B. (For simplicity, we have drawn the D_2 demand curve as though its vertical axis were at Q_1 instead of at the origin; therefore, the quantities taken at various prices by the D_2 customers should be read as beginning at Q_1.) The ideal price (setting aside the problem of financing the resultant deficit) would clearly be P_2, uniformly for all customers; or a system of perfect price discrimination that gave all D_1 and D_2 customers that price for their marginal purchases; or a lump charge to all customers giving them, then, the right to buy all they want at the P_2 price—provided that lump-sum charge did not exclude from the market any customers willing to buy some at the P_2 price.

Suppose, at the other extreme, that the only price discrimination possible is a crude separation of the D_1 and D_2 markets. Clearly, this would still be an improvement over the uniform P_1 price to all. If a lower price were set for the D_2 customers—the ideal one from their standpoint would be P_2—it would be possible to pick up their business and earn from it revenues sufficient to cover the full additional costs of supplying them. This means that neither the company nor the D_1 customers would be injured because of this additional business taken on at discriminatorily low prices: the unchanged P_1 price to the latter, on their OQ_1 sales, and the P_2 for the Q_1Q_3 sales to the D_2 market will still together cover ATC. Another way of saying this is that, by virtue of picking up the added Q_1Q_3 sales, the company has been enabled to choose the more efficient plant size appropriate for the larger output OQ_3, reducing its ATC from OP_1 to OP_3; as a glance at the figure will indicate, that new average cost is covered by the P_1 and P_2 prices, on the OQ_1 and Q_1Q_3 sales respectively.[29] The gain in social welfare is indicated by the

---

[29] We have simplified this demonstration by conveniently assuming that the $LRMC$ is constant (that is, horizontal) over the entire range of the incremental Q_1Q_3 output. A price set at $LRMC$ at the point of intersection with the D_2 demand happens, conveniently, to cover the total costs of that added increment of sales, CBQ_3Q_1. Whether the ideal price for the D_2 customers, set at that point of intersection, will in fact cover the total additional costs of their added sales—which is measured by the total area under the $LRMC$ curve—depends on the shape and slope of the $LRMC$ curve within the Q_1Q_3 range. If, for example, the D_2 intersects $LRMC$ while the latter is still declining, charging the D_2 customers only $LRMC$ at the margin will produce a deficit, denoted by the shaded area.

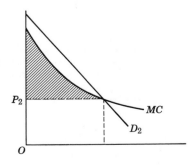

If instead D_2 intersects $LRMC$ in a rising range, the P price can produce a surplus (the next fig.).

Yet, in both cases the additional output is in a sense desirable (see note 17), since the area

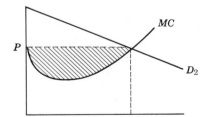

under the demand curve exceeds the area under the MC curve. In the first case, taking on the D_2 business at OP_2 would necessitate raising the price to the D_1 buyers above P_1 if total costs were to be covered; in the latter, the surplus can be applied to reducing P_1 as well.

The reader also should be reminded that price discrimination will not in all circumstances, even in correctly regulated industries, result in a larger volume of sales. Figure 6 illustrates a particularly easy case: where only one class of customers would have been served under a single-pricing scheme and discrimination enables the class of customers with the more elastic demand also to be served, the result will always be a higher output. See Miller, *op. cit.*, 397, and

triangle *ABC*—the difference between what the D_2 customers would have been willing to pay for the Q_1Q_3 purchases that they are enabled by the price discrimination to make and the added costs to society of supplying them.[30]

Who Deserves the MC Price?

As the antitrust laws recognize, price discrimination can be injurious to competitors of the discriminating seller and to the customers discriminated against; and it may accomplish a more effective nomopolistic exploitation of the latter. The idea that it is economically desirable to reduce rates down to marginal cost for "marginal buyers" is all very well; but how is one to decide which buyers are marginal and which are not?

In (impurely) competitive markets the "marginal business" is the business you either do not yet have or that you are in danger of losing. As the Robinson–Patman Act recognizes, a justification of selective price reduction on marginal business thus defined could be entirely circular: if it is all right to discriminate in favor of marginal buyers, and marginal buyers are all those whom the seller feels he has to favor in this way, all price discrimination is permissible. As far as causal cost responsibility is concerned, however, all customers are marginal.

Suppose, for example, the utility has two groups of customers, one, A, whose demand is stable, another, B, whose demand is increasing. And suppose expansion of the latter demand finally requires expansion of capacity. Does that mean, following our rules of peak responsibility pricing, that B are the marginal buyers on whom capacity costs alone should be imposed? Obviously not. True, it is the increase in B's purchases that precipitates the additional investment; but the additional costs could just as well be saved if A reduced their purchases as if B refrained from increasing theirs. So A's *continuing* to take service is just as responsible, in proportion to the amount they take, for the need to expand investment as B's increasing needs, and A should therefore be forced just as much as B to weigh the marginal benefits of the capacity to them against the marginal costs they impose on society by continuing to make demands. This reasoning clearly applies even when incremental investment costs per unit of capacity are rising and where, again, it might appear on first consideration that since it is the expansion of the B demands that is responsible for the supplier's incurring the higher costs, it is that group that ought to bear the additional burden. Even though B's demand is "marginal" in the temporal sense, both groups are marginal in the economic sense. Both should be forced to match those higher capacity costs against the satisfaction they derive from continuing to use the service.[31]

But what if, to come to the case closer at hand, long-run incremental costs are less than average total costs? Ideally, both A and B should be confronted with the low marginal opportunity costs to society of supplying the additional capacity. A might demand more capacity if offered the lower price, just as might B. But the ideal is unachievable: it is impossible to reduce the rates to

---

R. K. Davidson, *op. cit.*, 173–179. Our purpose has been merely to show that discrimination *can* improve welfare all around.

[30] By the same criterion, society continues to lose the potential addition to welfare *CEF* that it could have enjoyed had it found ways of extending the ideal price of P_2 to the D_1 customers as well.

[31] Suppose that A is the user of a piece of city land, acquired a long time ago, when land in the center of the city was plentiful and cheap. A would be irrational if he did not, as the demand and price for land rose, consider as the cost of continuing to hold on to what he has, not the historic price that was paid but the opportunity cost to society of his holding the land. As

the lower level for both buyer groups, because in that event total revenues would be inadequate. How then does one choose between the claims of A and B to the lower incremental cost?

The only generally acceptable answer would have to be on the basis of the comparative elasticities of the respective demands within the relevant range (between ATC and the relevant MC). Suppose, for example, that B's demand, though growing over time, is comparatively independent of price—this might well be the case, we have suggested, with respect to the demand for electricity for air conditioning—whereas A's, though not growing over time, would respond very sharply to a reduced price. In these circumstances, the intelligent decision would ordinarily be to lower the price not to B but to A.[32]

Why so? We know that it will pay any company, if it can separate the markets in which it sells, to discriminate between them on the basis of their respective elasticities of demand. A profit-maximizing company will equalize the marginal revenues it receives from the respective markets in which it sells (assuming variable costs are the same). If it could add more to its revenues by selling more in one than in the other, it would increase its sales efforts in the former and decrease them in the latter until the incremental revenues were once again equated. Since the difference between marginal and average revenue will be greater the less elastic is demand, the company will charge a higher price in the market with the less elastic and a lower price in the market with the more elastic demand.[33] This is merely an explicit version of the common sense notion that sellers will price in different markets on the basis of what the respective traffics will bear;[34] the more inelastic the demand, the higher the price a market will bear.

Public utility companies should, in certain circumstances, be encouraged to adopt the same type of system, forcing different customers to contribute to common costs (over and above the identifiable costs of serving them separately) on the basis of their respective abilities and willingness to pay or the value of the service to them. (See Figure 6.) At all levels of price at which there are customers in both categories, the demand D_1 is less elastic than D_2: the same price reduction or increase will bring a greater reaction by the D_2 than by the D_1 buyers. A price below P_1 is *necessary* to pick up the D_2 customers. They are willing and able to pay the full additional costs of serving them; so production on their behalf is economically justified.[35]

---

prices rose, he might at a certain point decide he was better off selling out and moving elsewhere. It would be economically inefficient for society as well if A were not forced to make such a calculation. From the point of view of the marginal opportunity costs of his using the land, he is just as much a marginal buyer as the new purchaser, B, even though he is not overtly in the market.

[32] The reason these statements are qualified ("the only generally acceptable answer," "the intelligent decision would ordinarily be"), as will be indicated, is that the problem requires a choice among different distributions of the benefits of decreasing costs among different classes of customers, a choice that cannot be proved right or wrong by economic reasoning alone.

[33] See, for example, George J. Stigler, *The Theory of Price*, 3rd ed. (New York: Macmillan, 1966), 209–213.

[34] This widely used expression is a very imprecise statement of the profit-maximizing condition. Most markets will "bear" prices much higher than a profit-maximizing monopolist would charge, in the sense that *some* sales would continue to be made at that price, but not enough to maximize the difference between total revenues and total costs. The economist will interpret the phrase as implying the equation of marginal cost and revenue.

[35] This is indicated by the fact that for at least some of its range, their demand, D_2, lies above the $LRMC$: note this is true also in the more complicated cases described in note 29. Perfect

This means that the D_1 customers, who are being discriminated *against*, need not be injured by the discrimination; instead, they can actually be benefited. If (in the case of short-run increasing returns) the rate reduction permits the fuller use of existing capacity, and the additional business taken on by the preferentially low rate covers anything more than the variable costs it entails, then the D_2 customers are making some contribution to the common costs that the D_1 customers would otherwise have to bear entirely by themselves. If instead, the question is one of permitting the construction of a larger plant than would otherwise be feasible, the lower rates to the D_2 customers make it possible for the firm to achieve economies of scale that would not otherwise be available. Once again, if the D_2 customers are made to pay anything in excess of the long-run incremental cost for which they are responsible, it would be possible for the company to reduce its rates to the D_1 customers below P_1 and still cover total costs. And it will of course be the function of effective regulation to require it to do so.[36]

Therefore, discriminatory rate reductions are not only justifiable but economically desirable, if the following possibilities exist.

1. The relevant cost of taking on the incremental business is less than the average cost of the total company operation without it.
2. The lower rates are required to elicit the additional business.
3. The elasticity of the demand in question is sufficiently in excess of unity that selective rate reductions could increase the system's total revenues by at least the additional costs incurred. Whether rates *should* be reduced to this end is a question we shall consider presently.

To these three conditions, there should be attached a warning.

4. Additional restrictions may have to be imposed in the event that the supplying company is competing with other suppliers or that the customers charged the different prices are in competition with each other— circumstances that we study in Chapter 6.

The Proper Limits of Discrimination

Figure 6 implies that the proper limits of discrimination are the prices P_1 and P_2: a price to the inelastic demand customers no higher than the ATC of serving them in the absence of discrimination; a price to the elastic demand customers no lower than the full additional costs of taking on that additional business. These are the rules that most authorities have adopted, and with which we concur.[37] One implies the other: as long as the favored customers pay their full additional costs, the others cannot on this account be

(and possibly even highly imperfect) price discrimination could theoretically extract more revenues than serving them would add to costs. However, see note 17.

[36] If the utility as a whole is not earning its permissible rate of return, then of course the customers paying the higher rates will receive no direct benefit, since any additions to revenues over costs consequent on extending the preferential rates to markets with elastic demand will serve only to bring the company's rate of return closer to the permissible level. It remains true in this case that D_1 customers need not be injured by the lower rates extended to the others (unless

they themselves compete with the D_2 buyers, a possibility we consider in the following chapter). Even if their rates are not actually reduced at once, they can benefit by the better financial condition of the company and its consequent superior ability to maintain and improve service over time.

[37] See, for example, Harry Gunnison Brown, *Principles of Commerce: A Study of the Mechanism, the Advantages, and the Transportation Costs of Foreign and Domestic Trade* (New York: Macmillan, 1916), Part III, 123–124, 172; Tyndall, *op. cit.*, 343, 347–348; Clemens, *Economics and Public Utilities*, 256; and the following pronouncement

led to pay more than the costs of serving them in the absence of discrimination. And both together imply the condition that discrimination be permitted only as long as it imposes no burden on the customers being discriminated against.

Such a rule would prohibit *internal subsidization*. Regulatory commissions, particularly in the transportation field, often consider it one of their responsibilities to assure the provision of maximum service, as long as the system's total revenues cover total costs. Under considerable political pressure from the affected localities or groups of customers, they interpret the public utility franchise as imposing an obligation on the company to maintain service in markets that are sparse and costly to serve, according to time schedules that are convenient to customers, at prices that do not cover even the avoidable, incremental cost of provision. This obligation is often used as a justification for limiting competition and restricting entry into the more remunerative markets, on the ground that if the profitability of the latter portion of the business were reduced, the common carriers would no longer be financially able to fulfill their less remunerative responsibilities. In the long run this must involve charging other customers more than the average total cost of serving them alone. Of course, society may choose to tax certain of its members in order to subsidize the provision of electricity, telephone, railroad, or air service to other classes of customers; all the economist can do is to underline the direct and indirect costs of providing the subsidy in this manner, that is, by setting certain prices above and others below the respective marginal social costs, instead of by direct monetary grants.[38]

But, in fact, an economic case could be made for extending the permissible limits at both ends. The ideal price would be at MC—the cost of the single last unit demanded. A price to the D_2 customers at that level might well not cover the full additional cost of serving them—that is, the cost of their entire, added increment. This could be so if the MC itself (and not just the ATC) were declining over some portion of that incremental output.[39] If, then, the

---

of the U. S. Supreme Court:

"Let it be conceded that if a scheme of maximum rates was imposed by state authority, as a whole adequately remunerative, and yet that some of such rates were so unequal as to exceed the flexible limit of judgment which belongs to the power to fix rates, that is, transcended the limits of just classification and amounted to the creation of favored class or classes whom the carrier was compelled to serve at a loss, to the detriment of other class or classes upon whom the burden of such loss would fall, that such legislation would be . . . inherently unreasonable. . . ." *Atlantic Coast Line Railroad v. North Carolina Corporation Commission* 206 U. S. 1, 25–26 (1907).
[38] For an illustration of the case against such a practice, see pp. 190–191, Chapter 7. There is no doubt that widespread internal subsidization of this type does prevail; we shall supply some examples, particularly in our discussion of "cream skimming," in Chapters 1 and 5, Vol. 2. But whether the alleged subsidization is real depends, of course, on whether the costs of the respective services cited have been computed according to the economically correct, marginal principles. The mere fact of price discrimination does not in itself demonstrate internal subsidization. Although in the long run it may well be that the disproportionate contribution to overheads by the customers being discriminated against— the D_1 market in our Figure 6—alone makes it possible for service to continue to flow to those paying a price closer to marginal costs, it seems anomalous to characterize their contribution as subsidization when (1) the favored customers do over the long-run incremental costs of servicing them and (2) the disfavored—a graceless word— pay no more, and possibly pay less, than they would if the discrimination were not practiced. But, as we shall see when the question is raised of where the respective rates ought actually to be set *within* the upper and lower limits just described, subsidization may be said to occur if the rates in the price-elastic market are set below the level that would *maximize* their net contribution (that is, over and above $LRMC$) to company overheads—because in this event the rates to the price-inelastic market could have been lower, while the company still covered total costs.

rules were altered to set the lower limit at marginal instead of full additional cost—and that *would* have to be the bottom limit, as far as economic considerations prevail—the upper limit could, indeed, would have to, exceed the ATC (P_1 in Figure 6) of serving the high-price market alone.

Whichever set of limits is adopted, the question remains of where the actual discriminatory prices should be set within those limits.

According to one standard of welfare economics, the prices of the various services should be marked up above MC in inverse proportion to their elasticities of demand. This prescription stems from the idea that the optimal pricing scheme will be the one that maximizes the surplus of all consumers taken as a group, subject to the constraint of raising sufficient revenue to cover total costs. Since total well-being, and hence total consumer surplus, is maximized when all goods are priced at marginal cost,[40] the solution, in situations where pricing above that level is unavoidable, is to minimize the amount of surplus sacrificed in this way. This will be achieved when the loss of consumer surplus that would result from a price increase sufficient to contribute one added dollar to overhead costs is equalized for all classes of service. If they were not equal, total consumer surplus could be increased by raising price in the market where the loss of surplus per dollar of net additional revenue was low and by reducing it where the ratio was high, since the surplus lost by the price increase in the former market would be smaller than the surplus gained by the reduction in the latter. If we begin from a situation where all prices are equated to *average* total cost, prices will go up in the inelastic demand markets and down in the elastic until the respective ratios to marginal costs for the various services, $(P - MC)/P$, are inversely proportional to their respective elasticities of demand.[41] Such prices will have the effect of reducing sales in all markets by the same percentage below what their respective levels would be if all prices were equal to marginal cost. Clearly, to achieve equiproportionate reductions in sales from that ideal level, prices will have to be raised much more above marginal cost for services with inelastic than with elastic demands.

But following such a rule would have the effect of favoring the D_2 over the D_1 customers. The ones with the less elastic demands, also, would be interested in taking additional quantities of service if the price to them were reduced below P_1. A decision to set the prices at the limits would in effect represent a decision to distribute the major part of the benefits of the increasing returns to the D_2 customers. Such an action could be justified on the ground that, since the surplus or welfare gain that the D_2 customers obtain from a reduction in price to MC exceeds what the D_1 customers lose, the former could compensate the latter. But without any arrangements for such compensation, this discriminatory pricing pattern would in effect distribute more income to the D_2 than to the D_1 group. As we have already seen, economics cannot provide a decisive answer to distributional questions such

---

[39] This possibility is illustrated in the first of the figures in note 29.

[40] See note 16.

[41] See William J. Baumol, "Reasonable Rules for Rate Regulation: Plausible Policies for an Imperfect World," in Almarin Phillips and Oliver E. Williamson, eds., *Prices: Issues in Theory, Practice, and Public Policy* (Philadelphia:

Univ. of Pennsylvania Press, 1967), 122–123, citing previous formulations by Alan S. Manne, Marcus Flemming, and Marcel Boiteux. Also the testimony of Baumol and of William S. Vickrey in FCC, *In the Matter of American Telephone and Telegraph Co. et al.*, Docket 16258, 1968; the latter's Appendix A is a particularly lucid explanation.

as these. It can supply no common denominator for comparing or adding up the psychic satisfactions that the D_1 patrons would get from their additional purchases with the corresponding satisfactions that would be enjoyed by the D_2 customers if the price to them were reduced to its lower limit—except to observe that compensation would be possible.[42]

Mainly for this reason—and also because of the difficulty of measuring demand elasticities—some economists have opposed the use of price discrimination in public utility rate making, advocating instead that the long-run marginal costs of as many classes of service as possible be identified and rates be set uniformly above those respective costs by whatever percentage required to bring in the necessary aggregate revenues. That is, instead of the various rates being set discriminatorily at varying percentages of marginal costs, in (inverse) dependence on the respective elasticities of demand, the price to marginal cost ratios would be constant for all classes of service.[43] Most economists would probably permit discriminatory departures from the rule for those categories of business that, by virtue of their high elasticity of demand, would be completely excluded by it from the market.[44]

Finally, some commentators, aware of the possible benefits of price discrimination to all parties but unwilling to sanction transfers of benefit from one group of customers to another, have proposed that discriminatory reductions be permitted *only* to the point of maximizing the benefit to customers discriminated *against*. By this rule, rates would be lowered in markets with elastic demand only if elasticity is great enough so that the discriminatory reduction results in those markets making an increased net contribution to common costs; and rates would be reduced only to the point

---

[42] That is, "maximizing the total consumer surplus" in the manner indicated involves equating a dollar of area under A's demand curve with a dollar under B's demand curve, and, where it will increase the total number of dollars of surplus, conferring benefits on consumer A and not on consumer B. It is impossible to add together incommensurable quantities in this way. How can we decide that the worth of a dollar to A is the same as to B? Even if we do so decide, by what right do we as economists decide it is proper to transfer income from one to the other?

[43] This is the arrangement of the French *tarif vert*. See James R. Nelson, "Practical Applications of Marginal Cost Pricing in the Public Utility Field," *Amer. Econ. Rev., Papers and Proceedings* (May 1963), LIII: 480.

[44] See the discussion by Baumol, in Phillips and Williamson, *op. cit.*, 120–121, and Vickrey, in his supplementary testimony in FCC, Docket 16258, 1969. The question of whether "ideal output" can be achieved equally well with prices proportional instead of equal to marginal cost has been extensively debated in the literature. The concensus seems to be negative, but that proportionality should produce tolerably good results with one major qualification: that for all primary and intermediate goods and services—

that is, for all inputs in the production process—severe distortions will result unless prices are equal to marginal costs. The reason for this exception is that if all inputs and intermediate goods were priced at some ratio in excess of marginal cost, that excess would be subjected to geometric expansion each time one of those inputs or one of the products in which it was then embodied was sold to the next level of production or distribution. The reader may recognize here the opposite side of the general case for vertical integration that it eliminates this progressive cumulation of interstitial mark-ups. (See the discussion of Figure 1, Chapter 6, Volume 2.)

Apart from this problem, the general opinion is that because setting prices in proportion to rather than equal to marginal costs leaves unchanged the (proportional) relationship between them, "the Proportionality Rule is likely to prove adequate." Lionel W. McKenzie, "Ideal Output and the Interdependence of Firms," *Econ. Jour.* (December 1951), LXI: 788; see also 785–803. See Ruggles, *op. cit.*, 110–111, 119 and the literature cited there; E. J. Mishan, *Welfare Economics*, Five Introductory Essays (New York: Random House, 1964), 20–22; Tibor Scitovsky, *Welfare and Competition, The Economics of a Fully Employed Economy* (Chicago: Richard D. Irwin, 1951), 356–362.

of maximizing that contribution.[45] The way to accomplish this would be to fix that lower price at the point at which marginal costs equalled marginal rather than average revenue, that is, at the monopoly profit-maximizing point. This would be P_4 in Figure 6, instead of P_2 At this price, the D_2 customers would take only Q_1Q_4, making the maximum contribution, above $LRMC$, to the reduction of price in the D_1 market below its P_1 level.[46]

It is important to emphasize that we are considering a situation in which the various categories of service have the *same* marginal costs and in which we are looking for guidance to decide how best to discriminate between them in a situation of decreasing costs. The purpose of a rule calling for reduction of rates on the more elastic services *only* to the MC = MR point is to maximize the benefit to other classes of service discriminated *against*. Analogously, it has been suggested that the rates for service off-peak might properly be set to maximize the contribution to overheads, thereby making possible a reduction in rates or an improvement of service at the peak.[47] But this proposal would have the very opposite effect from the one sought by the rule enunciated above. Here the marginal costs of serving the two classes of customers in question are different and the result would be to discriminate against the off-peak customers, charging them a price in excess of their marginal costs, in order to maximize the subsidy to the *favored* customers, that is, enabling the company to charge them a price as far *below* their marginal costs as possible.[48]

This does not mean that the peak customers should, in the presence of long-run decreasing costs, pay the full average total capacity costs. But a decision to charge them less, under the rules enunciated, would require a finding that it was the *peak* demand that was so highly elastic as to justify charging them a price containing a smaller markup above the (high) long-run marginal cost of serving *them* than is incorporated in the lower price charged the off-peak customers.

Of course, society might choose to make a different type of distributional decision. If it felt that customers in the market with more elastic demand were poorer or politically more deserving because they were in rural areas, it might well choose to confer all the benefits of the joint operation on that particular class of service, reducing those particular rates all the way down

---

[45] For evidence that the Interstate Commerce Commission attempts to follow this rule, see George W. Wilson, "The Effect of Rate Regulation on Resource Allocation in Transportation," *Amer. Econ. Rev., Papers and Proceedings* (May 1964), LIV: 164–165. In this event (see note 38) there is no way in which it could meaningfully be said that the customers paying the higher price were "subsidizing" the customers charged the discriminatorily favorable price.

[46] The reader may find this proposal for monopolistic pricing difficult to accept at first. The loss of the Q_4Q_3 sales reflects the consequence of the monopolist's equating MC to marginal rather than to average revenue or price. But here we are dealing with a situation in which all prices cannot be equated with MC and with various possible ways of handling the extraeconomic

problem of distributing the benefits of price discrimination.

[47] See, for example, Ponsonby, *op. cit.*, note 44, Chapter 4. Vickrey contends that AT&T's espousal of long-run incremental cost-pricing plus a markup sufficient to maximize net revenue on its (price-elastic) business services in its general rate case before the FCC (see pp. 156–157), with the balance of overheads being covered by the message toll telephone service comes to the same thing. It amounts, he asserts, to asking the off-peak users to subsidize the peak. Testimony in FCC Docket No. 16258, 1968, *op. cit.*, 8, 13–14.

[48] The effect would be similar to that of the Federal Power Commission's *Atlantic Seaboard* formula; it would encourage an uneconomic expansion of capacity. See pp. 98–100, Chapter 4.

to marginal costs or below.[49] And the economist could not say it was mistaken. Indeed, society might, for similar reasons, insist that the lowest of the rates be charged to particular classes of customers even if their demand were less instead of more elastic than others. But in this case, society could find that it had defeated its own purpose. If the demands of some of the politically *less* deserving customers were sufficiently elastic so that a preferential price reduction to them would add more to total system revenues than it would to costs, a failure to discriminate in their *favor* would involve passing up an opportunity to reduce rates to the politically more deserving customers as well.[50]

Why should it be necessary for the economist to develop and for society to enforce a rule that particular prices not be reduced below the point where marginal revenues equal marginal costs? Why would any private company consider going beyond that point anyhow? There are four possible reasons. First of all, the managers of the company, for reasons of their own, might prefer greater growth of the company to profit maximization. Second, they might be led to such an action by an excess of competitive zeal, predatory or otherwise, a possibility that we consider in Chapters 6 of this volume and 5 of Volume 2. Third, they might make mistakes. But fourth, it might be in their interest to do so because it might enable them more fully to exploit their monopoly power. If regulation is effective, it must mean that these companies are being restrained from charging at least some of their customers all that their traffic would bear. On the other hand, their regulators are under stern injunctions to permit them, as far as the market permits, to earn some minimum rate of return at least equal to the cost of capital on whatever investment is required to serve their customers.[51] Finally, any company will ordinarily be interested in maximizing the absolute total of its profits. This combination of circumstances creates an incentive for a regulated company to maintain or increase the aggregate of its investment, and hence its rate base, as long as its markets taken in the aggregate are capable of yielding up the requisite rate of return on incremental investments. Thus, it might be entirely rational policy to cut prices on some portions of the business, even though demand there did not have sufficient elasticity for the cut to increase total revenues more than costs, in order to justify additional investment, on which it might then earn the legally permissible return by raising rates in markets of inelastic demand—something it had previously been prevented from doing because of the regulatory limitation on total profits.[52] We have already suggested that such considerations probably exert an influence on public utility companies in the direction of improving the quality of service

---

[49] See, for example, the strong case by Vickrey for the Bell System's cutting long-distance rates sharply during the very early morning hours, partly on the ground that the MC at such off-peak times is virtually nil and partly because it would be the poor who might respond to the opportunity of phoning cheaply at these inconvenient hours. Testimony in FCC Docket 16258, *op. cit.*, 45–47.

[50] For a particularly illuminating illustration of the possible conflict between economically efficient pricing and an unwillingness to charge

higher rates to low-income than to wealthy countries, with a sacrifice of benefits to both if the latter consideration prevails, see Johnson, in Shepherd and Gies, *op. cit.*, 113–114, 134–138.

[51] Indeed (see note 64, Chapter 2), as a practical matter, the commissions are probably obliged to allow some margin above the bare cost of capital, partly because they can only roughly estimate that cost and partly in order to create a positive incentive to expand service.

[52] See the fuller discussions of this "A–J–W" effect in Chapter 2, Volume 2.

and refraining from imposing all their capacity charges on peak users.[53]

This particular distortion provides another illustration of the inadequacy of regulation that concentrates only on rate levels, in order to assure that the regulated companies earn no more than a specified average return on investment. As Troxel has pointed out, economic efficiency requires that the cost of capital be equated with not the *average* but the marginal rate of return on investment.[54] To prevent excessive *aggregate* investment, regulatory commissions must see to it not only that the *average* return permitted on total investment does not *exceed* the cost of capital, but also that no individual investments are made that earn *less* than the cost of capital.[55] This requires, among other things, that all discriminatory rate reductions be limited by the floor of long-run incremental costs (including the required return on incremental investment).

The kind of rate making that would be permissible under even these restrictive rules would almost certainly still strike the reader, the rate-payer, and most regulatory commissions as outrageously discriminatory. Consider the following illustration of the kinds of problems that face commissions today in passing on selective rate reductions proposed by electric companies in their increasingly avid competition for the home heating market, where, because of the competition of gas and oil, their demand is apparently highly elastic. (We reserve for Chapter 6 consideration of the relevance of the fact that it is the presence of competition that creates this elasticity.) Suppose the company has two groups of customers that it proposes to put in separate classes for purposes of rate making: A and B. Suppose their incomes and all other relevant economic characteristics are identical, and the only difference between them is that A customers heat their houses with electricity and B customers do not. Suppose also that the electric company proposes a lower rate to B, even though once those customers accept the offer the amount and timing of their purchases will be identical with that of A. The proposal is to give different treatment to customer classes identical in all ways, including the cost of serving them, except for the fact that A are already tied to the electric company and B are not.[56]

It is entirely conceivable, considering the long-run decreasing cost characteristics of the electricity industry, that a lower rate to class B would be defensible under the rules we have set forth; and that the consequence would be not only not to injure A but to benefit them. Such a differential could obviously not be justified under the cost-saving justification of the

[53] See pp. 24–25 and note 33, Chapter 4.

[54] See the discussion in note 74, Chapter 4.

[55] Troxel believes that the practice of telephone companies imposing a flat and uniform charge for all local telephone calls within a wide urban area, even though unit costs rise as service is extended to less densely settled outlying regions of the city, does create the possibility of "a marginal return at the suburban fringes below the cost of capital. That is, deficient returns to capital may occur at the extensive urban margin of telephone operations rather than in a whole metropolitan network." In *Shepherd and Gies, op. cit.*, 184.

[56] A "Request for Investigation" presented to the

Federal Trade Commission by the Virginia Petroleum Jobbers Association, *In the Matter of Promotional Payments by Electric Companies*, December 14, 1965, referring specifically to alleged practices by the Virginia Electric & Power Company, claimed:

"VEPCO will provide free underground wiring to builders of all-electric subdivisions and apartment houses. In contrast, where electricity is used only for lighting and for appliances, then *even though the amount of electricity used may be as great* as in an all-electric subdivision, underground wiring will be provided only at a prohibitive charge." Par. I, Sec. 3.

Robinson-Patman Act,[57] which would require that the difference in prices charged A and B be itself justified by differences in the respective costs of serving them—that is, that the rates not be discriminatory. Yet, the discrimination would be defensible in terms of the discrepancy between average and long-run marginal cost of the industry. The discrepancy might be politically objectionable or regarded as morally repugnant; but (apart from any possible deleterious effect on competition, which we consider below) it could be economically justified.

As in most of these discussions, we have concentrated our attention on pricing. The same principles would apply to nonprice methods of soliciting business.[58] Commissions have long grappled with the question, for example, of how to treat the appliance-selling activities of electric and gas companies. The general practice has been to require separate accounting for such activities in order to exclude their expenses or net losses from the utility cost-of-service and their revenues or profits from utility earnings.[59] Discussion of the merits of this procedure has run largely in terms of whether nominal losses on such sales are, like routine business advertising, an acceptable means of promoting sales of gas or electricity, hence a reasonable charge on the public utility part of the business; or really an unrelated activity that ought not to be permitted to burden rate-payers.[60] The correct economic approach, it would seem, would be to treat the costs of cut-rate appliance sales and advertising directed at particular kinds of customers as a form of rate making. The relevant questions would be: Are they discriminatory? If so do they meet our other tests—are they justified by the presence of decreasing costs, that is, by MC being less than ATC? Do the additional sales that they promote cover their long-run incremental costs, including the costs of promoting them? The purpose of asking these questions would be to decide not whether to segregate the appliance-selling business for purposes of rate regulation but whether, just as with the offering of straight-forward promotional rates, such methods of sales promotion should be permitted at all.[61]

In concluding, it is important to reemphasize the basic prerequisite: the presence of decreasing costs. Where it is not present, rate discrimination becomes very questionable. Consider, for example, the various promotional airline fares to which we have already alluded. As long as reduced fares are for standby service or travel on off-peak days or seasons they are not discriminatory; they merely reflect (perhaps even inadequately) the lower marginal costs of travel that makes no marginal demand on capacity. To the extent that they are offered only to select groups—young people under 21, wives and children accompanying husbands—they are discriminatory but the discrimination may be justified because (1) of the presence of short-run decreasing costs at times when capacity is in excess and (2) the demand by these classes of travelers may well be more elastic than by single unaccompanied adults, many of them traveling on business.[62] But to the extent that

---

[57] 15 U.S.C. 13(a) (1964 ed.).
[58] See the same observation applied to the appraisal of selective promotional expenditures in light of the principle of peak-responsibility pricing, note 16, Chapter 4.
[59] C. F. Phillips, *op. cit.*, 189.
[60] See for example, Troxel, *Economics of Public Utilities*, 241–245.

[61] An additional consideration that has been raised in many of these cases is whether such practices constitute unfair competition with local appliance dealers. We treat problems of rate making in the presence of competition in Chapter 6.
[62] The Civil Aeronautics Board allowed these tariffs to become effective in 1966. *American*

the purpose of such fares, or of the subsidies paid to the airlines that serve smaller towns, or the discriminatorily low rates on short-hop trips[63] is merely to "promote air travel" or the habit of using airplanes, without reference to whether the travel promoted is on peak or off peak, it seems to lack economic justification, in view of the apparent absence of economies of scale in the air transport business in the relevant range.[64] In short, there seems to be much uneconomic internal subsidization in this industry.

FULLY DISTRIBUTED COSTS

When public utility commissions or companies attempt systematically to construct or to appraise a rate structure, they do not ordinarily do so by calculating long-run marginal costs and demand elasticities. More often they use various methods of distributing or allocating total revenue requirements (including, as always, return on investment) among the several services or categories of service. The costs of electric companies will be fully distributed between residential, commercial, industrial, street lighting uses and the like; the costs of railroads will be divided between passenger and freight business; of telephone common carriers between message toll and their various business service offerings; of telephone and gas pipeline companies subject to both federal and state regulation between jurisdictional and nonjurisdictional business by the respective regulatory agencies. These totals are then reduced to costs per unit on the basis of some measure of the physical quantities taken by each group of customers—ton-miles, revenue passenger miles, kilowatt hours, MCF's, telephone message minutes or message-minute-miles—whatever seems appropriate. To the extent that the rates for these respective classes of customers are then based on or conform to such fully distributed costs, all services, by definition, will earn the same rate of return on the investment allocated to them; and the rates thus determined or justified are "completely nondiscriminatory," by definition.

Space does not permit any systematic summary of the various, often extraordinarily complex methods employed to distribute costs in this

Airlines, Standby Youth Fares, Order E-23137, January 20, 1966. A number of bus companies succeeded, however, in getting a Circuit Court of Appeals decision ordering the Board to hold hearings on the subject. *Transcontinental Bus System, Inc. v. Civil Aeronautics Board*, 383 F.2d 466 (1967). Also, a Federal Circuit Court of Appeals in 1969 ordered the CAB to hold hearings on the complaint of bus companies that the family fares are unjust and discriminatory. *Wall Street Journal*, June 17, 1969.

In 1969 the Board tentatively decided that neither the standby youth fare (which offers a 50% reduction for standby service) nor the "young adult" fares (a $33\frac{1}{3}\%$ discount on reserved-seat service) was "unjustly discriminatory." *Standby Youth Fares—"Young Adult" Fares*, Docket 18936, Opinion, August 25, 1969.
[63] See note 69, p. 153.
[64] See the discussion on this point at note 180, Chapter 5, Volume 2. The Board did, however,

offer in justification the alleged presence of an interesting type of dynamic long-run decreasing cost. The fares were justified, it argued, because the growing traffic volume that they promoted in turn made possible the more rapid development and adoption of new, more efficient, speedier and more commodious equipment and scheduling, providing "service at an increasing level of speed, comfort and convenience." *Loc. cit.*, note 62, above. As we have suggested, if the expansion of demand is causally related to the development of cost-reducing technology, this may properly be regarded as the kind of LRDC that could justify discrimination. In principle the same would be true of technological progress that provided improved service at constant cost. But the CAB's emphasis on service improvements intead of cost reduction may itself reflect an uneconomic bias. See our discussion of this point in the section on "The Regulation of Non-Price Competition: Air Transport," in Chapter 5 of Volume 2.

fashion.[65] In general, some costs can be directly assigned exclusively to one service or other—for example, railroad passenger agents to passenger service, box cars and freight terminals to freight. But most costs must be allocated at least in part because they are incurred in serving more than one class of customers—maintenance, depreciation, return, operating costs of locomotives, roundhouses, track and right of way, and so on. These common or joint costs may be distributed on the basis of some common physical measure of utilization, such as minutes, circuit-miles, message-minute-miles, gross ton-miles, MCF, or kwh employed or consumed by each. Or they may be distributed in proportion to the costs that can be directly assigned to the various services.[66] An ingenious variant of the latter was the "alternative justifiable expenditures" method devised by the Tennessee Valley Authority, which in general allocated the common costs of multipurpose river development schemes among the various services supplied (electric power, navigation, flood control) in proportion to which it *would* have cost to provide each of those services in the same quantity in single-purpose projects set up exclusively for them.[67]

Quite simply, the basic defect of fully distributed costs as a basis for rate making is that they do not necessarily measure marginal cost responsibility in a causal sense. They do not measure by what amount costs would be increased if additional quantities of any particular service were taken, or by what amount costs would be reduced if the service were correspondingly curtailed. They are average costs: the allocations among the various services

---

[65] For an excellent discussion and appraisal, see Bonbright, *Principles of Public Utility Rates*, Chapter 18.

[66] See for instance, Howard W. Nicholson, "Motor Carrier Costs and Minimum Rate Regulation," *Q. Jour. Econ.* (February 1958), LXXII: 142. For an example of a combination of these two methods, the ICC prorates running track maintenance on the basis of the gross ton-miles of passenger and freight service, common equipment repairs on the basis of the relative use in each service, and some other expenses in proportion to solely related expenses. ICC *Investigation of Costs of Intercity Rail Passenger Service*, Report transmitted to the Senate Committee on Commerce and House Committee on Interstate and Foreign Commerce, Washington, July 16, 1969, 15. See also *Separation of Operating Expenses between Freight and Passenger Service*, 302 ICC 735 (1958) and *Railroad Passenger Train Deficit*, 306 ICC 417 (1959). For other examples of plausible methods of allocating common costs, see note 36, Chapter 3.

[67] The method was actually slightly more complicated, in that those investment costs specifically attributable to the individual services were deducted both from the aggregate investment costs of the multipurpose project and from the estimated costs of the individual, single-purpose projects, with the residue of the former being distributed in proportion to the residues of the latter. See the Federal Power Commission,

Report on Review of Allocations of Costs of the Multiple-Purpose Water Control System in the Tennessee River Basin, Washington, March 23, 1949, 21–22. The FPC was later prevailed on to accept a similar method, the "relative cost method," for allocating the costs of production on joint-product leases between natural gas, on the one hand, and oil and various natural gas liquids, on the other, in order to ascertain a "just and reasonable" field price for the natural gas. The method involved distributing the joint costs of producing those same quantities in proportion to the actual costs of producing that same number of barrels of crude oil on leases in which oil was produced in the absence or virtual absence of natural gas, on the one hand, and that number of cubic feet of natural gas from virtually dry gas leases on the other. See *Phillips Petroleum Co.*, 24 FPC 537, 553, 623–625 (1960) and *Opinion and Order Determining Just and Reasonable Rates for Natural Gas Producers in the Permian Basin*, 34 FPC 159, 214–215 (1965). In advocating this method, at a later stage only for pricing gas that had already been discovered and committed to pipeline purchasers, the present writer emphasized that while it might be deemed to provide a just or a fair distribution of the joint costs, it did not provide an economic measure of the separate costs. Testimony in the *Permian Basin* proceeding, FPC Docket No. AR 61–1, 1962, tr. 7212–17, 7346–47. See also my *op. cit.*, *Amer. Econ. Rev.*, *Papers and Proceedings* (May 1960), L: 510–514.

are often made in part on the basis of the relative number of physical units of consumption or utilization by each, and the total allocated dollars are then divided by those physical units to get the unit costs. Also, being apportionments of historical costs, even when they do accurately reflect historical responsibility for the incurrence of these costs among the respective users, they do not provide a reliable measure of what will happen to costs in the future if particular portions of the business are expanded or dropped. Therefore, they do not tell whether a particular service is really profitable or unprofitable, in the sense that its continued provision at existing rates makes a net contribution to company revenues over and above the costs for which it is responsible, or whether, instead, it is a burden on the other subscribers.

This is a defect, of course, only to the extent that marginal costs diverge from average. The full distribution of costs that underlies the familiar two- or three-part tariff for gas and electricity, for example, with its separate customer, commodity (or energy) and demand charges, is in part along lines that reflect true causal responsibility: costs such as meter reading and billing do in fact depend on the number of customers, others (such as fuel) on the mere quantity taken, and others (capacity costs) on the amount the supplier may be called on to provide on demand at the time of the system's peak. Note that the distribution is not among classes of customers, as such, but along functional lines that recognize the various genuine determinants of cost. But the unit costs so determined are average, not marginal. They give no recognition, therefore, to the fact that some of the capacity is provided under LRDC conditions; and that the generation of electricity is subject to short-run increasing costs, with the result (see pp. 94–97, Chapter 4) that those charges ought properly to be high enough at times to make a contribution to overheads. The functional distribution itself may conceal interesting discrepancies between marginal and average costs. In the case of gas pipeline companies, for example, the costs of their own gas producing operations are placed among commodity costs, presumably on the ground that the cost of the gas itself obviously must vary with the number of cubic feet taken. But pipelines obtain most even of their *purchased* gas under long-term contracts that promise a certain maximum daily deliverability and often oblige the line to pay for certain minimum specified daily quantities of gas whether or not they take that much. Even though they pay a certain price per MCF, therefore, some part of the costs of the purchased gas is fixed, not variable, and is a function of the capacity required at the peak. Similarly, many of the costs of the pipelines' own production are fixed, representing the investment required to provide a certain production capacity. Therefore, the cost of the gas itself that the pipelines transport and sell is only partly variable with quantities taken, and hence belongs only partly in the commodity charge; part of it really belongs in the demand charge.

Again, one important component of the "separations procedures" used by the Federal Communications Commission to (fully) distribute Bell System investment costs between interstate and intrastate service (since it regulates only the former) is the allocation of those costs on the basis of relative minute-miles or relative minutes of use for the two purposes.[68] To the extent that capacity costs incurred do indeed depend on the number of minutes taken up

---

[68] See, for example, FCC, *In the Matter of American Telephone and Telegraph Co. et al.*, Docket Nos. 15011 and 16258, Interim Decision and Order, 9 FCC 2d 30, 93 and *passim* (1967).

and miles covered by individual messages, this allocation method does reflect the respective average cost responsibilities of the two services. But since this procedure treats all minutes the same, peak and off-peak, it fails to recognize the varying capacity cost responsibilities of calls made at different times. Moreover, being a measure of average historical instead of marginal cost, it ignores the very marked tendencies to decreasing cost in long-distance telephonic communication, which we have already described. Finally, it is simply not the case that all the costs thus allocated do in fact vary with minutes or miles of use.[69]

A particularly clear example of the lack of correspondence between average, fully distributed and marginal costs and of the irrationality of basing rates on the former is provided by the FCC's distribution between intra- and interstate jurisdictions of the costs of telephone "subscriber plant"—the equipment on the customer's premises and between those premises and the local office or exchange. (Net investment in Bell System subscriber plant amounted to $15.4 billion in 1966.) It decided in 1967 to do so on the basis of (1) the relative minutes of use of that equipment for interstate and intrastate service, which measure produced an allocation of only 4% to the former, (2) with a judgmental adjustment for the greater average *value* of a minute's use for interstate than for intrastate messages—producing a final allocation of 12% to the former.[70] But subscriber plant is in fact idle most of the time: it was used an average of only 29 minutes a day in the test period. It is simply available at all times for any and all calls. A doubling of any of these utilizations would cause the company no additional cost incurrence for subscriber plant: the marginal cost is therefore zero.[71] The FCC's adjustment for the different value of the different uses was a recognition that since neither the 4% nor any other allocation could produce a measure of relative marginal cost responsibility, the allocation would have to be based on demand considerations. But in so doing it failed entirely to recognize that the economically relevant demand characteristic in these circumstances would have been demand elasticity, as Commissioner Johnson implied in his concurring opinion,[72] and that the upward adjustment of the allocation to

---

[69] On these separation procedures, see also note 39, p. 100, Chapter 4 and Richard Gabel, *Development of Separations Principles in the Telephone Industry* (East Lansing: Institute of Public Utilities, Michigan State Univ., 1967). AT&T has pointed out, for example, that it was irrational of the FCC to allocate all the costs of interexchange plant on the basis of message-minute-miles, since some of that plant consists in terminals, the costs of using which have nothing whatever to do with the miles over which the messages travel. *Ibid.*, 9 FCC 2d 30, 100.

The CAB and the airlines have in recent years come to recognize the same serious defect in a passenger fare structure that was originally based on a uniform rate per mile. Since the costs at the terminal—ticket sales, baggage check-in, loading and unloading, landing and take-off—are essentially the same per passenger or per flight, regardless of the length of the trip, these costs are fixed when the dimension of output is the number of miles traveled. On the other hand,

obviously the costs of the flight itself will vary with the length of the trip. Combining the fixed and variable costs produces a "tapered" cost structure, one in which costs per mile decline the longer the journey. The CAB has pointed out and the airlines have come increasingly to recognize that at a uniform rate per mile the long trips have been subsidizing the short runs, and both parties have therefore been moving toward a more tapered fare structure. See, for example, *Wall Street Journal*, June 16, 1969, 34; *New York Times*, August 10, 1969, Sec. 3, 1; and the CAB Rates Division, Bureau of Economics, Staff Report, *A Study of the Domestic Passenger Air Fare Structure* (Washington, January 1968).

[70] *In the Matter of American Telephone and Telegraph Co. et al.*, Docket Nos. 15011 and 16258, 9 FCC 2d 30, 101–110.

[71] We set aside the increased possibility of busy signals, that is, of congestion costs.

[72] *Ibid.*, 128–129, 135–137.

long-run distance calls was, by this criterion, probably an adjustment in the wrong direction.[73]

A final illustration of the discrepancy between fully distributed and marginal costs is provided by the efforts of the ICC over the years to determine the separate costs of rail passenger and freight business, particularly in connection with the accelerating efforts of the roads to drop almost all their passenger service. The passenger business, taken as a whole, clearly no longer covers its long-run marginal costs. But the size of this deficit is greatly exaggerated if one compares passenger revenues with the fully distributed costs allotted to it by the Interstate Commerce Commission: as the commission has itself estimated, only about 75% of the cost thus determined would definitely be saved if the service were abandoned, the remaining 25% representing a distribution of common costs of freight and passenger traffic.[74]

In August of 1968, the ICC's Bureau of Economics pointed out that although the defit of the passenger operations for all Class I railroads on a fully allocated basis was $485 million in 1967, the extent to which passenger service revenues fell short of operating expenses related solely to those services was only $72 million; and whereas the former figures showed comparably large deficits all through the 1960s (and, indeed, deficits in every year since World War II), the latter showed annual surpluses from 1959 through 1966.[75] This is not to say that these "solely related operating expenses" are a full or correct measure of the avoidable costs of passenger operations. For example, passenger equipment has salvage value, the return on which is a genuine opportunity cost of continuing that service, and undoubtedly some portion of such common costs as track maintenance,

---

[73] In so doing, the FCC mystifyingly compounded what it recognized was already an inefficient discouragement of toll telephone calls, resulting from the fact that all the costs allocated to that service are recovered in toll charges, which exceed the marginal costs of (additional) calls, whereas the capital costs of local, intrastate calls are recovered largely in a monthly rental charge, which produces a zero price for additional calls. *Ibid.*, par. 301. It clung to the same logic in its later modification of these separations procedures. *In the Matter of Prescription of Procedures for Separating and Allocating,* . . . [etc.], Docket No. 17975, Report and Order, January 29, 1969 (16 FCC 2d 332), pars. 20–33.

In practice, the devising of separations procedures has been mostly a political process, involving a balancing of the interests of state and federal regulatory agencies. See the dissenting opinion of Commissioner Johnson, *ibid.* In particular, the modifications described both here and in Chapter 4 (p. 100, note 39), both of which had the effect of shifting costs—uneconomically, we have suggested—from the intrastate to the interstate level were apparently in response to the marked tendencies after World War II for their respective costs to move in the opposite directions. The state commissions, anxious to avoid the embarrassment of having to permit

continuous increases in local rates, pressed for separations that would tend to offset these divergent trends and, conceivably, the Bell System was willing to go along in order to diminish correspondingly the necessity of asking for such increases at the state level and of accepting reductions in interstate toll rates. According to a private estimate made in 1969 the overall effect of the change in separations was to keep interstate toll cost of service 12% higher, and state rates 10% lower (on a 1968 basis) than they would otherwise have been. AT&T's efforts to correct some of these distortions in recent years must have reflected the company's growing competition on the interstate part of its business, and its difficulties in meeting that competition as long as its interstate rate base was inflated in this way. See, for example, pp. 173–174, and the section on the national telecommunications network in Chapter 4, Volume 2.

[74] See ICC, *Investigation of Costs of Intercity Rail Passenger Service,* 1969, 48. See also the summary of the evidence in C. F. Phillips, *op. cit.,* 154–157; also J. C. Nelson, *op. cit.,* 284–296; and our discussion of the *Southern Pacific* decision, Chapter 2, Volume 2.

[75] *Transport Economics, Monthly Comment,* August 1968, 2–3.

repairs, and general administrative expenses could well be eliminated if passenger service were dropped.[76]

Therefore, in 1968 the ICC undertook an intensive study of the true avoidable costs of passenger service. Its analysis of the passenger operations of eight major intercity railroads concluded that these roads would eventually have saved $118 million more in expenses than they would have lost in revenues if they had not operated any passenger service in that year. In addition, they could have earned approximately $5 million on the salvage value of the facilities and equipment that would no longer be needed. On the other hand the $118 million includes some allowance for depreciation—evidently about $14,500,000—on the ground that this "is a properly assignable expense under generally accepted accounting procedures"[77]; but this is clearly not a real marginal cost that would have been avoided in an economic sense. (What would have been "avoided" would be the periodic accounting recording of depreciation, not any use of cash or real resources.[78]) The $118 million figure may be compared with the full ICC deficits of these roads measured with fully allocated costs, of $214 million.[79]

The basic defect of full cost distributions as the basis for pricing is, then, that they ignore the pervasive discrepancies between marginal and average cost. And, as this chapter has demonstrated, those discrepancies may require prices that take into account not just the costs but also the elasticities of demand of the various categories of service if the company is to recover its total costs. Whenever there is some separable portion of the demand sufficiently elastic that a rate below fully-distributed costs for it would add more to total revenue than to total costs, any insistence that each service or group of patrons pay their fully allocated costs would be self-defeating. It would force the firm to charge a price that would result in its turning away business that would have covered its marginal costs—in other words, would prevent it from obtaining from customers with an elastic demand the maximum possible contribution to overheads. Thus, under the guise of ensuring a fair distribution of common costs and preventing undue discrimination, it would be serving the interests neither of the patrons who would be prepared to take additional quantities if prices were closer to marginal costs, nor of the customers with the more inelastic demands.[80]

---

[76] On the other hand, not all solely related expenses are avoidable: for example, some of the expenses of passenger car and road locomotive repairs could not be eliminated. ICC *Investigation of Costs of Intercity Rail Passenger Service*, 1969, 49–52.

[77] *Ibid.*, 20; see also 37–38.

[78] A similar question might be raised about its inclusion of property taxes. These, in contrast with depreciation, are a genuine avoidable expense from the standpoint of the railroads; the question is whether they are a true social cost, representing a use of resources. To the extent that property—for example, passenger terminals in cities—could be used for other purposes, on which such taxes could in fact be paid out of commercial revenues, the taxes are properly included, as a reflection of the opportunity cost to society of using the property for the passenger

service. On the other hand, by this measure, railroad property is probably overtaxed. (See note 34, Chapter 7.)

[79] The biggest explanation of the difference is that only 74.4% of the expenses charged to passenger operations by the ICC separation rules could actually have been avoided by cessation of that service. See *ibid.*, i–iii, 47–48 and *passim.*

[80] See the testimony of Bonbright, Baumol and Froggatt, Bell Exhibits (in FCC Docket No. 16258, *op. cit.*, 1966). See, also, the testimony of Baumol in Verified Statement No. 67, January 20, 1966, *Canned Goods Between Pacific Coast and the East et al.*, Interstate Commerce Commission, Docket No. 34573 *et al.*; de Chazeau, *op. cit.*, *Q. Jour. Econ.* (February 1938), LII: 349–350, 355–356.

For an analysis and criticism of the "cost ascertainment system" of fully allocating costs

The most venerable and familiar illustration of this defect is provided by the historic inability of the railroads to charge uniform freight rates per ton-mile. What was the economic basis for charging higher rates per ton-mile for furniture than coal, or for watches than furniture—entirely apart from possible differences in the respective costs of carrying them? Or for charging lower rates to carry coal into towns with their own possible sources of supply than into towns with no potential local sources of production? The basis was that if the railroads charged uniform rates, all of them equal to the average total cost per ton-mile of traffic, they might have succeeded in getting the higher-value business, the watches and possibly the furniture and the coal delivered into towns with no local supply, but would have gotten very little if any of the lower-value business. The traffic in bulky, low-value per ton commodities, they discovered, was highly responsive to the rates charged. In contrast, the traffic in commodities with a high value per ton, for which the same rate per ton-mile would amount to a much lower proportion of their final sales price, was correspondingly price-inelastic. The former traffic would bear only a comparatively low rate, the latter a high rate at least before the truck offered a feasible alternative.[81] The consequences of a uniform, nondiscriminatory rate would have been an underutilization of rail capacity and a loss of traffic that could easily have covered incremental costs and made a contribution to common costs.[82]

A fully distributed cost analysis of the interstate and foreign communications services of the Bell System played a leading role in the FCC's comprehensive investigation of the rates and the rate structures of AT&T and its associated companies, initiated late in 1965. Following the directions of the Commission, the respondent companies prepared a Seven-Way Cost Study, which distributed the interstate and foreign costs of the System among seven major services mainly on the basis of their relative use of the common facilities: message toll telephone, teletypewriter exchange, wide-area telephone, telephone grade private-line, telegraph grade private-line, TELPAK, and all others. A comparison of these costs with the corresponding revenues produced calculations of the "profitability" of each of these services. The ratios of their net operating earnings to (allocated) net investments ranged for the 12-month period, September 1, 1963 to August 31, 1964, from 0.3% (on TELPAK) to 10.1% (on wide-area telephone service). Calling to the attention of the respondents the wide variation in earnings revealed by this analysis, the Commission instructed them:

---

employed by the U.S. Post Office and argument that it is irrelevant for rate making, or for deciding which services do or do not pay their way, along similar lines, see *Towards Postal Excellence*, Report of the President's Commission on Postal Organization, Washington, June 1968, 30–31, 130–135 and Annex, Vol. 2, Report on *Rates and Rate Making*.

[81] See section on transportation in Chapter 1, Volume 2.

[82] See the lucid statement by Ford K. Edwards, before the ICC, *Rules to Govern the Assembling and Presenting of Cost Evidence*, Docket No. 34013, Reply to the Report and Order Recommended

by Jair S. Kaplan, Hearing Examiner, February 28, 1967; and his "The Proper Function of Incremental Costs in Rate Making," a paper presented before the Federal Bar Association Twenty-second Annual Meeting, May 3, 1967; and George W. Wilson, "Value of Service Pricing for the Railroads," *Business Horizons* (Fall 1958), I: 88–97. As Edwards points out elsewhere, not only did 65% of railroad freight tonnage move in 1960 at rates below fully distributed costs, but some of the freight with the lowest *percentage* markup over out-of-pocket cost made the largest *aggregate* contribution to overheads. Testimony before the ICC, *Ingot*

"Respondents shall indicate the specific rate adjustments, if any, which they consider should be made on an interim basis in the light of such study results and the rate-making principles and factors advocated by them."[83]

The following table provides a truncated summary of the results. It combines the figures for the six business services, since the principal controversy is related to the low apparent earnings on these as compared with the 10.0% computed return on message toll telephone service.[84] It was the complaint by Western Union that AT&T's low rates on the former services, in the offer of some of which the two companies were competitors, were subsidized by the high profits in the monopoly MTT market that precipitated the inquiry.

table 2 Bell System Interstate Services (Total Day) for 12-Month Period September 1, 1963 to August 31, 1964 Earnings Statement Summary

	Message Toll Telephone	All Other Services	Total
Total revenues	$2,137,522	$ 562,352	$2,699,874
Total expenses, income charges and operating taxes	$1,710,799	$ 496,486	$2,207,285
Net operating earnings	$ 426,723	$ 65,866	$ 492,589
Net investment	$4,286,702	$2,271,704	$6,588,406
Ratio of net operating earnings to net investment	10.0%	2.9%	7.5%

Source. FCC *Special Interstate Cost Study*, Docket No. 14650, AT&T Exhibit 81, Attachment A, 4.

The interpretation of these data by Western Union and some of the FCC staff was, of course, that the various business services were not earning the 7.5% legal allowable return on investment, that the users of message toll telephone service were being overcharged in order to subsidize the business services and that Western was indeed being subjected to unfair, subsidized competition.

The FCC never did finally decide whether the data justified these conclusions.[85] We need observe only that they do not necessarily. The fundamental test of whether the MTT customers were subsidizing the rates on the business services is whether the latter covered their long-run marginal costs, including the 7.5% return on the *incremental* investment causally attributable to them. *If* (setting aside the allocations of the various expense items) the investment required for the Bell companies to provide message toll telephone service alone would have been not 4.3 but some $5.7 billion, and *if* the incremental investment costs necessary to introduce the various business services were not $2.3 billion but just short of $900 million, then the net operating earnings shown in table 2 would have represented a 7.5% return on the investments in both categories. In fact, the business services would have

Molds—Pennsylvania to Steelton, Kentucky, Docket 8038, April 21, 1964.

[83] *In the Matter of American Telephone and Telegraph Co. et al.*, Docket No. 16258, Memorandum Opinion and Order, 2 FCC 2d 142, 143 (1965). See also note 1, Chapter 3.

[84] Apart from WATS, returns on the business services ranged between 0.3 and 4.7%.

[85] See the inconclusive "Statement of Rate-Making Principles and Factors" that ultimately emerged from this phase of the investigation. *In the Matter of American Telephone and Telegraph Co.*, Dockets 16258, 15011 and 18128, Memorandum Opinion and Order, July 29, 1969.

been remunerative and imposed no burden on ordinary long-distance telephone callers.

But cost considerations alone could not determine whether the MTT customers might or might not have had a legitimate complaint about who was getting the LRMC price and who was being forced to make a disproportionately large contribution to overheads. Why, it must still be asked, should the former have attributed to them the full average costs of serving them alone and the latter only the requisite incremental investment? Justification for this kind of discrimination must be found in the comparative elasticities of demand for the two services. If demand for the various business services was the more elastic of the two, and if rates on those services had been set at a point that maximized their net contribution to aggregate system revenues, no rearrangement of the rates could have improved the situation for the patrons of the message toll telephone service.

If these various conditions existed, Western Union might have still claimed to be the victim of subsidized competition, in the sense that the prices with which it was having to compete were discriminatorily low. But if they were lowered only to the point of maximizing the benefit to the MTT customers, whose rates under any other system of pricing could only have been *higher*, it is difficult to see that the "subsidized" characterization could have any economic substance.[86] In any event, the presence of competition introduces a whole new set of considerations that we reserve for treatment in Chapter 6.

The Seven-Way Cost Study served to raise the question of whether these necessary conditions were in fact present in the telephone industry. But the study could not answer the question.

The other side of the coin is that where these conditions are *not* present—for example, for those segments of demand that do not have the requisite high elasticity—prices based on fully distributed costs have much to recommend them. This is so, at least in so far as they consist of identifiable, separate costs for the various classes of service plus a proportionate contribution to joint or otherwise inallocable costs. To the extent that the relation of marginal to average costs is the same for these different categories, this type of full-cost pricing amounts to fixing rates in proportion to marginal costs and, hence, retaining the same relative price relationships as would prevail under strict marginal cost pricing. We have seen that this comes tolerably close to avoiding any distortion of consumer choices among the various services. It may also have attractiveness on distributional grounds, since economics provides no assurance that there is any better way of distributing the advantages of joint operation and decreasing cost among the various classes of rate-payers.[87] Moreover, the respective average historic cost responsibilities of the various classes of service plus proportionate contributions to overhead will most likely strike the various rate-payers as equitable and nondiscriminatory. Where none of these categories of demand is sufficiently elastic for discriminatory rate reductions to confer advantages on all, any other pattern of rate making would involve making some customers better off at the expense of others.

---

[86] See notes 38 and 45, p. 143 and p. 145.   [87] See p. 145.

CHAPTER 6

Rate-Making in the Presence of Competition

We began Chapter 3 with the observation that some of the most challenging developments in public utility rate making in recent years have been the efforts of regulated companies to revise their rate structures in the face of competition. Our exposition of economic principles has thus far given no explicit recognition to this consideration. Yet it could not have been far beneath the surface: one of the two fundamental criteria for rate making in the presence of decreasing costs is elasticity of demand; and the most powerful determinant of the elasticity of demand for the services of any *single* company is the presence or absence of competing suppliers. In practice, therefore, the principal impetus to discriminatory price reductions is likely to be the desire of the public utility company to hold or to attract certain categories of customers from competitors. In addition, price discrimination raises the most serious questions when the customers being discriminated among are themselves in competition with one another, the danger being that the differences in the terms on which they are able to acquire public utility services—differences, being discriminatory, that are not explained by the relative costs of serving them—may distort that competition. How may the presence of competition, at the level either of the discriminating seller or his customers qualify the various principles set forth in our preceding chapters ?

In a way these problems are more intense in the public utility arena than in competitive industry generally. It takes monopoly power to hold price above marginal cost in the price-inelastic market. The fact that most public utility companies are physically linked to their customers in the supply of an essential service—the very fact that makes monopoly "natural" because it is usually inefficient to have more than one company linked in this way to customers in a particular area and because increasingly intensive use of that link involves decreasing unit costs—ties customers to them and makes those customers potentially victims of exploitatively high prices. Except for transportation, competitive pressures are typically confined to particular branches of business or particular locations. Even in transportation, where the pervasiveness of competition permits one legitimately to raise the question of whether the scope of regulatory supervision might not appropriately be sharply diminished and competitive forces given freer play, there can be little doubt that such competition would remain highly selective, with particular customers or classes of business, in particular locations, potentially well protected by competitive forces and others subject to the danger of considerable monopolistic exploitation.

Our examples will come mainly from the field of transportation, where we have had a rich history of regulation, extending back almost a century. From the outset, an important aspect of transportation regulation was aimed at controlling competition instead of merely regulating a monopolist. Indeed, it has been the prevalence and growth of this competition that has made it questionable to refer to the railroads as "public utilities" at all, or to attempt to apply to them the principles appropriate to "natural monopolists." Still, the competitive considerations in transportation, although different in degree and pervasiveness, are not different in kind from those applicable to rate making by electricity and gas distribution companies or communications common carriers.

The lessons to be learned from our long experience with intercarrier competition would seem to be these:

1. Long-run marginal costs are still the place to begin in assessing the validity of competitive rate reductions, and, particularly where the cost structures of the competing suppliers are widely divergent, LRMC will in most instances constitute a complete and sufficient test.

2. Not all rates will be set as low as long-run marginal costs, because competitive pressures will differ between different customers, classes of service, and localities; nor can all rates be set as low as LRMC and still cover average total costs. When the customers being discriminated between are in compet' .on with one another, selective rate reductions down to marginal costs give rise to a danger that competition at the buyer level will be distorted. When this danger arises, competitive rate reductions must be further scrutinized, to consider on the one hand whether they are conducive to a more efficient conduct of the business at the primary level, that is, on the suppliers' side, and, on the other hand, whether they contribute to an uneconomic diversion of business at the secondary level, that is, between competing buyers. The merits of discriminatory reductions are most likely to be questionable when the competitors have similar cost levels and structures.

3. Special consideration may have to be given to the institutional implications and consequences of discriminatory price competition. This would include the following: (a) the important stimulus that price competition imparts to keeping companies on their toes, energetic in cutting costs, enterprising in experimenting with price reductions, innovative in service, and (b) the possibility that competition will be predatory or destructive.

THE CENTRAL ROLE OF LONG-RUN MARGINAL COSTS

Apart from possible noneconomic considerations, society's interest is in having transportation, energy, or communications provided at the lowest possible cost, with due allowance for possible differences in the quality of services supplied or the costs imposed on the users.[1] And economic efficiency requires, additionally, that no business be turned away that covers the cost

---

[1] Trucks give door-to-door, and often speedier service than do railroads. The proper test of the desirability of these added services is whether customers are willing to pay the incremental cost

to society of providing that service. These basic goals are served by permitting rates to be set at long-run marginal costs. The consequence will be that, after consumers have made allowance in their choices for possible differences in the quality of the service, the competing company with the lowest long-run marginal costs will get the business; and the services will thus be provided by those companies which, in so doing, will impose the minimum opportunity costs on the economy at large.

This criterion is especially relevant in assessing proposed rate reductions by railroads in order to compete more effectively with trucks or barges. Railroads have heavy fixed costs, chronic excess capacity, and the widest discrepancy between marginal and average total or fully allocated costs. The other transport media, to a much greater extent, use variable factors: trucks are shorter-lived and both they and barges travel on roadways and rivers for which they pay on a variable basis, whether year-to-year in license fees or mile-by-mile in excise taxes on fuel and tires, in tolls, and so forth.[2] Moreover, both trucks and barges can more readily be taken off particular routes or branches of service (locomotives and freight cars can as well, but terminals and road beds cannot), so that for any particular market their entire cost is more nearly variable. And to a much greater extent than in the case of railroads their total costs vary in proportion with the mileage of each trip. This is true of the costs of drivers, fuel, and the depreciation of the trucks themselves.[3] Therefore, it is roughly true that the long-run marginal costs for the railroad carriage of particular commodities over particular routes, on the one hand, and the average total costs of trucks and barges, on the other,[4] represent the marginal opportunity costs to society of using these respective modes of transportation. In these circumstances, if railroad rates, set no lower than long-run marginal costs, succeed in taking business away from trucks and barges, it follows that it is efficient for society to permit them to do so.

---

of providing them. The market solution would be for the competing services to be priced at their respective long-run marginal costs, leaving the choice to customers, considering both the different rates and different qualities.

[2] The particular arrangements devised to recover these costs make them variable from the users' standpoint. The costs might be fixed from the standpoint of society, which is really what counts. But society is constantly adding to its highway capacity and is therefore in a position to alter promptly the size of those increments depending on the amount of traffic. Also, depreciation of the roads and the need for maintenance is in considerable measure a user cost; to the extent that trucks (particularly heavy trucks) curtail their use of highways, much of these costs can be avoided. These considerations apply much less to water transport. The principal distortion there, however, is that the users do not pay the full costs, fixed or variable, of maintaining and improving the waterways. This constitutes an even stronger argument for letting the choice be between the *marginal* costs of rails and the *total* costs of the barges. It would be even more conducive to efficiency if the latter were adjusted even higher to include the full

costs of providing these "road beds."

[3] Terminal and other overhead costs, which are fixed for a particular shipment, are higher for railroads. This combination of circumstances gives a competitive advantage to the trucks for shorter trips—up to about 300 miles—and to the rails for longer trips. The ATC of the rails decline as the length of trip increases, whereas the ATC of the trucks is more nearly constant. See George W. Wilson, "Effects of Value-of-Service Pricing upon Motor Common Carriers," *Jour. Pol. Econ.* (August 1955), LXIII: 341; Dudley F. Pegrum, *Transportation: Economics and Public Policy* (Homewood: Richard D. Irwin, 1963), 189–190 and Chapter 8; F. K. Edwards, "Cost Analysis in Transportation," *Amer. Econ. Rev., Papers and Proceedings* (May 1947), XXXVII: 449–452; and Merrill J. Roberts, "Transport Costs, Pricing and Regulation," in Universities-National Bureau Committee for Economic Research, *Transportation Economics*, esp. 3–12.

[4] Indeed, in as much as heavy diesel trucks and barges do not pay the full long-run marginal costs of the provision of roads or waterways, even their average total costs underestimate the real costs of transportation by these media.

This was roughly the comparison offered to the ICC and the U.S. Supreme Court in the famous *Ingot Molds* case.[5] The case involved a proposed reduction in a joint all-rail rate from $11.86 to $5.11 per ton, which would have taken all the business away from trucks and barges. The contesting parties essentially agreed that the fully distributed and long-run marginal costs for the railroads were on the order of $7.59 and $4.69 per ton, respectively, whereas for the barge-truck service both cost figures were approximately the same figure, $5.19 per ton.[6]

It should be emphasized that the foregoing reasoning applies not just to general but also to selective rate reductions. As long as a public utility company can take business away from its competitors at rates that cover long-run incremental costs for that business, both efficiency in the performance of the public utility function and the interest of all rate-payers recommend its being permitted to do so, all other things being equal. The competitive advantage may spring from simple differences in the efficiencies of firms in essentially similar industries, using essentially similar technology, or—as is much more likely and common in the public utility situation—differences in the respective technologies and cost structures, which have the effect of producing markedly lower long-run incremental cost for certain companies than for others. It is sometimes contended by trucking or barge companies, or by oil jobbers facing this discriminatory rate making, that the competition to which they are being subjected is unfair: their competitors are quoting discriminatorily low prices on those portions of the business in which they meet in competition, relying on the sheltered portions of their business for the greater contribution to overhead costs. However, the inequality of such competition resides in objective differences in the cost behavior and structure of the two industries. If following the rules outlined above results in business being taken away from the complaining companies, it is simply because the successful competitor is able to fulfill the function with a lesser expenditure of society's resources, not because it is subsidizing that competition out of high profits earned on its sheltered business. The consequence of its getting the competitive business is not to require recoupment from the higher-margin business but instead to permit reduction of that margin.

Some of the justices of the U.S. Supreme Court evidently found it difficult to understand or to accept this elementary proposition in the *Ingot Molds* case, as the following report of some of their colloquies on oral argument shows:

"Justice Byron R. White, and to a lesser extent, Chief Justice Earl Warren expressed concern that using out-of-pocket costs as a standard where competition exists might result in the rails' saddling shippers with higher rates, where there is no competition, so that overall costs could be met. . . .

"Justice White hammered at the theme that money lost by cutting rates below full costs 'must be recovered by some other traffic.'

---

[5] *American Commercial Lines, Inc., et al. v. Louisville & Nashville Railroad Co. et al.*, 392 U.S. 571 (1968).

[6] *Ibid.*, 575–576. The $4.69 figure for the rails, which was the ICC's estimate of "long-term out-of-pocket" costs, still included a 4% return on the portion of total investment allocated to this service under the Commission's method for full distribution of costs.

For a similar example, suggesting that the long-run marginal costs of communication by satellite might be below those of microwave radio but the average costs above, with the same conclusion—that the business should go to the former, see Johnson in Shepherd and Gies, *op. cit.*, 125–126.

". . . Justice Warren . . . remarked: 'If they [the railroads] don't get full costs in this situation where they had competition, don't they have to make that up where there are no competitors?'

"Mr. Friedman replied that 'obviously total operations must be borne by all customers.' But, he said, in this case since the rate is compensatory, the customers would be better off in the long run. He reasoned that through the rate cut the rails obtained traffic that it would not have otherwise and that the revenue acquired above out-of-pocket costs would go toward general overhead. . . .

"Later, Justice Fortas pointed out that the fixed costs of railroads are much greater than those of barge lines.

"'So if out-of-pocket costs are the standard, the railroads would always have an advantage. There is an enormous spread between fixed and out-of-pocket costs.

"'What you are saying,' he told Mr. Friedman, 'is that in every case the Commission has to allow the railroads to cut their rates within a marginal area and take business from barge lines.'"[7]

The point that the justices failed to see was that it was not a simple matter of one medium of transport having a lower ratio of variable to total costs than the other: there would be no logic in letting the business go to a firm merely because some portion of its total costs was lower than its competitors'. The advantage of the rails was that their long-run *marginal* costs—*including* fixed costs on any incremental investment that might have been required to handle the additional traffic—were lower than the long-run marginal costs of their competitors.

Clearly, the possibilities of this kind of competitive displacement are greatest where the technologies of the competing suppliers are sharply different, as in the case of railroads and trucks. It may similarly be true between electric companies and home heating oil distributors. But if the electric companies have a cost advantage in this competition, it does not lie in the mere fact that a much smaller proportion of their costs are variable than is the case of the oil jobbers, the major part of whose costs consist of the cost of purchased fuel oil. In fact, the latter companies receive their supplies preponderantly from highly integrated companies, which would presumably be prepared, if need be, to reduce the prices they charge for the oil down to *their own* variable costs. The relevant comparison of variable to total cost ratios would thus be between electric companies and vertically integrated oil producer-refiners. In any event, the principal possible advantage of the electric companies would not be that their *average*, short-term variable costs set a lower floor under their prices than is the case with the oil companies. It would be that they employ a technology with strong tendencies toward long-run decreasing cost; and they compete with an essentially extractive industry, whose inherent, static tendencies toward long-run increasing costs can be offset only by continuous technological progress. In these circumstances the former have a much lower ratio of *long-run marginal* to average cost than the latter. And to the extent that their LRMC are lower than for the oil companies, it is better for *all* their customers and for society as well if they get the business.[8]

---

[7] *Transport Topics*, April 29, 1968, 1.
[8] The lower marginal costs may be the result not of a difference in technology but of the presence of joint costs, in situations where the competitive

The marginal costs against which competitive rates should be judged are the costs of the company quoting or proposing to quote those rates, *not the costs of their competitors.*[9] Effective competition and economic efficiency alike require that lower-cost firms be encouraged, because of their own lower costs, to reduce their prices to take business away from their higher-cost competitors.[10] The basic economic objection to cartels and cartel-like arrangements is that they impede this process by forcing the lower-cost firms to price instead in consideration of average industry costs or the costs of their less efficient competitors. The same objection applies to the historic reluctance of the ICC to permit railroad companies to reduce rates to long-run marginal costs in situations where these are below the average total costs of trucks and barges.[11] The purpose has been the same—to preserve a fair share of the con-

---

business is "off-peak." For example, in one striking case, the ICC correctly approved sharply reduced rail rates on the carriage of coal from Kentucky to points in Florida on the ground that the rail cars would in any event be returning empty after having hauled phosphate rock from Florida to points northward of the Kentucky mines and that the reductions were required if the railroads were to get the business in competition with water carriers. The coal rates were judged compensatory because they were above the slight additional costs involved in hauling the cars back with coal in them *instead of empty:*

"The omission by the respondents of a proportionate share of the round-trip line-haul costs results in a short-term variable cost and the reduced rate based thereon is essentially a 'back haul' rate. Normally, the proper level of cost by which to judge a rate is the long-term out-of-pocket cost, which includes a proportionate share of the joint round-trip cost." *Coal—Southern Mines to Tampa and Sutton, Fla.*, 318 ICC 371, 382 (1962).

Although the reduction on the coal was clearly selective it was not discriminatory in economic terms: the rate resulted in effect from auctioning off the joint (return haul) capacity—like the cotton seeds in Figure 2, Chapter 3—at whatever price was required to clear the market. And despite the ICC's characterization, it truly covered long-run, not just short-run incremental cost, since the costs of the round trip would have been incurred whether or not the coal was carried. But there was an element of discrimination in that the roads asked and received permission to cut the coal rate on hauls only to Florida, not to intermediate points that did not enjoy the barge alternative. The justification for this type of discrimination is further analyzed in our discussion relative to Figure 7.

[9] See William Baumol *et al.*, "The Role of Cost in the Minimum Pricing of Railroad Service," *Jour. of Bus.* (October 1962), XXXV: 365. An earlier version of the Transportation Act of 1958,

attempting to give force to this economic principle, provided that in passing on proposed railroad rate reductions in competition with some other mode of transport, the ICC should "consider the facts and circumstances attending the movement of the traffic by railroad and *not by such other mode.*" See *American Commercial Lines v. Louisville & Nashville Railroad*, 392 U.S. 571, 580 (1968); also note 12, below.

[10] As we have already pointed out in this connection (see pp. 148–149, Chapter 5), the same type of economic rationale might justify the use of advertising or promotional allowances of one kind or another by the company with the cost advantage. Gas, oil, and electric companies have been offering various inducements to builders— outright gifts of money or offers to pay the costs of laying lines underground, for example—to induce them to install cooking and heating equipment using their respective services. The costs of these various nonprice inducements must be added to the long-run marginal costs of providing the public utility service, in determining whether the proposed rates are compensatory.

On the other hand, there could be institutional reasons for regulatory commissions insisting that all such interfuel competition be confined to the price of the fuel or energy itself to the ultimate user instead of being permitted to focus on the builder's decision about the kind of equipment to install. Any such decision would properly turn on the effectiveness of competition in the construction industry as a mechanism for getting the proper decisions made. This would include a consideration of whether the buyers of homes and commercial establishments whose builders had been influenced by such inducements were able to take intelligent account of the probable fuel or energy costs of the edifices they buy, when they come equipped to use one fuel or energy source rather than another. See the discussion of this problem on pp. 177–180.

[11] For a recent example see the ingot molds decision, *American Commercial Lines v. Louisville & Nashville Railroad*, 392 U. S. 571 (1968). See, also,

tested business for the latter carriers.[12] And so have the results; this anti-competitive and protectionist policy has contributed to inefficiency in our

the Commission's earlier decision, *New Automobiles in Interstate Commerce*, 259 ICC 475 (1945).

[12] See the discussion of these policies in the section on transportation, Chapter 1, Volume 2. The Interstate Commerce Act was amended in 1958 to instruct the Commission not to hold up the rates of a carrier to a particular level in order to protect the traffic of any competing transport medium. This might have justified its looking only at rail costs to test the validity of proposed railroad rate cuts. But the 1958 amendment still enjoined the ICC to give "due consideration to the objectives of national transportation policy," which includes recognizing and preserving "the inherent advantage of each" mode of transport. In so doing, the Commission therefore continues to look at the costs of all the carriers involved in the contested traffic, in order to assess their respective "inherent advantages."

The ICC would deny that its purpose in so doing is anticompetitive. Its avowed purpose is to prevent predatory competition by the carrier that happens to have lower out-of-pocket costs from taking the business away from the carrier with the "inherent cost advantage." But its method of determining that balance of advantage is by comparison of fully distributed costs. It was on this basis that it refused to permit the Louisville and Nashville and Pennsylvania Railroads to reduce rates on ingot molds in the direction of their own incremental costs in order to take the traffic away from the truck-barge combination. (See the relative cost data on p. 162.)

"We do not agree with respondents' arguments that fully distributed costs are an inappropriate or inadequate measure of the inherent cost advantages of competing regulated carriers . . . . [M]erely because a carrier is able, without incurring an out-of-pocket loss, to handle certain traffic at rates below fully distributed costs, and perhaps . . . to maximize thereby the contribution that such traffic would make to its overhead, does not necessarily mean that the carrier is the more efficient of the two. Carriers, such as the railroad respondents, do not, in the circumstances here present, possess an inherent cost advantage within the context of the national transportation policy. . . .

"In short, by reducing its rate below the level of the barge-truck full costs, the respondent railroads have unlawfully impinged upon the ability of the barge-truck mode competitively to assert its inherent cost advantage." *Ingot Molds, Pa. to Steelton, Ky.*, 326 ICC 77, 82, 85 (1965).

In fact, it is precisely the comparison of long-run marginal costs that, on grounds of economic efficiency, ought to determine which carrier has

the "inherent advantage." For a powerful argument to the same end, see the *Brief for the United States* in this case, *Louisville and Nashville v. U.S. and the ICC*, U. S. District Court, Western District of Ky., Civil Action No. 5227, Sept. 6, 1966, in which the Department of Justice, "confessing error," asked the Court to overturn the ICC. Interestingly, the Commission was perfectly willing to use out-of-pocket rail costs as its test of the compensatory character of reduced rail rates when the target of those reductions was the competition of unregulated truckers instead of other regulated carriers. *Grain in Multiple-Car Shipments—River Crossings to the South*, 325 ICC 752, 758–759, 770–776 (1965).

This comparison of carrier costs by the ICC has raised another interesting question in cases of rail-barge competition, where the latter carrier is subsidized: which measure of the barge costs ought the ICC to take into account in determining its "inherent advantage"—the (higher) real social costs of carriage or the (lower) monetary costs of the private carrier itself, the difference between the two being made up by government subsidy? If barge costs are to be considered at all in such cases, economic efficiency would surely require use of the first criterion—a comparison of the real, social long-run marginal costs of the two competing media. This question figured prominently in an important case in which the Southern Railway Company, using in part the justification of its having introduced "Big John" freight cars, proposed a reduction of approximately 60% in rates for grain shipped in multiple-car lots to a point in the southeast, principally in order to meet the competition of unregulated truckers. In consideration of the protests raised by competing barge-lines, the Commission approved instead a cut of only 53.5% in order to "preserve for the barge line the cost advantage they enjoy with respect to certain port-to-port movements." "Big John: ICC Cuts Against the Grain," *Railway Age*, July 22, 1963, 32. See 321 ICC 582 (1963) 616. The Commission's own Division 2 had recommended that the costs borne by the taxpayer be considered in determining which was the lower-cost mode, and had on that basis approved the 60% rail rate reduction. *Grain in Multiple-Car Shipments—River Crossings to the South*, 318 ICC 641, 683 (1963). But the full Commission reasoned that such a test would flout the will of Congress, which, in subsidizing water transportation, could logically be presumed to have expressed a wish that the mode of transportation obtain a larger share of the business than it could obtain in the open market. *Ibid.*, 321 ICC 582, 599 (1963).

transportation industry,[13] to the preservation of unnecessarily high rates, and to the chronic financial weakness of the railroads.[14]

But this statement of the continued validity of the long-run marginal cost test is only the beginning, not the end of the task of appraising competitive rate reductions. Against their possible contribution to a more efficient performance of the public utility function must be weighed their possibly deleterious impact on competition.

THE IMPACT ON COMPETITION AT THE SECONDARY LEVEL

As in competitive industry generally, price discrimination by public utility companies may have undesirable consequences either at the primary level —that is, on competition between the discriminating seller and rival suppliers —or at the secondary level—that is, on competition among customers of the discriminating monopolist. Once the principle is accepted that rates may not be reduced below long-run marginal costs, the first danger becomes of considerably less significance than the second, since this rule goes far toward preventing the cutting of rates to unremunerative levels. It also assures, therefore, that if competitors are displaced by the selective rate cuts, it will be because their marginal costs are higher and they deserve to be supplanted.[15] But distortions at the secondary level are inescapable in any system of price discrimination: not all customers will be charged the long-run marginal costs of serving them. In certain circumstances, the resultant inefficiencies at the buyers' level will outweigh the economic advantages at the primary level.

To begin with a fairly simple example, suppose we have the railroad depicted in Figure 7, which serves the localities A, B, C, and D and suppose, also, that the terrain from A to D is in all respects similar to that between A and C, so that there is no physical reason why the costs of carrying freight along one route are greater or less than along the other. However, suppose that both A and C are coal-producing centers, with the mines in A being lower cost than those in C: that, for example, the costs at C are $6 a ton and at

---

Commissioner Freas, dissenting, argued:

"Certainly it is no usurpation of Congressional power to say that in providing for fair competition under the mandate of the National Transportation Policy the true cost of providing a given service is properly the necessary criterion by which to judge a contention of cost advantage." *Ibid.*, 620. See references in this footnote above and Chapter 1, Volume 2, for the subsequent history of this case, and p. 197, Chapter 7 for a more general consideration of the problems raised by differential taxes and subsidies.

[13] For estimates that the annual excess costs run to billions of dollars see the Presidential Advisory Committee on Transport Policy and Organization, *Revision of Federal Transportation Policy*, in U.S. Department of Commerce, *Modern Transport Policy*, Washington, June 1956, 2. Merton J. Peck, "Competitive Policy for Transportation?" in Almarin Phillips ed., *Perspectives on Antitrust Policy* (Princeton: Princeton Univ. Press, 1965), 246.

[14] See, for example, the comparative profits data in note 76, p. 51, Chapter 2.

[15] The danger is not completely eliminated, first, because long-run marginal costs are difficult to compute and require the application of judgment —something each of the contesting parties is likely to do in the manner best suited to its own interest. In consequence, rates might well be cut below LRMC either unknowingly or in an excess of competitive zeal, with the regulatory commission unable to prove, decisively, that this had in fact occurred. This is the burden of a large part of the testimony of Harold H. Wein in the FCC's investigation of AT&T's rates, *op. cit.*, Docket 16258, where he emphasizes the threat to Western Union implicit in AT&T's discriminatory rates on competing business services. And second, as long as the LRMC of two or more competitors fall short of their ATC, there is the danger that competition between them might become destructive—a possibility that we consider at length in Chapter 5 of Volume 2.

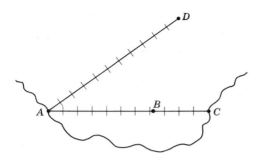

Figure 7. Rail-water carrier competition.

A $4.20 a ton, so that if the railroad is to get the business of carrying coal from *A* to *C* it cannot charge more than $1.80 for the trip.[16] Finally, suppose that the road's average cost for carrying a ton of freight from *A* to *C* exceeds $1.80, but that the incremental cost is below that figure. Would the roads be justified in reducing its rates selectively on coal from *A* to *C* in order, in effect, to compete successfully with *C*'s local mines? The competition in this case would be not with some other freight carrier but with local self-sufficiency.

The first answer is that since it is necessary for the railroad to reduce the *AC* rate below $1.80 in order to obtain the coal traffic, and since that business does cover its marginal costs, the reduction is justified. Is it justified however, even if the coal carried from *A* to the equidistant *D* and even to the less-distant *B*, neither of which has effective alternative sources of supply, continues to be charged an *ATC* of, for example, $2.20 and $2.00 a ton, respectively? The mine owners at *C* have no legitimate economic complaint: as long as the marginal costs to society of producing the coal at *A* and carrying it to *C* are less than the $6 a ton it costs to produce at *C*, efficiency requires that the coal business be taken over by the *A* firms. Nor, it would seem from our discussion of the proper limits of price discrimination in Chapter 5, do the customers at locations *B* and *D* have a legitimate complaint: the rates they are charged do not exceed the average total costs of serving them alone; the lower *AC* coal rates cover all the incremental costs of that traffic and possibly even contribute to the overhead costs that the *B* and *D* customers would otherwise have to bear entirely on their own.

But suppose the purchasers at *B*, *D*, and *C* are in some way or other in competition. Suppose, for example, that they are competing producers of coke. It costs just as much to mine a ton of coal at *A* and sell it at *C* as it does to mine and sell it at *D*, and more than to sell it at *B*; yet efficient use of the railroad has resulted in a delivered price of $6 a ton at *C*, compared with $6.20 at *B* and $6.40 at *D*. The coke plants will tend therefore to locate at *C* in preference to the other locations, despite the fact that the social costs, as far as coal production and transportation are concerned, are lower at *B*

---

[16] In most of these examples, it will be unnecessary to specify whether it is short-run or long-run marginal costs that are under consideration, since we have already discussed the circumstances under which the one or the other becomes the appropriate criterion. In this example, in addition, it is simplest to assume that the coal is produced under conditions of constant cost. This particular example is a modification of one that appears in Brown, *Principles of Commerce*, Part III, 64–65, 144–145, 166. In the various illustrations that follow, we draw heavily on the examples and discussion in Brown's book, Part III, Chapters 2, 4, 5, and 6.

and no higher at D than at C. Still, the railroad's discrimination confers no greater competitive advantage on customers at C than they would have enjoyed anyhow: the lower price of coal delivered in C merely reflects that location's natural advantage resulting from the fact that it has local mines capable of producing at $6 a ton. The railroad merely permits A's coal mines to match that price.

The fact remains that the ultimate result is not perfect; there will be some incremental resources of society devoted to carrying coal from A to C because of the lower rail rate that would otherwise be required to carry it only from A to B. It is important to see the precise cause of the difficulty: it is that *not all customers can be charged* only marginal costs, because MC is less than ATC and no public subsidy is available to make good the deficiency. Given the requirement that total revenues cover total costs, the victims of the price discrimination, B and D, pay no higher transportation rates than they would otherwise have to pay, even if there were no traffic between A and C; but to the extent that they compete with C, they *are* injured in that competition, and some misallocation of society's resources occurs, as some coal-using industries are diverted from them to C that would not leave if they too could get coal carried at MC.

Suppose, now, that the competition that necessitates a lower rate from A to C than to the other locations is competition not with local production at C but with a water carrier able to carry the coal along the rippling stream marked in Figure 7 at a long-run marginal cost (and average total cost) of $1.80 a ton.[17] The answer is the same. As long as the railroad can do the job at an LRMC less than $1.80, it is more efficient to let the railroad reduce its rates enough to the C customers to take over the traffic. As before, any advantages that the C customers thereby achieve over their B and D competitors are merely a reflection of their favorable location along a river; they could get their coal at $6 a ton, by water, even if the railroad did not quote the $1.80 rate to them. The fact remains that, in the ultimate solution, some coal will be carried by rail from A to C that would otherwise be carried, at lower social opportunity costs, to users who would have located at B. The solution, once again, is not ideal, because not all customers can be charged marginal costs.[18]

Our examples in this chapter so far have been of situations in which the competitors had markedly different cost structures—in particular where one of them and not the other had marginal costs markedly below average costs. The issue becomes much more difficult when the competition is between suppliers with similar cost structures. As we shall see, the main historical rationalization of railroad regulation and one important rationalization of the whole institution of regulated monopoly has been that

---

[17] This and other representative examples are briefly but clearly presented by Wilcox, *op. cit.*, 352–353, though without explicit consideration of the problems arising from the failure of all rates to be set at marginal costs.

[18] Not all the using industries will be driven, uneconomically, from B to C. Depending on the size of the rate differential, coal-using companies located at B may still have a competitive advantage over those at C when selling in markets west of B. But in markets east of B, the discriminatorily lower AC coal rates will tip the competitive balance progressively toward companies located at C, with the result that service of some customers between the two locations will involve hauling coal from A to C and then coke back westward towards B, when, at nondiscriminatory rail rates, the coal would go only to B and the coke on eastward toward C.

competition among *like* suppliers—two railroads, two gas, or two electricity distribution companies—is likely to become destructive and undesirably discriminatory, precisely because all of them have a similar wide gap between marginal and average costs.[19]

Suppose, then, that the competition in question is between two railroads. Assume, first, that one railroad runs directly from *A* to *C*, the other circuitously, as illustrated in Figure 8, where the respective terrains are such

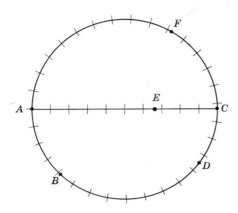

Figure 8. Rail-rail carrier competition.

that there is no reason to assume any physical difference in the costs per ton-mile over the one route as compared with the other. Competition might have the effect of depressing rates between *A* and *C* below the levels charged from between either of those points and the intermediate points on the circuitous line, *B* and *D*, or on the direct line *E*.

Under certain circumstances, a case could be made for permitting the circuitous route *ABDC* to reduce its rates between the terminal points in order to meet the competition of the direct route *AEC*. This would be so if the direct route had not yet been built, or were already fully utilized and therefore confronted with the decision of whether to add to its capacity, whereas the roundabout road was capable of carrying the *AC* business without additional capital expenditure or with less additional expenditure. In this case, the latter road might legitimately be permitted to reduce its rates between *A* and *C* sufficiently to handle or share the business, reflecting the fact that the cost to society of permitting it to do so, even though over a longer distance, would be less than having that incremental business taken on by the direct line. The customers at *B* and *D* would not be burdened by higher rates because of the reductions between *A* and *C* as long as the latter covered the long-run incremental costs of the business. Competition between them and the *A* and *C* customers might be distorted; as before, however, the favored customers might legitimately claim that the lower rates to them were a reflection of the fact that their business was sufficiently great to justify their being served by a direct route and that the roundaboutness of the *ABDC* route was properly attributable to the necessity for serving *B* and *D*— provided, that is, that the rates between *A* and those intermediate points did not exceed the average total costs of serving them alone.

It is difficult to imagine circumstances in which the presence of such competition would justify the direct route reducing *its* rates discriminatorily between *A* and *C* relative to those charged between *A* and *E*. The customers at *A* and *C* could point to no physical aspect of their location justifying their getting lower rates relative to marginal costs than the intermediate point, *E*. The resulting distortion in competition at the buyers' level, between *C* and *E*, would have no offsetting efficiency justification at the transportation end, since the lower rates between *A* and *C* would have as their purpose only some redistribution of the total business between the direct and the circuitous lines.[20]

Similarly, if competition between the two roundabout lines, *AFC* and *ABDC*, threatened to reduce the *AC* rates below those between intermediate points, there would seem to be no economic justification for permitting this arbitrary identification of the latter customers as marginal merely because they alone have competitive alternatives. From the point of view of the individual roads competing with one another, the *A* to *C* demand is clearly the more elastic. But the consequence of those selective rate reductions would not be a better use of the aggregate railway plant or performance of the transportation function at lower social costs. The distorting effect at the buyer end would have no offsetting social advantage.[21]

In the case of the railroads, the danger of selective, discriminatory competition is not, principally, that the customers or localities served by only a single road will have their rates increased to recoup revenue deficiencies on competitive business since the railroads as a group have not earned as much as 5% on investment in any five-year period since 1921—in contrast with the 5.75% that the ICC fixed as reasonable—and have exceeded 6% in only one year (1942) in that time.[22] Presumably, they have not been seriously restrained from charging the profit-maximizing price on noncompetitive business anyhow—in which event there is nothing left to recoup.[22a] In these circumstances, it would not seem rational for them to reduce competitive rates below LRMC in the hope of making good the resultant losses in those sheltered markets.[23] The main danger is that choices will be distorted at the buyer or customer level by virtue of the fact that some rates are set at

---

[20] On these cases, see Brown, *Principles of Commerce*, Part III, 40–49, 120–126.

[21] See *ibid.*, 97–103; also Baumol, et al., "Statement of Clarification," *Jour. of Bus.* (July 1963), XXXVI: 351 note. George Wilson points out that where the traffic in question has a low elasticity of demand for transportation service generally, the ICC will step in to "prevent the unraveling of the rate structure" caused by the competition between two regulated carriers: "It will force a kind of compulsory cartel and . . . will generally maintain rate levels well above any measure of ATC." *Op. cit.*, *Amer. Econ. Rev.*, *Papers and Proceedings* (May 1964), LIV: 165.

[22] James C. Nelson, *op. cit.*, 199, 228 and note 76, Chapter 2.

[22a] But see Chapter 1, Volume 2, at note 27.

[23] This is not to suggest that there can have been no recoupment by railroads from monopolistic traffic of losses suffered on competitive traffic

during these years. First of all, not all companies have failed consistently throughout this period to earn the allowable rate of return. (*Ibid.*, 215, 460, 464.) The successful companies could have had an incentive to fight for unremunerative competitive business, with the expectation of being permitted then to make up revenue deficiencies in other markets. Second, we must allow for the inevitability of ignorance, uncertainty, and irrationality. Long-run marginal costs are difficult even to define in workable terms, not to mention to measure incontrovertibly. In these circumstances, it is entirely possible that railroads might have been induced by competition to reduce certain rates below incrementally remunerative levels; and when, as occurred regularly during the period 1946 to 1952, they turned to the ICC to request general rate increases—freight rates were raised 78.9% in this period (*ibid.*, 125 note)—they might have justified

marginal cost and others above—a danger that is particularly extreme when the favored and nonfavored customers are in competition with one another.

In the other public utility industries there is the first danger as well: that in competing for residential heating, cooking, industrial power, or communications customers the companies may be willing to set rates below long-run marginal costs—in expectation, conscious or otherwise, of being enabled in this fashion to expand their rate base and to recoup on the portions of their business in which they do not encounter such competition.[24]

Even if no rate is permitted to go below LRMC, and even if the several companies genuinely try to follow the rule of cutting rates on price-elastic business only to the point of maximizing the benefit to the other customers, competition still creates a genuine danger of selective reduction that will be a burden on the customers not so favored. The key to this paradox is the difference between what constitutes profit (or net revenue) maximization from the standpoint of the individual firm, acting independently, and of the industry, acting as a single entity. Each individual competitive price cut may be wholly compatible with the above-outlined rules, if regarded narrowly from the point of view of the individual firm making the proposal. Each competitor, individually, may be able to point out that, taking the prices of his rivals as given, he must be permitted to cut his rates in order to get or keep the business in question and to maximize its net contribution to overheads; and that his other customers would only be injured if he were denied the opportunity of doing so. And he would be right, *ceteris paribus*. But each rate reduction by one firm, justified in this manner, creates the opportunity, indeed the necessity, for a corresponding reduction, similarly justified, on the part of his rivals; and so on, until the bottom limit of marginal cost is reached. From the standpoint of all competing firms, taken as a group, the total effect of the successive reductions may well be mutual frustration. Their *combined* net revenue (over and above incremental costs) from the competitive markets probably will have been sharply reduced; if the competition is pure, it will have fallen to zero.

This is of course precisely the way in which competition is supposed to work: demand for the product of each individual competitor being highly elastic, price is driven down to marginal cost and supernormal profits are eliminated. But where marginal costs are below average total costs and the competition is between regulated companies—two or more railroads, gas and electric companies, AT&T and Western Union—one or more of which is capable of recouping any losses in net revenue from certain markets by higher rates in others, the result will be absolutely higher charges in the noncompetitive markets than would otherwise have been necessary.

---

greater increases on the noncompetitive portions of their business than they would have been able to do otherwise.

Conversely, a major explanation for the increasing financial difficulties and loss of business by the railroads to competing carriers has been their continued, irrational adherence to value-of-service pricing (using rate structures inherited from the days when they enjoyed something close to a national transportation monopoly) in situations where, because of the increasing intrusions of trucks, the markets would no longer

bear those rates. (See Chapter 1, Volume 2.) In the face of this widespread evidence of their failure to behave like intelligent profit-maximizers, it would surely be an extreme example of the economist's confusing his deductive models with the real world if he were to deny the possibility of unremunerative rate reduction and recoupment on the ground that this is something no intelligent profit-maximizer would do.

[24] See Chapter 2, Volume 2, for the fuller appraisal of this danger.

Whether or not recoupment takes place, distortions will have been introduced at the buying end by the fact that some rates exceed marginal costs by more than others, without economic justification or compensating advantage.

It is impossible to lay down general economic rules telling regulatory commissions how heavily to weigh the possible efficiency advantages of price discrimination at the sellers' level against the possible inefficiencies or distortions thereby introduced at the buyers' level—a problem, enormously accentuated by the uneven incidence of competition among public utilities. However, the following guidelines seem reasonable.

1. Discriminatory, competitive rate reductions should not be permitted unless they make for a more efficient performance of the supplying function. This means that competition (or some other device) should be permitted to allot the business to the medium with the lowest long-run marginal costs, when there are substantial differences in the respective levels of those costs. But it also means that selective rate reductions are suspect where they have no justification other than the fact that the favored customers happen to have competitive alternatives that other customers do not enjoy. In that event the only effect is to introduce distortion at the buying level.

    This generalization does not answer the question of what commissions are to do when both of the foregoing circumstances are present (as may frequently be the case): (a) one competitor does have lower marginal costs than another and (b) because competition prevails only in some markets and not in others, it will tend to drive certain rates all the way down to those marginal costs, which will mean lower net revenues from this particular business and, hence, a possibly objectionable burden on the customers who have no such protection. The problem becomes one of devising arrangements that will achieve the efficient redistribution of the business at the supply end while minimizing the injury (more precisely, maximizing the benefit) to those other customers. Since the question of whether competition ought to be restricted and some other device used to achieve this end is essentially an institutional one, we reserve the major part of its consideration for Volume 2. In principle, it would seem that the ideal result could be achieved by keeping the rates of the competing suppliers above their respective marginal costs by the same absolute amounts[25] and reducing them toward those respective marginal costs only to the extent justified by the elasticity of their *combined* demand—that is, only as long as marginal revenue to all competitors taken together exceeded marginal cost.[26]

---

[25] Competitive rates should differ by the absolute difference in marginal supply cost instead of in proportion to those marginal costs because of the reason provided in our third rule.

[26] I am indebted to H. Roseman for this suggestion. Suppose, to take a very simple example, the LRMC of supplying a particular residential heating market with natural gas is $1.20 per therm, and with electricity $1.00. The efficient distribution of the business could just as well be effected at respective rates of $2.20 and $2.00 as at $1.20 and $1.00. If the total demand for therms (for natural gas and electricity, together)

is inelastic, there would seem to be no justification for permitting competition to drive promotional rates on new business to the lower levels, forcing an increase in the rates to other customers (let us say, those with heating equipment already installed, for whom no promotional rate reductions are proposed). So a regulatory commission could impose the nondiscriminatory $2.20 and $2.00 pattern.

This example assumes, of course, that only regulated companies are involved in the competition. Where the gas and electric companies are competing also with unregulated heating oil

The problem in cases of discriminatory rate making in competitive situations is to decide whether we are confronting a "rail–water carrier" or a "roundabout-rail–roundabout-rail" competition, of the types described in Figures 7 and 8. In both situations, conceivably, it is only the presence of competition between points A and C that makes the demand elastic for the individual, competing carrier. But in the first case, because of the differences in the cost *structures* of the competitors *and* the fact that the AC traffic would have been served at lower costs than the AB and AD even in the absence of discrimination, we concluded that economic efficiency would be served by permitting the discrimination. In the second, the absence of these two conditions called for a prohibition of the discriminatory rate cutting.

This has been the unrecognized issue in the FCC's lengthy investigation of the rate structure of AT&T, in its Docket No. 16258. The development of microwave radio resulted in the 1960s in many large business and governmental bodies setting up their own, private communications systems. AT&T responded by reducing its rates on certain business services discriminatorily, in the direction of its long-run marginal costs, and this in turn brought objections not only by its own competitors, such as Western Union, but also by Motorola, Inc., a manufacturer that had been supplying equipment for the private systems. In defense of these rate reductions, AT&T argued that in view of (a) its great economies of scale and (b) the elasticity of the demand of these business users— consequent on their ability, now, to serve some of their own needs—it would be in the interest of both efficiency in the performance of the communications function and of AT&T's *other* customers to permit it to reduce these particular rates down toward LRMC. This defense fails explicitly to recognize that if this was a "rail-rail" situation, the mere fact that the business demand was elastic from the standpoint of any single, competing supplier did not justify the competitive rate reductions.[27]

However, the situation could well be of the "rail–water carrier" variety. What made the entry of competitors into the provision of private micro- wave service economically feasible was the fact that their average total

---

distributors, there may be no alternative to permitting whatever rate reductions are required, down to marginal costs, to achieve the efficient distribution of the business.

It is important to qualify these observations by pointing out that they take no account of the institutional case for free price competition, which we consider at length in Volume 2. Given the institutional weaknesses of regulation, price competition, although discriminatory, may be the most effective mechanism for producing efficient results.

[27] Bonbright alone of the AT&T witnesses explicitly recognizes that this problem may arise in reference to the competition between that company and Western Union.

"What here gives rise to such difficulty is . . . that both enterprises are presumed . . . to be supplying their services under conditions of declining unit costs. . . .

"Under these special conditions . . . a plausible case can be made for the establishment by regulation of a floor of minimum rates higher than mere incremental . . . costs. . . . Unless this were done, both companies might feel constrained to hold or lower their competitive rates down close to, or right at, barely incremental cost levels. If this should be the actual experience, the revenues from the competitive services would yield little or no contribution to the coverage of the unallocable corporate overhead costs. . . .

". . . serious consideration should be given to the proposal . . . that actual rates be set at levels reasonably designed to maximize *the combined net earnings* of the two regulated telecommunications systems on their directly competitive business." Stress supplied. Testimony in FCC Docket No. 14650, AT&T Exhibit 89, mimeo., 27–29, December 8, 1965. Note the similarity to our suggestion in note 26.

costs were less than the rates that they had been charged by AT&T, which were based on the latter company's ATC. Whereas the ATC of the private microwave facilities were for all practical purposes the same as their LRMC,[28] the LRMC of AT&T, because of its enormous economies of scale, were far below its ATC—precisely the rail–water carrier situation. In these circumstances, if AT&T could obtain some or most of the business by reducing its rates toward its own LRMC, it would seem that it should be permitted to do so, because (a) the result would be to have the communications function performed at lower marginal cost to society and (b) as long as the rates were reduced only to the extent necessary to get the business, other customers would not only not be injured—since the large private users had the alternative (corresponding to the availability of water transport to AC in Figure 7) of getting their communications at lower costs anyhow—but would be positively benefited by the contribution that the price-elastic business would make to the common costs of the system.

2. Where the competitive necessity for the selective rate reductions to particular customers merely reflects the latter's "natural advantages," the reductions should be permitted, even though competitors less well situated may have to pay higher rates relative to the marginal costs of serving them and some inefficiency may be introduced. Examples of such natural advantages would be those enjoyed by customers located on a river route, where the average total costs of water transportation are less than the average total costs of rail; or by customers supplied by a local producer (for example, of brick) whose costs of production can be successfully competed with by distant suppliers (for instance, of building stone) if the latter are charged transport rates below average total but above LRMC; or perhaps by homeowners in the process of deciding on a new heating system, who have the opportunity to install oil at favorable rates; or by large users of communications services who have a choice of installing their own, private microwave systems.[29]

3. Where the customers are in direct competition with one another *and* the favored buyers enjoy no such "natural entitlement" to the lower rates, the rates charged them should differ only by the absolute amount of the differences in the incremental costs of serving them.[30] Other things being

---

[28] There are apparently great economies of scale in microwave ccmmunications (see pp. 125–126, Chapter 5), but in as much as the private users were confined to supplying their own needs, the costs relevant to their decision of whether to do so themselves would have been the average total costs of that operation. Whether it was desirable for the FCC to have so confined them depends on whether the provision of common-carrier communications service is a "natural monopoly," a question that we consider in Chapter 4, Volume 2.

[29] It is sometimes easier to state this principle than to apply it in particular situations. The question of what is a "natural" advantage and what is the consequence of defective institutions —like the mere availability of competitive alternatives to some customers and not to others—

is one to which we shall return in our discussion of institutional issues in regulation. See in particular the discussion of "the discrimination problem" in the cream-skimming section of Chapter 5, Volume 2.

[30] "Even if a utility company, by the skillful practice of discrimination, could and would thereby reduce *all* of its rates, including the rates which it charges to those customers who are discriminated against, the practice should nevertheless be forbidden if it would seriously prejudice the competitive business relationships between these consumers and those other consumers who would receive a preference." Bonbright, *Principles of Public Utility Rates*, 384.

See *ibid.*, 374–377 for a fuller discussion of whether rate differentials should be proportional or equal to the absolute differences in marginal costs.

equal, the rates charged by the same railway or by competing railways for carrying brick and stone should differ only by the difference in the long-run marginal costs of carrying each: only then would the purchasers receive the correct signals about their choice between the two. The same would be true of the respective rates charged for raw materials and the finished products into which they are converted. If rates differ by more than this amount, the processing industry will tend to be inefficiently located, too near either to the source of raw material or the market.[31] This does not mean that identical charges per ton are appropriate. If the road carrying the brick has chronic excess capacity, possibly because the greater portion of the traffic is in the opposite direction and it has many freight cars that would otherwise return empty, whereas the road carrying the stone would have to expand capacity to supply the entire demand, their respective long-run marginal costs will differ, and so should their rates.

This third rule would apply whenever there is a high cross-elasticity of demand between services: direct competition between two customers is only one possible source of this.[32] Bonbright offers another example: if a commercial customer has the choice between buying low- or high-voltage power, the former of which imposes on the supplier the extra costs of stepping down the voltage of its distribution network, the difference in the rates for the two should reflect, as accurately as possible, the absolute costs of making the transformation.[33]

IMPACT AT THE PRIMARY LEVEL AND OTHER INSTITUTIONAL CONSIDERATIONS

We should also consider the danger that discriminatory rate reductions may be predatory in intent or effect: that they will eliminate competition at the level of the discriminating seller. We shall not devote much attention to this possibility in the present chapter, because here we are concerned with the principles of efficient public utility pricing, not with the institutional arrangements for following those principles. Whether competition, regulated or unregulated, is likely to prove destructive or predatory is one of the many operational questions that must be confronted whenever one undertakes to translate the *a priori* rules into functioning social institutions; and these institutional problems form the subject matter of Volume 2.[34] We confine our present discussion to enunciating and briefly illustrating the relevant principles and governing considerations.

1. Reducing rates to marginal costs is exactly the way in which competition is supposed to achieve an efficient allocation of business at the primary level. It would be a confusion of means and ends to forbid rate reductions to that level merely in order to protect individual competitors against

---

[31] See the discussion in Brown, *Principles of Commerce*, Part III, 160–169.
[32] Cross-elasticity of demand is a measure of the sensitivity of purchases of product A to changes in the same direction in prices of product B. If two users of transportation service are in direct competition, a discriminatory reduction in the price of transportation to the one will tend

to result in a transfer of business to him and therefore a reduction in purchases of transportation service by the other.
[33] Testimony in FCC, *In the Matter of American Telephone and Telegraph Co. et al.*, Docket No. 16258, Bell Exhibit 25, May 31, 1966, mimeo., 33–34.
[34] See especially Chapters 4–6.

displacement, when displacement of higher (marginal) cost suppliers is the very result competition is supposed to produce.

2. The presence of competition does, however, increase the desirability of setting the lower limit at long-run instead of short-run marginal costs. Whereas it might be desirable to permit a regulated monopolist to reduce rates temporarily to the latter level when it has excess capacity, the possibility that such reductions might be predatory or destructive makes this kind of pricing much more objectionable in a competitive situation. This still does not mean that rail rates need to cover the capital costs of such quasipermanent installations as road beds, rails, and terminals, except insofar as taking on additional business will indeed entail additional maintenance or investment costs for these facilities.

3. The possibilities of selective, predatory rate-cutting might conceivably be controlled, as some writers have suggested,[35] by permitting the regulated companies to reduce such rates as they chose, subject to the condition that they might not raise them again in the future unless it could be demonstrated that their costs had somehow changed in the interim.[36] Such a provision might deter a railroad, for example, from cutting its rates temporarily to unremunerative levels, in expectation of raising them once it had succeeded in driving out competition. But it would not necessarily be effective in preventing such unremunerative pricing as long as the regulated companies were not fully exploiting their monopoly power elsewhere, because in one of their subsequent general rate investigations, a general revenue deficiency—which, given the variety of circumstances that would almost certainly have changed in the interim, could hardly be traced to any particular rate reductions on any particular business—could serve as the basis for regulatory permission to raise the general rate structure.

4. There remains the possibility that although it may be more efficient for society, in the static sense, to permit a public utility company to take the business away from its rivals by reducing rates on competitive services to marginal costs, there may be some dynamic loss if the result is the elimination of those competitors. If it were true, for example, that because of the Bell System's superior size or integration Western Union were incapable of competing with it in providing business communications services, at rates fully covering AT&T's long-run marginal costs, efficiency would seem to require that Western Union go out of that business. It would seem anomalous to try to retain the protection that competition affords *customers* by protecting Western Union *against* competition, by holding up the Bell System rates. Yet it remains a possibility that preserving the competitor and the stimulus to Bell's performance of its continued presence might in the long run contribute

---

[35] See, for example, Baumol, in Phillips and Williamson, *op. cit.*, 118–119.

[36] The 1910 amendment of the Interstate Commerce Act contained such a provision:

"Whenever a carrier by railroad shall in competition with a water route or routes reduce the rates on the carriage of any species of freight to or from competitive points, it shall not be permitted to increase such rates unless after hearing by the commission it shall be found that such proposed increase rests upon changed conditions other than the elimination of water competition." The Act to Regulate Commerce, Section 4, as amended by the Act of June 18, 1910, c. 309, par. 8, 36 Stat. 547.

See, however, *Skinner & Eddy Corp. v. U.S., et al.*, 249 US 557 (1919), which placed a very narrow construction on this provision.

sufficiently to a greater and more varied innovation, to continual improvements in the industry's service and efficiency to outweigh the static welfare loss involved in keeping it alive. This assessment could only be made in each particular instance, considering all the alternatives available to customers—including, in this particular case, their own private microwave relay systems—and the presence of other sources of competitive pressures and innovation. However, economists would probably agree that anyone arguing merely to protect a competitor from extinction would have to sustain a very heavy burden of proof before they would be convinced that the way to preserve competition and its advantages is to restrict it.

5. The determination of whether unregulated competition is the best device for achieving economically efficient pricing and, if not, what controls ought to be imposed can be made only on the basis of an appraisal of the particular technological and economic circumstances of each individual case. Central to any such inquiry must be a consideration of how perfectly competition would work or could be made to work in the situation under examination.

The way in which serious market imperfections or the presence of important externalities might require regulatory intervention is interestingly illustrated by the increasingly intense competition between electric, gas, and fuel oil companies for the residential and commercial heating market that developed in the 1960s. This competition, apparently increasingly, took the form of offering developers and builders inducements of one sort or another to influence the type of equipment they installed—loans, cash payments, free or cut-rate undergrounding of electricity lines, insulation, installation of appliances and equipment, advertising allowances and so on.[37] The reason for this is obvious: once the house has been built, the choice of *kind* of fuel or energy is essentially determined, and the costs of converting equipment already installed usually preclude a shift to an alternative fuel at that point. We have already suggested that advertising or promotional payments might well be justified as a means of getting business distributed to the lowest-cost supplier, provided the costs of these various outlays are incorporated in the LRMC floor below which price should not be permitted to go.[38] But a question remains of whether this type of competition, focusing on influencing the decision of the builder or developer instead of the homeowner or business man concerning the kind of fuel that will be used in his completed house or store is likely to get the proper economic choices made.

This depends in turn on the effectiveness of competition in the construction market, which would determine whether these promotional payments get translated into lower prices of the buildings sold and

---

[37] A survey by a subcommittee of the House of Representatives Committee on Small Business of the promotional payments by public utility companies in the 1963 to 1966 period disclosed that about one-half went to builders, developers, or owners of tracts of homes or apartments, another 8% to appliance or equipment dealers, about 17% to trade associations, and probably only slightly more than one-quarter directly to

the ultimate customer. *Promotional Practices by Public Utilities and Their Effect upon Small Business*, House Report No. 1984, 90th Cong. 2d Sess., Washington, December 31, 1968, 106, 109 and Wallace F. Lovejoy, "The Impact of Competition Among Public Utilities: Gas Versus Electricity," paper presented at the Public Utilities Institute, Michigan State Univ., March 25, 1969, 6–13.
[38] See note 10.

whether buyers have a sufficiently wide choice among buildings in desired locations with various types of equipment and appliances already installed. It would depend also on whether the buyers are able intelligently to weigh the respective merits of buildings with different purchase prices on the one hand and different prospective fuel or energy costs on the other. The more imperfect the market, the greater the danger that competition in bribing builders may result in the latter making installation decisions that are not in the interest of the prospective buyer, hence of society.

It has been claimed, for example, that these subsidies are less likely than direct reductions in the prices of gas, electricity, or heating oils to be passed on to the person who ultimately buys the house or store; and that inducements of this sort may lead builders to install equipment that saddles the ultimate buyer with higher heating costs than he would otherwise care to incur. It is difficult to accept such claims without careful investigation. If competition among builders is ineffective and buyer ignorance creates additional opportunities for exploitation, it is not clear why builders would not have been fully exploiting those opportunities before any promotional allowances were offered. They would in any event be under systematic temptation to put in the equipment that was least expensive to install, since this would minimize their own outlays, saddling the ignorant buyer with the burden of unnecessarily high maintenance and operating costs in the future. To contend that the introduction of the promotional allowances would result in even greater exploitation, with builders merely pocketing the monetary payments, would be tantamount to arguing that any competition among suppliers of building materials or other inputs is not only fruitless but possibly injurious to the ultimate buyer. Such a position would not be tenable, as a general proposition. The general assumption must be that any reductions in production cost, whether of competitors or monopolists, will tend in the short or long run to be passed on.

On the other hand, the introduction of promotional allowances to the builders does create a new incentive and opportunity, a possibility of builders increasing their profits by installing less efficient equipment and leaving the ultimate buyer stuck with higher heating bills. It does introduce a new possible source of distortion of the builder's decision. One cannot prove by purely deductive reasoning that there may not be serious lags in the transmission of these benefits into the price of the house, or that the ultimate purchaser has either sufficient knowledge and ability to make the necessary comparisons of initial outlays and operating costs, or a sufficient number of alternatives of roughly comparable quality and attractiveness to him among which to choose, so as to protect him from exploitation by this sort of competition. Whether the introduction of this new element in the builder's calculus has the desirable effect of offsetting the preexisting distortion (inducing builders now to install the more efficient equipment by making it comparatively less costly to them), or accentuates the distortion, or merely introduces an alternative method of exploiting buyer ignorance is a question that is impossible to resolve in *a priori* terms. The generalization remains valid: the more effective is competition in the construction market and the information available to buyers, the greater is the likelihood that promotional rivalry among public utility companies will be beneficial. It must be recognized that it *is* a form of competition and a form that tends to push effective price closer to long-run marginal cost.

However, there is another possible source of distortion. To an electric or gas company, it is essentially a matter of indifference whether it competes in the home-heating markets by the offer of various promotional allowances to builders, or via rate reductions to homeowners, except for the fact that the former method permits the finer degree of price discrimination, with the inducements being extended only to those with the elastic demands—that is, the customers in process of making up their minds. In either case, if an allowance to a builder induces him to install electric heating equipment, the public utility can be certain, because of its monopoly, that the current or gas will thereafter be purchased from it. The benefits of its promotional allowances, in brief, are internal to it.

Consider the case of the individual fuel oil dealer, in contrast. If he offers a promotional allowance to a dealer to install oil-burning equipment, he has far less assurance that the homeowner will buy the oil from him. The benefits of this promotional device will be largely external—that is, they will tend to flow in large measure to his competitors. Only if all the fuel oil dealers could organize themselves, as a monopoly, would they be as certain as the electric company that the benefits of promotional allowances to builders would all flow to them. Such an organization would encounter the institutional obstacle of the antitrust laws. But, apart from those laws, there would always be the temptation for the individual dealer to stay outside of the organization, refusing to bear his proportionate share of the burden of the promotional allowances, because he could not in any event be prevented from reaping some of the benefits.[39]

We make no effort to resolve these various conflicting considerations. Since we are in any event dealing with regulated monopolies, the question is not ordinarily one of removing all controls. If regulation of rate structures is required in order to prevent injurious discrimination, regulation of promotional competition is equally required and for the same reason.[40] It is conceivable that a decision by regulatory commissions to confine interfuel or energy competition to competing quotations in the price of the gas or electricity itself might be the most effective institutional device for achieving the benefits of competition while avoiding the dangers and distortions of unregulated discrimination.[41] Conceivably, alterations of published rates afford inadequate play for the strong competitive forces that have emerged

---

[39] This point, essentially, was made by the Virginia Petroleum Jobbers Association, in its request of the FTC for investigation of the promotional practices of the Virginia Electric & Power Company and the Appalachian Power Company, *In the Matter of Promotional Payments by Electric Companies, Request for Investigation*, December 14, 1964, Par. III, sec. B. 2. However, to the extent that these promotions are heavily financed by a relatively small number of major integrated oil companies, the force of this consideration is diminished.

[40] We must also consider the legitimate com-

plaints of independent appliance dealers and plumbing and heating contractors, who have had to face the competition of sales-below-cost by public utility companies that have been willing to take these nominal losses on appliance sales and installations in order to increase their sales of gas and electricity at rates that afford a margin of return on investment well in excess of the cost of capital. See *Promotional Practices by Public Utilities and Their Effect on Small Business, op. cit., passim.*

[41] For an interesting example of the use of a direct promotional rate in the gas–electricity

in these industries; and to confine competition to those rates would diminish its effectiveness in forcing costs down and in probing the great opportunities for improved consumer welfare inherent in elasticity of demand and the tendency of unit costs to decrease with increased output.[42]

Once one moves from the rules of statically efficient pricing to the prerequisites for dynamic improvement of industry performance, it becomes essential to ask what degree of price competition is most conducive to the alert, aggressive extension and improvement of service. In general, this consideration probably argues for more instead of less freedom to compete in price, particularly in industries such as these, which, by virtue of the prevalence of long-established, government-protected monopoly, might tend to fall easily into conservative and unimaginative ways of doing business. Increasing returns to scale afford opportunities for improvements in welfare; but they must be aggressively explored if the benefits are to be realized. Yet there must also be attached the condition that regulators remain alert to the danger of utility companies using their monopoly profits in sheltered markets to squeeze enterprising rivals out of competitive areas. This is the basic paradox of the institution of regulated monopoly.

CONCLUSIONS

The testing of competitive rates must begin with marginal costs; other things being equal, rates equal to incremental cost are compensatory and are not a burden on other customers. In the presence of competition, long-run, not short-run, marginal costs should set the floor.

The costs that are relevant in applying this test are the costs of the company proposing to cut its rates, not those of its competitors.

Not all rates would tend to be driven by competition to marginal costs because the intensity of competitive pressures will differ between different customers, classes of service, and markets; nor can they be equal to marginal costs and still cover average total costs. Price discrimination becomes inevitable, then. When the customers being discriminated between are in competition with one another, directly or indirectly, such discrimination raises the danger of distortion and inefficiency in the distribution of businesss In these circumstances, the possible contribution of selective rate reduction. to greater efficiency on the supply side must be weighed against their possible undesirable effects at the buying end.

---

competition, a special rate offered by a natural gas company for total-energy installations, see Federal Power Commission, *Northern Natural Gas Co.*, Docket No. RP69-5. A Presiding Examiner, citing other cases in which the Commission had approved promotional rates for space heating and to facilitate competitive sales for industrial uses, recommended approval of the offering, although it allegedly would not cover fully distributed costs, on the ground that "The proposed rate offers better than a fair chance of providing an increase in the use of natural gas, and an excess of revenues over incremental costs, and will impose no undue financial burden on other customers on Northern's system." *Initial Decision*, issued February 11, 1969.

[42] For an excellent review of the economic arguments for and against this method of competition, see the testimony of Irwin M. Stelzer, William J. Baumol, and James W. McKie, the comments by the first two on the testimony of the third and the latter's response, House of Representatives, Subcommittee on Activities of Regulatory Agencies, Select Committee on Small Business, 90th Cong. 2d Sess., *Promotional Practices by Public Utilities and Their Impact upon Small Business*, Hearings, Washington 1968, 589–645, 677–695 and, for a broad survey of the case for competitive rate making in the same context, Irwin M. Stelzer, Bruce C. Netschert, and Abraham Gerber, "Competitive Rates and Practices by Electric Utilities," *ibid.*, A 171–289.

The justification at the selling end depends on a contribution being made to the fuller use of existing plant or a fuller achievement of economies of scale in the entire supplying industry, considering both the company that obtains and the company that loses the business as a result. Where the resources displaced are readily shiftable in the comparatively short run, efficiency in the entire industry can be enhanced. Where, instead, the competition is between suppliers with essentially similar cost structures, it is not necessarily true that the transfer of business from one supplier to the other contributes to greater efficiency; in these circumstances, and particularly when there is some danger of distortion at the buying end, price discrimination may be unjustifiable.

Special provisions must also be made against the possibility that the selective price cuts may eliminate competition—not in order to protect competitors automatically regardless of their respective long-run marginal costs, but in order to prevent predatory competition, to guard also against the possibilities of recoupment of the losses by the surviving firm either in charges to other customers or by raising rates in the competitive market once the competition has been eliminated, and also to preserve the dynamic advantages of continuing competition.

CHAPTER 7

Qualifications: Practicability, Externalities, Second-Best and Noneconomic Considerations

These are the principles of economically efficient public utility pricing. Formulating them was the easy part of the job. Most public utility executives and regulators would probably acknowledge their validity, while taking pains at the same time to point out that economic efficiency is not the sole test or purpose of their performance. But they would also hasten to emphasize that these principles fall far short of providing workable rules for the guidance of their accountants or engineers. The task of translating these principles into actual price schedules is so extraordinarily difficult that it is entirely possible to accept their validity while at the same time concluding that the task of following them is an impossible one. Few would go as far as to abandon the effort entirely. But all would point out, and correctly so, that even the most sophisticated and conscientious effort to apply these principles inevitably involves large doses of subjective judgment and, at the very best, can achieve only the roughest possible approximation of the desired results. The uncertainty of the resulting estimates and the impossibility of devising and enforcing rate structures that fully embody them counsel a rounding of the edges, a tempering of the principles themselves. Such a tempering is not necessarily objectionable even on purely economic grounds: as we have already pointed out, the economic costs of ascertaining and enforcing economically efficient rates, in particular circumstances, can well outweigh the efficiency advantages that such rates are supposed to achieve.[1]

This is additionally, and most troublesomely, the case in the presence of competition, particularly competition between sellers of widely divergent size and financial staying power. Permitting selective rate reductions down to

---

[1] For an illuminating example of the enormous effort and expense required to measure the costs of handling particular kinds of railway freight in Western Canada, see W. J. Stenason and R. A. Bandeen, "Transportation Costs and Their Implications: An Empirical Study of Railway Costs in Canada," in Universities-National Bureau Committee for Economic Research, *Transportation Economics*, 125.

LRMC is the basic economic rule for intermodal competition. In view of the possible incentives of regulated companies to reach out for business at rates below LRMC and the uncertainty and arbitrariness about the precise definition, measurement, and enforceability of that minimum, one cannot ignore the danger of predatory competition that attempts to apply the principle may in practice involve.

Noneconomic goals usually require similar modifications of these principles. The desire to distribute the business "fairly" among competing suppliers and the difficulty of estimating marginal cost both argue against permitting one rival or the other to cut prices below fully-distributed costs in competitive situations. Considerations of national security might similarly call for preserving a variety of alternative modes of supply, even though only one of them deserves to survive on the basis of efficiency calculations alone. National security may also join with uncertainty about the location and stability of peak demands in counseling against strict adherence to peak responsibility pricing because the national interest may call for construction of a larger capacity than would be supported by the market demand of peak users alone. Considerations of fairness or the desire to protect the small user against discrimination combine with the impossibility of accurately measuring relative demand elasticities in counseling compromises with the principle of constructing rate structures on the basis of value of service.

Even if we stick to purely economic criteria, there are two other hurdles that have to be confronted: externalities and the problem of second best. First, if the supply of a public utility service involves social costs in addition to those reflected in the books of the supplying company, or benefits to the community at large in addition to those that accrue to the individual purchaser, those costs and benefits somehow must be brought to bear on the process of deciding how much shall be produced, how, and by whom. Second, if prices in the economy generally are not uniformly set at social marginal cost, if output decisions outside the public utility arena are influenced by monopoly, taxes, and subsidies that fall with different weight on different services, then the efficient price for the utility service must no longer necessarily be set at marginal cost either.[2]

We must therefore examine these four new sets of considerations that must be brought to bear on the pricing, hence on the investment and output, decisions of public utility companies:

1. Administrative considerations, having to do with the practicability of measuring the relevant private parameters of efficient price and embodying them in rates;
2. The necessity of adjusting private costs and output decisions to reflect external costs and benefits;
3. Second-best: what prices will produce the efficient allocation of resources in a world of imperfect competition and differential taxes and subsidies; and
4. How society twists the market process and outcome to serve social goals other than those embodied in the market system's concept of economic efficiency.

---

[2] See the general discussion of these principles at pp. 69–70, Chapter 3.

All four considerations are so closely intertwined in practice that we shall find it impossible in most cases to discuss one without alluding to one or more of the others.

ADMINISTRATIVE CONSIDERATIONS

It is extraordinarily difficult to convert economic principles into actual rates. There are two types of practical problems: estimation and application. In practice these are interrelated—there is no point in trying to estimate the different marginal costs of different units of service (different customers, in different geographic locations, or at different times, or services of different specifications) if it is infeasible to embody those differences in rates; conversely, there is no point in attempting to set up fine distinctions in rates where differences in the respective costs cannot be estimated with tolerable accuracy or reliability.

The simplest way to illustrate the principles is to assume production of a standardized service, as in Figure 6 or note 25, Chapter 5, where the unit costs depend on the level of output. Or two standardized services, as in Figure 4 of Chapter 4. But public utility companies supply an enormous variety of services and the behavior of the unit costs of each in relation to the volume of output will vary enormously depending on the particular *dimension* along which output is being expanded. A major source of the tendency toward long-run decreasing costs, for example, is increasing *intensity* of use—when customers within a given geographic area consume additional electricity or gas or make more telephone calls. The behavior of unit cost is very different when the expansion of service occurs, instead, by taking on additional customers. Here again it will vary depending on whether those additional customers are in regions already served, in which case their incremental patronage may also entail a greater intensity of use, or in outlying geographic areas, in which event the opposite tendency might be involved. If it is impractical to vary charges from city block to city block, depending on the concentration of purchases, or from customer to customer, depending on whether his patronage involves a more or less intensive use, it is not clear *which* marginal cost should govern rates.

Therefore, it makes sense for an electricity or gas company, following the familiar classifications of the three-part tariff, to compute separately marginal energy, customer, and capacity costs involved respectively in supplying additional kwh or cubic feet to existing customers, serving additional customers, and meeting additional demands at the peak. But these three dimensions of cost are far from exhaustive. Marginal customer and capacity costs will both vary also from customer to customer, subject to, for example, the distance between them, the consequent differences in the time required to read their meters, and in the amount of sales per mile of distribution line or pipe.[3]

---

[3] See the proposal of Vickrey to levy the costs of electric, gas, and telephone mains, ducts, and poles against landowners on the basis of their frontage-feet or area, regardless of how much or even whether they use the service. He points out that this dimension is often reflected in charges for water or sewer service, but rarely for other services. A tennis court, even one that might have no telephone or use no electricity or gas itself, would be levied a charge reflecting the additional distribution capacity required to get past it to other customers. The effect, Vickrey recognizes, is similar to that of a tax on land itself. *Op. cit., International Encyclopedia of the Social Sciences*, XII: 463.

Transportation and communication common carriers are in a better position to reflect some of these dimensions of cost-incurrence in price because they can vary their charges for carriage between different pairs of localities or for different commodities. But, here again, there is no single dimension of output that influences the behavior of cost in a single direction. Cost per ton-mile will vary with increasing volumes of business for different routes with varying gradients and other cost-influencing physical characteristics and will also respond differently to an increase in tonnage, with distance constant, than to distance, with tonnage constant. The variation in costs per message-minute-mile will vary similarly depending on whether the increase is in the number of messages, minutes, or miles, on the type of information transmitted (different kinds of messages—voice, data, television video, audio—use different numbers of circuits), and on whether the additional sales are on peak or off peak. The marginal cost of carrying a ton will change with reference to the density of the commodities carried—a ton can take up part of a boxcar or many boxcars. The marginal cost will be greater if the freight is to be carried (or messages transmitted or computer results provided) rapidly and with a high priority on crowded track (or circuits or computers), and it will be less if it is to be carried slowly. It will be slight if the bulk of the traffic is in the opposite direction, so that the particular business in question is in a sense off peak, and it will include the total capacity costs if it is in the direction of the major flow of traffic. It also will include varying proportions of the joint costs of the round trip depending on which direction's demand will press on the limits of capacity with varying distributions of the joint costs between the two.[4] The cost will be different depending on whether the traffic is regular and can be planned for in advance, or sporadic.[5]

These considerations bring us to the second major problem in estimating marginal costs: their height will depend on the elasticity of demand. Marginal costs that are continuously low in the presence of excess capacity will jump to a much higher level if rates set on the basis of them elicit an expansion in the volume of traffic sufficient to give rise to congestion. Of course, the costs that are relevant are future, not past costs. Therefore, all the accounting and statistical records in the world can do no more than hint at their level, except in the unlikely event that the industry operates under constant costs, in both the static and dynamic sense. Even where separate production costs are conceptually measurable, because the proportions of the various services can be altered, and *a fortiori* where they are not—that is to say, in the presence of joint costs—the estimation of demand elasticities becomes an inescapable part of the task. And that, as we shall see, is a very difficult exercise, the results of which will always be subject to considerable uncertainty.

The difficulties in estimating demand weigh heavily against any cut-and-

---

[4] This is the case of the shifting peak, illustrated in Figure 4, Chapter 4.
[5] For an excellent survey of the problems of estimating costs in transportation, by an author who recognizes the economic necessity of attempting to base rates on them, see Wilson, *Essays on Some Unsettled Questions in the Economics of Transportation*, Chapter 2 and especially 40 and 77, on which many of these observations are

based; for the same with respect to electricity, see Turvey, "Practical Problems of Marginal-Cost Pricing in Public Enterprise: England," in Phillips and Williamson, *op. cit.*, 124–132. For a brief reference to the six parameters selected by Vickrey to approximate the response of operating costs on the New York subways to various changes in service and traffic, see Bonbright, *Principles of Public Utility Rates*, 346 note.

dried application of peak-responsibility pricing. Peaks shift over time, in response to relative rates, changes in consumer habits, technology, and so forth. In view of the political difficulty of sharply increasing off-peak rates when the demand in question turns out instead to fall at the peak, and the inefficiencies that may be introduced at the buyer level by rates set excessively low on the mistaken assumption that they ought to bear no portion of capacity costs, public utility executives and regulators alike are understandably reluctant to follow the rule of imposing all of the capacity costs on peak consumption if there is the slightest possibility that in five or ten years the pattern may change.[6] This reluctance is reinforced by the feeling that it is "only fair" for all users who benefit from the existence of capacity to pay part of the costs.

The practical problems of converting marginal cost calculations for different items of service into different rates are equally complex. We have already suggested the difficulties of basing rates on short-run marginal costs, which are particularly volatile. Whether they can be employed is almost entirely a matter of whether particular portions of business sufficiently small so as not to produce congestion can be, if necessary only temporarily, singled out for this particular kind of treatment; and whether the inconvenience to customers of fluctuations in rates outweighs the efficiency advantages of basing rates on SRMC.

Whether peak-responsibility pricing can be consistently applied depends on the ability to enforce separate peak and off-peak rates so that each applies to the appropriate portion of the service. Most residential and commercial customers in the United States have only watt-hour meters, measuring simply their total consumption of electricity during the period in question. Introduction of pricing that would encourage them to cut down their consumption during the peak portions of the day and increase it correspondingly during off-peak hours must wait until meters capable of recording these separate purchases can be installed.[7] This immediately raises a question of whether the costs of more elaborate metering would be justified by the benefits.[8] But

---

[6] Originally, when the peak traffic was westward, the railroads set low rates for the eastward movement of Pacific Coast lumber. It took 15 years for them to obtain permission to raise those rates, after the lumber traffic had the effect of shifting the peak to the eastward direction. See Marvin L. Fair and Ernest W. Williams, *Economics of Transportation*, 1st ed. (New York: Harper & Brothers, 1950), 430–432.

Apparently AT&T similarly underestimated the elasticity of demand for long-distance telephone calls when it instituted its famous $1.00 rate for calls after 9 P.M. and all day Sunday. Considerable congestion resulted and it appears that additions to capacity were required. *Wall St. Journal*, April 16, 1964, 32.

[7] According to Vickrey, Électricité de France now implements its Tarif Vert by use of "a small relay sensitive to signals at a nonstandard frequency emitted from the central station," which permits time-of-day tariffs to "relatively small customers at very little cost." "The Pricing of Tomorrow's Utility Services," paper presented

at Occidental College, June 19–24, 1966, processed. For discussion of this and other metering devices in use or under development, see Melvin Mandell, "Inside Industry," *Dun's Review and Modern Industry* (November 1961), LXXVIII: 97–102E, and H. S. Houthakker, "Electricity Tariffs in Theory and Practice," *Econ. Jour.* (March 1951), LXI: 22, 24 note 1.

Industrial customers will usually have meters that measure their maximum consumption, as the basis for assessing a demand or capacity charge; but most of them measure only the noncoincident demand—that is, they measure the maximum consumption at the time of the user's peak, without regard to whether it coincides with the peak of the system. Bonbright, *Principles of Public Utility Rates*, 361; see also pp. 96–97, Chapter 4.

[8] See Turvey, "Peak-Load Pricing," *Jour. Pol. Econ.* (January–February 1968), LXXVI: 104–107. The entire article provides convincing support for Turvey's argument that "the theoretical 'solutions' to the peak-load problem are a

in the absence of such devices, the familiar pattern of charges for residential and commercial use—with a minimum, high per kwh charge for the first block of consumption, to cover the customer costs, and with progressively lower per unit charges for subsequent blocks—though making sense as a rough device to reflect the decreasing average costs of more intensive utilization,[9] also has the opposite, inefficient consequence of encouraging additional consumption at low marginal rates without regard to whether those increments are taken on or off the system peak.[10] Obviously, there are immense problems in fashioning separate rates for separate classes of patronage, where the marginal costs differ. The problem is not simply one of classifying customers into different groups and charging varying rates to them, but also of varying the charges to *each* customer depending on the type of service he takes and the cost of the service. On the other hand, it would not be impossible to vary fares on the New York City subway system or commuter railroads with the length of the trip—as in the London underground—and with the time of day,[11] just as is done with toll telephone calls.

The discussion of practical problems so far has concentrated on the difficulties of measuring the marginal costs of different categories of service and equating rates to them. Additional problems of estimation and administration are introduced by value-of-service pricing, that is, by price discrimination, the outstanding one of which is the uncertainty that attaches to all estimates of demand elasticity. All the econometrician or statistician has to work with is historical data showing volumes of sales of various kinds at various prices; from these he must infer a causal relationship between price and quantity that will enable him to predict the effect on the latter of a change in the former. But consider the many difficulties. First, price is rarely a unique single number. Most public utility services are sold under complex tariffs, in which the charge depends on the number of uses, type of equipment employed, length of the use (for example, minutes or miles or both), time of use, and so on. One can combine these various dimensions of price into an index number, but if that index changes over time, it could be because specific prices had changed or because the mix of uses had changed, and ordinarily it will be both. Second, and closely related, quantity of sales is not a unique number either, for the same reasons. Third, if the analysis is to be of time series, there has to be a record of experience of substantial price change over time, so that the associated volume changes may be measured. Or, if

---

beginning, not an end. . . . While the matters which then have to be examined are less suited to the tools of the armchair economist, they are both important and fascinating." *Ibid.*, 113.

[9] This is an instrument for offering each customer a price that reflects the marginal costs of the system. Impecunious customers, who might willingly take more power at the marginal rate, may be dissuaded from ever reaching those lower brackets by the higher rates which they must pay for their initial, smaller blocks of consumption. See, for example, Tyndall, *op. cit.*, *Q. Jour. Econ.* (August 1951), LXV: 348, 357–358; also Davidson, *Price Discrimination in Selling Gas and Electricity, passim.*

[10] For a finding of a similar tendency in Australia, see H. M. Kolsen, *op. cit., Econ. Record*, XLII (December 1966), 562–565, 570–571. Kolsen singles out for special criticism the promotional rates for all-electric homes. On the other hand, the installation of special water-heating rates, when the water heater is equipped to go on principally during the night and is separately metered, conforms much more directly to correct, marginal-pricing principles. See the brief descriptions of current practice on pp. 96–100, Chapter 4.

[11] Vickrey, *op. cit., Amer. Econ. Rev., Papers and Proceedings* (May 1963), LIII: 453–454; also his "A Flexible Change-Free Collection System for Buses and Subways," processed, May 10, 1966. See, also, references to some of his other suggestions, note 60, Chapter 4.

the analysis is cross-sectional (with comparisons of different markets or companies with varying price-quantity relationships), there must be significant price differences to which volume differences may be associated. Fourth, and most important, volume of sales will always be affected by a vast number of other determinants that can never be anything but very imperfectly separated out in order to ascertain the effect of price alone. This difficulty is particularly severe in the analysis of time series, when so many determining factors will have been changing simultaneously. And fifth, the statistical measures are inevitably measures of past relationships, or of relationships that have developed over the past. These cannot provide decisive answers to the crucial question, which is how quantities purchased will change *in the future* if rates are varied from wherever they are now set.[12]

In addition, since perfect discrimination (the pricing of each individual sale separately) is impossible, there are the problems of distinguishing and enforcing classifications of business and groupings of customers for purposes of discrimination. The groupings can be based on location, time, volume, type of use, income, age, or some other attribute of users. All raise problems of enforcement; all involve complex distributional effects; all will be economically imperfect; and all will inevitably raise noneconomic questions about what is fair, politically acceptable, and so on.

As might be expected, problems such as these appear with particular frequency in competitive situations, for it is (imperfect) competition, above all, that drives sellers into devising more and more ingenious (and discriminatory) forms of promotion to attract business away from rivals. When an electric or gas company instructs its salesmen to obtain a fixed percentage of the house heating market, by whatever means necessary, and the latter respond by offering all sorts of special deals and allowances to individual builders of new homes, the notion of a separate effective price for each customer, such as is involved in perfect discrimination, begins to seem not entirely unrealistic. Competitive suppliers of fuel or energy, building contractors and appliance dealers, small builders who feel they receive less favorable treatment than large ones, and customers with furnaces already installed—who are less likely to be wooed in this way—will all complain that this type of competition is unfair to them.[13]

Similarly, airline companies have developed a great variety of promotional fares in their competition, with special rates for young persons between the ages of 12 and 22, reductions up to 50% for servicemen in uniform, varying discounts for family members travelling together, and excursion fares, with the precise discounts varying between airlines and depending on the day of the flight and whether the passenger is guaranteed a seat or takes the risk of "standing by." It may well be, as we have already suggested, that young people have a sufficient elasticity of demand for travel on a standby basis to justify offering them special rates for this type of travel; but there may well be wealthy young people whose demand is not sufficiently elastic, and, on the other hand, poor people over 21 years of age who justifiably might be accorded a similar privilege on the economic grounds enunciated in our

---

[12] This summary of problems draws heavily on the account by Irwin M. Stelzer and Jules Joskow, *Utility Rate-Making in the Competitive Era* (New York: National Economic Research Associates, 1966).

[13] See the reference to these complaints on pp. 177–180, above.

Chapter 5. Therefore, the designation of the group on the basis of age or family status of travelers is, at best, only a rough and arbitrary approximation to the kind of discrimination that would be economically justified. Even if plans such as family discounts did represent the closest possible approximation of devices for separating various parts of the market on the basis of their respective elasticities of demand, they too would inevitably be imperfect unless they were confined to situations in which marginal costs were less than average total costs. Senator Monroney has commented in these circumstances,

"The promotional fare structure is 'getting so crazy . . . that you have to travel at $3:02\frac{1}{2}$ in the morning, in the dark of the moon with six children, two of whom have to be blondes . . . . it seems to me that the regular travelers are entitled to some consideration.' "[14]

And he is not necessarily wrong, even on economic grounds.

NONECONOMIC CONSIDERATIONS

The foregoing discussion has already illustrated how noneconomic considerations inevitably intrude in the very practical process of devising and administering economically efficient rate structures. They influence the decision of which customers or groups of customers should receive the benefit of rates closer to marginal costs, where price discrimination is justified because of the presence of decreasing unit costs. Consider, for example, the following court decision justifying a city's supplying water free of charge to a school while charging other users on the basis of their consumption:

"It is urged . . . that the court must necessarily conclude . . . that in delivering free water to the Normal School there would be a cost to the city which the plaintiff . . . and water consumers, would be compelled to pay. . . . [S]o far as appears from this record, there may be a surplus of water in the city which may be disposed of without any extra expenditure in the operation of the water plant."[15]

The fact that the marginal cost might have been zero (the water was delivered by gravity flow) did not explain why the school in particular was singled out for the benefit of marginal-cost pricing, in preference to other users.

Noneconomic considerations intrude even when the intention is to charge all customers rates equal to marginal cost. In principle, each individual electricity customer could be charged according to his own complex individual structure of rates and lump sum charges, reflecting precisely the costs of serving him—the capital cost of hooking him up and providing him with generation, transmission and distribution capacity, and the variable costs of reading his meter, mailing his bills and generating, transmitting, and distributing power to him. But the system would be excessively complex and expensive to administer. Therefore it becomes necessary to group customers for purposes of pricing even in the absence of increasing returns.[16] But all such groupings, departing from individual cost responsibility, involve

---

[14] *Wall Street Journal*, October 9, 1967, 32.
[15] *Fretz v. City of Edmond et. al.*, 66 Okla. 262, 263; 168 Pac. 800, 801 (1916).

[16] See Turvey, *Optimal Pricing and Investment in Electricity Supply*, 98–106.

averaging; and the application of average group costs to individual buyers is inevitably to some extent arbitrary and unfair. Different groupings would produce different averages and no one individual's cost responsibility will, except by accident, be the same as the average. They therefore raise both administrative questions—what kinds of cost groupings can be developed, measured, and enforced and at what cost—and distributional issues—what kinds of customer classifications are fair or politically acceptable?

Social or political objectives are especially obvious in the practice of internal subsidization—where some services or markets pay less than their marginal costs, thus clearly imposing a burden on other users. The practice is often rationalized on distributional grounds, the desire being to make the service more widely available to people who could not otherwise afford it. Internal subsidization of service to rural areas may be justified also on the ground that by helping to keep the population dispersed, it contributes to reduced social and psychological tensions. There is also a possible economic justification—in the event that the particular use subsidized confers economic benefits on others besides the individual purchaser. Making telephone service and electricity available on the farm benefits city dwellers as well because it holds down urban congestion. Since a good deal of governmental economic activity and collective consumption involves precisely the provision of services that are believed to confer large external benefits—outstanding examples are public education and public health[17]—it is not surprising that the social or political objectives that are brought to bear on public utility rates often involve, explicitly or implicitly, a purely economic judgment that the private market provides insufficient consumption because the external benefits are large.

Internal subsidization provides an apt opportunity for demonstrating how an economist would go about explaining or measuring the costs of such departures, on political or social grounds, from the norm of economic efficiency. Ralph Turvey does so, using the familiar example of uniform electricity rates to rural and urban customers, where the marginal costs of serving the former greatly exceed the latter, in the manner shown in Figure 9.[18] At a uniform price equal to the weighted average of their marginal costs, C_a, the rural customers will take OR, the urban OU kwh. If instead the rates were differentiated according to their respective marginal costs, the rural customers would buy none, the urban OU'.

Ignoring the problem of interpersonal comparisons—that is, setting aside for the moment the possibility that a dollar may be worth more to rural than to urban customers—it is possible to show that society would be better off with the differential prices, by the total of areas A and B. That is to say moving the price in each market to its marginal cost would increase total transactions surplus by this amount, following the demonstration of our note 16 in Chapter 5. B represents the difference between the added costs imposed on producers by the UU' output for the urban market (the area

---

[17] See Francis M. Bator, *The Question of Government Spending* (New York: Harper & Brothers, 1960), Chapters 6 and 7.

[18] *Optimal Pricing and Investment in Electricity Supply,* 97–98. Actually the relative positions of the three marginal cost curves is simplified. When the quantities taken in the two markets are the same, the weighted average *MC* would presumably be halfway between the other two. The particular weighted average shown in Figure 9 might be construed as the one that would prevail when the rural customers take OR and the urban OU, as they would at the uniform price equal to that average cost, C_a.

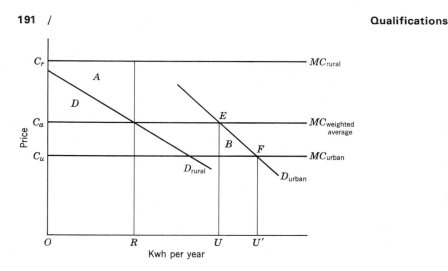

Figure 9. Hypothetical illustration of the welfare costs of internal subsidization.

under MC_{urban}) and the value of that additional output to urban customers (the area under D_{urban}). Area A represents the difference between the cost saving from eliminating the OR sales in the rural market (the area under MC_{rural}) and the value of those sales to the rural customers (the area under D_{rural}).

This also means that the urban buyers could give the rural ones monetary compensation sufficient to offset the latter's loss of consumer surplus from those purchases (measured by the area of triangle D) and still remain better off themselves—they benefit not only by B but also from the C_a to C_u price cut on the OU they had been buying. The producers are by assumption indifferent between the two pricing schemes, since they in either case recover only their incremental costs.

Of course, society might still decide that the internal subsidization is a worthwhile device for transferring income from urban to rural customers; and the economist can not say it is wrong. He can only point out that this is an inefficient way of making the transfer, since it involves taking away the entire area C_uC_aEF from the former in order to confer a benefit of only the area D upon the latter. He might also question whether society really thinks the result is an improved distribution of income. Internal subsidization is a very crude device for promoting egalitarian objectives. Uniform subway fares, regardless of distance, subsidize commuters who live in outlying districts of cities at the expense of commuters in the central city; uniform electricity and telephone rates for metropolitan areas ignore the lower costs of the more intensive consumption in the center city and benefit suburbanites.[19]

There are many extraeconomic considerations that may seem to society to dictate departures from marginal-cost pricing and the allocation of resources that it would produce (for example, the national pride that played so large a role in inducing us to devote tens of billions of dollars to landing a man on the moon and the far more meager appropriations for the deplorably pacific "War on Poverty"). These considerations and the ways in which they

---

[19] See our discussion along similar lines of the purportedly egalitarian argument for departing from peak responsibility pricing, pp. 102–103, Chapter 4.

may qualify the principles of economic efficiency are so obvious that little purpose would be served by an extended listing or appraisal of them.[20]

Most of the cases are mixed. As we have already observed, most qualifications of purely efficient pricing on so-called social or political grounds can be rationalized by the presence of external costs or benefits, which must be taken into account on grounds of economic efficiency as well. When the ICC refused to permit railroad abandonments of passenger service, it did so on the basis of a variety of considerations: the national interest in preserving different transport media for possible emergency; a desire to maintain the quality of life in out-of-the-way communities; a feeling that the external benefits of continued passenger service to such communities may have justified the continuation even though private revenues fell short of private costs; recognition of the fact that railway property has traditionally been disproportionately heavily taxed. The ICC believed that such distortions should not drive out a railway service that might otherwise be privately remunerative. They also hoped that state and local governments might be persuaded to change those policies and supply subsidies instead.[21]

The flat charge for local telephone service in most cities supplies an interesting final illustration of the complicated mixture of administrative, economic, and extraeconomic considerations that impinge on utility rate making. In a sense, the flat charge is inefficient because it involves a zero price for additional local calls, whereas their MC is certainly not zero: in 1969, New York City telephone subscribers witnessed the costs of congestion and the New York Telephone Company was made aware of the consequences of its failure to have provided sufficient capacity to meet the unanticipatedly large increase in demand in the years immediately preceding. On the other hand, (1) most customers apparently prefer the flat charge because it gives them the freedom to make local calls freely, without having to worry about their bills; (2) a flat rate is also preferred by the phone companies because when they charge on a per call basis they incur additional costs—of equipment to count the calls, employees to handle customer complaints about their bills, and so forth; (3) also, the incremental costs of local calls are well below average costs because of economies of scale when the dimension along which output is expanded is the number of calls made per subscriber.

---

[20] They would explain, for example, the 1956 amendment to the Federal Aviation Act (eliminated in 1960) that authorized reduced-fare air transportation on a standby basis to "ministers of religion," 49 USC 1958 and 1964 eds., Sec. 1373 (b); the fact that reduced fares for military personnel were upheld on national security grounds by the same Circuit Court that sent the standby youth and young adult fares back to the CAB for further examination (see note 62, Chapter 5); the below-cost postal rates on newspapers and magazines; the FCC's authorization of special low communication rates for newspapers (*In The Matter of AT&T*, 34 FCC 1094, 1098–99, 1963) (an FCC examiner recommended in 1969 that this discount on telegraph, telephotograph, and other private-line services be eliminated, *Wall Street Journal*, June 18, 1969,

21); and AT&T's offer of interconnection service to the Corporation for Public Broadcasting on an interruptible basis at about 15% of normal commercial rates, *Wall Street Journal*, March 19, 1969, 16. According to Turvey:

"Greek members of parliament do not pay for their telephone calls and telegrams (with the result that their constituents visiting Athens frequently ask to use their telephone), the parents of large families in France pay extra low rail fares and Swedish university students pay concessionary prices at the state opera. In none of these cases, so far as I know, is the motive that of a monopolist seeking to exploit different elasticities of demand." In Phillips and Williamson, *op. cit.*, 133.

[21] See our discussion of some of the problems in Chapter 2, Volume 2.

These are all strictly economic considerations. Customers prefer to buy one service (the privilege of making unlimited local calls) instead of another (the privilege of making local calls at some positive price per call). And if they are willing to pay the higher marginal costs of the former service in preference to the latter—to pay, that is, whatever it adds to the costs of a telephone company to let subscribers have unlimited local calling at a zero price per call—then giving them the more costly service is unobjectionable on economic grounds. For the telephone companies, the difference in the marginal costs of the two services is narrowed when the greater costs of administering the latter are taken into account.[22] Point (3) suggests that the distortion introduced by the zero marginal price for individual local calls would be exaggerated if we compared it with the average cost of making such calls. In any event, point (1) should be decisive: provided the prices accurately reflect their respective marginal costs (which would take points 2 and 3 into account), customers should have the service they prefer.

As long as it is infeasible for the telephone company to offer *each* individual subscriber his choice of service, at prices clearly reflecting the marginal costs he individually would impose on the system by taking the one or the other, distributional considerations are inescapably introduced. The choice of service then becomes a collective one and all subscribers are forced to take the only one that is available or go without, and to pay some sort of average cost instead of what they individually impose. Specifically, the flat monthly charge, based inevitably on average company cost experience, presumably transfers income from those who use their phones sparingly to those who use it freely for local calls. Internal subsidization is inherent in any averaging or customer grouping system, and society could conceivably decide that this sort of income transfer is unjust, for example, that it involved the poor subsidizing the wealthy. If it did so, the economist might reasonably question its underlying factual assumption; but if its facts were right he could not, on grounds of economic efficiency, say it was wrong to have reached such a decision.

EXTERNALITIES

We have emphasized the "public" character of the public utility industries as consisting partly in the unique relationship between the supply of transportation, communication and energy and the process of economic growth. Everyone's economic activities indirectly affect the welfare of others—effects that do not enter into his own decisions. (Your very presence on this planet takes up space that could otherwise be empty, blocks my view and, through your demand for food, induces farmers to use just a little more insecticide that helps pollute my lakes.) Externalities are ubiquitous. The external effects of public utility company operations are particularly great.

---

[22] James R. Nelson includes "the less metering the better" as one aspect of the desire for rate simplification that, on the one hand, consumers seem to desire and, on the other, is basically hostile to marginal cost pricing. He is right, of course. "Practical Problems of Marginal-Cost Pricing in Public Enterprise: the United States," in Phillips and Williamson, *op. cit.*, 139. But the *costs* of metering are properly weighed in deciding to what extent rate differentiation on the basis of marginal costs is in fact economically efficient; and if consumers strongly dislike metering, this too must be considered in deciding what is the efficient outcome.

On the cost side, their possible contributions to air pollution, to thermal and nuclear pollution of lakes and rivers, to the hazard of leakages and explosions (in the case of gas pipelines), to "visual pollution," to destruction of the wilderness and scenic beauty with their poles, transmission lines, dams, and reservoirs have all been the subject of intense and mounting concern and controversy in recent years. On the external benefit side are their afore-mentioned contributions to economic growth (with its own full measure of external costs!)[23] and, along with, for example, water and sewerage systems, to the general welfare. (It is in *my* interest to have you use water freely— perhaps more freely than you would if you had to pay the MC of supplying it to you—especially if I ride on the subway next to you.) Commuter train and local air service benefit not only commuters and air travelers but people who own real estate in the communities they serve.

As we have already suggested, almost every case in which public utility prices and output decisions are influenced by social or political considerations also can be rationalized on the basis of external economic benefits. The reduced air fares for clergymen no doubt contributed indirectly to the enhanced spiritual satisfaction of the community at large, as perhaps its later withdrawal made happier the staunch anticommunists who have objected to clerical expressions of opposition to the Vietnam war. The reduced telegraph, telephoto, and postal rates for newspapers undoubtedly reflect the external benefit to society (over and above the benefit to buyers, advertisers, and subscribers) of the wider transmission of news and comic strips to which they contribute. And so on.

Perhaps the most important observation to make about the implications of externalities for public utility pricing is that they really have nothing to do with the economics of regulation. In principle, there is no difference between the way society should handle the location of an electric generating plant, or dam, or gas pipeline[24] and that of a steel mill or a ski resort,[25] or the possible contributions to air or visual pollution of an oil refinery or private automobile on the one hand or a coal or oil-burning power station on the other. On the benefit side, every time any businessman hires and trains an unskilled worker or provides opportunities on equal terms for the member of a minority group he is probably generating an external benefit by contributing also to the diminution of social and political tensions. (A member of the Students for a Democratic Society might for this reason regard it as an external *dis*economy, if he ever attended his economics classes. Economic values like any others are inherently subjective.) There is nothing inherent in the economics of the public utility industries or their regulation that makes it appropriate for them to do more or less along these lines than unregulated

---

[23] E. J. Mishan, *The Costs of Economic Growth* (London: Staples Press, 1967).

[24] "Report on Power Plants Urges Planning to Control Pollution," *New York Times*, January 5, 1969, reporting the submission of a study to the President by the energy policy staff of his Office of Science and Technology:

"If placed indiscriminately and without built-in controls, they will pollute our air and water and despoil our land. Areas of great natural beauty will become ugly eyesores. Opportunities for healthy recreational activities will be lost forever." *Ibid.*

"FPC Plans Rules to Protect Environment in Path of Gas Pipelines; Opposition Seen," *Wall St. Journal*, June 9, 1969, 12, reporting the formulation of proposed aesthetic guidelines.

[25] On the latter see the *New York Times Magazine*, August 17, 1969, Sec. 6, 24 and ff.

companies.[26] The decision to subsidize the provision of electricity or telephone service to particular members of the populace or areas of the country is in principle no different from the decision to provide them with a decent diet, medical care, housing and education. None of this is to deprecate the importance of these things being done in fuller measure; but it is an argument against doing so in the former case by internal subsidization and in the latter by other devices, merely because the former industries happen to be regulated anyway.

The second general observation is that the mere identification of external benefits does not suffice to justify unlimited, or, indeed, any, subsidies to consumption. It does not create an unlimited case, for example, for the internal or external subsidization of passenger railroad service that the passengers themselves have deserted.[27] Since external benefits are ubiquitous, the conclusion that each calls for a subsidy involves concluding that more of almost everything should be produced—hardly a solution to the problem of the optimum allocation of scarce resources. Nor do they lessen the force of the case for using a price equated to marginal cost for the strictly economic purpose of restricting wasteful consumption. (My interest in your liberal use of water does not extend to putting you in a position where it does not pay you to hire a plumber to repair your leaky faucet, as is said to contribute to immense wastage in cities that do not charge users directly for their water; and it must be tempered by a recognition of the social costs imposed whenever the City of New York buries another upstate town under water to give itself an additional reservoir.[28])

There is no substitute for the application of judgment in cases such as these. And, the economist must admit, his own criteria are not necessarily decisive. But this does not justify his criteria being ignored; an intelligent regulatory decision cannot be made without assessing costs and benefits.

THE PROBLEM OF SECOND BEST

The final problem in translating principle into policy is that of the "second best." Deviations *anywhere* else in the economy from optimal pricing and resource allocation make it impossible to conclude *as a general proposition* that application in any single sector of the normative rules that we have been developing will be desirable. No single policy decision can be determined to be optimal except on the basis of a general equilibrium analysis of the situation in the entire economy, which takes into account all the ways in which that equilibrium will be altered by the adoption of any particular policy for any particular part of the economy—manifestly an impossible task.

---

[26] Because public utility companies have an unusually close link and identification with their local communities, they may be expected to take the leadership in attacking the problems of urban poverty and decay. We can use all the leadership, talent, and money possible directed to the solution of problems such as these. But this has nothing to do with the economics of regulation. For a summary of the problems along with a strong argument that it is desirable for public utility companies and regulation to pursue "externality-solving policies and programs" and social goals, see Warren J. Samuels, "Externalities, Rate Structure, and the Theory of Public Utility Regulation," a paper presented at a conference of the Institute of Public Utilities, Michigan State University, 1969. For an argument closer to the one made here, see Bonbright, *Principles of Public Utility Rates*, Chapters 7 and 8.

[27] See, for example, Ward Bowman, "The New Haven, a Passenger Railroad for Nonriders," *Jour. Law and Econ.* (October 1966), IX: 49–59.

[28] Noel Perrin, "New York Drowns Another Valley," *Harpers Magazine* (August 1963), CCXXVII: 76–83.

This general proposition means that, as a matter of pure economics, adoption of any particular economic policy on the basis of the rules we have expounded could well end up doing more harm than good in practice. But the observation applies equally to the policy of having *no* policy. Most economists would draw the conclusion, from this dilemma, that a conscious policy is better than an unconscious one; that, therefore, the important contribution of the theory of the second best is not that it recommends a policy of no policy but that it emphasizes the need for considering, as best as one can, the implications for any particular policy of the presence of sub-optimal conditions elsewhere in the economy; and that as a practical matter it is not impossible to make informed judgments about the ways in which *the most directly relevant* imperfections elsewhere might suggest modification of the rules.[29] In short, here as elsewhere, there is no substitute for judgment when one comes to the job of applying our principles—judgment in identifying the imperfections elsewhere that bear most directly on the wisdom of the policy under consideration and in deciding in what way those imperfections counsel modification of that policy.[30]

The first task, then, is to decide what relationships elsewhere in the economy are sufficiently close and important to require consideration.[31] The most obvious relationships would be between prices and marginal social costs of close substitutes, complementary products, or products using the public utility service as input. Turvey lists four major possible reasons for pricing electricity above its nominal marginal costs:

"(a) Important close substitutes sell at significantly above marginal cost or generate external economies

"(b) Products in whose production electricity constitutes a major input sell at significantly below marginal cost or involve large external diseconomies

"(c) Important close complements sell at significantly below marginal cost or generate large external diseconomies

"(d) Major inputs of the electricity industry are bought at significantly below marginal cost or involve large external diseconomies."[32]

The second, and probably even more delicate, exercise of judgment involves a decision of how to modify the rules to take account of any particular deviations from first-best conditions elsewhere. The answer will depend

---

[29] The reader will have to make his own allowances for the possibility that most economists expressing such an opinion—including this one—may not be unbiased. It is very difficult for any one but a pure theorist—"pure" in more than one meaning of the word—to admit that he simply does not know enough to be able to give useful advice, for which he is often well paid.

[30] See note 18, Chapter 3. See also E. J. Mishan, "Second Thoughts on Second Best," *Oxford Econ. Papers* (October 1962), n.s. XIV: 205–217 and Turvey, *Optimal Pricing and Investment in Electricity Supply*, 87–88.

[31] "The sort of non-optimality which has to be disregarded can be illustrated by two extreme examples. Take first, the existence of a large

excess of the price of shaving cream over its marginal cost. This will make the use of electric razors larger than it would be in a 'first-best' situation, but it would nevertheless be absurd to suggest adjusting the price of electricity to compensate for it. The non-optimality is, by assumption, known but it is totally insignificant. Second, consider the point that income taxation may cause labour inputs to be non-optimal. [On this, see note 15, Chapter 5.] Since this affects the whole economy the effect is not trivial, but as its implications for electricity are wholly unknowable there is no point in fretting about it." *Ibid.*, 88.

[32] *Ibid.*

largely on whether those deviations must be taken as given and ineradicable. But they may themselves be influenced by whatever decision is taken about the utility price. For example, the fact that the price of oil in the United States is held considerably above marginal cost by the domestic system of production and import control might be taken as an argument on allocational grounds for holding the regulated price of natural gas similarly high. On the other hand, a price of gas held closer to its marginal cost will undoubtedly help hold in check the cartel-controlled price of oil.[33]

The solution will depend also on the net effect of *all* relevant deviations from first best. Probably the most important distortion is created by the unusually severe weight of taxation on public utility companies.[34] This is true, first, even of taxes such as those on corporate profits and property, which are taxes on capital. Since production of public utility services is unusually capital-intensive, if such taxes are shifted forward at all they will raise these prices by a greater percentage than the prices of products that use less capital relative to other inputs. Second, property and excise taxes are evidently levied discriminatorily heavily on utility services. Consider, for example, the special excise taxes on common carriers, which confer an advantage on the many private carriers that compete with them. The subsidies that important competing carriers enjoy[35] operate in the same direction, effecting an uneconomic underutilization of railway services. Common carrier commuter transit media, similarly, are exposed to the competition of the private automobile, which does not pay the full external costs of the congestion it imposes on the central city in rush hours.[36]

All of these factors, if they are indeed the most important ones, strengthen the general case for adopting first-best pricing of public utility services— permitting at least marginal cost pricing below average total cost (and perhaps even prices below marginal cost) for those services whose demand is elastic. In these circumstances so does the phenomenon of decreasing average cost. A tax that is shifted forward gives rise to a greater increase in price and reduction in output, hence a greater departure from optimality, in a decreasing than in an increasing cost situation. This is because the price in the former case has to be raised to cover not just the tax but also the higher average cost attributable to the lower level of output, whereas in the latter case the price can rise by less than the tax, because reduced output entails reduced unit costs.[37]

---

[33] See my "Economic Issues in Regulating the Field Price of Natural Gas," *Amer. Econ. Rev., Papers and Proceedings* (May 1960), L: 514–517, in which I try to assess these offsetting considerations, including also the effects of the tax preferences that affect the supply and price of natural gas and oil alike. Also R. Rees, "Second-Best Rules for Public Enterprise Pricing," *Economica* (August 1968), n.s. XXXV: 269–270 and Turvey, *Optimal Pricing and Investment*, 88–89.

[34] See Clemens, *Economics and Public Utilities*, 523–526; Dick Netzer, *Economics of the Property Tax* (Washington: Brookings Inst., 1966), 23–27; Garfield and Lovejoy, *op. cit.*, 385–390. For the documentation of these and other distortions that uneconomically discourage use of the railroads,

see Chapter 2, Volume 2; also Haskel Benishay and Gilbert R. Whitaker, Jr., "Tax Burden Ratios in Transportation," *Land Econ.* (February 1967), XLIII: 44–55, which concludes that rails bear four to twelve times the tax burdens of motor carriers.

[35] See note 12, Chapter 6 and Ann F. Friedlaender, *The Dilemma of Freight Transport Regulation* (Washington, D.C.: The Brookings Institution, 1969), 103–11.

[36] See notes 60, 64, Chapter 4. Also Bonbright, *Principles of Public Utility Rates*, 402–405.

[37] See C. Lowell Harriss, "Taxation of Public Utilities: Considerations for the Long Run," *Taxes* (October 1965), XLIII: 663–664; and Clemens, *Economics and Public Utilities*, 542–543.

The above-marginal cost prices of such major competitors as petroleum and automobiles are the principal factors operating in the opposite direction. We have already pointed out that second-best considerations constitute the main economic case for allowing public utility companies a rate of return equated to comparable earnings instead of the cost of capital.[38] It is possible, on the basis of the foregoing considerations, to show that the argument is a tricky one and probably more wrong than right. Since public utility companies are highly capital-intensive, a one percentage point increase in their rate of return on capital will mean a greater percentage increase in their total costs and final sales prices than in industry generally. Thus the attempt to raise their returns to a level comparable with that of industry generally, in order to prevent a distortion in consumer choices between their services and others, will instead produce a distortion in the opposite direction —excessively discouraging their purchase. Once considerations of second-best are introduced, it becomes necessary to consider *all* possible distortions. On balance second-best considerations probably argue more often for pricing utility services below marginal cost than above.

To this conclusion must be added the institutional consideration that we treat at greater length in Volume 2: that the principal virtue of setting rates at marginal cost is the virtue of competition; it exerts the maximum pressure on competitors to improve their own efficiency and service offerings. Competition is particularly important where reduced prices make possible the fuller exploitation of static economies of scale; it also exerts pressures to bring the prices of substitute products closer to first-best levels; and it is a powerful stimulus to dynamic improvement in industry performance.

CONCLUSION

The decision about what kinds of modifications second-best considerations recommend can be made only by looking at the facts in each individual case.

No set of economic principles can substitute for the use of judgment in their application. There is no point in attempting to make estimates of marginal cost for categories of service more refined than can in fact be distinguished for purposes of rate making. There is no point in attempting greater precision in the design of rates, in decreasing-cost situations, than can be justified in terms of *probable* differences in costs or in demand elasticity. If the prices of substitutes are markedly above or below their respective marginal costs, or if the burden of taxes differs markedly from one product to another, or if one or the other involves major externalities, a public utility company or regulatory commission ought to take such discrepancies into account in setting the rates under its own jurisdiction.

In view of the pervasive uncertainties with respect to the measurement of marginal costs and elasticities of demand, certain dangers are introduced by following the economic principles we have enunciated. It becomes difficult to be sure whether rates reduced below fully distributed costs really do cover their long-run marginal costs and are compensatory. It becomes less clear whether such rates constitute a burden on other customers.

But any system of pricing involves the exercise of judgment. The question is whether that judgment should be employed in order best to apply economic-

---

[38] See note 80, Chapter 2.

ally efficient principles or irrational principles.[39] The fact that the elasticity of demand is difficult to estimate does not make it more sensible to assume that demand has no elasticity at all. The anxiety to avoid burdening certain customers by charging others less than fully distributed costs does not justify burdening them even more by refusing a utility permission to reach out for additional business, when a discriminatory rate is necessary to get it and where it seems reasonably probable that it will cover its full additional costs. The fact that off-peak consumption at certain times of the day or year is close enough to the peak to make it reasonably probable that the peak might shift is no excuse for forcing customers also to bear capacity costs at times that are unlikely to become peaks.[40] The fact that future costs are difficult to estimate does not make it rational to cling to past costs, when there is clear reason to believe they are wrong. The use of correct principles is still far from solving all the problems of intelligent public utility pricing; but it is the correct place to begin.

---

[39] "An approximation, even one subject to a wide margin of error, to the correct answer is better than the wrong answer worked out to seven decimal places." Vickrey testimony in FCC Docket 16258, 7.

[40] See Bonbright, *Principles of Public Utility Rates*, 358, 360, 365–366; also Little, *The Price of Fuel*, 146, who proposes that the demand charge be distributed among time periods in accordance with their respective probabilities of coinciding with the peak.

Selected Bibliography

American Economic Association, *Readings in Price Theory*. Chicago: Richard D. Irwin, 1952.

Barnes, Irston Robert, *The Economics of Public Utility Regulation*. New York: F. S. Crofts & Co., 1942.

Bauer, John, and Gold, Nathaniel, *Public Utility Valuation for Purposes of Rate Control*. New York: The Macmillan Co., 1934.

Baumol, William, et. al., "The Role of Cost in the Minimum Pricing of Railroad Services," *Journal of Business* (October 1962), XXXV: 357–366.

Bonbright, James Cummings, *Principles of Public Utility Rates*. New York: Columbia University Press, 1961.

Brigham, Eugene F., "The Effects of Alternative Tax Depreciation Policies on Public Utility Rate Structures," *National Tax Journal* (June 1967), XX: 204–218.

Brown, Harry Gunnison, *Principles of Commerce, A Study of the Mechanism, the Advantages, and the Transportation Costs of Foreign and Domestic Trade*. New York: The Macmillan Co., 1916.

———, "Railroad Valuation and Rate Regulation," *Journal of Political Economy* (October 1925), XXXIII: 505–530.

———, "Railroad Valuation Again: A Reply," *Journal of Political Economy* (August 1926), XXXIV: 500–508.

Bryan, Robert F., and Lewis, Ben W., "The 'Earning Base' as a 'Rate Base,'" *Quarterly Journal of Economics* (February 1938), LII: 335–345.

Clark, John Maurice, *Studies in the Economics of Overhead Costs*. Chicago: The University of Chicago Press, 1923.

Clemens, Eli Winston, *Economics and Public Utilities*. New York: Appleton-Century-Crofts, Inc., 1950.

———, "Price Discrimination in Decreasing Cost Industries," *American Economic Review* (December 1941), XXXI: 794–802.

Davidson, Ralph K., *Price Discrimination in Selling Gas and Electricity*. Baltimore: Johns Hopkins Press, 1955.

de Chazeau, Melvin G., "The Nature of the 'Rate Base' in the Regulation of Public Utilities," *Quarterly Journal of Economics* (February 1937), LI: 298–316.

———, "Reply," *Quarterly Journal of Economics* (February 1938), LII: 346–359.

Fellner, William, "The Influence of Market Structure on Technological Progress," in American Economic Association, *Readings in Industrial Organization and Public Policy*. Homewood, Ill.: Richard D. Irwin, 1958, 277–296.

Garfield, Paul J., and Lovejoy, Wallace F., *Public Utility Economics*. Englewood Cliffs, N.J.: Prentice-Hall, 1964.

Glaeser, Martin Gustav, *Public Utilities in American Capitalism*. New York: The Macmillan Co., 1957.

Hirshleifer, "Peak Loads and Efficient Pricing: Comment," *Quarterly Journal of Economics* (August 1958), LXXII: 451–462.

Kahn, Alfred E., "Economic Issues in Regulating the Field Price of Natural Gas," *American Economic Review, Papers and Proceedings* (May 1960), L: 507–516.

Kolsen, H. M., "The Economics of Electricity Pricing in N.S.W.," *Economic Record* (December 1966), XLII: 555–571.

Lewis, William Arthur, *Overhead Costs: Some Essays in Economic Analysis.* New York: Rinehart, 1949.

Lipsey, R. G., and Lancaster, Kelvin, "The General Theory of Second Best," *Review of Economic Studies* (1956), XXIV: 11–32.

Little, I. M. D., *A Critique of Welfare Economics.* 2nd ed. Oxford: Clarendon Press, 1957.

——, *The Price of Fuel.* Oxford: Clarendon Press, 1953.

Locklin, D. Philip, *Economics of Transportation.* 6th ed. Homewood, Ill.: Richard D. Irwin, 1966.

Lyon, Leverett S., and Abramson, Victor, *Government and Economic Life, Development and Current Issues of American Public Policy.* Washington: The Brookings Institution, 1940.

Meek, Ronald L., "An Application of Marginal Cost Pricing: The 'Green Tariff' in Theory and Practice," *Journal of Industrial Economics* (July and November 1963), XI: 217–236 and XII: 45–63.

Miller, Merton H., "Decreasing Average Cost and the Theory of Railroad Rates," *Southern Economic Journal* (April 1955), XXI: 390–404.

Morgan, Charles Stillman, *Regulation and the Management of Public Utilities.* Boston: Houghton Mifflin Co., 1923.

Morton, Walter A., "Rate of Return and the Value of Money in the Public Utilities," *Land Economics* (May 1952), XXVIII: 91–131.

Nelson, James C., *Railroad Transportation and Public Policy.* Washington: The Brookings Institution, 1959.

Nelson, James R., *Marginal Cost Pricing in Practice.* Englewood Cliffs, N. J.: Prentice-Hall, Inc., 1964.

——, "The Role of Competition in the Regulated Industries," *Antitrust Bulletin* (January–April 1966), XI: 1–36.

Phillips, Almarin, and Williamson, Oliver E., ed., *Prices: Issues in Theory, Practice, and Public Policy.* Philadelphia: University of Pennsylvania Press, 1967.

Phillips, Charles F., Jr., *The Economics of Regulation.* rev. ed. Homewood, Ill.: Richard D. Irwin, Inc., 1969.

Ponsonby, G. T., "The Problem of the Peak, with Special Reference to Road Passenger Transport," *Economic Journal* (March 1958), LXVIII: 74–88.

Priest, A. J. G., *Principles of Public Utility Regulation: Theory and Application.* Charlottesville, N.C.: Michie Co., 1969.

Robinson, Joan, *The Economics of Imperfect Competition.* London: Macmillan and Co., Ltd., 1933.

Ruggles, Nancy, "Recent Developments in the Theory of Marginal Cost Pricing," *Review of Economic Studies* (1949–50), XVII: 107–126.

Shepherd, William G., "Marginal-Cost Pricing in American Utilities," *Southern Economic Journal* (July 1966), XXXIII: 58–70.

——, "Regulatory Constraints and Public Utility Investment," *Land Economics* (August 1966), XLII: 348–354.

——, and Gies, Thomas G., *Utility Regulation, New Directions in Theory and Policy.* New York: Random House, 1966.

Smidt, Seymour, "Flexible Pricing of Computer Services," *Management Science* (June 1968), XIV: B-581–600.

Steiner, Peter O., "Peak Loads and Efficient Pricing," *Quarterly Journal of Economics* (November 1957), LXXI: 585–610.

Trebing, Harry M., and Howard, R. Hayden, *Rate of Return under Regulation, New Directions and Perspectives*. East Lansing, Mich.: Institute of Public Utilities, Michigan State University, 1969.

Troxel, Emery, *Economics of Public Utilities*. New York: Rinehart and Co., 1947.

Turvey, Ralph, *Optimal Pricing and Investment in Electricity Supply, An Essay in Applied Welfare Economics*. London: George Allen and Unwin, Ltd., 1968.

——, "Peak-Load Pricing," *Journal of Political Economy* (February 1968), LXXVI: 101–113.

Tyndall, David G., "The Relative Merits of Average Cost Pricing, Marginal Cost Pricing and Price Discrimination," *Quarterly Journal of Economics* (August 1951), LXV: 342–372.

United States, Interstate Commerce Commission, *Investigation of Costs of Intercity Rail Passenger Service*. Washington, July 1969.

Universities-National Bureau Committee for Economic Research, *Transportation Economics*, A Conference of the Universities-National Bureau Committee for Economic Research. New York: National Bureau of Economic Research, 1965.

Vickrey, William S., "Pricing in Urban and Suburban Transport," *American Economic Review, Papers and Proceedings* (May 1963), LIII: 452–465.

——, "Pricing Policies," in *International Encyclopedia of the Social Sciences*. New York: The Macmillan Co. and The Free Press, 1968, XII: 457–463.

——, "Some Implications of Marginal Cost Pricing for Public Utilities," *American Economic Review, Papers and Proceedings* (May 1955), XLV: 605–620.

——, "Some Objections to Marginal Cost-Pricing," *Journal of Political Economy* (June 1948), LVI: 218–238.

——, Testimony in Federal Communications Commission, *In the Matter of American Telephone and Telegraph Co.*, Dockets 16258 and 15011, Networks Exhibit No. 5, July 22, 1968, mimeographed.

Wallace, Donald A., "Joint and Overhead Cost and Railway Rate Policy," *Quarterly Journal of Economics* (August 1934), XLVIII: 583–619.

Wellisz, Stanislaw H., "Regulation of Natural Gas Pipeline Companies: An Economic Analysis," *Journal of Political Economy* (February 1963), LXXI: 30–43.

Wilcox, Clair, *Public Policies Toward Business*. 3rd ed. Homewood, Ill.: Richard D. Irwin, Inc., 1966.

Wilson, George Wilton, *Essays on Some Unsettled Questions in the Economics of Transportation*. Bloomington, Ind.: Graduate School of Business, Indiana University, 1962.

——, "Effects of Value-of-Service Pricing upon Motor Common Carriers," *Journal of Political Economy* (August 1955), LXIII: 337–344.

——, "The Effect of Rate Regulation on Resource Allocation in Transportation," *American Economic Review, Papers and Proceedings* (May 1964), LIV: 160–171.

Index